IFIP Advances in Information and Communication Technology 404

IFIP – The International Federation for Information Processing

IFIP was founded in 1960 under the auspices of UNESCO, following the First World Computer Congress held in Paris the previous year. An umbrella organization for societies working in information processing, IFIP's aim is two-fold: to support information processing within its member countries and to encourage technology transfer to developing nations. As its mission statement clearly states,

> IFIP's mission is to be the leading, truly international, apolitical organization which encourages and assists in the development, exploitation and application of information technology for the benefit of all people.

IFIP is a non-profitmaking organization, run almost solely by 2500 volunteers. It operates through a number of technical committees, which organize events and publications. IFIP's events range from an international congress to local seminars, but the most important are:

- The IFIP World Computer Congress, held every second year;
- Open conferences;
- Working conferences.

The flagship event is the IFIP World Computer Congress, at which both invited and contributed papers are presented. Contributed papers are rigorously refereed and the rejection rate is high.

As with the Congress, participation in the open conferences is open to all and papers may be invited or submitted. Again, submitted papers are stringently refereed.

The working conferences are structured differently. They are usually run by a working group and attendance is small and by invitation only. Their purpose is to create an atmosphere conducive to innovation and development. Refereeing is also rigorous and papers are subjected to extensive group discussion.

Publications arising from IFIP events vary. The papers presented at the IFIP World Computer Congress and at open conferences are published as conference proceedings, while the results of the working conferences are often published as collections of selected and edited papers.

Any national society whose primary activity is about information processing may apply to become a full member of IFIP, although full membership is restricted to one society per country. Full members are entitled to vote at the annual General Assembly, National societies preferring a less committed involvement may apply for associate or corresponding membership. Associate members enjoy the same benefits as full members, but without voting rights. Corresponding members are not represented in IFIP bodies. Affiliated membership is open to non-national societies, and individual and honorary membership schemes are also offered.

Etiel Petrinja   Giancarlo Succi
Nabil El Ioini   Alberto Sillitti (Eds.)

Open Source Software: Quality Verification

9th IFIP WG 2.13 International Conference, OSS 2013
Koper-Capodistria, Slovenia, June 25-28, 2013
Proceedings

 Springer

Volume Editors

Etiel Petrinja
Giancarlo Succi
Nabil El Ioini
Alberto Sillitti
Free University of Bozen/Bolzano
39100 Bolzano, Italy
E-mail: {etiel.petrinja, gsucci, nelioini, asillitti}@unibz.it

ISSN 1868-4238   e-ISSN 1868-422X
ISBN 978-3-642-38927-6   e-ISBN 978-3-642-38928-3
DOI 10.1007/978-3-642-38928-3
Springer Heidelberg Dordrecht London New York

Library of Congress Control Number: 2013940259

CR Subject Classification (1998): K.5.1, D.2, K.6, K.4, K.3, D.3, D.1

Typesetting: Camera-ready by author, data conversion by Scientific Publishing Services, Chennai, India

Printed on acid-free paper

Springer is part of Springer Science+Business Media (www.springer.com)

Preface

The 9th International Conference on Open Source Systems of the IFIP working group was again organized in Europe after three successful editions organized in North America, South America, and Africa. This year we received several high-quality contributions, both full papers and short papers, and two workshop proposals. The conference hosted a doctoral consortium and invited distinguished speakers. The success of this year's edition was possible thanks to the contributions of the Organizing Committee, the Program Committee, workshop organizers, the Doctoral Consortium Committee, and the authors of the contributed manuscripts coming from over 20 countries. We are also thankful to the organizers of the previous conferences for all their suggestions.

We were positively surprised this year to receive contributions, from all continents, showing the truly international scope of the Open Source Systems conference and the diffusion of open source initiatives worldwide. The open source that was initially based on a rich set of free software initiatives proved to be a viable and often highly successful alternative to traditional, closed source, software development. Several key topics in open source software research were introduced in previous editions of the conference. Based on enlightening study results presented in key journals and conferences, the open source approach proved to be not limited only to software development but showed that it can also be extended to affine domains such as publishing, education and also tangible products development. These initiatives were addressed by some interesting contributions presented during this year's Open Source Systems conference.

This book is a collection of 18 carefully peer-reviewed full paper contributions and 3 short paper contributions. At the end of the volume, readers can find the presentation of the topics covered in two workshops held together with the main conference. The first part of this volume is dedicated to studies focused on the innovation and sustainability of open source systems initiatives. The second section is dedicated to contributions focused on practices and methods adopted by open source systems communities. A section is dedicated to innovative technologies for managing open source systems development and execution of open source software. Two studies focus on two important aspects: information security in open source projects and the adoption of open standards. The last section containing full papers is dedicated to business models and licensing aspects in open source initiatives.

We believe that this book will be a valuable milestone for the open source software research community and that it adds new insights into this still-growing area. We hope that the content will further enrich the open source research community, the producers, integrators, and final users of open source systems, and will be useful to readers who are part of communities where openness is considered a valuable resource. Our thanks go particularly to all developers, documentation writers, translators, and in general to all contributors to open source initiatives that make our field of study interesting.

April 2013

Etiel Petrinja
Giancarlo Succi
Nabil El Ioini
Alberto Sillitti

OSS2013 Conference Organization

Conference Officials

General Chair

Giancarlo Succi   Free University of Bozen-Bolzano, Bolzano, Italy

Program Chair

Etiel Petrinja   Free University of Bozen-Bolzano, Italy

Organizing Chairs

Davide Dozza   Make-IT, Italy
Alberto Sillitti   Free University of Bozen-Bolzano, Italy

Proceedings Chair

Nabil El Ioini   Free University of Bozen-Bolzano, Italy

Doctoral Consortium Chairs

Björn Lundell   University of Skövde, Sweden
Gregory Madey   University of Notre Dame, USA
Klaas-Jan Stol   Lero, University of Limerick, Ireland

Industry Chairs

Marjan Hericko   University of Maribor, Slovenia
Stephane Ribas   INRIA, France
Andrej Kositer   Agenda Open Systems, Slovenia

Public Sector Liaison Chair

Jelena Vlasenko   McGill University, Canada

Tutorials Chair

Greg Madey   University of Notre Dame, USA

Workshops Chair

Ivica Crnkovic   Mälardalen University, Sweden

Social Media Chair

Sulayman K. Sowe   United Nations University Institute for Advanced Studies, Japan

Publicity Chair

Imed Hammouda   Tampere University of Technology, Finland

Publicity Co-chairs

(Asia)   Tetsuo Noda, Shimane University, Japan
(USA)   Lutz Wrage, Carnegie Mellon, USA
(Canada)   Jelena Vlasenko, McGill, Canada
(Central and South America)   Carlos Denner Santos Jr., University of Brasilia,
                              Brazil
(Central and East Europe)   Stefan Koch, Bogazici University, Turkey
(W. Europe, Scandinavia)   Jonas Gamalielsson, University of Skövde,
                              Sweden

Program Committee

Alberto Sillitti   Free University of Bozen-Bolzano, Italy
Andrea Capiluppi   University of East London, UK
Anthony Wasserman   Carnegie Mellon Silicon Valley, USA
Björn Lundell   University of Skövde, Sweden
Carlos Denner Dos Santos   Universidade de Brasilia, Brazil
Charles M. Schweik   University of Massachusetts, USA
Chintan Amrit   University of Twente, The Netherlands
Cornelia Boldyreff   University of East London, UK
Daniela Cruzes   Norwegian University of Science and
                               Technology, Norway
Davide Tosi   University of Insubria, Italy
Diomidis Spinellis   Athens University of Economics and Business,
                               Greece
Dirk Riehle   University of Erlangen-Nuremberg, Germany
Etiel Petrinja   Free University of Bozen-Bolzano, Italy
Fabio Kon   University of São Paulo, Brazil
Francesco Di Cerbo   SAP Labs, France
Gregorio Robles   Universidad Rey Juan Carlos, Spain
Gregory Madey   University of Notre Dame, USA
Guy Martin   Red Hat, USA
Imed Hammouda   Tampere University of Technology, Finland
Jesus M. Gonzalez-Barahona   Universidad Rey Juan Carlos, Spain
John Noll   Lero - the Irish Software Engineering Research
                               Centre, Ireland
Jonas Gamalielsson   University of Skövde, Sweden
Klaas-Jan Stol, Lero   University of Limerick, Ireland
Luigi Lavazza   Università degli Studi dell'Insubria, Italy
Maha Shaikh   London School of Economics, UK
Marcos Sfair Sunye   Federal University of Paraná, Brazil

Netta Iivari	University of Oulu, Finland
Patrick Wagstrom	IBM T.J. Watson Research Center, USA
Rafael Prikladnicki	PUCRS, Brazil
Reidar Conradi	Norwegian University of Science and Technology, Norway
Richard Torkar	Blekinge Institute of Technology, Sweden
Sandro Morasca	Università degli Studi dell'Insubria, Italy
Stefan Koch	Bogazici University, Turkey
Wasif Afzal	Blekinge Institute of Technology, Sweden
Witold Pedrycz	University of Alberta, Canada
Yeliz Eseryel	University of Groningen, The Netherlands

Table of Contents

FOSS Technologies

Security and Open Standards

Business Models and Licensing

Part II: Short Papers

Technological Innovation and Resource Bricolage in Firms: The Role of Open Source Software

Aarti Mahajan[1,*] and Bart Clarysse[1,2]

[1] Ghent University, Ghent, Belgium
[2] Imperial College, London, UK
{aarti.mahajan,bart.clarysse}@ugent.be

Abstract. Technological resources have been an important source of innovation in companies. They play a key role in the development of new products and services. However, the upfront investment in technical resources to enable the development of these new products and services can be quite high. Therefore, managers ask for well elaborated business cases before making investments. These business cases rely on market research to back up their assumptions rather than in-market testing. We argue that the advent of open source software (OSS) creates an opportunity space for companies to build low-cost prototypes and test their ideas in the market. Little is known about how OSS plays a role in allowing these firms to enhance product development. Using qualitative case studies, the paper sheds light on how OSS acts as a bricolage mechanism for technological innovation in the ICT services industry.

Keywords: Open Source Software, Bricolage, Case study, Resource constraints, Opportunity Recognition, OSS Adoption.

1   Introduction

Most firms face substantial resource constraints during firm creation and firm growth (Shepherd et al., 2000). Several authors have studied resource constraints such as lack of finance (Berchicci & Hulsink, 2006), physical resources constraints (Garud & Karnoe, 2003) or technological resources constraints (Stuart et al., 1999). Resource-constrained firms cannot make the necessary upfront investments in technical resources to develop new products and services.

Baker & Nelson (2005) present Levi-Strauss' (1966) concept of bricolage-*"making do with what is at hand"* as a mechanism to address resource scarcity. Using bricolage, firms are able to create something from nothing by exploring resources which are ignored or rejected by other firms (Baker & Nelson, 2005). Firms in resource-poor environments typically engage in bricolage by using resources at hand, or by combining resources for new purposes.

Resources at hand typically include personal knowledge and capabilities, initial investment and personal network. However, technological resources may also play an

---

* Corresponding author.

E. Petrinja et al. (Eds.): OSS 2013, IFIP AICT 404, pp. 1–17, 2013.

important role in bricolage. Technological resources, comprising the technology-software, system, platform, etc. are the backbone of the software & information communication technology (ICT) service industry. The degree of novelty and protection in ICT requires considerable investments in order to access technological resources. A cheaper option for firms is to invest time in developing technology in-house using their technical knowledge and know-how. Open Source Software (OSS) presents an emerging alternative to access technology quickly and cheaply in a context where time and money are crucial. Free availability of source code, zero cost and access to knowledgeable community are the major features of OSS which attract firms to adopt OSS (Fitzgerald, 2006). OSS presents an opportunity space for firms to experiment with technological resources. Moreover, OSS presents several networking opportunities for individuals and firms, enabling 'network bricolage' (Baker et al., 2003).

The literature has so far largely ignored the role of technological resources, and specifically OSS to enable bricolage in the product/service development process. This is an important omission in contexts where technological resources are central to the value proposition of the firm. In this article, therefore, we address the following research question: How do organizations confronted with resource constraints, irrespective of their size and position in the industry life cycle, embrace the opportunity provided by OSS and manage innovation to create value for their firm?

We begin by reviewing the literature on bricolage and OSS adoption. We then introduce the resource pool provided by OSS as a bricolage mechanism in firms to allow technological innovation through experimentation. We proceed to three case studies to examine how OSS as a technological resource facilitates value creation and innovation in micro, small and large firms by allowing them to experiment and bricolage in ICT services industry. We end with results, discussion and conclusions.

2   The Concept of Bricolage

The availability of resources presents firms with opportunities to experiment and create value for the firm. Demand and supply gaps lead to opportunity creation, while access to resources confines the choice of opportunities (Thakur, 1999). Availability of resources is highly valuable to young and nascent ventures (Hitt et al., 2001), initially to survive and later to grow (Sirmon & Hitt, 2003; Hoegl et al., 2008). However, financial, technical and human resources are often not available when required (Bruderl et al., 1992). When discovering opportunities and facing challenges of resource scarcity, entrepreneurs often make decisions using bricolage (Baker & Nelson, 2005). Bricolage allows these young and nascent ventures to deal with routine problems, and is seen to have a positive effect on innovation in nascent and young firms (Anderson, 2008; Senyard et al., 2011).

Bricolage as a process of resource use and development is conspicuous in firms characterized by resource-poor environments (Baker & Nelson, 2005). Despite these resource constraints, some ventures survive by solving problems and exploiting opportunities (Mahoney & Michael, 2005). Levi-Strauss (1966) suggested bricolage as a mechanism for opportunity creation by using resources at hand, recombining resources for new purposes, and making do with existing resources. Previous studies on bricolage in small- and medium-sized enterprises (SMEs) and large organizations have been limited to its role in facilitating innovation. Few authors have studied the use of bricolage in ICT firms to develop new products or services (Ciborra, 2002; Ferneley & Bell, 2006). Ferneley and Bell (2006) studied the concept of bricolage to integrate business and IT innovation in SMEs. SMEs are recognized for their flexibility, and ability to respond rapidly to changing environment, but they are reluctant to adopt information systems, primarily due to lack of strategic planning (Levy et al., 2001) and financial constraints (Foong, 1999). Similarly, MNCs face a number of hurdles which prevents them from reaching their full potential, uncertainty avoidance being the key hurdle (Halme et al., 2012). Halme and colleagues introduced the term intrapreneurial bricolage as entrepreneurial activity within a large organization, characterized by creative bundling of resources, in contexts of resource scarcity (Halme et al., 2012). In order to bricolage, the internal bricoleur- the person who engages in bricolage within an organization, needs organizational space to experiment and innovate (Ferneley & Bell, 2006). For innovation to occur, the internal bricoleur needs access to technology, which managers are often reluctant to invest in.

While the role of bricolage in innovation has been studied, the literature has largely ignored the resource configuration of firms engaging in bricolage. Several authors have addressed technological resources as key success factors in high technology industries (Henderson & Clark, 1990; Zahra, 1996; Autio et al., 1997). Not only do technological resources help in formulating the value proposition in the ICT industry, they also play a major role in understanding and evaluating the commercial potential of technological advances (Cohen & Levinthal, 1990). Research shows that technological knowledge resources impact firm performance (Lee et al., 2001; Clarysse et al., 2011) and that the quality and diversity of technological resources leads to breakthrough innovation (Srivastava & Gnyawali, 2011). The authors argue that the type of resources plays a key role in value creation for ICT firms The authors further emphasize that technological resources are the backbone of ICT firms, and are a primary source of innovation. The authors propose that availability of technological resources shapes the value proposition of the firm, which in turn facilitates innovation through bricolage.

3   Open Source Software

The importance of technological resources in high-technology industries has received ample attention in the management literature. In the ICT industry, ventures need to keep up with the rapid rate of technological evolution. Technological resources in ICT industry are protected by intellectual property rights in the form of patents and copyrights with a view to gain market share and obtain investments from venture capitalists (Bell & McNamara, 1991). Firms in resource-scarce environments either need to buy these technological resources (software, platform, etc.) or need to reinvent the wheel and develop the technology in-house. With the rapid changes in ICT industry, firms find it difficult to invest time and money in technological resources. Open Source (OS) provides a solution for firms to use technology as a resource at hand, and manage innovation through bricolage.

Open Source has been widely accepted as a collaborative development process in the software industry. Open Source Software (OSS) is software available in source code form; it can be modified by users, and can be redistributed even in modified form without paying the original developers (Riehle, 2009). Development is undertaken by people dispersed all over the world, forming a virtual community via the Internet (Hertel et al., 2003)

Research on OSS suggests that OSS drives innovation and spurs novel business models (Ebert, 2007). Bonaccorsi and Rossi (2006) observed that a key motivation for OSS entrepreneurial ventures in collaborating with OSS communities was that it allowed small and new firms to be innovative. With a robust, high-quality, feature-rich software, and a strong community of developers creating and testing the software, OSS acts as an important source of opportunity for small and large firms. OSS has surpassed the notion of being free software developed by "techies", and is being extensively embraced by organizations owing to its 'high quality at zero cost' facet. Not only individuals and SMEs, but also large corporations and government organizations have depicted a strong increase in adopting OSS. Deploying OSS products in their operation environment as end users has been the most common manner of organizational adoption of OSS (Fitzgerald & Kenny, 2004; Ven et al, 2008). Hague & colleagues argue that adopting OSS is more than simply using OSS products (Hauge et al., 2010). Integrating OSS components into one's own software is another popular way of organizational adoption of OSS (Ajila & Wu, 2007; Ven & Mannaert, 2008). Participating in OSS development, providing own OSS products, and using OSS development practices within the organization are other ways in which organizations adopt OSS (Hauge et al., 2010).

These studies on OSS adoption have focused more on the collaboration process with the communities and the impact of OSS on firm performance. The key aspect of OSS as an opportunity space and technological resource that drives value creation and technological innovation tends to be sidelined in this research.

4   OSS Bricolage in Firms

The concepts of OSS and bricolage have been previously discussed by Feller and Fitzgerald (2002). They addressed the approach of collaborative development in OSS communities, where developers and users bring together their knowledge resources to develop solutions rapidly. The use of these communities enables a process of bricolage. Communities of users and developers interacting over Internet have proved to be valuable innovation inputs (Hargrave & Van de Ven, 2006). Participation and/or collaboration with a OSS community can facilitate bricolage in firms. We define OSS bricolage as "*making use of OS software/platform and the OS community as materials at hand*". OSS bricolage may apply to ventures in Software and ICT industry. Starting a business in software and ICT industry is comparatively quite straightforward with the need for few resources. In contrast, industries like biotech, pharmaceuticals and manufacturing are less likely to engage in bricolage due to the high importance assigned to the protection of intellectual property rights.

In ICT, individuals set up micro-firms by exploring the freely available software, while SMEs and large firms tend to exploit the OSS community for their knowledge pool. Micro firms are confronted with resource shortage at startup, while SMEs and large firms are keen to expand their resource base in order to grow. OSS not only helps these firms to manage innovation, it also presents several resources for OSS entrepreneurial ventures to build on.

4.1   Technological Resources

Technological resources include patents, technological knowledge and skills which are not only valuable, but also difficult to reproduce by other firms (Lee et al., 2001). Patents lead to technological value creation and allow firms to commercialize their intellectual property. In the software sector, copyrights overrule patents. Software code is protected by copyright, while OSS code is freely available under copyleft. Rather than buying expensive licenses on copyright protected software, OSS allows entrepreneurs to experiment and build prototypes with freely available software code. Founders of micro firms and developers in large firms can syndicate their technical knowledge and expertise to work further on the freely available OSS to build their own product/service portfolio.

4.2   Human Resources

The acquired knowledge, skills and capabilities of the founders, managers and employees constitute the human resources of the firm (Coleman, 1988). The success of the firm is hugely influenced by qualified managers and founders of the firm (Colombo & Grilli, 2005). Since human capital focusses on individual attributes, and these ventures tend to be young and small, founders play a critical role in the success of micro firms. Participation in an OSS community enables firms engaging in OSS bricolage to attract knowledgeable developers willing to perform customization of the software.

4.3   Social Capital Resources

Several researchers have validated the importance of networks and partnerships for firm performance (Gabbay & Leenders, 1999; Elfring & Hulsink, 2003). Social capital allows firm to build up their resource base with the help of other partners. For young and small firms, the social capital resources provide access to information, technical knowledge, market know-how and complementary resources (Eisenhardt & Schoenhoven 1996; Hitt et al., 2001). Collaboration with OSS communities has displayed positive effect on the innovation performance of the venture (Piva et al., 2012). An OSS community consists not only of the core developers of the software, but also testers, end users and vendors of the software. Owing to their community participation, members tend to know the working of the software as a result of which most of them proceed to form micro firms. The community itself acts as the greatest social capital for these ventures. The community not only helps with development and testing of the software, it can also act as a great marketing and distribution tool for micro firms. Large organizations often allow their developers to work on development of OSS in order to build up their knowledge and professional network.

4.4   Financial Resources

Technology based firms generally require capital in order to invest in R&D. Firms with access to financial resources are more likely to pursue innovative strategies (Kang 2000; Teece 1992) as financial resources guarantee the firm's survival over longer periods (Dobrazynski, 1993). Lack of financial resources does not affect the performance of OSS micro firms, as the need for significant investments is rare. While keeping costs at minimum, founders of OSS micro firms tend to bootstrap. For SMEs and large firms, adopting OSS instead of their proprietary counterparts helps them cut costs and invest in other activities.

Limited by financial and human resources, firms balance their internal R&D efforts by networking intensively with external third parties that are likely to contribute valuable knowledge and competences (Stuart & Sorenson, 2007). With fairly addressable human and financial resources, entrepreneurial ventures regard OSS primarily as a *technological and social bricolage mechanism.* SMEs and large firms have quite some resources at hand, and OSS as a technical resource can provide them with a platform to expand their value proposition. Moreover, OSS bricolage in these organizations can pave the way for more resources which are necessity for higher levels of innovation (Rothaermel & Deeds, 2006).

5   Data and Methods

In the absence of prior research on the processes of bricolage associated with OSS in ICT service firms, a case study approach seems most appropriate for interpreting these processes (Yin, 1984; Eisenhardt & Graebner, 2007; Leitch et al., 2010). We adopt a case study approach to explore how dependence on OSS and OSS community helps facilitate technological innovation in ICT service firms. In particular, we examine the nature of the resource configuration associated with OSS in order to develop a framework for OSS adoption in these firms.

There were several reasons to select the ICT services industry: Firstly, owing to the code-sharing conditions enforced by majority of OSS licenses, it is difficult to build commercial products with OSS. Secondly, very few companies provide a 100% product portfolio. Thirdly, service companies are more likely to innovate with the newer releases of OSS.

In order to look at the adoption of the OSS under different degrees of resource scarcity, we studied its use in a resource-constrained micro-enterprise, a medium sized company which can afford the use of proprietary software while still being in a constraint environment, and a large company which is not resource constrained. We interviewed the founders and/or the department heads of the product development department in each case[1].

---

[1] Interviews were semi-structured with open-ended questions in English. Two authors conducted the interviews, while a third author was not a part of the interviews in order to avoid any confirmatory biases. The interviews were audio-taped and notes were taken. The interviews were transcribed verbatim and the text was read and re-read several times to identify themes and sub-themes.

With regards to the micro firm, we interviewed the founders of a Dutch web development company, JWebs. As an initial stage in identifying a suitable micro firm, several micro firms adopting OSS were interviewed at the first Joomla![2] international conference. JWebs was considered relevant for the research owing to its size- the two founders never employed any other employees in the five years of company founding, and high dependence on Joomla! OS content management system.

Mobixx represents an example of a Belgian SME trying to carve a space for itself in a niche market of mobile web. Interviews were conducted with two founders and four employees of Mobixx. The company contact was obtained through the professional network of one of the authors. Since one of the founders of Mobixx works in close collaboration with the authors, it was easy to obtain access to the company data throughout the company lifecycle.

To study OSS adoption in a large firm, we interviewed the director of application development of Dutch bank in the Netherlands. The authors identified this case by interviewing five projects relating to intrapreneurship in large organizations. The director had initiated and managed the adoption process from start to finish, and provided the authors with the required information for the case study.

The primary data source is the interviews conducted with the people involved in the bricolage process, namely the founders or department heads. The interview data is complemented by other secondary data- press releases, corporate presentations and company archives, depending on availability.

6   Bricolage in Micro[3] Firms: OSS Adoption in a Website Development Company

In this case, founder1 had a degree in computer science and had used his knowledge to control sound and lights in the theatre industry for nearly two decades. After initially working with the .NET framework, he started coding in PHP in 2007. He founded JWebs in 2007, along with founder2 as a creative designer, with a view to building custom websites and applications. Dynamic websites demanded the use of a content management system (CMS), and founder1 initially built a CMS from scratch using .NET and later reworked it in PHP. He was soon confronted with the difficulties of extending and maintaining the CMS.

> *"If my customers wanted additional features, I had to write extensions specifically for them. All customers had different requirements, and it was quite time consuming to customize the CMS for each one of them."*

---

[2] Joomla! is one of the most popular Open Source content management systems today with a large community consisting of more than 500,000 forum members. Until 2010, Joomla! has been downloaded 25 million times and there are more than 30 million websites running on Joomla

[3] We use the definition of the European Commission for defining micro firms as firms with less than 10 employees and turnover of less than 2 million euros : http://ec.europa. eu/enterprise/policies/sme/facts-figures-analysis/ sme-definition/index_en.htm

Having switched to PHP from .NET, he was presented with a wide variety of OS CMS to work with. Fascinated by the community and extendibility of Joomla!, he embraced Joomla! in 2008. Joomla! CMS served the purpose of a PHP-based CMS. Not only was Joomla! easy to work with, but there was also a list of free and cheap extensions available and ready-to-use.

> *"When I bumped into Joomla!, I realized that I was reinventing the wheel. With Joomla!, I did not need to write specific extensions for customers any more, I could find it or buy it without spending more time developing them myself. Also I did not need to customize them for different websites; the available extensions were ready-to-use."*

In comparison to PHP-based OS CMS, very few .NET OS CMS were available in the market at that time. As a result, the extensions for .NET OS CMS were highly priced, and PHP-based OS CMS was the way to go. Customers of JWebs did not know what a CMS was, all they wanted was a good website, and be sure that the website could be easily updated. Since the end users did not care about the backend and just required a website that worked, founder1 decided to migrate all his existing websites to Joomla!.

> *"Another reason to move towards Joomla! was that it is a community and there is not one person who is at the top making decisions."*

The large community of Joomla! also helped the founders to expand their professional network. Activities like Dutch Joomla! days allowed founder1 to meet fellow Joomla! users and developers from Netherlands.

> *"People interact here and become friends and partners, rather than competitors. At the end of the day, everyone is limited with the number of resources and cannot commit to all projects."*

To summarize, JWebs adopted OSS due to its ease of use and extensibility. Over the years, Joomla! has become an integral part of their value proposition. Not only does Joomla! provide these resource-constrained individuals with a free platform for use, it also provides micro companies like JWebs with a space to advertise themselves to the target market. OSS like Joomla! presents a huge potential for extension developers and service providers to set up micro-businesses and make profits by exploiting OSS. As founder1 defended the concept of open source:

> *"One idea of open source is that you don't put any energy in protecting it, otherwise there is less time spent for coding, and more for workarounds."*

7   Bricolage in SMEs: OSS Adoption in a Small Mobile Internet Company

The case study presents innovation in a Belgian mobile Internet company with the help of OSS. Mobixx started in 2006, at the time when mobile Internet was still in an early stage of market development. After a first successful pilot project, Mobixx was officially founded in December 2007 with two founders, one project manager, three software engineers and four freelance software developers. The value proposition of Mobixx was a technological solution to adapt website content to any mobile device in real time, while adding specific applications like flexible mobile payment system, location specific information, targeted advertisement, etc. The founders were highly dependent on their strong personal and professional network in order to bring the product to market. Due to lack of customer profile, Mobixx was confronted with a diversity of customers who expected high level customization and experimentation with the technology.

> *"In the beginning, the founder just sold projects to customers. We often had to push reality to deliver everything that was promised to the customer"* (Interview with Software Engineer, 16 Nov 2007)

To meet the customer demands, the company had to be flexible with the technological resources they used. This triggered them to use OS components to build part of their value proposition. Use of OS components allowed the developers to easily respond to the varied customer requests. At zero costs, and in no time, the components can be downloaded and used with no need to negotiate and buy a license for use. One of the major components of their technology platform- the device detection database- was based on OS WURFL mobile device database which was continuously updated. The use of OS components enabled the company to instantly respond to opportunities with no significant financial commitment.

> *"The bazaar model that the open source community uses in the only way to be able to follow the quick innovations that characterize web technologies. Without a large community, maintaining such a project and pushing its possibilities to its limits is impossible."* (Press article, 3 October 2008)

In addition, one of the venture capitalists involved had previously invested in OS companies, instigated by the success story of Red Hat. The venture capitalist intended to push the business model of Mobixx in the direction of Open Source. As a result, Mobixx also provided an OS platform at a later stage under a dual license.

In summary, the evidence from Mobixx suggests that small firms with sufficient resources may be able to benefit from OS in order to widen their value proposition. SMEs are often confronted with speed and timing issues in their early stage, and free availability of technological resources can help strengthen their value proposition and meet their market needs. Technological innovation with the help of OS components assists small organizations in nascent markets to quickly compete with incumbents aiming to be fast followers in their industry.

8   Bricolage in Large Firms: OSS Adoption in a Large Bank

The case study involves bricolage at the application development department of Dutch retail bank. In the recent past, Information Technology has come to play an important role at the heart of the banking sector. The banking sector has moved from outsourcing IT services to having its own IT department. Dutch bank has nearly 2000 employees in their offices in The Netherlands. With the radical changes in information technology, banks are continuously under pressure to have innovative solutions, while being under cost pressure. As the interviewee suggested, the narrow focus on application development at Dutch bank circumvents the need to be entrepreneurial and look for creative solutions in the outside world.

> *"Last month, I took a week off together with my boss and signed for a fantastic web conference in California. I had a fantastic week with developers of Yahoo! and Facebook. We would have expected our people that actually do the work (of application development) to be there. But there was nobody. People are so frightened and under cost pressure. No team manager allows his people to fly for a week to the States to actually find out what Yahoo! and Google are doing. I truly think there is a great opportunity but also a great need. If we are not careful, in 10 years people will not see the value of bank anymore."* (MVD, Director Application Management, Dutch Bank)

After MVD's manager attended a Google conference in 2011, he was impressed by the Android operating system. With MVD's previous IT education and expertise, he and his manager started working on the development of a mobile banking application. Although they had the required background, he did not have formal financial support or dedicated resources from the department. To start with, he needed a software platform to build his application on. MVD went back to his roots and thought about OSS. During his Ph.D. years, he was a Java developer. Contributing to Java had helped him to know the language well and comfortably work with it. They started up a Java community and decided to bricolage, i.e. use resources at hand. Technological resources were no more an issue. Java was freely available, and they had the knowledge of source code. To gather human resources, MVD set up a Java community and encouraged people to come together for free pizzas every Tuesday evening, where they would work on developing something cool. This became an enormous success, and 50 people decided to dedicate their free time to the community. OS technology of screen scrapping was used to evoke the same request normally done by browsers. The knowledge pool resulted in a fully-working mobile application in 2.5 months. This prototype built using OSS answered all questions about the working and feasibility of the application, which normally would not have been possible without resources.

Although they had a fully-working application, the next challenge was to get it into production. Due to several technical reasons, the prototype developed with OSS could not officially advance to production. Additionally, there had been several failures of projects in the past. Thankfully, the prototype proved the success and potential of the mobile application.

> *"We had a fully-working version but that's not the official way to get into production for many technical reasons. Then you see that it really helped, because all the questions- does it work, is it feasible, they are all gone!"* (MVD, Director Application Management, Dutch Bank)

The only problem that MVD still faced was to institutionalize several processes and get it up and running for the bank. They placed an official program in the application development group to replace the version built in the free time using OSS, with a formally developed application. The success of the prototype gained them credibility and legitimacy, guaranteed them a budget for the development, and also speeded up the development, which was practically impossible with a handful of developers.

Although large organizations are perceived to have several resources at hand, the resources are in fact tightly held and face several constraints. Due to rigid structures and control, employees in large organizations find it difficult to move from their assigned task and work on something creative and entrepreneurial. OSS allows these firms to bricolage in order to seek resources for technological innovation and gain credibility.

9   Results

Using qualitative case studies, our aim has been to shed light on how OSS acts as a bricolage mechanism for technological innovation in resource-constrained contexts within the ICT services industry. The degree of bricolage in service firms tends to vary based on the size of the firm. This can be accounted to the difference in the firms' initial resource configuration as well as the growth perspective of the firm. Based on our case study research, table 1 below summarizes the differences in the use of OSS between firms of different sizes.

Table 1. Differences between the three case studies

	Micro firm	SME	Large firm
Type of OSS	OS project/ system	OS database	OS platform
Dependence on OSS	High	Medium	Medium
Use of OSS	Firm level	Firm level	Department level
Type/Degree of innovation	Incremental/ Low	Incremental/ Medium	Radical/ High
Resources at hand	Software skills	Software skills, professional network	Software skills, professional network, commercial channels, infrastructure
Resources needed	Technical, Social	Technical, Financial	Technical, Financial
Why OSS	Value offering, network, marketing channels	Satisfying customer demands, expand market (Speed and timing)	Gaining credibility within firm

Micro firms startup with scarce resources. Mostly the resources consist of the software skills of the founders, and their expertise based on degree to which they are involved in the OSS community. As a result, they are highly dependent on OSS for technological resources as well as the network. OSS allows them to build their value proposition, while the OSS network provides them with marketing channels and allows them to easily target their customer group. The OSS community helps them build a professional network which opens up possibilities for business partnerships to enable them to work on bigger projects, while still staying small. The regular updates and releases of OSS spurs little innovation opportunities for the service companies, but promises persistence to the firm. For micro OSS firms engaging in extended product development for OSS, innovation opportunities are higher with every new major release of OSS. The speed of innovation for micro firms is influenced by OSS release plan. As a result, micro firms are more likely to work with successful OSS, which is under continuous development by an active community. Micro firms highly dependent on OSS projects and systems tend to remain small, and their future business perspective includes technical superiority and contribution to OSS project, than growth in terms of revenues and employees.

Unlike micro firms, **SMEs** already have some resources at hand. SMEs have a better insight into market requirements, and the value proposition is already in place at start-up. While software skills and expertise are at hand, SMEs are typically confronted with vague customer demands in a niche market and require more resources due to time constraints. In order to gain competitive advantage in a niche market, SMEs need to satisfy customer requirements by competing on their own expertise, rather than collaborating with peers and OSS community. Speed and timing are crucial in a niche market; SMEs are on a constant lookout for existing technological resources which could add strengthen their value proposition to address varied customer requirements. As seen in our case study, the availability of an OS database can be very useful for SMEs who are faced with time constraints, and hence cannot reinvent the wheel. While dependence of SMEs on OSS is of medium importance, they can benefit from OSS bricolage in order to rapidly adapt their value proposition and expand their customer reach. Free availability of several OSS also allows SMEs to experiment and constantly innovate their value proposition. OSS bricolage in turn helps them to display flexibility and allows them to gain access to financial resources through venture capital.

Large firms are the least likely to be confronted with resource constraints at the firm level, but several departments in large firms find it difficult to get hold of these resources, owing to the hierarchy, control and structure in large firms (Damanpour, 1992; Dougherty, 1992; Halme et al., 2012). Consequently, innovation activity in large firms is limited to specific departments. In spite of the existing knowledge and skills prevalent in some departments, the department heads find it difficult to encourage innovation owing to the lack of resources. Departments in large firms foresee the availability of OSS platforms as a resource-seeking mechanism. As seen in the case of Dutch bank, these departments use OSS platforms to build a working prototype of their products. Working on mature OSS platforms assures high level of security. Departments in large firms profit from OSS bricolage for radical innovations. Building working prototype using OSS platforms as technological resource allows these departments to gain credibility within the firms and showcase their innovations to higher management, in order to seek further resources.

10   Discussion

Our analysis suggests there are important strategic differences in the way in which OSS is harnessed in resource-constrained firms of different sizes. These differences concern the extent to which OSS is used for exploration or exploitation activities.

Micro firms innovate through OSS bricolage, and **explore** OSS with a view to strengthening their value proposition and increasing their technical expertise. Micro firms act as real OSS partners and contribute back to the OSS community. However, it is much more difficult for them to **exploit** OSS as they typically have few customers. Thus, although OSS allows these companies to easily enter the opportunity space and to get off the ground following a lean start-up philosophy (Reis, 2011), it is difficult for them to monetize on OSS. We expect that this is a typical scenario in micro enterprises. Only a few OSS start-ups have escaped this through the attraction of venture capital[4]. Micro OSS firms are comfortable working with successful OSS which is under development by an active community.

In contrast, SMEs are not deterred from experimenting with either developing or mature OSS. Alongside using OSS for iterating their value proposition, they sometimes tend to contribute their expertise back to the OSS, thus **exploring** and **exploiting** OSS. As these companies have an installed customer base to which they have sufficient credibility, they can exploit OSS components without taking too much risk. Their customers will pay for the "consulting" rather than straight license fees although the OSS technology is the basis for the work they are doing. Since these companies typically do not have R&D departments, the OSS community becomes the enlarged R&D department of the company. This implies that these companies also engage in giving "back" to the community and **explore** at the same time. These companies are probably the most important sources of innovation for the community. For them, OSS resembles open innovation in a true sense.

Finally, large firms play it safe by incorporating mature OSS which has been in the market for a long time, and which tends to pose minimal security risks. Consequently, large firms tend to **exploit** OSS to gain access to more valuable resources. For large companies, OSS tools have become a sense giving instrument to convince the different management layers that a new product or service can be useful. Especially in an environment such as a bank, where new technologies tend to be cognitively distant from the mainstream understanding in the company, it is important to visualize and even prototype new ideas and services. OSS is an ideal fast and low cost way of

---

[4]   For a related research, the authors conducted an online questionnaire survey to study the product developers and service providers for Joomla! OS CMS. Out of the 170 firms, as many as 93% of the firms started with less than 3 employees, and 91% of these remained with less than 5 employees within 1-5 years of their founding. None of these 170 firms received any venture capital or external funding.

prototyping. Without OSS, a traditional business case would have to be made and an upfront investment would be needed. It is unlikely that managers would have been convinced to invest in this.

11   Conclusion

In sum, our article makes the following contributions relating to how OSS acts as a bricolage mechanism for technological innovation in the ICT services industry. We have shown that OSS creates an opportunity space. However, that opportunity space is contingent upon different company types. Our case studies show that for micro start-ups, OSS provides an opportunity to explore, but does not easily translate in "exploitation". For SMEs with a customer base, exploitation is more likely and OSS becomes a space for open innovation. In large companies, exploitation is the most likely objective of the use of OSS tools. Overall, these findings provide insights suggestive of how bricolage can be used to access and coordinate technological resources in rapidly changing resource constrained environments. As such, our findings help extend understanding of how different contexts help shape innovative entrepreneurial activity (Zahra and Wright, 2011). We hope that our insights resulting from a focus on analysis of a small number of cases will provide the departure point for future larger studies that encompass further variety in the nature of entrepreneurial ventures adopting OSS.

References

Ajila, S.A., Wu, D.: Empirical study of effects of open source adoption on software development economics. Journal of Systems and Software 80(9), 1517–1529 (2007)

Alvarez, S.A., Busenitz, L.W.: The entrepreneurship of resource-based theory. Journal of Management 27(6), 755–775 (2001)

Anderson, O.J.: A Bottom-up perspective on Innovations. Administration and Society 40(1), 54–78 (2008)

Autio, E., Yli-Renko, H., Salonen, A.: International growth of Young Technology-based Firms: A resource-based network model. Journal of Enterprising Culture 5(1), 57–73 (1997)

Baker, T., Miner, A.S., Eesley, D.T.: Improvising firms: bricolage, account giving and improvisational competencies in the founding process. Research Policy 32, 255–276 (2003)

Baker, T., Nelson, R.E.: Creating something from nothing: Resource construction through entrepreneurial bricolage. Administrative Science Quarterly 50(3), 329–366 (2005)

Barney, J.B.: Resource-based theories of competitive advantage: A ten-year retrospective on the resource-based view. Journal of Management 27(6), 643–650 (2001)

Barney, J.B., Ketchen, D.J., Wright, M.: The Future of Resource-Based Theory: Revitalization or Decline? Journal of Management 37(5), 1299–1315 (2011)

Bell, C., McNamara, J.: High-tech Ventures: The Guide for Entrepreneurial Success. Addison-Wesley Publishing Company, Inc., US (1991)

Berchicci, L., Hulsink, W.: Of Bikes and Men: Innovation patterns and strategic entrepreneurship in the human-powered vehicle sector. Strategic Entrepreneurship: The Role of Networking, Vrije Universiteit Amsterdam, July 3-4 (2006)

Bonaccorsi, A., Rossi, C.: Comparing motivations of individual programmers and firms to take part in Open Source movement: From community to business. Knowledge, Technology and Policy 18(4), 40–64 (2006)

Bruderl, J., Preisendorfer, P., Ziegler, R.: Survival chances of newly founded business organizations. American Sociological Review 57(2), 227–242 (1992)

Clarysse, B., Wright, M., Van de Velde, E.: Entrepreneurial origin, technological knowledge, and the growth of spin-off companies. Journal of Management Studies 48(6), 1419–1442 (2011)

Cohen, W.M., Levinthal, D.A.: Absorptive-capacity- A new perspective on learning and innovation. Administrative Science Quarterly 35, 128–152 (1990)

Coleman, J.S.: Social capital in the creation of human capital. American Journal of Sociology 94, S95–S120 (1988)

Colombo, M.G., Grilli, L.: Founders' human capital and the growth of new technology-based firms: a competence-based view. Research Policy 34, 795–816 (2005)

Damanpour, F.: Organizational size and Innovation. Organization Studies 13, 375–402 (1992)

Dobrzynski, J.H.: Relationship investing. Business Week 3309, 68–75 (1993)

Dougherty, D.: Interpretive barriers to successful innovation in large firms. Organization Science 3(2), 179–202 (1992)

Ebert, C.: Open Source drives innovation. IEEE Software 24(3), 105–109 (2007)

Eisenhardt, K.M., Schoonhoven, C.B.: Resource-based view of strategic alliance formation: Strategic and social effects in entrepreneurial firms. Organization Science 7(2), 136–150 (1996)

Eisenhardt, K.M., Graebner, M.E.: Theory building from cases: Opportunities and Challenges. Academy of Management Journal 50(1), 25–32 (2007)

Elfring, T., Hulsink, W.: Networks in Entrepreneurship: The case of High- Technology Firms. Small Business Economics 21, 409–422 (2003)

Feller, J., Fitzgerald, B.: Understanding open source software development. Addison Wesley (2002)

Ferneley, E., Bell, F.: Using bricolage to integrate business and information technology innovation in SMEs. Technovation 26(2), 232–241 (2006)

Fitzgerald, B.: The transformation of open source software. MIS Quarterly 30(3), 587–598 (2006)

Fitzgerald, B., Kenny, T.: Developing an information systems infrastructure with open source software. IEEE Software 21(1), 50–55 (2004)

Foong, S.: Effect of end user personnel and systems attributes on computer based information systems success in Malaysian SMEs. Journal of Small Business Management 37(3), 81–87 (1999)

Gabbay, S.M., Leenders, R.T.A.: The structure of advantage and disadvantage. In: Leenders, R.T.A., Gabbay, S.M. (eds.) Corporate Social Capital and Liability, pp. 1–16. Kluwer, New York (1999)

Garud, R., Karnoe, P.: Bricolage versus breakthrough: distributed and embedded agency in technology entrepreneurship. Research Policy 32(2), 277–300 (2003)

Halme, M., Linderman, S., Linna, P.: Innovation for inclusive business: Intrapreneurial bricolage in multinational corporations. Journal of Management Studies 49(4), 743–784 (2012)

Hargave, T.J., Van de Ven, A.: A Collective Action Model of Institutional Innovation. Academy of Management Review 31(4), 864–888 (2006)

Hauge, O., Ayala, C., Conradi, R.: Adoption of open source software in software-intensive organizations- A systematic literature review. Information and Software Technology 52, 1133–1154 (2010)

Henderson, R.M., Clark, K.B.: Architectural innovation: the reconfiguration of existing product technologies and the failure of established firms. Administrative Science Quarterly 35, 9–31 (1990)

Hertel, G., Neidner, S., Herrmann, S.: Motivation of software developers in Open Source projects: an Internet-based survey of contributors to the Linux kernel. Research Policy 32, 1159–1177 (2003)

Hitt, M.A., Ireland, R.D., Camp, S.M., Sexton, D.L.: Strategic entrepreneurship: Entrepreneurial strategies for wealth creation. Strategic Management Journal 22(6-7), 479–491 (2001)

Hoegl, M., Gibbert, M., Mazursky, D.: Financial constraints in innovation projects: When is less more? Research Policy 37(8), 1382–1391 (2008)

Kang, D.: The impact of family ownership on performance in public organizations. A study of U.S. Fortune 500, 1982-1994. Academy of Management Meeting, Toronto (2000)

Lee, C., Lee, K., Pennings, J.M.: Internal capabilities, external networks, and performance: A study on technology-based ventures. Strategic Management Journal 22(6-7), 615–640 (2001)

Leitch, C.M., Hill, F.M., Harrison, R.T.: The philosophy and Practice of Interpretivist Research in Entrepreneurship: Quality, Validation, and Trust. Organizational Research Methods 13(1), 67–84 (2010)

Levi-Strauss, C.: The Savage Mind. University of Chicago Press, Chicago (1966)

Levy, M., Powell, P., Yetton, P.: SEMs: Aligning IS and the strategic context. Journal of Information Technology 16, 133–144 (2001)

Mahoney, J.T., Michael, S.C.: A subjectivist theory of entrepreneurship. In: Alvarez, S.A., Agarwal, R., Sorenson, O. (eds.) Handbook of Entrepreneurship, pp. 33–53. Kluwer, Boston (2005)

Piva, E., Rentocchini, F., Rossi-Lamastra, C.: Is Open Source software about innovation? Collaborations with the Open Source Community and Innovation Performance of software entrepreneurial ventures. Journal of Small Business Management 50(2), 340–364 (2012)

Reis, E.: The Lean Startup: How today's Entrepreneurs use continuous innovations to create radically successful businesses. The Crown Publishing Group, New York (2011)

Riehle, D.: The Commercial Open Source Business Model. In: Proceedings of Americas Conference on Information Systems (2009)

Rothaermel, F.T., Deeds, D.L.: Alliance type, alliance experience, and alliance management capability in high-technology ventures. Journal of Business Venturing 21(4), 429–460 (2006)

Senyard, J.M., Davidsson, P., Baker, T.: Resource constraints in innovation: The role of bricolage in new venture creation and firm development. In: Maritz, A. (ed.) Proceedings of the 8th AGSE International Entrepreneurship Research Exchange, Swinburne University of Technology, Melbourne, pp. 609–622 (2011)

Shepherd, D.A., Douglas, E.J., Shanley, M.: New Venture Survival: Ignorance, external shocks, and risk deduction strategies. Journal of Business Venturing 15(5-6), 393–410 (2000)

Sirmon, D.G., Hitt, M.A.: Managing resources: Linking unique resources, management and wealth creation in family firms. Entrepreneurship Theory and Practice 27(4), 339–358 (2003)

Srivastava, M.K., Gnyawali, D.R.: When do relational resources matter? Leveraging portfolio technological resources for breakthrough innovation. Academy of Management Journal 54(4), 797–810 (2011)

Stuart, T.E., Hoang, H., Hybels, R.C.: Interorganizational endorsements and the performance of entrepreneurial ventures. Administrative Science Quartely 44(2), 315–349 (1999)

Stuart, T.E., Sorenson, O.: Strategic Networks and Entrepreneurial Ventures. Strategic Entrepreneurship Journal 1, 211–227 (2007)

Teece, D.J.: Foreign investment and technological development in Silicon Valley. California Management Review 34(2), 88–106 (1992)

Thakur, S.P.: Size of investment, opportunity choice, and human resources in new venture growth: Some typologies. Journal of Business Venturing 14(3), 283–309 (1999)

Ven, K., Mannaert, H.: Challenges and strategies in the use of open source software by independent software vendors. Information and Software Technology 50(9-10), 991–1002 (2008)

Ven, K., Verhelst, J., Mannaert, H.: Should you adopt open source software? IEEE Software 25(3), 54–59 (2008)

Yin, R.K.: Case Study Research: Design and Methods. Sage, London (1984)

Zahra, S.: Technology Strategy and Performance. A study of corporate-sponsored and Independent Biotechnology Ventures. Journal of Business Venturing 11(4), 298–321 (1996)

Zahra, S., Wright, M.: Entrepreneurship's next act. Academy of Management Perspectives 25(4), 67–83 (2011)

Empirical Study of the Relation between Open Source Software Use and Productivity of Japan's Information Service Industries

Keisuke Tanihana and Tetsuo Noda

Shimane University
{keisuke_tanihana,nodat}@soc.shimane-u.ac.jp

Abstract. This paper analyzes the relation between OSS (Open Source Software) use and the performance of Japanese information service industry. We first estimate the market value of OSS, an issue which only a few studies have specifically addressed. The results are then used to analyze the economic effect of OSS. Although our study has some methodological limitations regarding the calculation of the market value of OSS, we demonstrate that the economic effect of OSS is generally positive.

1 Introduction

This paper examines the relation between the use of Open Source Software (OSS) and the productivity of the Japanese information service industry from an economic perspective. OSS has recently become an indispensable resource in the information service industry. As Raymond (1998) has shown, the spread of open software development is associated with the increasing participation and contribution of information service enterprises. These enterprises use OSS primarily to enhance their competitive advantage. The open source community continually updates the software on a voluntary basis and, although this input is quite independent of enterprise needs, information service enterprises are the beneficiaries of this process. Chesbrough (2003) accurately described this as "open innovation" process to denote not only the enrichment of an enterprise's "inner" resources, but also the increasing importance of using "outer" resources such as OSS, especially when enterprises regard their competitiveness and growth in productivity as indispensable.

We adopt the view of OSS as an "outer" resource to analyze the business model in the Japanese information service industry in terms of its productivity.

2 Research Design

Tanihana and Noda (2011) used the concept of "open innovation" to study the relation between software development style and the use of OSS by showing the connections between "inner" and "exterior" resources. This section of our paper is devoted to explaining the theoretical background of OSS.

E. Petrinja et al. (Eds.): OSS 2013, IFIP AICT 404, pp. 18–29, 2013.

2.1   The Concept of "Connection"

Although the cost of duplicating software is almost negligible, the results of OSS development are made freely available. Therefore, unless there is a scarcity of talented developers, OSS may be regarded as a kind of public good that is non-competitive and non-exclusive. In the view of Ghosh (1998), all enterprises i(i=1, 2, n) can use OSS because of these two attributes. This relation is defined by formula (1):

$$OSS_1 = OSS_2 = \ldots = OSS_n \tag{1}$$

Ghosh (1998) highlighted the ease of duplicating software. In our view, the open style business model accompanying information oriented economy and copyright strengthen his opinion about OSS. We will examine the concept of "open" from the perspective of changes to an enterprise's business style[1].

The use of OSS reduces an enterprise's transaction costs, as defined by Coase (1937), and changes its economic structure and business model from economy of scale to economy of "connection," as noted by Miyazawa (1986a, 1986b, 1988). Economy of "connection" is a concept that is not applicable to a single enterprise, but rather the synergy effect produced by many enterprises sharing their technological expertise.

On the other hand, Raymond (1998) used the expression "cathedral and bazaar," to distinguish between software development styles, likening the OSS development style, which is open to any other developer, as a bazaar style. In this style, OSS developers are "connected" through the Internet, thereby producing value[2]. On this point, it is thought that the development of OSS beyond the "inner" organization indicates the existence of an economy of "connection."

2.2   Open Innovation and OSS Utilization

In considering the development of OSS, the connection of "inner" resources with "outer" resources is a vital point. In our view, the development of OSS and its business model is based on the concept of "open innovation" advocated by Chesbrough (2003).

To strengthen their competitive advantage, enterprises generally keep the results of their R&D activities secret, an attitude which Kokuryo (1995) argues may be characterized as a manifestation of independent management. However, under an "open innovation" process, an enterprise's R&D activities are connected to "outer" resources, thereby creating new value. In other words, changes to a business model occur from the reductions in transaction costs, as defined by Coase (1937), with the with the economy of "connection" serving as a driving force for "open innovation." In considering the development of OSS, the connection of "inner" resources with

---

[1]   Regarding changing business styles in enterprises, Kokuryo (1995) points out the change in the form of information processing from centralized to distributed processing.

[2]   Raymond's (1988) statement that "Given enough eyeballs, all bags are shallow." is another interesting way of expressing the "connect" effect.

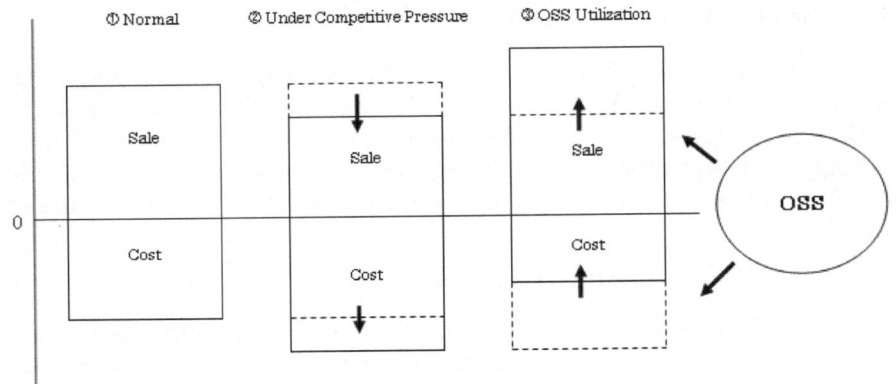

Fig. 1. Structure of Sale, Cost and OSS in Information Service Enterprise

"outer" resources is a vital point. In our view, the development of OSS and its business model is based on the concept of "open innovation" advocated by Chesbrough (2003).

To strengthen their competitive advantage, enterprises generally keep the results of their R&D activities secret, an attitude which Kokuryo (1995) argues may be characterized as a manifestation of independent management. However, under an "open innovation" process, an enterprise's R&D activities are connected to "outer" resources, thereby creating new value. In other words, changes to a business model occur from the reductions in transaction costs, as defined by Coase (1937), with the economy of "connection" serving as a driving force for "open innovation."

The Linux Foundation (2010) has shown that approximately 70% of contributions to OSS are by business enterprises, and that OSS activities are included in profit growth activities. Thus, enterprises use OSS to enhance their competitiveness. Kunai (2010) points out that revenue is generated from a contribution to the OSS community, whereas Fukuyasu (2011) considers the leveraging effect of using OSS. In the latter's view, the cost of developing OSS is shared among contributors, and all market players can enjoy the results produced by the contributors. Consequently, the positive economic effect of OSS takes the form of cost reductions and increased profits because of the leveraging effect of R&D activities.

Thus, for business models that use OSS, the vital point is that value, which cannot be created through independent management, is produced through the "connection" between "inner" and "outer" resources. In addition, OSS is a standard technology produced by the community independently of the enterprises contributing to it. Thus, it is a kind of infrastructure characterized by non-competition and non-exclusion.

We shall consider the business model that uses OSS from the perspective of value addition. Figure 1 shows the relation between sales and costs in information service enterprises. We define the difference between the sale of products or services and development or management costs as value added to an information service enterprise. It is well established that a fundamental objective of all enterprises is to maximize their value added activities.

However, as the center of Figure 1 shows, competitive pressure on services and products is a daily and commonplace necessity. Because each enterprise has to deal with this pressure, price competition will be unavoidable. As a result, there is a fall in sales. On the other hand, under competitive pressure, it is necessary for each enterprise to produce more attractive products and services with a greater market appeal than before. This triggers a rise in development costs. That is, under competitive pressure, because its sales fall and its costs rise, each enterprise will face a reduction in its added value.

The context in which OSS is used is shown on the left side of Figure 1. Because OSS is generally made freely available, enterprises are able to reduce development costs by replacing internal resources with external resources, or by "connecting" both. Similarly, it will be possible for each enterprise to generate profits and surpass its rivals in technology and competitive advantage by "connecting" its own products or services with OSS-based technology, which is developed out-side the enterprise. This process appears to facilitate competitive pricing by enterprises.

As already mentioned, our hypothesis is that using OSS can potentially enhance an information service enterprise's capacity to create added value. Therefore, we attempt to grasp the structural and quantitative effects of OSS in this paper.

2.3 Model for Empirical Analysis

To analyze the economic effects of OSS, we have to consider the effect of "connection" with respect to resources. If the "connection" between "inner" resources and OSS as "outer" resource is considered, an information service enterprise i's production structure can be expressed by formula (2), as follows:

$$V_{i,t} = AK_{i,t}^{\alpha}L_{i,t}^{(1-\alpha)}OSS_t^{\gamma} \tag{2}$$

Formula (2) is a kind of Cobb-Douglas production function[3], according to which, given technology A, value in an information service enterprise i $V_{i,t}$ consists of its capital input $K_{i,t}$ and labor input $L_{i,t}$. These resources exist in the "inner" organization. On the other hand, OSS_t constitutes the "outer" resources, which develop independently of each enterprise i. In other words, the relation indicated in formula (2) shows the "connection" between "inner" resources and "outer" resources that lies behind the "open innovation" business model[4].

If formula (2) is logarithm-zed and deployed, it is possible to obtain formula (3), which specifies the determinants of labor productivity in an information service enterprise.

$$ln\left(\frac{V}{L}\right)_{i,t} = lnA + \alpha ln\left(\frac{K}{L}\right)_{i,t} + \gamma lnOSS_t \tag{3}$$

---

[3] This production function is a fundamental technique in economic growth factor analysis.
[4] This relationship revealed by formula (2) is based on public goods economic analysis model, which is studied by Ashauer (1989) and Ford and Porter (1991).

In formula (3), the level of labor productivity *(V/L)* depends on the level of ratio of capital equipment *(K/L)* and OSS input. In this formula, the value of coefficient γ is important. When γ is positive and significant statistically, OSS gives positive effect to the level of labor productivity in Japan's information service industry.

3   Data Resources and OSS Market Value

3.1   Data Resources

$V_{i,t}$: Value added in information service enterprises
For the data on value added, we used "Currently Survey of Selected Service Industries" released by Japan's Ministry of Economy, Trade and Industry.
<http://www.meti.go.jp/statistics/tyo/tokusabido/index.html>

$K_{i,t}$: Capital input in information service enterprises
For the above, we used data from the "Currently Survey of Selected Service Industries" released by Japan's Ministry of Economy, Trade and Industry.
<http://www.meti.go.jp/statistics/tyo/tokusabido/index.html>

$L_{i,t}$: Labor input in information service enterprises
Labor input is composed of the number of workers and the number of labor hours in this paper. For data on the number of workers, we used the "Currently Survey of Selected Service Industries" released by Japan's Ministry of Economy, Trade and Industry. We obtained the labor hours data from the "Monthly Labor Survey Statistics" released by Japan's Ministry of Health, Labor and Welfare.
<http://www.mhlw.go.jp/toukei_hakusho/toukei/>

w_t: Wages for programmer
We used the "Basic Survey on Wage Structure" published by Japan's Ministry of Health, Labor and Welfare for the data on the wages for programmers.
<http://www.mhlw.go.jp/toukei_hakusho/toukei/>

3.2   Calculation of OSS Market Value

Although software is an intangible asset, quantitative evaluations, such as price, are required to determine the economic effect of OSS. In software development, the person-month scale is generally applied. On the other hand, the value of software is evaluated in terms of market transactions. In our view, the difference between the standards of the person-month scale and the market price makes it difficult to evaluate the economic effect of OSS.

Moreover, there are no official statistics, such as price and market value, for OSS. Although OSS increasingly resembles economic activity in recent years, it was not necessarily developed to obtain evaluation and market share data at the outset. This is one reason why it does not lend itself easily to quantitative assessments in relation to measurements such as price and market value. Therefore, to evaluate the market value of OSS, it is necessary to change from an obscure standard such as person-month to something more obvious, such as price.

Other scholars have undertaken a few quantitative assessments of OSS. MacPherson et al. (2008) calculated the development cost of Fedora9, and estimated it at 10.8 billion dollars. Glott and Haaland (2009) also evaluated the development cost of Debian as approximately 12 billion euros. Furthermore, Garcia-Garcia and Magdaleno (2010) estimate the market value of the Linux kernel (version 2.6.30) at 1 billion euros. For their monetary assessments of OSS, MacPherson et al. (2008) and Garcia-Garcia and Magdaleno (2010) used a Constructive Cost Model (COCOMO), which calculates a process and a period for software development[5]. COCOMO is a method that is advocated in Boehm (1981) and it can estimate the effort that goes into software development on a person-month scale, based on a line of source code. Multiplying such effort estimates by wages makes it possible to evaluate the monetary value of OSS. We shall use the same method to estimate the market value of OSS in this paper. For this purpose, we shall use the following formula.

$$EFFORT_t = a(KSLOC_t)^b \prod_{j=1}^{m} C_j \qquad (4)$$

Formula (4) is a basic COCOMO, in which the man-month scale effort $EFFORT_t$ depends on the kilo source line of code $KSLOC_t$ and cost factors C_j. Coefficients a and b are the parameters which are determined by the scale and the environments in software development; these are computed by regressing past development projects as reported in Boehm (1981). Based on MacPherson (2008), we set coefficient a at 2.4 and b at 1.05[6]. For the number of lines of source code, we adopt statistics released by Ohloh, which is a project that publishes statistics and information about OSS[7,8].

In COCOMO, cost factors are composed of 15 variables, including hardware, human resources, and project environments. A coefficient was assigned to each of these factors. Then, based on Wheeler (2004), we assigned to the development of OSS a cost factor parameter of 2.4. Wheeler (2004) has demonstrated that software development not only requires a labor force, but also the capacity to meet the costs of tests, facilities, and management. Because the proportion of labor force input is one of the cost factors in software development, it is necessary to count the variable multiplied by a cost factor coefficient of 2.4 as a development cost.

---

[5] The development effort calculated by basic COCOMO does not depend on the kind of programming languages, but rather the number of lines of source code. On this point, it seems that COCOMO maintains the objectivity of calculation. However, it is necessary to realize that this technique does not take into consideration the programming language.

[6] There can be three levels to a software development project in COCOMO: Organic, Semi-detached, and Embeded. That is, each parameter is set as a=2.4, b=1.05 at Organic, a=3.0, b=1.12 at Semi-detached, and a=3.6, b=1.20 at Embedded.

[7] Ohloh is a project which supplies information about OSS development, publishing about 550,000 project trends as at April 2012. See<http://www.ohloh.net>.

[8] Ohloh divides the number of lines of source code into "code", "comments", and "blanks". In this paper we use "code" to refer to the number of lines of source code.

According to MacPherson et al. (2008) and Garcia-Garcia and Magdaleno (2010), OSS development costs and market value can be calculated by multiplying effort by wages. Based on these studies, we define the market value of OSS by formula (5), as follows.

$$OSS_t = \left(\frac{EFFORT_t}{12}\right) w_t \qquad (5)$$

In formula (5), man-year scale effort ($EFFORT_t/12$) is obtained by dividing the man-month effort by 12 (i.e. 12 months). Next, multiplying person-year effort by programmer's wages w_t enables us to calculate the market value of OSS for every year as OSS_t[9]. Because in economic theory, marginal cost and price are equal at market equilibrium point, effort for OSS development is equal to its market value[10].

4   Empirical Result

4.1   Labor Productivity

Table1 shows the trend in labor productivity per Person-hour in Japan's information service industry for the period 2001 to 2009. Based on "Currently Survey of Selected Service Industries" published by Ministry of Economy, we divided this industry 8 enterprise groups in according to the number of its workers in Table1.

Regarding the labor productivity trend, three points can be deduced from Table 1. First, the level of labor productivity in an enterprise employing 500 or more workers is higher than that of other enterprises. This accounts for the discrepancies among enterprises within the same industry, as noted by Tanihana and Noda (2012). Second, Table 1 shows that the overall fluctuation of labor productivity is reduced, along with the scale of business expansion[11]. Moreover, after 2009 labor productivity level in this table reduces. It is caused by economic recession of those days.

From these features, it is obvious that an information service enterprise with over 500 workers, a so-called "big vendor", firmly maintains a high level of productivity. Again, it is possible to see the difference between big vendors and small vendors in terms of labor productivity in the Japanese information service industry.

---

[9]   There are two problems concerning programmer's wages. First, the wage level in Japan is lower than that of other countries. For example, programmers in Japan earned on average 3.5 million yen in 2000s. However, MacPherson et al.(2008) estimated that programmers earned $7.5 thousand in 2008. Garcia-Garcia and Magdaleno (2010) estimate that programmers in Europe earned €31 thousand in 2006. Compared with these results, Japanese programmers' earn a low wage. Therefore, the possibility of an underestimation of market value of OSS cannot be denied. Second, OSS development is global, so using the Japanese average wage level is somewhat unfavorable. Ideally, we would use the time series data to reveal the developer's nationality and the proportion of their respective contributions. However, we were unable to obtain the data for such a calculation.

[10]   Then, we calculated the real   OSS market value with the price index.

[11]   This figure shows that management becomes stable according to expansion of business scale. The gap of labor productivity in this figure results from   vertical Japanese industrial (keiretsu-like) structure. See Tanihana and Noda (2012).

Table 1. Labor Productivity per Per-hour in Japanese Information Service Industry

(Japanese yen
(exclude coefficient of
variation))

Enterprise's scale	1–4	5–9	10–29	30–49	50–99	100–299	300–499	over500
2001	1891	1530	1355	956	1029	1406	1095	2355
2002	761	1557	959	1114	1032	1451	1190	2237
2003	1927	1270	1134	1249	1098	1244	927	2315
2004	1646	1493	1112	979	1065	1149	1136	2066
2005	2708	2440	1729	1198	1320	1558	1528	2836
2006	1495	2380	3795	2657	2899	2788	1699	4037
2007	1519	4185	1590	1180	1450	1497	1773	4451
2008	1413	1671	2101	1300	1412	1585	1065	3221
2009	603	1137	1164	901	1178	1220	950	2817
Average	1551	1962	1660	1282	1387	1544	1263	2926
Coefficient of Variation	0.40	0.48	0.53	0.39	0.14	0.32	0.25	0.27

4.2 OSS Market Value

Table 2 shows OSS market values estimated using formulas (4) and (5). This paper discusses the Linux kernel, MySQL, PostgreSQL, Apache HTTP Server, Perl, Ruby, Python, PHP, Ruby on Rails, and Open Office, which were objects of this study. Today, each of these 10 objectives are well known and widely used in the field of business. In table 2, the estimated period ranging from 2001 to 2010, except a small part.

Table 2. OSS Market Value

(Millions of Japanese Yen)

	Linux kernel	MySQL	Postgre SQL	Apache HTTP Server	Perl	Ruby	Python	PHP	Rubyon Rails	Open Office
2001	–	1,207	1,290	1,834	7,304	358	2,404	1,378	–	13,158
2002	18,126	2,812	1,503	2,136	9,177	427	2,531	2,173	–	16,266
2003	23,768	3,404	1,591	3,874	11,020	604	3,259	4,556	–	22,224
2004	25,828	3,526	1,813	4,840	12,064	1,252	3,754	5,374	–	31,930
2005	30,259	6,122	2,145	6,474	12,428	1,842	4,082	7,002	95	40,203
2006	106,910	6,288	2,169	6,349	13,136	1,886	4,147	7,956	242	39,585
2007	110,868	5,261	2,340	6,294	13,485	1,990	4,511	9,144	354	40,959
2008	118,928	5,393	2,541	6,347	14,081	2,347	3,712	10,410	384	47,888
2009	134,224	5,388	2,627	6,758	14,407	3,081	3,407	11,847	577	48,523
2010	173,518	6,415	3,069	8,408	–	4,012	3,599	13,679	532	50,079

First, the Linux kernel typifies today's OSS movement. Table 2 shows that its market value was approximately 173.5 billion Yen in 2010. Table 2 clearly shows that no OSS has had the same market value as the Linux kernel during the period of this study. The reason for the high economic value of the Linux kernel is the high accumulation of its source code[12].

Open Office is one of the office suite programs originally developed by Sun Microsystems and released as OSS in 2000. According to table 2, its market value was approximately 50 billion Yen in 2010. This figure ranks second to that of the Linux kernel.

On the other hand, Ruby on Rails is OSS that was still in the developmental stage. Because Ruby on Rails appeared in 2004, sometime after the other OSS, the accumulation level of its source code is low. This seems to explain its lower economic value.

4.3   Contribution of OSS to Labor Productivity

Table 3 shows the estimated contribution of OSS to the Japanese information service industry using a regression of formula (3). Our research objects are enterprises, which are categorized into 8 groups based on the "Current Survey of Selected Service Industries."

First, the estimated result shown in the second line of the upper section is the production structure of enterprises that do not use OSS. Because the elasticity of the ratio of the capital equipment is 0.292, it is reasonable to conclude that the Japanese information service industry can enhance its productivity or ability to create added value through the enrichment of "inner" resources.

The estimated results of the Linux kernel are produced in the third line of the upper section, which shows that the contribution of the Linux kernel, when measured in terms of its elasticity, was 0.307. We can conclude from this that the use of the Linux kernel has a positive economic effect on the Japanese information service industry.

We chose MySQL and PostgreSQL as the research objects in database server. Their results are shown in the fourth and fifth line of the upper section, respectively. The estimated elasticity of MySQL was 0.357 and for PostgreSQL it was 0.486. Based on these results, the Japanese information service industry could possibly enhance their labor productivity with these OSS.

The estimated elasticity of the Apache HTTP Server is indicated in the sixth line of the upper section, showing an estimated result of 0.278. From this, it is plausible to conclude that the Apache HTTP Server has had a positive effect on the labor productivity of the information service industry in Japan.

As regards programming languages, we estimated the economic effect of four languages: Perl, Ruby, Python, and PHP. The elasticity estimates are shown in the seventh line of the upper section, as well as the second, third, third, and fourth lines of

---

[12] The market value of the Linux kernel grew rapidly between 2005 and 2006. This was due to the rapid increase in code accumulation.

Table 3. The Contribution of OSS to Productivity in Japanese Information Industry

OSS type	With no OSS	Linuxkernel	MySQL	PostgreSQL	ApacheHTTPServer	Perl
Covered Period	2001-2009	2002-2008	2001-2009	2001-2009	2001-2009	2001-2009
C	-4.860	-13.058	-12.821	-14.941	-11.000	-16.807
ln(K/L)	0.292(2.641)**	0.293(3.112)***	0.287(2.672)***	0.351(3.118)***	0.305(2.801)***	0.321(2.864)***
ln(OSS)	–	0.307(5.271)***	0.357(3.212)***	0.486(2.395)**	0.278(2.772)***	0.521(2.011)**
Covered Period*The Number of Enterprise	72	56	72	72	72	72
Hausman-test (p-value)	0.830	0.852	0.995	0.886	0.968	0.947
fixed effect or random effect	random	random	random	random	random	random
$\bar{R}^2$	0.086	0.347	0.203	0.148	0.172	0.126
OSS type	Ruby	Python	PHP	RubyonRails	OpenOffice	
Covered Period	2001-2009	2001-2009	2001-2009	2005-2009	2001-2009	
C	-7.779	-24.60	-6.078	-2.667	-11.01	
ln(K/L)	0.333(2.996)***	0.263(2.538)**	0.330(2.953)***	0.495(3.007)***	0.324(2.934)***	
ln(OSS)	0.150(2.423)**	0.890(4.215)***	0.163(2.215)**	-0.048(0.491)	0.261(2.477)**	
Covered Period*The Number of Enterprise	72	72	72	40	72	
Hausman-test (p-value)	0.918	0.992	0.929	0.998	0.939	
fixed effect or random effect	random	random	random	random	random	
$\bar{R}^2$	0.150	0.278	0.138	0.261	0.153	

Note: t-values are in parentheses. **Significant at 5% level, ***Significant at 1% level.

the lower section. Although the estimated results are limited by the number of OSS selected for our study, we can still conclude that, generally speaking, OSS programming languages have had a positive effect on the Japanese information industry.

The estimated results for Ruby on Rails are shown in the fifth line of the lower section. Although its elasticity was -0.048, which indicated a negative economic effect, its t-value was 0.491. Therefore, Ruby on Rails seems not to have had any economic effect on the Japanese information service industry.

We estimated the economic effect of Open Office as an office suite OSS. The results are shown in the sixth line of the lower section. Judging from our results, we can conclude that Open Office has had a positive economic effect on Japan's information service industry.

5   Conclusion

The paper has discussed OSS from the viewpoint of a "open innovation". The free availability of OSS and the near zero cost in duplicating it are both aspects that are guaranteed by licenses, which leads us to view OSS as a kind of infrastructure or public good.

Information service enterprises use OSS in the bid to strengthen their productivity and competitive advantage. Through the "bazaar" process, OSS is developed in a community that is organized independently from the enterprises contributing to such development.

Information service enterprises are able to create value by "connecting" OSS with their "internal" resources. Chesbrough defines this process as "open innovation" to denote a change in business model from a scale-intensive to a "connection"-intensive approach. It is therefore necessary to consider the effect of such a "connection" when analyzing the economic effect of OSS.

To conduct an analysis from an economic viewpoint, it is necessary to factor in the market value of OSS. For this purpose, we used COCOMO to calculate the market value. This calculation depended on effort. We found that the Linux kernel, and Open Office software have a high market value. In the case of Linux kernel, this is because their early appearance has facilitated the buildup of their source code, while the Open Office software's high value is attributable to the fact that it was originally developed as proprietary software, and has built up its source code since then. However, to calculate the market value of OSS, we had to rely on statistics for only Japan. Since the development of OSS is global, we concede that our exclusive reliance on Japanese statistics is not ideal. We had no other choice, though, because we were unable to obtain any data that provided a percentage breakdown of developers' respective nationalities and contributions. We would like to improve upon the method used in calculating the market value in a future study.

The calculation of the market value of OSS enabled us to estimate the contribution of OSS to labor productivity in the Japanese information service industry. We chose ten different kinds of OSS as our research object. The results of our analysis shows, broadly speaking, that although OSS has a positive economic effect on Japan's information service industry, each OSS has a variety of economic effects.

OSS has recently become an indispensable resource in the information service industry. This paper clarifies the relation between technical and economic productivity. In this connection, we can infer from our results that in order to create value and strengthen their competitiveness, information service enterprises will face subjects in style of OSS use. In other words, this will be essential in deciding which OSS will have a significant economic effect on the information service enterprise. However, to profit from the use of OSS, improvements to internal resources, such as talented developers, will also have to be made by such enterprises.

References

1. Ashauer, D.A.: Is Public Expenditure Productive? Journal of Monetary Economics 23, 177–200 (2001)
2. Boehm, B.: Software Engineering Economics. Englewood Cliff, New Jersey (1981)
3. Chesbrough, H.: Open Innovation. Harvard Business School, Boston (2003)
4. Coase, R.H.: The Nature of the Firm. Economica, 386–405 (1937)
5. Ford, R., Pierre, P.: Infrastructure and Private-sector Productivity. OECD Economic Studies 17, 63–89 (1991)

6. Fukuyasu, N.: Economic Model about Open Source. The Linux Foundation (2011),
   `http://www.ospn.jp/osc2011-spring/pdf/`
   `osc2011spring_tne_linux_foundation.pdf`
7. Garcia-Garcia, J., Magdaleno, M.I.A.: Commons-based Innovation The Linux Kernel Case
   (2010), `http://iri.jrc.ec.europa.eu/`
   `concord-2010/posters/Garcia-GarcGa.ppt`
8. Ghosh, R.A.: Cooking-pot Markets: An Economic Model for the Trade in Free Goods and
   Services on the Internet. First Monday 3(3) (1998), `http://firstmonday.org/`
   `htbin/cgiwrap/bin/ojs/index.php/fm/issue/view/90`
9. Glott, R., Haalamd, K.: Open Source and Regional Promotion. This document is prepared
   for the lecture in Shimane University, July 17 (2009)
10. Kokuryo, J.: Open Network Management. Nikkei Inc., Tokyo (1995)
11. Kunai, T.: Let's go with Linux. LINUX.COM (2010),
    `https://jp.linux.com/whats-new/column/kunai`
12. The Linux Foundation, Linux Kernel Development (2008),
    `http://www.linuxfoudation.org`
13. MacPherson, A., Proffitt, B., Hale-Evans, R.: Estimating the Total Development Cost of a
    Linux Distribution. The Linux Funndation (2008),
    `http://www.linuxfoundation.org/sites/main/files/`
    `publicpublica/estimatinglinux.html`
14. Miyazawa, K.: Distribution Structure in Highly Informative Society: Development of
    Network-type System. Toyo Keizai Inc., Tokyo (1986a)
15. Miyazawa, K.: Industrialized Society: Pursuit of the Economy of Connection through
    synergy between knowledge and technology. Nihon Keizai Shinbun, Tokyo (1986b)
16. Miyazawa, K.: Economics of System and Information. Yuhikaku Inc., Tokyo (1988)
17. Raymond, E.: Cathedral and Bazarr (1998), `http://www.catb.org/`
    `~esr/writings/cathedral-Bazarr/cathedral-Bazarr/`
18. Suematsu, C.: Open Source and The IT Strategy in Next Generation. Nikkei Inc. (2004)
19. Tanihana, K., Noda, T.: Open Source Software and Productivity of Information Service
    Industries. In: JSIS&JASI Proceeding, The Japan Association Social Informatics, Tokyo,
    pp. 357–362 (2011)
20. Tanihana, K., Noda, T.: Study on Production Structure of Information Service Industry in
    Japan. Journal of Economics Memoirs of the Faculty of Law and Literature, 93–120
    (2012)
21. Wheeler, D.A.: SLOCCount User's Guide (2004),
    `http://www.dweeler.com/sloccount/sloccount.html`

How Healthy Is My Project? Open Source Project Attributes as Indicators of Success

James Piggot and Chintan Amrit

Department of IEBIS
University of Twente
The Netherlands
j.j.h.piggott@student.utwente.nl,
c.amrit@utwente.nl

Abstract. Determining what factors can influence the successful outcome of a software project has been labeled by many scholars and software engineers as a difficult problem. In this paper we use machine learning to create a model that can determine the stage a software project has obtained with some accuracy. Our model uses 8 Open Source project metrics to determine the stage a project is in. We validate our model using two performance measures; the exact success rate of classifying an Open Source Software project and the success rate over an interval of one stage of its actual performance using different scales of our dependent variable. In all cases we obtain an accuracy of above 70% with one away classification (a classification which is away by one) and about 40% accuracy with an exact classification. We also determine the factors (according to one classifier) that uses only eight variables among all the variables available in SourceForge, that determine the health of an OSS project.

1   Introduction

Determining what makes a software project successful has been a research topic for well over 20 years. The first model that defined the factors influencing software success was published in 1992 by Delone and McLean [1], as the Information Systems Success Model. Since then there has been a considerable effort in research to determine what can be done to minimize project failure. However, factors that influence commercial projects differ from those known as FLOSS or Free/Libre Open Source Software. Attempts at remedying this gap have focused on statistical models that focus on certain aspects of a software development lifecycle. Only recently, has historical data been used to determine the changing nature of factors for success during a projects lifecycle[2].

  In this paper we use machine learning in the form of decision trees, to predict the development stage of an Open Source project based on project metrics[1], project constraints and circumstance. This model will serve as an indicator of OSS project health that will enable developers to determine accurately in what stage their

---

[1] We use the terms metric and attribute to mean the same concept in this paper.

E. Petrinja et al. (Eds.): OSS 2013, IFIP AICT 404, pp. 30–44, 2013.

project is in and what is necessary to improve project success. For organizations seeking to use OSS it can also be used to determine what risks are associated with sponsoring a project.

Previous research has tried to understand which indicators influence a project's success and how these indicators are interrelated but there have been very few working models[3]. What this paper proposes is that, through machine learning we can model which available project metrics are of importance in determining OSS project health. Our method differs from previous attempts at building a model, which were based on statistical correlations that approximated success factors without revealing how they actually influenced project's status [4-6].

In the last few years a considerable number of papers have been published that have tried to determine what the indicators of OSS project success are and how these indicators are interrelated. Often a number of these metrics are empirically tested on OSS projects found on SourceForge[2], a key OSS depository. In this paper we try to estimate the status of a project based on various metrics related to an OSS project. We also determine the accuracy of the subjective status of an OSS project in SourceForge that is provided by the OSS project leader. To this extent, we extend the research work on the problems with reporting the status of a software project [7], to OSS projects. For the purposes of this research we use SourceForge to obtain a data sample and use longitudinal data collected from 2006 to 2009. We have limited the sample to projects starting in 2005, in order to observe all stages of a project's lifecycle.

2   Literature Review

Recent research on OSS success factors has focused on enlarging the scope of influences, common elements found cite factors such as user/developer interest [2], the critical number of active developers [8] and software quality [5].

Ever since the publication of the Information Systems Success model by Delone and Mclean[1] researchers have attempted to define in what way factors that influence Open Source Software differ from those of commercial software. Early research showed that due to geographical dispersal of developers and lack of formal managerial methods, coordination becomes more difficult [9], this has been off-set by the proliferation of software forges that act as a single locale for communication and development for a project as well as a download site for users. To determine which metrics found on a software forge can be used to determine project success, an explanation of the IS success model is in order.

2.1   Open Source Health

In order to gauge the success of the Open Source projects we studied in this paper, we looked into literature on measuring Open Source success.

---

[2] http://www.sourceforge.net

Crowston et al. [3] collect data on the bug tracker and the mailing list of the projects to determine the health of the projects. They propose that the structure of the OSS community determines the health of the community and state that an onion structure is one of the better OSS community structures. Subramanian et al. [2] measure an Open Source project's success by measuring user interest, project interest and developer interest. They measure user interest by calculating the number of project downloads and to measure the developer interest in the project, Subramanian et al. [2] count the number of active developers in the project. Finally, they measure project activity by calculating the number of files released in the project [2].

Other authors such as Stewart et al. [10] find that licence choice (i.e. how restrictive the licence is) and organizational sponsorship (i.e its affiliation with a for-profit company or university) determine how successful the OSS projects are. In addition to these measures, Sen et al. [11] also find subscriber base (i.e. the number of individuals who chose to be updated about the project developments) and number of developers to reflect the "healthiness" of an OSS project [11]. Chenglur-Smith et al.[12] work on similar lines, and predict that a OSS project's age and size help in the sustainability of the project (i.e. its ability to retain interest and continue to attract developers) [12]. Amrit and Hillegersberg [13], on the other hand, explore the core-periphery shifts of development activity and its impact on OSS project health. They find that a steady movement of developers away from the core of the software code is indicative of an unhealthy OSS project [13].

Regarding the techniques used to analyse OSS data, English and Schweik [14] produce a six-part classification for OSS projects. They base this classification on phone interviews with OSS developers, manual coding of a sample of OSS projects from SourceForge.net, and theoretical insights from Hardin's "Tragedy of the Commons". English and Schweik operationalize these definitions and test them on 110,933 SourceForge projects, with low error rates. Wiggins and Crowston [15] extend this research and analyse another SourceForge data set. Of 117,733 projects, they classify 31% as abandoned at the Initiation stage, 28% as abandoned at the Growth stage, and 14% as successful at both the Initiation and Growth stages.

Though the dependent variables of English and Schweik [14] are well thought out, they do not explore the relationship of their classification with the existing classification of projects in SourceForge. Furthermore, their focus is by and large to determine the number of successful and unsuccessful OSS projects and to classify projects into their six categories. In this paper, we also try to determine the factors that affect the heath of an OSS project. Specifically, we try to predict the subjective classification provided by the project managers and developers of the different SourceForge projects in order to (1) check the validity of the subjective classification and (2) if the classification is indeed valid, one can use the classifier to determine the variables that affect project health.

2.2   Success Factors

Previous research has focused on using three well known metrics to determine project success with the added benefit they have corresponding metrics on SourceForge [2, 3].

The use of longitudinal data from past projects hosted by SourceForge.net to determine OSS success is also an innovation in recent studies [2]. They divide the independent variables into two groups; time-variant and time-invariant and determined how they affect the success measures. The outcome of this study validates the idea of using historical data, as they have proved that past levels of developer and user interest influence present interest. The effect of this change in popularity is that lead-developers and project managers should better anticipate the future need for resources and manage both the internal and external network size of a project [16].

The choice of software license can also have a detrimental influence on the success of a project [4]. They find that if more effort is necessary to complete the project, developers tend to choose less restrictive licenses such as those from the No-Copyleft or Weak-Copyleft categories as opposed to Strong-Copyleft. This even holds true when developers prefer to use more restrictive licenses to ensure that derivative work is adequately protected. The choice of license can be influenced by external factors such as royalties and network effects. As such the preferred license can differ from the optimal license. Other research has shown that when a project has managed to pass through the initial stages of its lifecycle with a less than optimal license it will not severely influence future success [17].

A difficult topic to study relates to determining what factors influence OSS projects in both the initial stage and in the growth stage. As data from a project's initial stages is often absent, this resolves to determining what time-invariant factors can influence the growth stage. Research has found that the initial stage of an OSS project is indeed the most vulnerable time period as a project competes for legitimacy with other similar projects in attracting developers.

3   Methodology

3.1   Data and Variable Definitions

In order to build a model that approximates the status value of a software project on SourceForge we need to gather factors that might influence developers to assign a particular value of status.

Table 1. Overview of SourceForge's status classification

Classification Number	Development Stage
1	Planning
2	Pre-Alpha
3	Alpha
4	Beta
5	Production / Stable.
6	Mature
7	Inactive

3.2   Dependent Variables

To determine the success of software project we try and categorize what status (stage) of development a project has reached.

3.2.1   Project Status

The current progress of a software project can be placed in one of five development stages according to the System development life cycle: these are Requirements Planning, Analysis, Design, Development and Maintenance [2]. Another way to describe a projects progress is through terms such as Planning, Alpha, Beta and Stable. Shifts in progress are marked by improvements in completeness, consistency, testability, usability and reliability [2].

SourceForge.net maintains a system of 7 status designations (Table 1). The numbers 1 through 6 are for Planning, Pre-Alpha, Alpha, Beta, Production/Stable and Mature The last status is an outside category for projects that are Inactive. Previous research [2] makes it clear that it can be expected that projects reaching advanced stages of their life cycle will be more in favor with users and those in earlier stages, as their input goes beyond mere maintenance. As more users make use of the software, they also generate more bug reports, feature requests and feedback/suggestions. In turn developers develop more patches. As such, the latter stages of development are marked by more development activity related to patches, bugs and feature requests. The use of historical data in previous research [2] shows that increased numbers of developers and users will show later on in increased project activity. To better mark this relationship between different time periods within a project we have selected projects on SourceForge that have valid data from a period of four years from 2006 to 2009. The 7 stage status category used by SourceForge is considered by some [2, 11], an awkward use of the typical lifecycle definitions used in software development. SourceForge uses only vague descriptions for each, and much is left to developers to decide the status their project is in. Especially the difference between pre-alpha and alpha, as well as between production/stable and mature, may be cause for confusion. To overcome this, we also consider the binary project status representing whether the project is active, and the project status variable that has four categories; namely Planning, Alpha and Beta and Stable. To achieve the four stages of the project status, we collapsed the inactive and planning stages to the Planning stage, we aggregated the stages Pre-Alpha, Alpha to Alpha stage and Production/Stable and Mature to the Mature category.

Projects on SourceForge.net can also be differentiated along a different dimension, that of project activity. It can be reasonably assumed that both projects in the planning stages and those that are inactive do not have either code to download or developers to work on the project. As such they should be markedly different from those projects of which code is available for download and alteration. We propose to check for ways in which projects that are inactive differ from those that are active, apart from the aforementioned variables.

3.3   Time-Invariant Variables

Variables that can influence the success of an OSS project can be divided into two groups – time-invariant factors and time-variant factors. The variables included have been previously identified in literature as affecting OSS success [3, 11].

For time-invariant variables we have chosen those that define a project in general terms such as license [4], the operating system that can be used and the programming language [2] in which the code is written, to determine if they are factors that have an influence on the project status. Each variable is divided into binary variable categories such as Strong-CopyLeft, Weak-Copyleft and No-Copyleft for license and after which each project is assigned either the value 0 or 1 to show if it supports a particular feature.

The time-invariant variables have been further augmented with simple numerical variables that list the number of features of each category that a project supports. So for license, there is a variable that would count the number of licenses used by a project.

License

The license used by a project can influence the amount of support it gets, as it affects the interests of users and developers [10]. Software licenses can be broadly divided into three groups based on the level of restrictiveness that would determine whether users can distribute derivatives or modify the software (copyfree).

These categories are Strong-Copyleft, Weak-CopyLeft and No-CopyLeft. Licenses such as GPL (General Public License) and BSD (Berkeley Software Distribution) License are grouped into these categories depending on whether they support issues such as 'copyfree' or not. Various research papers already use this division of licenses and where licenses fall into [9, 10]. However, numerous licenses cannot be exactly assigned to any of the three categories because they do not conform the GPL format. As far as possible, they are assigned based on the effect these licenses have on user and developer choices.

Operating System

The operating system used for development and use of a project can have a severe impact on its popularity as it determines how many users it could potentially reach as well as what type of license the developer intends to use [2]. Traditionally open source software has used UNIX, Linux and its derivatives for development, which caused OSS to be somewhat excluded from other operating systems such as Windows and Mac OS X. With the popularity of languages such as a Java that make portability possible Windows has become an increasingly more popular for OSS developers. Previous research[2] has indeed focused on these three categories of operating system: the Windows-family, UNIX (also includes Linux and POSIX) and a other category that includes MAC OS X. They prove that UNIX and Linux type operating system have a negative correlation with user interest, but a positive correlation with developer interest and explain this based on the roots of the OSS community who frequently started their career on UNIX and Linux machines.

We have expanded the number of OS groupings to also include 'OS Independent' as a category to denote the increasing popularity of portability. Mac OS X has also been grouped into a separate category as an acknowledgement of its increasing popularity. Other operating systems were left out of this study. The increase in number of categories should allow for better rules to be deduced from our data mining efforts.

Similar to the license variables these categories denote binary variables and an outside category has been added that counts the number of operating systems supported by a project.

Programming Language
The effects of the programming language used in a project has previously solely focused on the C-family of languages, while others where either excluded from study or aggregated into one category [2, 3]. This study intends to rectify this deficiency to also include popular languages such as Java and PHP as separate categories without denying the continued importance of C-type languages.

Because the C programming language was used for the implementation of UNIX is has remained popular with UNIX and Linux developers ever since [2]. Despite memory allocation problems it has remained a favorite for projects that have more stringent processing and real-time requirements. Through the prevalence of high quality compilers and the importance of derivative languages (C++ C# and Visual C++) the use of C can be associated with more developers and project activity [2].

For our study we have expanded the number of language categories to 5 and included 'C-family', 'Java', 'PHP', 'Python' and 'Others' as separate categories.

3.4   Time-Variant Variables

The three success measures previously mentioned that have their roots in the IS Success Model also have their equivalents in OSS projects found on SourceForge. These are Project Activity (number of files, bug fixes and patches released), User Activity (number of downloads) and Developer Activity (number of developers per project). Crowston et al. (2006)[3] discovered that these measures are interrelated as developers are often users which means that the number of downloads and developers is thus correlated. Project Activity is also closely correlated with User Activity as the latter often download the latest software releases, developers tend to flock to such projects as well. We use the above three metrics as the basis for our time-variant variables.

Other variables include the number of donors, forum posts, mailings lists, feature requests and 'Service Requests' that allow users to ask for help from developers. Our dataset also includes the project age in days from 2009 backwards as a control variable. Combined, we have constructed a dataset that contains 38 variables including 35 independent variables and three variations of one dependent variable, i.e. project status with 7, 4 and 2 project statuses.

3.5   Dataset Sampling

SourceForge.net is the largest web portal for the development of Open Source Software, it acts as a repository for code, as a tracking system for bugs and features and as a communication outlet for those involved in software development. As of November 2012 it hosts some 300,000 projects that differ in a wide range of categories such as intended audience, the topic of the project, the license used as well as technical attributes in which projects can distinguish itself; programming language, OS supported as well as the Graphical User Interface used. For the purpose of this study it is impossible to gather data directly from SourceForge through a screen scraper as the servers of Sourceforge.net cannot distinguish this activity from more nefarious ones such as a Denial of Service attack.

The dataset used has thus been obtained through a third source which has made the data publicly available [18]. FlossMole.org contains data collected for the period 2006 to December 2009 from which a dataset was compiled of 125,700 projects. Unfortunately, many projects had missing data, due to the fact that no data was entered by developers, or project portals were not maintained, or the screen scraper that collected data often did so wrongly, which corrupted portions of the dataset.

Our dataset initially contained 125,700 projects and most projects had incomplete data for the time period 2006 to 2009. Hence, upon cleaning the data we were left with 28,282 rows in our database,

4   Experiment Methodology

We used the SPSS 2.0 decision tree analysis able to analyze the data and predict project status. In our research we chose the CHAID[19] and the CART[20] method of data classification, in order to handle over 35 independent variables some of them being categorical, numeric and non-parametric.

Decision trees can suffer from over-training, whereby the trees continue to grow and might afterwards not be able to validate test-data because it uses rules learned from the training data that are incompatible with the test data. Both CHAID and CART use different ways to limit the growth of decision trees.

CHAID
Which stands for 'Chi-squared Automatic Interaction Detection' uses a statistical stopping rule to keep the tree from growing to impossible sizes. CHAID has the advantage of being able to handle categorical variables. Other research using this method indicate that it excels at analyzing all the factors that can possible influence a dependent variable but it's result at predicting these value with subsequent data samples is often poor.

CART
Also known as 'Classification and Regression Trees' builds a tree based on theory quite different from CHAID. CART uses a non-parametric approach which can work with both categorical and numerical variables, and also has the ability to model the complex interactions among the variables[20]. It first grows the tree to its full size and afterwards it prunes the tree until the accuracy of the tree is similar for both the training dataset and the test dataset.

The reason why we chose CHAID and CART is that while both classifiers can work with categorical variables and use different theoretical models, they are also comparable in some aspects (lift in response)[21].

Cross Validation

With both methods of growing a decision tree we have used our dataset in two ways. The first is cross-validation of the entire data sample whereby data is partitioned multiple times over in both trainings sets to build the tree and test sets to validate the tree.

This is a process whereby data is manually split into training and test sets. For the purposes of this study we used a 50-50 data split in order to avoid overtraining.

5   Results

Below are the results of for each of the three types of project status. The results include both the CHAID tests as well as the Cross-validation and data-split methods.

The accuracy with which our classification tree has been able to determine the correct project status can be seen in tables 2 and 3.

5.1   Data Split

The results in table 2 have been obtained through a 50-50 data split (to prevent overtraining) and represents the results of the training set. The method obtained two results of importance, the first is the exact match of 39.6 % whereby of the 24582 data samples 9729 achieved the correct corresponding status value. For a 7-fold category this result can be considered acceptable (as compared to $1/7 \sim 0.14$ for random chance). The second method, or 1-away result, shows what percentage of data samples either had exactly the correct status value, or were just 1 value off the mark. The accuracy for this is 76.2 % and suggests that the results are closely distributed around the correct value. This result validates the decision tree that was grown from the rules deduced from this test.

Table 2. Results of the CHAID decision tree with 7 stage project status

	Categories.							Accuracy.	
	1	2	3	4	5	6	7	Exact match	1-away
1	3246	539	115	344	113	0	27	74.0%	86.3%
2	1770	809	189	1029	257	0	16	19.9%	68.0%
3	967	368	400	2083	534	0	10	9.2%	69.2%
4	786	262	279	3469	1175	0	9	58.0%	78.8%
5	386	109	213	2478	1734	0	3	35.2%	85.4%
6	39	14	10	184	132	0	0	0.0%	34.8%
7	180	34	32	120	47	0	71	14.7%	14.7%
								39.6%	
									76.2%

Exact match = 39.6%.
number of hits / total cases = 9729 / 24582.
1-away match = 76.2%.
(number of hits + number of 1-away hits) / total cases
= (9729 + 9013) / 24582.

5.2   Cross-Validation

For the cross-validation method, the final score seems to closely match those of the data split method. However, for status value corresponding to Planning (1) and Inactive (7) the results differ significantly, as this method partitions the data set multiple times it would average out the more extreme values obtained through the data-split method.

Table 3. Status results through cross-validation

	Categories.							Accuracy.	
	1	2	3	4	5	6	7	Exact match	1-away
1	6008	1352	288	691	181	0	43	70.2%	85.9%
2	3043	2084	590	1913	471	0	8	25.7%	70.5%
3	1711	924	1364	3551	1230	0	15	15.5%	66.3%
4	1420	664	910	6693	2328	0	27	55.6%	82.5%
5	666	386	718	4321	3710	0	5	37.8%	81.9%
6	72	45	70	283	275	0	0	0.0%	36.9%
7	358	76	73	236	93	0	70	7.7%	7.7%
								40.7%	
									76.0%

Exact match = 40.7%.
Number of hits / total cases = 19929 / 48966.
1-away match = 76.0%
(number of hits + number of 1-away hits) / total cases
= (19929 + 17294) / 48966.

Both results validate our method to classify software projects found in SourceForge.

5.3   Four Stage Project Status: Planning, Alpha, Beta and Stable

In table 4 are the results of our efforts to classify projects in the four categories popularly described in literature. The test results were obtained using the CHAID method with a 50-50 split of the dataset.

The accuracy of 45.4% is better than the score for the 7-fold status category, though it's predictive value is especially undermined by the low score in its efforts to classify projects in Beta stage. This could be seen as proof that this stage is a subjective stage that is hard to classify through machine learning. The 1-away score of 86.0 % once again proof that the scores are distributed around the correct value though for a 4-fold category the value loses in importance.

This result validates that out method works to determine the correct stage in its lifecycle a software project is in.

Table 4. Results of CHAID for 4 stage project status

	Categories.				Accuracy.	
	1.	2.	3.	4.	Exact match	1-away
.	1877	2081	157	73	44.8%	
.	1270	5049	1274	858	59.4%	
.	424	2405	1837	1327	30.7%	
.	201	1621	1384	2094	39.5%	
					45.4%	
						86.0%

Fig. 1. Stage results

Growing method; CHAID.
Exact match = 45.4%.
Number of hits / total cases = 10857 / 23932.
1-away match = 86.0%.
(number of hits + number of 1-away hits) / total cases
= 20598 / 23932.

5.4   Binary Project Status: Active and Inactive

We get an accuracy of 82.4% for classification of projects based on a binary status of active or inactive. The results can be considered to be better, if we consider that the inactive state is an aggregation of the Planning status and the Inactive status, they share many things in common but also have crucial differences for the former can have developers assigned to it.

Table 5. Results of CHAID for a binary project status

	Categories.		Accuracy
	1	2	
1	1226	3539	25.7%
2	789	18985	96.0%
			82.4%

5.5   Cross Validation Result

The cross-validation method seems better able to determine whether a project is active (1), because the method splits the dataset 10 times and tests each iteration we can presume that the lower score for the above 50-50 data split is an aberration.

Table 6. Results of CHAID, CV for binary project status

	Categories.		Accuracy
	1	2	
1	3498	6972	36.9%
2	2474	37023	93.7%
			82.8%

This result of 82.8% accuracy, shows that our method can successfully distinguish active projects from inactive projects.

6   Discussion

The results of our classification show a nearly 40% accuracy for an exact match of the subjective classification and a 76% 1-away match (Table 2) indicates that subjective classification performed by the OSS project leader is quite accurate and correlates with the project data. This is quite unlike what is reported for commercial projects [7]. The errors and implications of this finding can be a subject for future research.

By using the CART method of decision tree analysis, we obtained a model for status classification, as shown in Figure 2. The tree shows that numerical metrics such as downloads, donors, developers and forum posts are far more explanatory of project health than time-invariant metrics such as license used, or the operating system supported.

This is in-line with earlier research [2]. However, this should not be surprising as those time-invariant metrics are usually decided upon when the project is initiated, and change little over its lifecycle. When they do change, they change only to suit users and developers. On the other hand, time-variant metrics, by their definition, can gauge what popularity a project has presently obtained. The order of importance that metrics have taken in the model is also as expected and follows established literature [2, 3].

In the early stages of a project lifecycle, the ability to attract developers is of vital importance in order to be able to develop software along the stated goals. In the latter stages of the software life cycle, it can be expected that users and developers generate more forum posts. This model also shows that the number of donors is an indication as to whether the project has status 4, 5 or 6. This can serve as an indicator, for example, that a project sponsor can have a positive influence on project success. This is in line with the findings of Stewart et al.[10].

The number of SVN commits relates to the number of changes developers have uploaded to the central software repository on SourceForge. In the model (Figure 2) it is closely related with the number of developers on a project in the early stages of the software lifecycle. The number of CVS commits denotes the number of official software releases and surprisingly is not part of the model obtained.

The choice of license is also not an important factor in determining whether a project will be able to continue to succeed in the growth stage. This validates other research [10, 17] but for the most part contradicts long established views on how a project would compete for resources.

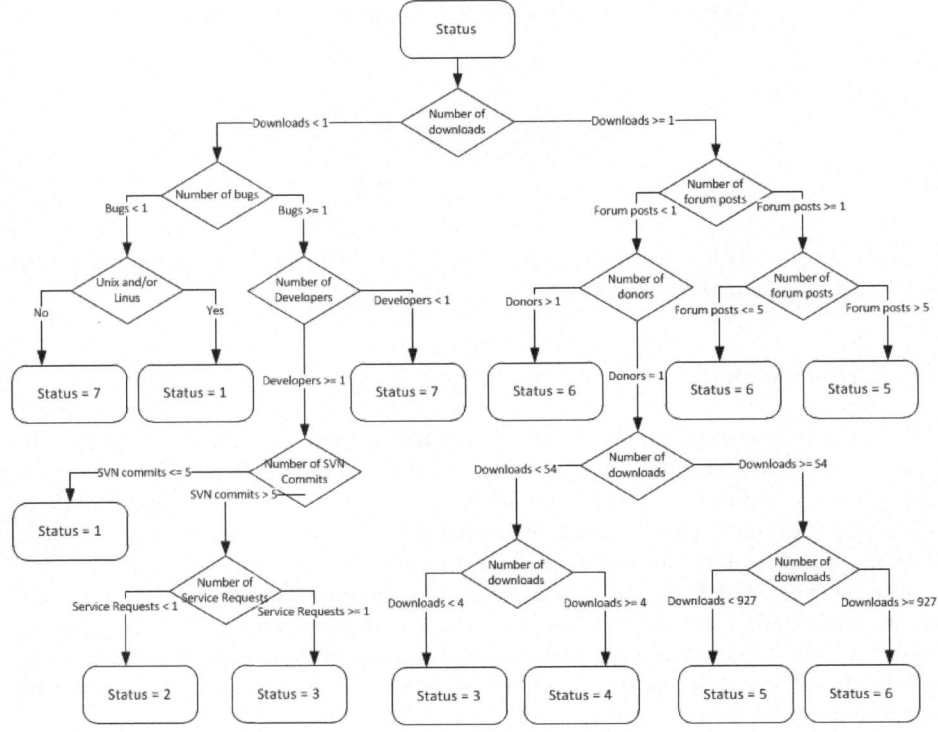

Fig. 2. The CART decision tree for our data

Even though our dependent variable is the SourceForge subjective classification done by the OSS project leaders, we can definitely say that given the predictive accuracy of 1-away classification, the classification model does reflect the stage/health of the OSS projects. As validation of this claim, we find that most of the important variables are also mentioned by other authors[2, 3, 5, 6]

With our model we have managed to predict the status of a project with reasonable accuracy. The model in figure 2 shows this when status 7 (inactive) is reached after a combination of few downloads few active developers and only a small number of bug reports have been generated.

7   Conclusion

We make two primary contributions with this research: (i) we demonstrate that the subjective project status (especially the 1-away value) reflects the actual health of the OSS project. This finding is in line with that of [2] and shows that, in this respect OSS projects differ from commercial projects [7] (ii) we determine the variables that affect project status and in turn affect project health based on nearly 30 K projects over a period of four years.

Our research shows that with a limited set of just 8 variables (Figure 3), we can gauge the status of a software project on SourceForge. Analyzing these 8 attributes of the OSS project can help alert Project controllers that their project is either poorly supported or will become obsolescent in the near future due to lack of developer interest. For prospective developers and sponsors this model can give an idea, whether a project is on track to pass through the early difficult stages of a software life cycle on schedule and is in fact not already failing.

We think our results can provide further research opportunities in projects that also suffer from users and developers being flooded with data, whose accuracy cannot be interpreted easily. Crowd funding sites such as Kickstarter[3] offers an index of project that are considered 'popular' and 'most funded' but there may be lopsided metrics as projects size, ambition and accessibility can negatively influence them.

References

[1]   DeLone, W.H., McLean, E.R.: The DeLone and McLean model of information systems success: a ten-year update. Journal of Management Information Systems 19, 9–30 (2003)

[2]   Subramaniam, C., et al.: Determinants of open source software project success: A longitudinal study. Decision Support Systems 46, 576–585 (2009)

[3]   Crowston, K., et al.: Information systems success in free and open source software development: theory and measures. Software Process Improvement and Practice 11, 123–148 (2006)

[4]   Comino, S., et al.: From planning to mature: On the success of open source projects. Research Policy 36, 1575–1586 (2007)

[5]   Lee, S.Y.T., et al.: Measuring open source software success. Omega 37, 426–438 (2009)

[6]   Midha, V., Palvia, P.: Factors affecting the success of Open Source Software. Journal of Systems and Software (2011)

[7]   Snow, A.P., Keil, M.: The challenge of accurate software project status reporting: a two-stage model incorporating status errors and reporting bias. IEEE Transactions on Engineering Management 49, 491–504 (2002)

[8]   Mockus, A., et al.: Two Case Studies of Open Source Software Development: Apache and Mozilla. ACM Transactions on Software Engineering and Methodology 11, 309–346 (2002)

[9]   Wang, J.: Survival factors for Free Open Source Software projects: A multi-stage perspective. European Management Journal (2012)

[10]   Stewart, K.J., et al.: Impacts of license choice and organizational sponsorship on user interest and development activity in open source software projects. Information Systems Research 17, 126–144 (2006)

[11]   Sen, R., et al.: Open source software licenses: Strong-copyleft, non-copyleft, or somewhere in between? Decision Support Systems (2011)

[12]   Chengalur-Smith, I., et al.: Sustainability of free/libre open source projects: A longitudinal study. Journal of the Association for Information Systems 11, 5 (2010)

---

[3] http://www.kickstarter.com/

[13]   Amrit, C., van Hillegersberg, J.: Exploring the impact of socio-technical core-periphery structures in open source software development. Journal of Information Technology 25, 216–229 (2010)

[14]   English, R., Schweik, C.: Identifying success and abandonment of FLOSS commons: A classification of Sourceforge. net projects. Upgrade: The European Journal for the Informatics Professional VIII 6 (2007)

[15]   Wiggins, A., Crowston, K.: Reclassifying success and tragedy in FLOSS projects. In: Ågerfalk, P., Boldyreff, C., González-Barahona, J.M., Madey, G.R., Noll, J. (eds.) OSS 2010. IFIP AICT, vol. 319, pp. 294–307. Springer, Heidelberg (2010)

[16]   Sharda, R., Delen, D.: Predicting box-office success of motion pictures with neural networks. Expert Systems with Applications 30, 243–254 (2006)

[17]   Wang, J., et al.: Human agency, social networks, and FOSS project success. Journal of Business Research (2011)

[18]   Howison, J., et al.: FLOSSmole: A collaborative repository for FLOSS research data and analyses. International Journal of Information Technology and Web Engineering (IJITWE) 1, 17–26 (2006)

[19]   Kass, G.V.: An exploratory technique for investigating large quantities of categorical data. Applied Statistics, 119–127 (1980)

[20]   Breiman, L., et al.: Classification and regression trees. Chapman & Hall/CRC (1984)

[21]   Haughton, D., Oulabi, S.: Direct marketing modeling with CART and CHAID. Journal of Interactive Marketing 11, 42–52 (1997)

Identifying Success Factors
for the Mozilla Project

Robert Viseur[1,2]

[1] University of Mons (FPMs), Rue de Houdain, 9, B-7000 Mons, Belgium
robert.viseur@umons.ac.be
[2] CETIC, Rue des Frères Wright, 29/3, B-6041 Charleroi, Belgium
robert.viseur@cetic.be

Abstract. The publication of the Netscape source code under free software license and the launch of the Mozilla project constitute a pioneering initiative in the field of free and open source software. However, five years after the publication came years of decline. The market shares rose again after 2004 with the lighter Firefox browser. We propose a case study covering the period from 1998 to 2012. We identify the factors that explain the evolution of the Mozilla project. Our study deepens different success factors identified in the literature. It is based on authors' experience as well as the abundant literature dedicated to the Netscape company and the Mozilla project. It particularly highlights the importance of the source code complexity, its modularity, the responsibility assignment and the existence of an organisational sponsorship.

1   Introduction

After the launch of the GNU project in 1984 and the emergence of Linux in 1991, the Mozilla project was probably one of the most important events in the field of free and open source software at the end of the nineteenth century (Viseur, 2011). It was a pioneering initiative in the release of proprietary software, while commercial involvement in the development of free and open source software has accelerated over the last ten years (Fitzgerald, 2006). Netscape was the initiator. The company had over 50% browser market shares, facing up to Microsoft. The challenge was huge. Netscape had to be allowed to maintain its pace of innovation and to sustain its business facing one of the main actors in the software market.

The Netscape decision was inspired by Eric Raymond's essay entitled *"The Cathedral and the Bazaar"*. The author presented his experience with the Fetchmail free software and proposed a set of best practices. "*Release early. Release often.*" is still remembered (Raymond, 2001). However, the Mozilla project was not as smooth sailing. Netscape has seen its market share decline over the last few years. The development team was finally fired in 2003. Success of the project resurfaced in 2004 with the lighter Firefox browser. In December 2012, Firefox had a market share of almost 30% in Europe (statcounter.com).

E. Petrinja et al. (Eds.): OSS 2013, IFIP AICT 404, pp. 45–60, 2013.

This adventure was studded with victories as well as failures. The implementation of the project needed to find solutions to organisational, legal, technical and economic issues.

Our study is based on the author's knowledge but also on the abundant scientific literature dedicated to the Netscape company and the Mozilla project. Our goal is to identify the success factors for the Mozilla project.

We organised this study into four sections. The first section presents the historical context. The Mozilla project comes from the Netscape browser that dominated the Web browser market between 1993 and 1997. The second section presents success factors that we will use in our case study. The third section develops the case study. The fourth section discusses the results.

2   Historical Context

The authorship of the World Wide Web is attributed to CERN (info.cern.ch). Tim Berners-Lee and Robert Cailliau implemented the technical foundations for an open sharing of information on the Internet (Berners-Lee and al., 1994; Ceruzzi, 2012; Grosskurth and Godfrey, 2006). CERN put the system in operation at Christmas 1990. It also published a library ("libwww") and a line mode browser. The merit of making the W3 accessible to a wider audience is often attributed to NCSA (www.ncsa.illinois.edu). In 1993, Marc Andreessen presented the Mosaic graphical Web browser. This one offered a significantly improved user experience and was massively distributed over the network. A part of the Mosaic development team joined Netscape. Marc Andreessen was a co-founder. Netscape gave birth to popular Web browsers. In 1994 Netscape developed its software (clients and servers) for the World Wide Web. Netscape dominated the market until 1997 (Cusumano and Yoffie, 2000).

Microsoft lagged behind the market. However the commercial issue went beyond the Web browser market (Halloul, 2005). Indeed, Microsoft faced the risk that Netscape Navigator and Java would lead to a platform able to replace the Windows operating system (Sebenius, 2002). Microsoft succeeded in about six months to offer a product similar to Netscape. Microsoft relied on a strategy of vertical integration. Internet Explorer was tightly integrated with the Microsoft Windows operating system and came free with it (Wang and al., 2005). Microsoft Windows dominated the operating systems for personal computers. Its users were fairly indifferent for the tool and they tended to use the software installed by default. Some aspects of Microsoft strategy could be criticised. After the failure of a market sharing agreement, Microsoft used its dominant position within its network to prevent Netscape from selling browser with profit (Halloul, 2005). Microsoft imposed Internet Explorer with agreements (for example with computer manufacturers). It organised a policy of systematic incompatibility (format war) (Liotard, 2007). In 1998 Netscape joined legal actions against Microsoft for anti-competitive practices (Descombes, 2002; Halloul, 2005; Krishnamurthy, 2009, Wang and al., 2005).

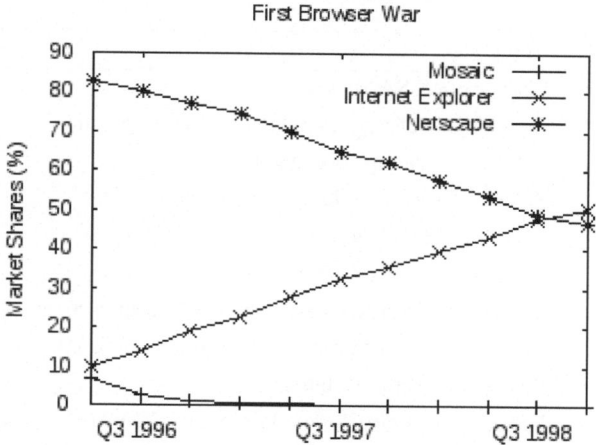

Fig. 1. Netscape market share (first browser war)

The Netscape company announced the release of the source code of Communicator 5 (including the browser) in January 1998. The source code was made available in May 1998. The stakes were high: to allow Netscape to maintain its pace of innovation and sustain its business against a competitor playing a key role in the software industry.

The fifth edition of Netscape did not achieve a commercial future. The sixth edition was released in late 2000. Its instability, its incompatibility with many sites and its heaviness disappointed fans and users, resulting in a significant loss in market share. The number of downloaded copies continued to rise steadily. However, in terms of market share, after a peak of 90% in mid-1996, the Netscape market share decreased gradually in favour of Microsoft, at a rate of about 1% per month (Cusumano and Yoffie, 2000; Descombes, 2002). From 18% in early 2001, the Netscape market share decreased to 12% in mid-2001. The 7.1 version was released in June 2003 and was based on Mozilla 1.4. It corrected the most troublesome defects. However, the harm was done. Microsoft won the first round of the browser war.

Netscape was acquired by AOL Time Warner in March 1999. In July 2003, AOL Time Warner decided to fire the latest Netscape developers. The development of the Netscape browser was stopped (however several Netscape branded software were sporadically released after 2003). The Mozilla project was then supported by the Mozilla Foundation, established on 15th July 2003. The Firefox browser was released in 2004. Its market share increased regularly, mainly to the detriment of Microsoft Internet Explorer. This growth came to a halt in 2008 with the launch of Google Chrome / Chromium, based on the Webkit open source rendering (or layout) engine. The Mozilla Foundation is absent from Web mobile market and has tried to regain the initiative since 2011 with the launch of the Boot to Gecko project (renamed Firefox OS).

Table 1. Important milestones of Mozilla project

Year	Event
1993	Release of NCSA Mosaic.
1994	Creation of Netscape Communications Corporation.
	Release of Netscape Navigator.
1995	Release of Microsoft Internet Explorer.
1998	Launch of Mozilla project.
1999	Acquisition of Netscape by AOL Time Warner.
2000	Release of Netscape 6 based on Mozilla source code.
2003	Death of Netscape. Creation of Mozilla Foundation.
2004	Release of Firefox Web browser.
2008	Release of Google Chrome / Chromium Web browser based on Webkit.
2011	Launch of Boot to Gecko project.

Our research covers the period from 1998 (release of Communicator 5 source code and launch of the Mozilla project) to 2012.

3   Success Factors for Open Source Projects

Several investigations were devoted to the topic of success factors for open source projects.

Comino, Manenti and Parisi (2007) are concerned about the definition of success. They identified different types of measures: the use of software, the size of the community (or the level of activity, measured for example by the output per contributor) and the technical achievement of the project. Their study leads to three conclusions: first, the restrictive licenses, such as GPL, have a lower probability of reaching a stable or mature release; second, projects dedicated to advanced users have a higher probability of evolving in the development status; and third, the size of the developer community increases the chances of progress up to a certain size, after which this effect decreases. This might be explained by the appearance of coordination problems in large projects.

Fershtman and Gandal (2007) were specifically interested in the output per contributor (lines of code). They concluded that this production is lower if the license is restrictive; it is higher if the software is dedicated to developers (rather than end users) and is lower if the software is written specifically for Linux. The restrictive nature is defined according to three levels (rather than two), with a distinction between permissive licenses (e.g. BSD), license with weak reciprocity (e.g. LGPL) and licenses with strong reciprocity (e.g. GPL).

Stewart, Ammeter and Maruping (2005) focused on the type of the license and the existence of an organisational sponsorship. They showed that a sponsored project became more popular over time, and the popularity of the project (i.e. the success among users) had a positive effect on its vitality (i.e. the success among developers).

However the impact of the type of the license is not resolved by this study. These results must be seen alongside those of Roberts, Hann and Slaughter (2006) regarding the Apache project. They showed that being paid to contribute is associated with a higher level of contribution on the source code.

Midha and Palvia (2012) used the "cue utilisation theory" (CUT) to determine the factors influencing the success of open source projects. The factors are categorised as extrinsic and intrinsic factors. The extrinsic factors are the type of license, the number of available translations, the size of the user base (since the software exists), the size of the developer base and the responsibility assignment. The intrinsic factors are the complexity and the modularity of the source code. The authors also distinguished two kinds of success: the technical success (i.e. the activity of developers) and the current market success (i.e. the popularity of the project).

They reached following conclusions:

- The technical success does not influence the market success.

- The negative impact of restrictive licenses depends on the status of the project. If we consider the criterion of market success, the negative impact of restrictive licenses only takes place for the first version of the software. It tends to disappear with time. If we consider the criterion of technical success, the negative impact of restrictive licenses does not occur in the early stages of the project but in the following stages. The authors explained this finding by the fact that the license is one of the only pieces of information available to users when the software appears and that the first developers see the restrictive licenses as a protection against the risks of ownership.

- The user base positively influences the market success and the technical success (except in the early stages of the project).

- The number of translations positively influences the success on the market.

- The technical success is positively impacted by the delegation of responsibilities, negatively influenced by the complexity and positively influenced by the modularity.

For our case study, we retain the following factors: the complexity, the modularity, the type of license, the number of available translations, the size of the users' base, the size of the developers' base, the responsibility assignment and the existence of an organisational sponsorship.

These factors are included in the CUT theory. We added the organisational sponsorship (as an extrinsic factor), whose the positive impact is underscored by several studies.

4   Case Study: The Mozilla Project

4.1   The Complexity

Jamie Zawinski (1999) was a veteran of Netscape and one of the initiators of the Mozilla project. He pointed to the fact that the released code was too complicated and difficult to change. As a result, few people contributed and a complete rewrite of the browser was necessary, which delayed the project by six to ten months. This rewrite gave birth to a new rendering engine named Gecko/Raptor.

This need for rewriting was also justified by the objective to propose a rendering engine complying with the Web standards and by an erosion of design, which results in iterative development practices implemented by Netscape (Cusumano, 2007; Reis and Pontin, 2002; van Gurp and Bosh, 2002).

4.2   The Modularity

The release of Netscape and the launch of the Mozilla project were accompanied by the provision of valuable development tools. These tools are used to develop the software itself (XUL, Gecko, etc.) and for the organisation of collaborative work (Bugzilla, Tinderbox, etc.) (Reis and Pontin, 2002).

After rewriting the released software, the Mozilla project has been gradually moving towards a stable release. Mozilla 1.4 can be considered as the first fully exploitable release. The Mozilla project has a modular structure. Mozilla technologies can be used by other software and benefit from additional external contributions. The HTML rendering engine, called Gecko, is used as a basis for other browsers like Camino or Galeon. In response to heavy criticisms, Mozilla has been subsequently split into lighter applications. Mozilla Firebird (now Mozilla Firefox) and the Mozilla Thunderbird mail client emerged in 2004.

The extensions (addons.mozilla.org) are considered as an important competitive advantage and mobilise a large community of developers. They can meet very specific needs and attract new users (Krishnamurthy, 2009). In July 2012, more than 85% of Firefox users used at least one extension, for an average of five extensions by user. These extensions cover features as diverse as ad blocking, video downloading, browser interface customisation and Web page debugging. The Mozilla Foundation also claims more than 25,000 developers for extensions and three billion downloads worldwide.

4.3   The Type of License

The creation of a new software license, called Mozilla Public License (MPL), was a part of the project. It was written to regulate the coexistence between the community and the companies. More than 75 third-party modules were used in the browser. Lawyers regard the MPL as original (Montero and al., 2005). It is a license with weak copyleft. It differs notably from the distinction between modified works and wider works. If the first one must remain under MPL, the second one can use a third-party licensed for the original parts. Sun Microsystems was inspired by this license for the Common Development and Distribution License (CDDL). The Open Source Initiative approved MPL 1.1 as well as newer MPL 2.0.

The choice of a software license to cover the new project was a project within the project (Hamerly and Paquin, 1999). The very permissive BSD license did not protect the developers' contributions enough in case of use without compensation by a third party. The GPL was more restrictive (it imposes a conservation and a propagation of the license) but it was considered untenable for commercial developers. A new license, called Netscape Public License (NPL), was submitted to developers in March 1998. It seemed very unpopular and was quickly deemed unacceptable by the community because Netscape had been granted special rights. The NPL then became Mozilla Public License (MPL). It was identical to the NPL but skipped over the clause giving the possibility for Netscape to transfer the code licensed under NPL in a product not covered by this license. The source code of the browser subsequently evolved from the original NPL coverage to the MPL coverage (Di Penta and German, 2010). The LGPL and GPL later appeared in the development, in order to address problems of incompatibilities with third-party projects (de Laat, 2005).

4.4   The Size of the User Base

The Mozilla project had its roots in the Netscape products and could benefit from the sympathy of a portion of the former user base.

Firefox 1.0 was downloaded two million times in the first two days (Baker, 2005) and surpassed one billion downloads in late July 2009 (Shankland, 2009). Foundation estimated the number of users at 300 million compared to 175 million a year earlier.

4.5   The Size of the Developer Base

Recruiting new developers was not easy to start the project. According to Jamie Zawinski (1999), the scope of the project entailed a significant delay before they contributed. As a result, a small change could take several hours. The complexity of the code further aggravated this problem. The efforts of the leading contributors were not rewarded. The contributors expected compensation, such as having the ability to change the commonly used browser version and thus see the effects of their own changes. However, the released sources were not those of the commercially distributed version of the browser (4.x branch). Netscape released a code which lacked many features and was full of bugs. The development capabilities were shared between two versions: the 4.x branch (it underwent several changes, from 4.5 to 4.78) and the Mozilla branch. The activity on the proprietary branch did not benefit from the open source branch. The open source development was slowed down by dispersion of resources. The same applied for the commercial branch.

Rewriting the project allowed it to reach its cruising speed. However, changes were then made following the withdrawal of AOL Time Warner, although these were not necessarily visible for an outside observer. The transition was accompanied by a significant decrease in activity of developers and a significant change in the composition of the group of most active developers (Gonzalez-Barahona and al., 2007).

The adoption of Firefox slowed after the release of Google Chrome / Chromium. This was accompanied by tensions within the community, and some departures occurred (Champeau, 2011). The discord focused on the relationship between the contributors in the community and the official structures of the Mozilla project. The fast release cycle that Firefox inaugurated in 2011 in the wake of Chrome (this cycle is particularly interesting on a marketing plan) was also the subject of heated debate. The results of this new policy did not seem negative, with a largely preserved stability and faster correction of errors (Khomh and al., 2012).

4.6   The Responsibility Assignment

The Mozilla project maintains a centralised decision-making structure. The whole project is managed by a small group of developers (Krishnamurthy, 2005; Mockus and al., 2002; Nurolahzade et al., 2009). This small group delegated tasks and roles. They appointed, in particular, the module owners who are responsible for selecting and implementing changes.

The users can share their report bugs, vote to prioritise them and discuss their resolution. In practice, the development of Mozilla is bug-driven, in other words, led by the bugs (den Besten and Dalle, 2010; Pontin and Reis, 2002). The term "bug" covers defects, enhancements and changes in functionality. The bug reports are encoded, numbered and sorted. If they are confirmed, their correction is planned according to severity and priority. A manager is appointed for each bug. The proposed changes to the source code are finally attached to the bug in the form of patches. These operations are managed through Bugzilla, a Web-based bug tracking system developed in Perl for the needs of the Mozilla project.

The design process is open and User Experience practitioners work in the bug tracker. However, a User Experience director lead the design and *"some decisions are made behind the scenes"* (Bach and Carroll, 2009). Community can be conservative with design explorations.

The hierarchical organisation of the Mozilla project is the source of frequent disputes but ensures the coherence of development. This structure is perhaps a relic of the past strong involvement of commercial organisation in the development process (as well as the contributions below the expectations after the launch of the project). The history of the project is also that of a transition from commercial to open source development model (Baker, 2005). However, the Mozilla project is distinguished by the large number of contributions made by members at the periphery of the community, which tends to show the relevance of this mode of organisation for a project of this scale (Wang and Carroll, 2011). Taking the votes on the outskirts of the community into account would be low (Dalle and al., 2008).

The gradual shift in the market towards the WebKit open source rendering engine raises questions about the ability of the Mozilla project to accommodate large external contributors.

4.7   The Organisational Sponsorship

From May 1998 to July 2003, the Mozilla project was supported by Netscape, owned since March 1999 by AOL Time Warner. Since July 2003 the Mozilla Foundation has overseen the development of the Mozilla project and has received a $2 million donation from AOL Time Warner (Baker, 2005).

Table 2. Organisational sponsorship for Mozilla project

Period	Sponsor
May 1998 – March 1999	Netscape.
March 1999 – July 2003	Netscape / AOL Time Warner.
July 2003 - present	Mozilla Foundation.

The Mozilla Foundation derives its income from agreements with commercial search engines. Google accounts for 95% of its revenues. The Mozilla Foundation (www.mozilla.org) announced that it earned $52.9 million in 2005 with its browser. In comparison, the revenues amounted to $2.4 million in 2003 and $5.8 million in 2004. The Foundation employs 70 employees on a permanent basis. It is dependent on and owes its financial survival of this agreement to Google. Mozilla Foundation and Mozilla Corporation (trading subsidiary) expenditures rose to $8.2 million in 2005. Software development accounted for $6,075,474 compared to $768,701 to $1,328,353 for marketing expenses and general administrative expenses.

Support also came from Unix vendors such as IBM, HP and Sun, who put their research and common development capabilities into the Mozilla project and were able to focus on their own needs (West and Gallagher, 2006).

4.8   Language Translations

In 2012, Firefox was available in over 70 languages. The Mozilla project ensures long efforts to empower translation (see in particular Mozilla Translator).

4.9   Technical Success

The release of Netscape and the launch of the Mozilla project were accompanied by the provision of valuable development tools. These tools are used to develop the software itself (XUL, Gecko, etc.) and for the organisation of the collaborative work (Bugzilla, Tinderbox, etc.) (Baker, 2005; Reis and Pontin, 2002).

After rewriting the code, the Mozilla project has a modular structure. Moreover Mozilla technologies can be used by other software and benefit from additional external contributions. The HTML rendering engine, called Gecko, was used as a basis for other browsers like Camino or Galeon.

In hindsight, it appears that the development tools developed for the Mozilla project sometimes struggled to spread beyond the projects of the Foundation. This is especially true for XULRunner application framework launched in 2007 (Stearn, 2007). XULRunner should bring a runtime environment independent of the operating system for XUL-based applications, a description language for graphical user interfaces based on XML created as part of the Mozilla project. The lack of development environment dedicated to these tools, the gaps in the documentation and the gradual rise of Ajax frameworks help to explain this result in halftone.

The market success came back in 2004, especially with Firefox. This Firefox breakthrough restarted the browser war that Microsoft won a few years earlier. Several technical elements contributed to the success of Firefox: the protection against popups, the software security (Internet Explorer is regularly criticised in this regard, and viruses and security issues caused inconvenience in the summer of 2004), the tab system, the compliance with Web standards and the ability to create extensions (Baker, 2005; Krishnamurthy, 2009).

4.10   Market Success

Promoting the Project

The Mozilla project was well promoted in 2003. Rewards were offered to the project by newspapers, such as Linux Journal that promoted Mozilla as one of the 10 best Linux products. The marketing efforts of the Mozilla Foundation amplify this comeback.

From a marketing perspective, the Mozilla Foundation became more focused on end users (Baker, 2005; Viseur, 2011). It changed the former site, which contained some major flaws, especially from a "commercial" point of view, which was presented as a site for developers with too much complexity for the normal user. There was too much information which was also poorly structured. For example, multiple versions of the Mozilla site were proposed in footnotes. A beta version could have masked a stable version. However, the end user may not know what is involved in beta (it was the second trial period of a software product before its official publication). Improvements were made with the release of version 1.4 of the browser (mid-2003). The latest stable version was clearly shown (upper left corner of the page). The installation files were classified by an operating system (Linux, Mac and Windows). The information sought by the user was directly accessible. Mozilla also introduced the concept of "product". This is familiar to end users, considers the customer and involves a minimum of strategic thinking. A line of products is highlighted. The end user can choose between the classic Mozilla browser and a new lighter browser called Firebird (now Firefox). This development of a line of products was associated with the development of a brand strategy (Mozilla Application Suite, Thunderbird, Firebird, etc.). The name Firefox is registered as a brand. References (such as awards from magazines and quotes from recognised people) were clearly identified in order to give credibility to the products and to reassure new users attracted to the Web site. Contributors were not neglected. Information intended for testers and developers appeared in a different colour at the bottom of the page. The supported operating systems and tools available were also highlighted. The new initiatives, such as telephone support, sales of CDs and gifts, were pointed across the site.

The Mozilla Foundation subsequently continued its marketing efforts. It launched the Spread Firefox initiative in September 2004 (Baker, 2005). After testing the traditional advertising with the purchase of an advertising page (funded by the community) in the American press, the Mozilla Foundation tested viral marketing in

2005. FunnyFox site (www.funnyfox.fr) hosted three humourous ads made by the Pozz (www.pozz-agency.com) French communication agency: The Office, The Mobile and The Notebook. The goal was that these three Flash movies were to be widely distributed at the initiative of users and spread all over the Internet. The Foundation then went further in co-creation. This marketing technique for involving customers and users in the design, the development, the promotion or the support of new products and services was applied to the creation of advertisements. Mozilla launched a contest called Firefox Flicks (www.firefoxflicks.com) in late 2005. The goal was to create a marketing campaign to tap into the creative energy of amateur and professional filmmakers in order to present Firefox to a wider audience.

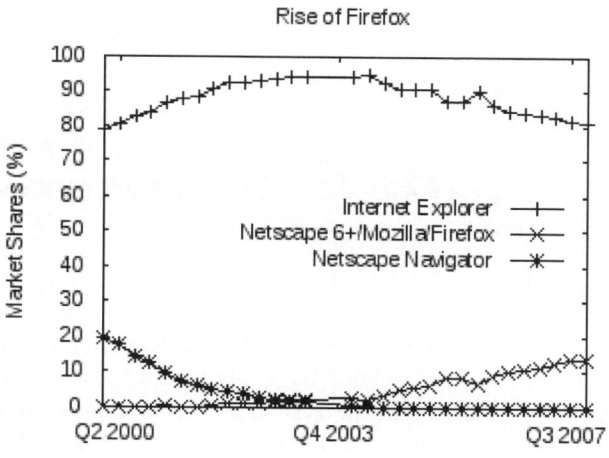

Fig. 2. Firefox market share

The community has also been tapped. Krishnamurthy (2009) identifies three missions supported by the community: the development of the brand, the creation of traffic and the conversion of new users (providing banners, writing positive comments, voting on websites dedicated to software, etc.).

Organisation of the Competitors

The new browser war may have reached a point in September 2008 with the launch of Google Chrome (www.google.com/chrome). Google was motivated by improving the user experience with rich Internet applications (Corley and Hunsinger, 2011), i.e. applications running in a Web browser with characteristics similar to applications running on the workstation. Google offers this type of product (Youtube, GMail, etc.). Google faced stability and speed problems with existing browsers during testing. Google therefore decided to release its own browser.

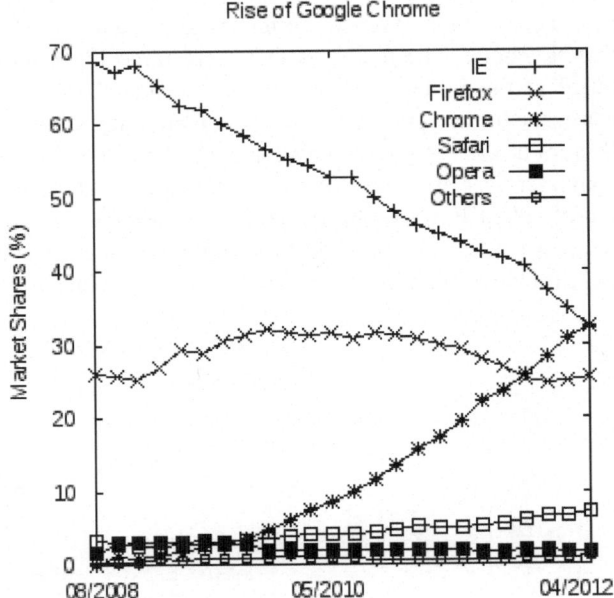

Fig. 3. Google Chrome / Chromium market share

Google Chrome is a browser based on WebKit (webkit.org). WebKit is an open source project which launched in 2005 by Apple for its Safari browser. It is forked from the source code of KHTML, the HTML rendering engine used by Konqueror, the file manager and Web browser combined with the KDE desktop environment (Grosskurth and Godfrey, 2006; Viseur, 2012). Apple was joined on this project by Nokia, Palm and RIM (in practice, Webkit-based browsers dominate the mobile platforms). Chromium is the Chrome free software release (www.chromium.org). The Mozilla ecosystem is particularly fuelled by companies wishing to have a functional browser on platforms other than Microsoft Windows. It is now challenged by a new ecosystem mainly composed of companies that sometimes frontally compete (Google and Apple, for example).

Google Chrome has proven to be fast and stable (process isolation). Google Chrome is frequently offering new versions and its park is quickly renewed through an automatic update system (Baysal and al., 2011). The new product was vigorously promoted by Google, for example by using video spots. It quickly became the third most widely used browser, behind Internet Explorer and Firefox. In practice, the evolution of market shares shows a stabilisation of Firefox browser, a decrease of Internet Explorer and a growth of Google Chrome (gs.statcounter.com). In May 2012, Chrome had a market share of 32.43%, compared to 32.12% and 25.55% for Internet Explorer and Firefox respectively. The competition from Chrome tends therefore to erode the market share of the Internet Explorer common competitor.

It raises new questions about the future of the agreement between Google and the Mozilla Foundation, and about the financial sustainability of the Foundation. In the long term, the motivations behind the release of Chrome also question the evolution of the Web required by major companies. The border between the Internet and the desktop tends to gradually subside, as between the Web pages and applications.

The competition from Google Chrome / Chromium is also consistent with that of the Webkit rendering engine, especially in mobile systems. Most mobile browsers use Webkit. Mozilla is marginalised on these platforms as they become proportionately more important. The use of tablets and smartphones already becomes, for example, dominant for consulting media Web sites during certain periods of the day (comScore). Mozilla is trying to reposition itself in the market with the Boot to Gecko project, an open operating system for mobile devices.

5   Discussion and Perspectives

The influence of intrinsic factors seems to be well emphasised in this case study. The excessive complexity of the released code hindered the start-up of the project and kept potential contributors away, which resulted in a small amount of contributions and a complete rewrite of source code. This suggests the need for thorough preparation before publishing the source code. This rewrite was accompanied by a significant modularisation of source code. The modularity of the browser was enhanced with Firefox that proposed a very popular system of add-ons.

Two external factors stand out: the responsibility assignment and the organisational sponsorship.

The Mozilla project has a centralised decision-making structure and differs from other projects by a module ownership mechanism. It is sometimes a source of tension but this organisation ensures the coherence of the project. The project continues to benefit from many contributions, such as bug reports or corrections ("patches").

The Mozilla Foundation ensures the coherence in the project development and the promotional activity for popularising its software to a wider audience. The impact of the Netscape teams' dissolution also highlighted the impact of the organisation support on the development process of a large-scale and complex project.

In the case of Mozilla, a decision cannot be made regarding the impact of the type of license on the success of the software. However, there was a lot of controversy after the publication of the NPL license illustrated the importance of the license in the eyes of the community and the attention paid to the risks of ownership. Note that the main competitor (Google Chrome / Chromium) is based on a rendering engine that is also covered by a license with weak copyleft.

The technical success depends on the point of view. The Mozilla Firefox project helped to impose open standards for Web site development. One objective of the project was therefore achieved. The market success is undoubtedly linked to the technical success in securing the application or offering modularity ("add-ons"). The success of the Google Chrome / Chromium competitor is also explained by its technical quality and better functioning with websites using technologies for rich clients (e.g. Flash and Ajax). As for disadvantages, the technologies on which the Mozilla browsers are based (e.g. Gecko), or that derived from these technologies (e.g.

XULRunner), encountered difficulties to export to other projects. It is interesting that most software vendors using an open source rendering engine based their product on Webkit and not on Gecko. Regarding further research on this point, it might be instructive to identify the factors that encourage or discourage the reuse of open source components. The highly centralised project organisation may explain the difficulty to collaborate with other key partners.

The market success came back in 2003 and especially in 2004 with the release of Firefox. Firefox was lighter and modular. It benefited not only from its technical qualities but also from the high number of marketing campaigns. Emphasis is placed on the originality of implementing marketing techniques without a classic commercial structure.

The project now faces a major challenge due to the evolution of the market and the arrival of new competitors. The Web evolves gradually under companies' pressure from a world of documents, developed using standards, to a world of heavier and complex applications (Taivalsaari and Mikkonen, 2011). The release of Google Chrome fits into this context. Another development is the rise of the mobile Web. If the situation on the workstation is currently competitive with balanced market shares between Internet Explorer, Firefox and Chrome, the mobile systems market evolves to a monopoly to the benefit of the Webkit rendering engine that powers most mobile browsers (Hernandez, 2009). The mobile operating systems offer a preinstalled browser and the success of Boot to Gecko will determine the future of the Foundation due to the growing importance of a mobile Web.

References

Bach, P.M., Carroll, J.M.: FLOSS UX Design: An Analysis of User Experience Design in Firefox and OpenOffice.org. In: Boldyreff, C., Crowston, K., Lundell, B., Wasserman, A.I. (eds.) OSS 2009. IFIP AICT, vol. 299, pp. 237–250. Springer, Heidelberg (2009)

Baker, M.: The Mozilla Project: Past and Future. In: DiBona, C., Stone, M., Cooper, D. (eds.) Open Sources 2.0, The Continuing Evolution. O'Reilly Media (October 2005)

Bar, M., Fogel, K.: Open Source Development with CVS. Paraglyph Press (2003)

Baysal, O., Davis, I., Godfrey, M.W.: A Tale of Two Browsers. In: MSR 2011, May 21-22 (2011)

Berners-Lee, T., Cailliau, R., Luotonen, A., Nielsen, H.F., Secret, A.: The World-Wide Web. Communications of the ACM 37(8), 76–82 (1994)

Ceruzzi, P.E.: Aux origines américaines de l'Internet: projets militaires, intérêts commerciaux, désirs de communauté. Le Temps des médias (18), 15–28 (2012)

Champeau, G.: Mozilla interroge sur son avenir et ménage sa communauté. Numerama, 23 août (2011)

Comino, S., Manenti, F.M., Parisi, M.L.: From planning to mature: On the success of open source projects. Research Policy 36(10), 1575–1586 (2007)

Corley, J.K., Hunsinger, D.S.: Why are People Using Google's Chrome Browser? In: CONISAR Proceedings (2011)

Cusumano, M.A., Yoffie, D.B.: Competing on Internet time. Touchstone (2000)

Cusumano, M.A.: Extreme programming compared with Microsoft-style iterative development. Communications of the ACM 50(10), 15–18 (2007) de Laat, P.B.: Copyright or copyleft? An analysis of property regimes for software development. Research Policy 34, 1511–1532 (2005)

Dalle, J.-M., Masmoudi, H., den Besten, M.: Channeling Firefox Developers: Mom and Dad Aren't Happy Yet. In: Russo, B., Damiani, E., Hissam, S., Lundell, B., Succi, G. (eds.) Open Source Development, Communities and Quality. IFIP, vol. 275, pp. 265–271. Springer, Boston (2008)

Dalle, J.-M., den Besten, M.L.: Voting for Bugs in Firefox. In: FLOSS Workshop 2010 (2010)

Descombes, S.: Saga Netscape/Microsoft: histoire d'un renversement. Journal du Net, 23 août (2002)

Di Penta, M., German, D.M.: An Exploratory Study of the Evolution of Software Licensing. In: ICSE 2010, Cap Town, South Africa, May 2-8 (2010)

Elie, F.: Économie du logiciel libre. Eyrolles (2006)

Fitzgerald, B.: The transformation of open source software. MIS Quarterly 30(3), 587–598 (2006)

Gonzalez-Barahona, J.M., Robles, G., Herraiz, I.: Impact of the Creation of the Mozilla Foundation in the Activity of Developers. In: Proceedings of the Fourth International Workshop on Mining Software Repositories (2007)

Grosskurth, A., Godfrey, M.W.: Architecture and evolution of the modern web browser. Preprint submitted to Elsevier Science (2006)

Halloul, R.: Le réseau stratégique et la concurrence illustrés par le cas M/N (Microsoft versus Netscape). Innovations (21) (2005)

Hamerly, J., Paquin, T.: Freeing the Source: The Story of Mozilla. In: Open Sources: Voices from the Open Source Revolution. O'Reilly (January 1999)

Harrison, W.: Eating your Own Dog Food. IEEE Software (May/June 2006)

Hernandez, E.A.: War of Mobile Browsers. Pervasive Computing, 82–85 (2009)

Iansiti, M., MacCormack, A.: Developing products on Internet time. Harvard Business Review, 108–117 (Septembre-Octobre 1997)

Khomh, F., Dhaliwal, T., Zou, Y., Adams, B.: Do faster releases improve software quality? An empirical case study of Mozilla Firefox. In: 9th IEEE Working Conference on Mining Software Repositories (MSR), pp. 179–188 (2012)

Krishnamurthy, S.: About Closed-door Free/Libre/Open Source (FLOSS) Projects: Lessons from the Mozilla Firefox Developer Recruitment Approach. Upgrade 6(3) (June 2005)

Krishnamurthy, S.: CASE: Mozilla vs. Godzilla - The Launch of the Mozilla Firefox Browser. Journal of Interactive Marketing (2009)

Liotard, I.: Les nouvelles facettes de la propriété intellectuelle: stratégies, attaques et menaces. Management & Sciences Sociales (4), 1–14 (2007)

Midha, V., Palvia, P.: Factors affecting the success of Open Source Software. Journal of Systems and Software 85(4), 895–905 (2012)

Mikkonen, T., Taivalsaari, A.: Apps vs. Open Web: The Battle of the Decade. In: Proceedings of 2nd Workshop Software Eng. for Mobile Application Development (MSE 2011) (2011)

Mockus, A., Fielding, R.T., Herbsleb, J.D.: Two case studies of open source software development: Apache and Mozilla. ACM Transactions on Software Engineering and Methodology 11(3) (July 2002)

Montero, E., Cool, Y., de Patoul, F., De Roy, D., Haouideg, H., Laurent, P.: Les logiciels libres face au droit. Cahier du CRID (25), Bruylant (2005)

Nurolahzade, M., Nasehi, S.M., Khandkar, S.H., Rawal, S.: The role of patch review in software evolution: an analysis of the Mozilla Firefox. In: Proceedings of the Joint International and Annual ERCIM Workshops on Principles of Software Evolution (IWPSE) and Software Evolution (Evol) Workshops, pp. 9–18 (2009)

Raymond, E.S.: The Cathedral & the Bazaar (Musings on Linux and Open Source by an Accidental Revolutionary). O'Reilly Media (2001)

Reis, C.R., Pontin de Mattos Fortes R.: An Overview of the Software Engineering Process and Tools in the Mozilla Project. Working paper (February 8, 2002)

Roberts, J.A., Hann, I.-H., Slaughter, S.A.: Understanding the Motivations, Participation, and Performance of Open Source Software Developers: A Longitudinal Study of the Apache Projects. Management Science 52(7), 984–999 (2006)

Sebenius, J.K.: Negociating Lessons from the Browser Wars. MIT Sloan Management Review (Summer 2002)

Shankland, S.: Firefox: 1 billion downloads only part of the story (July 31, 2009), http://news.cnet.com

Stearn, B.: XULRunner: A New Approach for Developing Rich Internet Applications. IEEE Internet Computing 11(3), 67–73 (2007)

van Gurp, J., Bosch, J.: Design Erosion: Problems & Causes. Journal of Systems & Software 61(2), 105–119 (2002)

Viseur, R.: Associer commerce et logiciel libre: étude du couple Netscape / Mozilla. In: 16ème Conférence de l'Association Information et Management, AIM, Saint-Denis (France) (25 mai, 2011)

Viseur, R.: Forks impacts and motivations in free and open source projects. International Journal of Advanced Computer Science and Applications (IJACSA) 3(2) (February 2012)

Wang, J., Carroll, J.M.: Behind Linus's law: A preliminary analysis of open source software peer review practices in Mozilla and Python. In: 2011 International Conference on Collaboration Technologies and Systems (CTS), May 23-27 (2011)

Wang, T., Wu, L., Lin, Z.: The revival of Mozilla in the browser war against Internet Explorer. In: ICEC 2005, pp. 159–166 (2005)

West, J., Gallagher, S.: Patterns of Open Innovation in Open Source Software. In: Chesbrough, H., Vanhaverbeke, W., West, J. (eds.) Open Innovation: Researching a New Paradigm, ch. 5. Oxford University Press, Oxford (2006)

Zawinski, J.: Resignation and postmortem (March 31, 1999), http://www.jwz.org

Is It All Lost?
A Study of Inactive Open Source Projects

Jymit Khondhu[1], Andrea Capiluppi[1], and Klaas-Jan Stol[2]

[1] Department of Information Systems and Computing
Brunel University, United Kingdom
[2] Lero—The Irish Software Engineering Research Centre
University of Limerick, Ireland
j_khondhu@hotmail.co.uk, andrea.capiluppi@brunel.ac.uk,
klaas-jan.stol@lero.ie

Abstract. Open Source Software (OSS) proponents suggest that when developers lose interest in their project, their last duty is to "hand it off to a competent successor." However, the mechanisms of such a hand-off are not clear, or widely known among OSS developers. As a result, many OSS projects, after a certain long period of evolution, stop evolving, in fact becoming "inactive" or "abandoned" projects. This paper presents an analysis of the population of projects contained within one of the largest OSS repositories available (SourceForge.net), in order to describe how projects abandoned by their developers can be identified, and to discuss the attributes and characteristics of these inactive projects. In particular, the paper attempts to differentiate projects that experienced maintainability issues from those that are inactive for other reasons, in order to be able to correlate common characteristics to the "failure" of these projects.

Keywords: Open Source, Inactive Projects, Maintainability Index.

1 Introduction

The vast diffusion of Open Source Software (OSS), and the availability of several (hundreds of) thousands of OSS projects, has started to show that this online phenomenon is not always successful [21,19]. A lack of activity by developers, and a low interest by users, show that many OSS projects, after a certain long period of evolution, stop evolving, and in fact become "inactive" projects. This phenomenon has been observed before, and metrics have been developed to automatically detect inactivity, or to correlate which characteristics are more relevant to such inactive projects [18]: how many days, months or years in *"lack of activity"* are necessary to tag a project as inactive? How much should two subsequent releases be apart to declare that a project's development is inevitably facing a downturn? On the other hand, is a specific programming language more likely to cause inactivity in projects? A specific application domain (games, office productivity, etc.)? A specific OSS license?

E. Petrinja et al. (Eds.): OSS 2013, IFIP AICT 404, pp. 61–79, 2013.

Although the semi-automatic detection of inactivity can produce useful insights on the general trends of large sets of OSS projects, any set of assumptions used to produce figures of inactive projects could be criticized for its inclusion criteria, or for not being validated with external factors. One could inadvertently misclassify dormant projects as "inactive"; projects could be renamed in the meantime, or even just moved to dedicated repositories.[1]

The information on such inferred inactivity has relevant external effects: from an end-user's point of view, organizations and private users would not want to invest money or time to deploy or evaluate inactive projects, or those with few or no contributors to perform future maintenance. From a developers' point of view, the original authors should take the responsibility to inform others that they are no longer interested (or able) to support or enhance their project. Or, as Raymond [15, p.26] suggested:

> "When you lose interest in a program, your last duty to it is to hand it off to a competent successor."

This would introduce one of the most powerful mechanisms in OSS development, namely the possibility for another developer to take over the project from one or more previous developers who lost interest in it [15,3]. Thus, we identified two key motivations for accurately labelling inactive or abandoned projects:

1. The ability to clearly distinguish alive projects from the clutter, so as to give confidence to potential users and adopters;
2. To implement one of the most powerful mechanisms of OSS development, namely the ability for other developers to "take over" inactive or abandoned projects, in order to sustain a new phase of development, managed and sustained by someone other than the original creators.

This paper studies the abandonment of OSS projects without inferring their lack of activity with measures. It studies the abandoned projects by spidering a specific HTML tag (i.e., < inactive >) that the authors are encouraged to use in specific cases for their projects on SourceForge.[2] When developers do not intend to continue working on their projects any longer, they have the ability of placing such a tag onto the SourceForge "main" project page,[3] thus sending a clear indication to potential users about the lack of maintenance and support; but also to other developers, who can follow a specific process to become the new maintainers and owners of the project, if they want to do so.[4]

A fundamental reason for studying abandoned projects is to analyze what type of resources have been left behind when developers "moved on", their quality,

---

[1] As an example, the Moodle CMS was moved from SourceForge to its own dedicated repository, after they have "outgrown it."

[2] http://sourceforge.net

[3] See for instance the main page of the *busiprocess* project, http://sourceforge.net/projects/busiprocess/.

[4] The process is detailed, for the SourceForge repository, at http://sourceforge.net/apps/trac/sourceforge/wiki/Abandoned%20Project%20Takeovers.

and whether one of the reasons for such abandonment is because those resources have become ultimately unmaintainable. Both as a user and as a prospective new contributing developer, it is important to understand the quality of an abandoned project and its resources, its general maintainability, and how it progressed over time, also in relation to taking over "control" of the overall project, or potentially the reuse of some of its carefully designed internal components [5]. Therefore, this paper has three objectives:

1. To *quantify* the phenomenon of abandonment of OSS projects on the Source-Forge repository;
2. To *investigate* whether the abandonment of these projects should be linked with issues of maintainability of the source code itself;
3. To *discuss* the quality of the resources that were left behind for others to reuse or "upcycle."

The remainder of this paper proceeds as follows. Section 2 presents the research design. Section 3 presents the results of our study. Section 4 positions this study with respect to previous work in this area. We conclude in Section 5.

2   Research Design

2.1   Research Strategy

We adopted the *Goal-Question-Metric* approach as the overall research strategy [2].

Goal. The overall goal of this study is to develop an understanding of the scale, nature and characteristics of abandonment of OSS projects. We defined two sub-goals: (1) to quantify abandonment of OSS projects, and (2) to evaluate the quality of the code that was left abandoned by developers.

Questions. This paper addresses the following research questions:

1. How many "active," "dormant" and "inactive" projects exist in SourceForge?
2. Do these categories achieve similar growth patterns?
3. Do these categories result in comparable quality and maintainability attributes?

Metrics and Definitions. We used the following metrics and definitions in this study:

- **Category of Projects**: in this study we aim to produce three clusters of projects: the "active" ones, whose activity is updated and recent; the "dormant" ones, whose activity is visible in the past evolution, but it has stopped (for any reason) for a defined period (e.g., one year, two years, etc.); and the "inactive" ones, that have been explicitly tagged as such by the previous developers.

- **Latest Update**: in this study we will extract the latest recorded activity for any Sourceforge project by parsing the specific `dateUpdated` tag on each project's summary page.
- **Inactive Project**: in principle, the inactivity of an OSS project should be evaluated by pre-defining an interval of time when no development effort is registered by its contributors, in terms of commits, messages on the mailing lists or public releases. The SourceForge repository places the specific $< inactive >$ HTML tag[5] on the project pages that show no sign of activity. This could be either be directly communicated by a project's administrators (i.e., an "abandoned" project), or inferred from activity logs (i.e., an "inactive" project). The possibility of isolated inactive projects, and the availability of the source code, is one of the fundamental characteristics of OSS development, which allows new developers to take over and manage an abandoned project [3].
- **Number of lines of code (LOC)** measures the physical size of the program code, excluding blank lines and comments.
- **Percentage of lines of comments** with respect to the number of lines of code (PerCM) describes the documentation and self-descriptiveness of the code.
- **Halstead Volume (HV)**. Halstead [10] defined four metrics that can be measured from a program's source code: n1 (the number of distinct operators), n2 (the number of distinct operands), N1 (the total number of operators) and N2 (the total number of operands). Based on them, Halstead defined program vocabulary n (given by n = n1 + n2) and program length N (given by N = N1 + N2). Finally, he defined Volume, a composite metric given by the formula $V = N * (LOG2n)$.
- **Cyclomatic Complexity (CC)**. Proposed by McCabe [13], this metric counts the number of independent paths in the control flow graph of a program component. Its value depends on the number of branches caused by conditional statements (`if-then-else`). It measures the structural complexity of the component.
- **Maintainability Index (MI)**: based on the definitions above, the Software Engineering Institute (SEI) has developed a maintainability index defined as follows:

$$171 - 5.2ln(HV_{avg}) - 0.23CC_{avg} - 16.2ln(LOC_{avg}) + 50.0sin\sqrt{2.46COM} \quad (1)$$

where HV_{avg} measures the average Halstead metric per module (function, method, class, file or the whole system), CC_{avg} the average McCabe index per module and LOG_{avg} the average lines of code per module.

2.2   Data Collection and Analysis

In this subsection we detail the steps undertaken to perform this empirical study.

---

[5] `<span id="dev-status" class="inactive">inactive</span>`

1. **SRDA database query**: in order to have an initial list of all the projects contained in the SourceForge archive, we queried the SRDA database [9].[6] In the data-dump of September 2012, the total number of SourceForge projects retrieved in the SRDA database is 174,845, and their unique names were recorded.

2. **Status extraction**: each of the project IDs was used to compose a URL relative to the SourceForge online structure.[7] The retrieved page contains a generic summary of the status of the project, along with information on its programming languages, the intended audience, the date of the latest update to the project and so on. The tag "inactive" was searched for all the projects, and a subpool of **inactive projects** was identified. This additional attribute is not available from the SRDA database, and it had to be specifically extracted.

3. **Latest activity extraction**: from the same summary page, we extracted, per project, the latest recorded date of activity, which is automatically copied by SourceForge from the list of activities of the project.[8] The information on the latest activity date served to discriminate between an "active" and a "dormant" project. If no activity was registered throughout the last year since the analysis (i.e., since November 2011), a project was categorized as "dormant" (instead of abandoned as proposed in [19]). As a result of this step, we obtained a subpool of **active projects**, and another subpool of **dormant projects**. The inactive projects, when their latest activity flagged them also as dormant, were discarded from the subpool of dormant ones, in order to have mutually exclusive subsets.

4. **Sampling of projects**: three equally sized samples of 25 projects each were randomly extracted from the three subsets of projects ("active," "inactive" and "dormant"), respectively. An SQL "random" statement was used to extract the three samples. Each of the projects in all the samples IDs was used to compose a URL relative to retrieve the relative code repository in the SourceForge online structure.[9]

5. **Three-point selection**: considering the number of revisions of a project, three data points were considered:

   - *Initial Point – IP*: this point refers to the first revision that was committed into the code repository of the project;
   - *Final Point – FP*: the last available point in the evolution log, corresponding to the latest available revision N contained in the repository of the project;

---

[6] The table that lists the projects is named *trove_agg*.

[7] The homepage of any Sourceforge project 'p' hosted appears in the form `http://sourceforge.net/project/p`.

[8] This is coded within the summary page of each project and marked with the `<dateUpdated>` tag.

[9] The repository of any Sourceforge project 'p' can be found under their "develop" page under `http://sourceforge.net/project/p/develop`, and marked with the `<code>` tag.

- *Middle Point – MP*: considering the final point, the middle point is evaluated dividing by two the overall number of revisions N contained in the repository. In this way, we observed a system in three points not temporally, but *logically* equidistant.

6. **Evaluation of size**: the size of each project in the samples of the three categories ("active," "dormant" and "inactive") was evaluated using the sloccount[10] tool, that measures the physical lines of code (SLOCs) rather than the overall number of lines in a class, file or a whole system. The size was evaluated in the three points mentioned above (IP, MP and FP), and boxplots were produced to compare the growth in size of the projects in the different samples.

7. **Calculation of the Maintainability Index (MI)**: the maintainability index (MI) can be used to evaluate single functions, classes, files, compounds (as packages, namespaces, etc.) and even a system as a whole. The general understanding of such index is that with an $MI \geq 85$, the function or the compound can be considered to have a good maintainability; with an index $85 > MI \geq 65$ the compound has a moderate maintainability; while for a $MI < 65$ the compound should be considered as a difficult to maintain compound, signaling low quality pieces of code. In this work, the index was used to compare and contrast the projects within the abandoned sub-pool, and to evaluate the changes in such index when considering the evolution of the projects, before the abandonment, rather than as an absolute measure. The MI was evaluated for all the systems in the three samples, and along the three points forming their life-cycles: an automated Perl script[11] from the Understand suite[12] was used to evaluate the MI of each compound, as well as the system-wide MI.

3   Results

As outlined in Section 2, we defined two sub-goals. The first, that of quantifying the abandonment of OSS projects, is addressed by research questions one and two listed in Section 2.1. Subsections 3.1 and 3.2 address these research questions, respectively. The second goal, that of evaluating the quality of the code left behind by developers is operationalized by research question three, and is addressed in Subsection 3.3.

3.1   A Classification of Project Activity Status

To address the first research question, *How many 'active,' 'dormant' and 'inactive' projects exist in SourceForge?*, we conducted a characterization of the pool

---

[10] http://www.dwheeler.com/sloccount/

[11] Available at
http://scitools.com/plugins/perl_scripts/acjf_maint_index_halstead.pl

[12] Understand by Scitools, http://scitools.com/index.php

of over 174,000 projects in SourceForge (as of November 2012), into three major clusters: "active," "inactive" and "dormant."

The inactive cluster was the easiest to evaluate: as reported in the sections above, the specific "inactive" tag was searched in each of the projects' summary pages. As depicted in Figure 1, the pool of SourceForge projects contains over 10,000 projects tagged as "inactive" by their own developers (as of November 2012). The inactive projects represents around 6% of the overall population of the hosted projects.

The "active" and "dormant" clusters of projects were evaluated more subjectively: given the date of sampling (DS) at 11/2012, and knowing the date of the latest activity (LA) for each project, at first it was decided to evaluate as "active" those projects whose latest update was within a year (i.e., 365 days) of the date of sampling, "dormant" otherwise. We used the formulas below:

$$LA - DS < 365 \implies active \tag{2}$$

$$LA - DS > 365 \implies dormant \tag{3}$$

Using this approach, over 86% of Sourceforge projects were classified as "dormant," i.e., there is no recorded activity in their latest year on SourceForge. Only some 7% of projects have experienced an update within the last year. These initial three clusters are visible in the left part of Figure 1.

Using two years (i.e., 730 days) as a threshold for the latest activity, some 65% of projects were classified as "dormant," while some 28% were classified as "active" (that is, development occurred in the last two years). This second set of clusters are visible in the right-hand side of Figure 1.

These results form an updated picture of what is well known of OSS portals by researchers and practitioners: on the one hand, OSS portals tend to host an increasingly large number of projects. On the other hand, the large number of inactive and dormant projects has started to become an issue of space (i.e., should abandoned projects be erased from repositories?), as well as of credibility of the overall OSS community (i.e., are OSS projects doomed to failure?).

A further investigation of the inactive projects resulted in a clustering of three subsets:

1. **Inactive "moved" projects**: some of those projects were moved from SourceForge to their own servers, and were tagged as inactive (but "moved") to indicate to interested developers where to find the up-to-date releases or the repository that hosts the source code. The number of moved projects represents some 14% of the overall inactive projects.
2. **Inactive "stale" projects**: a larger portion of the inactive projects are additionally tagged as "stale" projects, therefore indicating to other interested developers that the project is properly "dead" and it could benefit from

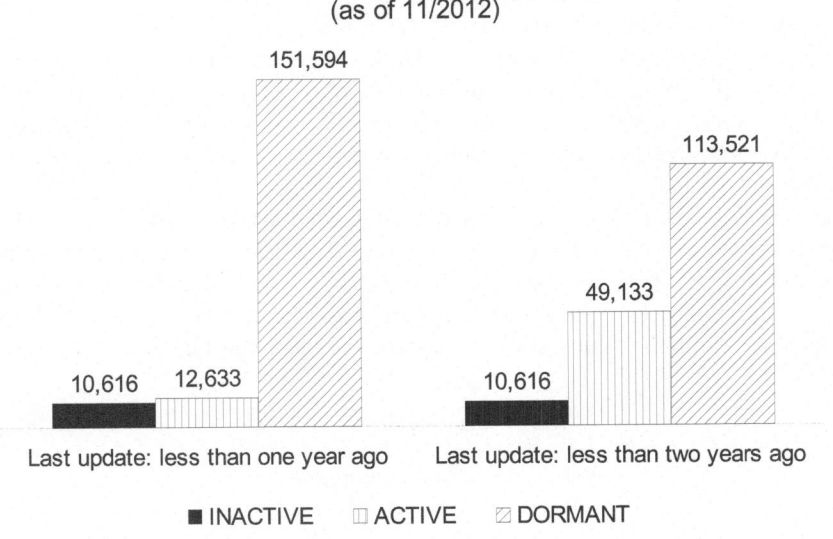

Fig. 1. Clusters of "active," "inactive" and "dormant" projects in Sourceforge, using different thresholds (as of 11/2012)

further attention and development.[13] SourceForge makes sure also to record the date since when those projects were declared as "stale," which becomes an additional piece of information for the evaluation of such systems. Over 60% of the inactive projects are also categorized as stale, as shown in Figure 2.

3. **Other inactive projects**: the remaining 23% of the inactive projects provide no further information on specific details regarding when the project was declared inactive.

The remainder of the analysis in this paper focuses only on the projects which were appropriately tagged as "stale" by their developers, to produce a more thorough understanding of what sort of resources were left behind by the original developers for others to take over.

3.2   Growth Patterns across Categories

The second research question was defined as: *do these categories achieve similar growth patterns?* As described above, three points were considered: the size of a project in its "first revision" under the versioning system (i.e., its initial

---

[13] For instance, by being developed in a parallel branch onto another OSS repository as GitHub, as anecdotally reported in
http://www.quora.com/What-is-the-appeal-of-GitHub-com

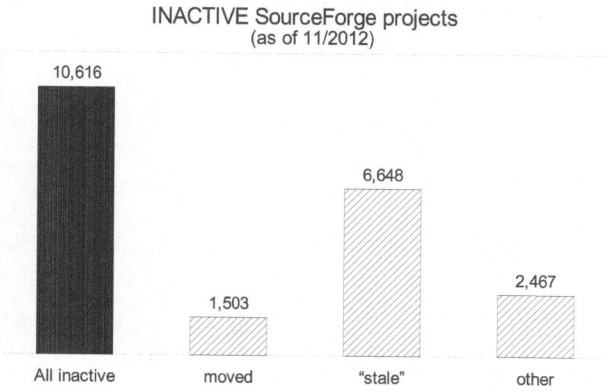

Fig. 2. Distribution of inactive projects in SourceForge (as of 11/2012)

point – IP); in its latest revision (i.e., its final point – FP); and in the revision midway between the first and the latest (i.e., its midway point – MP). The size of the systems was evaluated with the *sloccount* tool for the IP, MP and FP points. The size in SLOCs of the systems are shown, per point, in the Appendix section (Tables 2, 3 and 4).

The distribution of size per project and point, and across samples was visualized using boxplot diagrams to take into consideration the distribution of very diverse projects in the same sample. The distribution per sample, and relative to the initial point (IP) is shown in Figure 3. The other boxplot distributions, albeit similar to the one reported below, are not displayed due to space limitations.

The boxplots in Figure 3 show that the distribution of size (in SLOCs) among the "active" projects is generally larger than the other samples ("dormant" and "inactive"). Such disparity is clearly visible (albeit not reported as a graph) also in the other analyzed points (MP and FP): the outliers of the dormant and inactive projects (shown in Figure 3) exacerbate the difference between few outstanding projects and the more general projects in the MP and FP points.

Despite the large variances (indicated by the whiskers and the outliers of Figure 3), we report the averages and medians of these distributions among samples and in the three points IP, MP and FP (Table 1). In both the average and median measurements, and across samples, the average system increases its size along the three points, but the average active system achieves a growth of 7 times (or 6 times for the medians) between the initial and final points of its growth. "Dormant" and "inactive" projects appear less distinguishable in what they achieve in their growth.

The results of the growth analysis suggest that there is a difference between the analyzed samples, hence between the described clusters: "active" projects begin as larger (in size) than both "dormant" and "inactive" projects, and they grow considerably larger than the other samples along their lifecycle. Whether

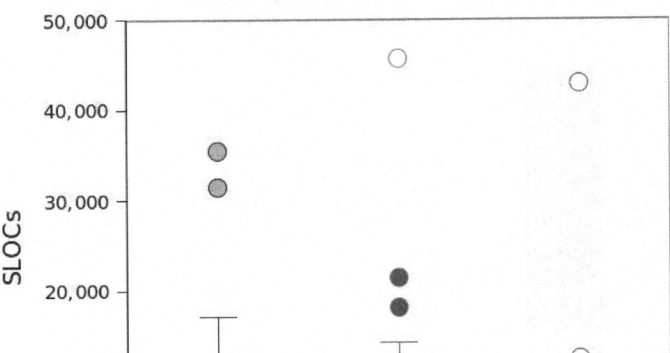

Fig. 3. Boxplots of size (in SLOCs) across samples, initial point (ip)

Table 1. Size growth in the sample of "active," "dormant" and "inactive" projects – Average and median values (in SLOCs)

Average	IP	MP	FP
Active	7,680	24,486	50,189
Dormant	5,585	12,361	16,862
Inactive	4,056	7,775	15,014

Median	IP	MP	FP
Active	4,789	12,361	20,217
Dormant	1,114	3,047	4,520
Inactive	720	2,163	3,267

or not a dormant project returns in an active state, the difference with active projects still persist.

These differences in size will be evaluated in the next section by monitoring their maintainability indexes along the three selected points.

3.3   Quality and Maintainability across Categories

The third research question defined in Section 2 was: *do the categories result in comparable quality and maintainability attributes?* The overall objective of this is to assess whether there is a difference in the quality of projects across the different categories (active, inactive and dormant).

In this section, the issue of quality is discussed by measuring and monitoring the Maintainability Index [14] of the projects composing the abandoned sub-pool. The index has been used several times in the past [8], especially to evaluate the effect of the index on the resulting maintenance needed, but the index has also been exposed to various criticism [11].

Code quality is a multi-dimensional attribute that cannot be evaluated only by a static analysis, as the one that we performed and reported below. Nonetheless, the maintainability index (MI) offers an advantage over other low-level metrics and measurements (such as the Kemerer and Chidamber suite of object-oriented metrics, the cyclomatic complexity or others): such index can be used to evaluate single functions, classes, files, compounds (as packages, namespaces, etc.) but also whole systems.

In this study, MIs were used more to compare and contrast the projects within the samples, and to evaluate the changes in such index when considering the evolution of the projects, before the abandonment, rather than as an absolute measure.

The maintainability indexes for the projects composing the samples are reported in the right-hand side of Tables 2, 3 and 4 included in the appendix) for the IP, MP and FP points. In particular, we were interested in two aspects: (1) whether the maintainability indexes are comparable across samples and categories; and (2) whether the projects in the "inactive" sample have clearly issues with their quality, reflected in low maintainability indexes.

Figure 4 shows the distribution of MIs within the samples in the initial point (IP, top of the figure) and of the latest available revision (FP, bottom of the figure). Two things can be observed: first, that the "active" sample shows a boxplot which achieves less variability between IP and FP (reflected in a more compact boxplot). Second, the difference between samples is not evident. The average scores in the maintainability indexes show that "active" projects are slightly higher than the other samples, but in general the samples seem to decrease their quality with their growth. This is more evident in those projects that achieve large changes of size (reflected in Tables 2, 3 and 4).

The second aspect that was investigated was related to the relative change in overall maintainability between the initial and the final point of each project, and it was measured with a Delta, defined as:

$$Delta(MI)_p = \frac{MI(fp)_p - MI(ip)_p}{MI(ip)_p} \qquad (4)$$

where $MI(fp)_p$ represents the maintainability index at the final point for project 'p' and $MI(ip)_p$ the MI in the initial point for the same project 'p.' No relative changes were recorded in proximity of smaller changes, i.e. when the Delta was less than 1%. If the Delta was positive, nil or the change was minimal, we put a ✓ in the last column of Tables 2, 3 and 4. If there was a substantial negative change, we recorded it with a X in the same column.

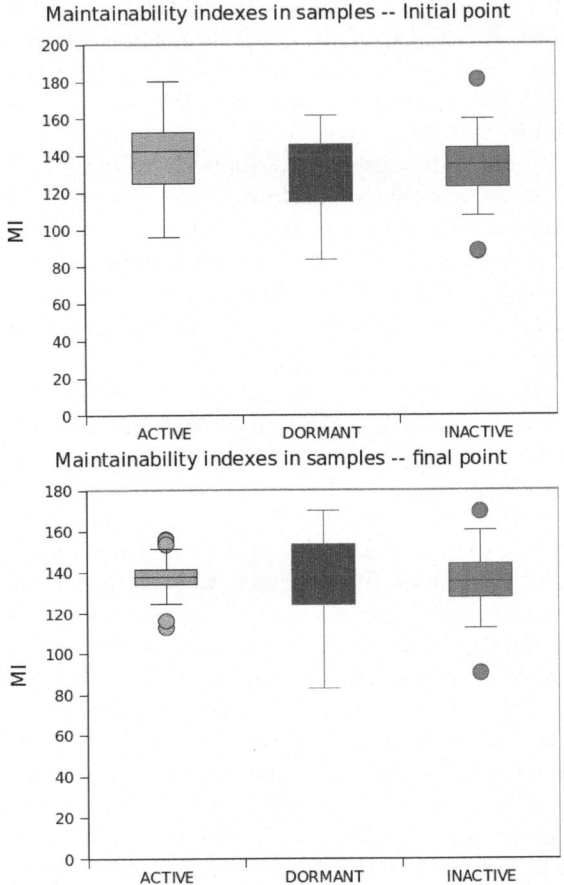

Fig. 4. Boxplots for the maintainability indexes across samples, initial point (IP, top) and final point (FP, below)

As shown in the tables, 14 projects in the "active" sample scored a positive change (or an equal score) between IP and FP in their MIs. On the other hand, 11 projects experience a substantial negative change in their MIs. The proportion of "dormant" projects with an increasing or stable MI to those with a decreasing MI is 16 to 9; the proportion for "inactive" projects is 17 to 8. This shows that the majority of "dormant" and "inactive" systems are left (or abandoned) with a similar or increased maintainability, in comparison to their initial status.

If the results were confirmed in a larger sample, or the whole population of inactive projects, the implications would be straightforward:

– From a *developer's* perspective, one would want to take over projects which are inactive, and that showed some degree of growth (otherwise they could

Table 2. Size growth and maintainability indexes in the sample of "active" projects

Project ID	SLOCs			Maintainability Index			$\Delta \geq 0$?
	IP	MP	FP	IP	MP	FP	
adirectoryimp	10,818	11,918	12,202	152.43	156.34	156.06	✓
Cw-evolver	2,449	4,147	5,994	120.73	123.63	131.53	✓
eid2ldap	444	5,697	7,606	122.75	139.79	134.35	✓
Enrich-ege	780	139,857	88,878	170.17	141.71	141.6	X
eps2pgf	2,372	8,014	19,315	153.13	153.11	155.68	✓
fenixweb	8,555	8,777	9,817	138.95	140.35	140.31	✓
flugbuchz	12,313	5,941	47,587	137.33	134.87	135.85	X
fluidcubed	749	774	887	132.35	144.72	144.55	✓
foxtrot	450	2,161	5,156	143.28	140.03	137.59	X
ieplugin4rm	14,071	18,619	25,355	144.58	144.72	140.68	X
javajson	318	2,620	3,345	95.83	138.65	137.84	✓
loconetovertap	557	5,107	9,622	145.57	140.97	129.66	X
micepfl	6,812	39,458	47,716	122.5	137.23	135.26	✓
midiagentsystem	4,789	9,007	13,329	145.81	141.66	140.92	X
mythtvplayer	9,545	11,700	20,217	133.07	132.23	133.27	✓
oswing	31,476	64,856	128,879	145.53	143.62	144.64	✓
quartica	17,086	12,205	101,063	154.78	149.78	137.09	X
rcpforms	1,861	22,039	74,036	161.3	139.66	137.62	X
resteasy	2,220	79,237	151,681	180.08	155.32	151.46	X
spl	35,488	55,560	257,447	125.08	151.88	135.24	✓
vizkit	6,444	9,542	40,130	142.37	139.2	141.01	✓
xith3d	5,658	51,062	122,811	169.66	153.38	153.62	X
xmms2-qtcli	1,157	2,074	2,486	138.65	126.97	124.68	X
yaco	15,397	41,445	58,550	96.88	116.34	112.82	✓
zmkk	201	325	605	104.68	115.7	116.22	✓

be perceived as "toy systems" that were developed over a short time and abandoned soon after storing in an OSS repository);

– From a *commercial stakeholder's* perspective aiming to participate in OSS development [6], the project to take over (or get involved in) should have a certain minimum degree of quality and maintainability. The MI could be a useful metric to show this quality of compounds, such as files, classes, modules and even the whole system, at various points of its evolution, and ensuring that the quality or maintainability was not compromised too significantly in its evolution. The MI may be a simple alternative to the plethora of more extensive evaluation methods and frameworks that have been proposed so far to evaluate open source products [20].

However, further research is needed to investigate this in more detail and to confirm these findings.

Table 3. Size growth and maintainability indexes in the sample of "dormant" projects

Project ID	SLOCs			MaintainabilityIndex			$\Delta \geq 0$?
	IP	MP	FP	IP	MP	FP	
build-status	1,075	1,075	1,572	154.73	154.73	153.59	✓
dbtoolbox	7,146	8,541	9,214	161.47	160.14	159.95	✓
dekware	45,693	46,181	46,644	113.36	113.36	111.79	X
dynolab	190	553	841	146.22	178.44	170.14	✓
emfincpp	260	1,229	3,226	154.24	154.53	154.53	✓
fit7h-projects	66	192	201	143.08	124.21	123.98	X
gcts	1,114	1,611	642	148.75	147.92	155.48	✓
gerber2eps	1,201	9,616	9,652	135.62	126.74	127.1	X
hemus	14,229	88,665	139,147	111.36	104.78	99.24	X
jrdesktop	6,206	11,327	12,104	127.46	139.36	138.63	✓
libnary	9,159	9,792	10,059	86.01	90.92	89.82	✓
llads	381	46,843	56,182	114.81	124.15	124.22	✓
msgtext	253	4,431	4,520	111.97	135.17	135.02	✓
nexplorer	18,111	19,574	19,523	142.06	149.51	150.54	✓
numenor	348	1,981	2,734	135.55	138.92	142.37	✓
osgmaxexp	4,229	6,632	8,448	139.94	140.55	137.48	X
overflowandroid	308	5,140	2,055	111.18	112.16	86.18	X
psimpl	4,051	3,047	10,283	133.69	133.7	127.28	X
siprop	21,429	68,828	108,816	153.39	158.3	158.41	✓
svnauthzctl	905	941	1,075	83.65	82.65	82.95	✓
tbltools	1,804	2,949	5,688	145.66	140.11	146.52	✓
vmatrixlib	1,048	1,108	1,377	139.98	148.04	146.3	✓
yahoofinanceapi	1,288	1,834	2,339	138.09	142.41	148.17	✓
ybwopenpilot	820	1,729	1,949	161.9	156.33	153.98	X
zcommons-mojos	454	800	1,212	140.05	130.82	130.82	X

4   Discussion

4.1   Comparison to Related Work

This study positions itself in the area of the categorization of OSS projects: the abandonment of OSS projects has been extensively studied in the past in [19,12] and in [7,4], firmly establishing that the vast majority of OSS projects suffers from the "abandonment tragedy." What the present study contributes is an understanding of how developers are currently handing over projects to others, by means of signaling the inactivity of their projects through a specific tag. Also, different from other studies, we did not try to predict the inactivity or projects based on specific coding characteristics (such as languages, application domain, and so forth), but we used readily available identifiers to infer a project's inactivity.

The maintainability of OSS packages has been studied, in a slightly different formula by Samoladas et al. [16], and was also reproduced with OSS projects by Heitlager et al. [11]. Rather than analyzing single compounds, we have used

Table 4. Size growth and maintainability indexes in the sample of "inactive" projects

Project ID	SLOCs			Maintainability Index			$\Delta \geq 0$?
	IP	MP	FP	IP	MP	FP	
aesop-server	489	489	489	128.12	128.12	128.12	✓
arduinoforum	508	576	1,426	124.42	123.03	112.33	X
artgarden	1,990	2,349	2,649	132.97	133.39	130.96	X
carjam	2,484	2,495	3,267	153.72	153.54	147.18	X
cgiscaler	42,901	29,488	58,958	135.67	135.9	137.47	✓
cherrygis	9,374	9,510	10,436	135.19	135.46	138.24	✓
csamegame	2,753	2,753	2,753	129.06	129.06	128.69	✓
cuatroenraya	189	342	1,190	128.99	127.88	115.77	X
doubles	1,028	3,857	6,130	107.31	132.27	124.25	✓
foobar1914	665	1,051	1,904	139.89	167.5	169.52	✓
gimp-vs	1,536	6,073	151,164	107.48	118.58	125.27	✓
icbor	576	7,907	3,488	116.74	140.23	139.76	✓
icepidgen	921	919	13,061	180.88	181.01	144.27	X
icerp	577	2,163	4,763	146.57	159.44	148.71	✓
javimojamucho	154	704	1,457	144.43	145.74	160.45	✓
jnetclip	285	285	285	135.39	135.39	135.39	✓
kino	7,328	93,385	81,883	123.13	122.63	127.73	✓
minigames	428	428	404	87.96	87.96	90.35	✓
pycdk	104	152	152	88.32	131.74	131.74	✓
tankz	634	705	848	139.15	135.03	139.05	✓
timeedition	10,532	10,532	10,532	156.66	156.66	156.66	✓
tuxnotebook	12,353	12,375	9,903	117.96	117.9	114.31	X
unlesbar	720	1,974	3,713	159.78	155.53	152.72	X
utopicengine	2,710	2,947	3,370	136.7	141.58	141.19	✓
webappservicefi	151	913	1,136	144.11	129.09	129.09	X

the MI as a system-level metric, but without inferring quality or maintainability in an absolute way, rather pointing at a relative change between points of the evolution.

Existing studies on the maintainability of OSS projects have shown that evolving software tends to decrease its quality and maintainability [1,17]. We found that this is not necessarily true, given a pool of projects and analyzing their growth of lines of code and maintainability indexes.

Maintainability studies have been performed also to predict the quality of OSS projects using well-known design metrics [23]: using the MI metric as a response, and object-oriented metrics (such as the depth of inheritance tree, average response per class, etc.) as input factors, it was found that OSS projects written in Java show a dependency between the MI and the control flow of the program itself, hence validating the MI as a metric for maintainability. We used this result to acknowledge the value of MI as a metric.

Finally, it has been noted that studies of maintainability in the OSS domain are flawed by the quality of data that is available for investigation [22]. Given the number of resources that OSS projects make available (change logs, mailing lists, source code, etc.), and the diversity in quality in each source, it becomes inevitable to avoid a strict comparison between projects to assess which one has more quality. What we produced in this study was rather an assessment, per project and not inter-project, of how these quality measurements change, and how to interpret them.

4.2   Limitations of This Study

We are aware of a few limitations of this study, which we discuss next. Since we have not studied any causal relationships, we do not discuss threats to internal validity.

Construct Validity refers to the extent to which a concept is correctly operationalized, i.e., whether the researcher is measuring what he or she meant to measure. In particular, a key construct that we operationalized is abandonment of OSS projects, for which we defined three categories: active, dormant, and inactive. We relied on (ex-)maintainers of OSS projects who have indicated their projects to be inactive, using the `inactive` tag; active and dormant projects were distinguished by measuring the latest activity for each project (see Section 3). As shown in Fig. 1, results depend on how the terms "active" and "dormant" are operationalized.

Growth of OSS projects was another construct that we measured, which we operationalized using source lines of code (SLOC) as a metric. We believe that SLOC is the most useful metric to measure size, as it is source code that developers are dealing with. (For that reason, measuring size using memory footprint or number of files or classes, to mention two alternatives, is less useful). Important here is that we only measured the projects at three points: the initial point (size of first revision in the source repository), the final point (last revision in the source repository), and the middle point which is logically positioned between IP and FP.

External Validity refers to the extent to which a study's findings can be generalized, or in which other settings the findings are valid. While the results of the classification of SourceForge projects into clusters has been performed on *all* in the SourceForge repository, we extracted three samples (size 25) that were randomly chosen from the three sets of projects (active, dormant and inactive). While the samples were chosen at random (using SQL's random statement), a different and larger set of samples may result in a different set of findings. Replication and extension of this study should be performed so as to overcome this limitation.

Reliability of a study refers to the degree to which a study can be repeated while attaining the same results. In this paper, we have provided an extensive description of the research method and operationalization, as well as pointers to relevant sources and tools. This description can help other researchers to replicate or extend this study using the same methodology. While results of one study can be "revelatory," research results need to be replicated and confirmed with other studies and research methods, so as to triangulate findings.

5   Conclusion and Future Work

This paper positioned itself in the practice (and duty) of OSS developers to hand off their project to other developers when they lose interest in its further development. The study started off by clustering the population of SourceForge projects into three clusters, using both objective (i.e. the "inactive" tag that can describe an OSS project), and subjective indicators (i.e., the amount of days that a project remains without updates) to draw an updated picture of the status of the projects on one of the largest OSS portals. We isolated projects that are inactive because they have been moved to another portal, and other projects that have been classified as "stale," and therefore properly abandoned by the original developers. We further identified as "dormant" those projects whose latest date of activity was over a year from the date of the analysis (November 2012). Projects with updated activity were characterized as "active."

Using a sample of "active," "dormant" and "inactive" projects, we investigated whether differences could be detected in terms of the projects' overall growth: we found that "active" projects start generally as larger than "dormant" and "inactive," and that they grow consistently larger than the other two clusters.

Finally, we investigated whether projects in the different categories show differences between them by using the maintainability index (MI): we selected this metric since it produces a useful system-wide measurement, ensuring not to use it as an *absolute* measure, but rather observing its *relative change*. The study revealed that the majority of "inactive" projects' MIs increase or remain stable. This result is important for other developers and potential commercial stakeholders to evaluate whether a project is worth taking over, or whether its quality has degraded excessively.

We identified a number of potential research directions for future work. Firstly, this study should be replicated on a larger sample of projects, so as to confirm these results, which will help in improving the generalizability of these findings. Secondly, whether or not the maintainability index is a useful metric to reflect the quality of an open source project as perceived by commercial stakeholders remains an open issue. While this paper presents quantitative results, we believe that triangulation of these results through qualitative studies would be the next step so as to increase the confidence in the findings presented in this paper.

Acknowledgements. The authors would like to thank Dr Angela Lozano for the feedback on an early draft of the paper. This work was supported, in part, by Science Foundation Ireland grant 10/CE/I1855 to Lero—the Irish Software Engineering Research Centre (www.lero.ie).

References

1. Bakota, T., Hegedus, P., Ladanyi, G., Kortvelyesi, P., Ferenc, R., Gyimothy, T.: A cost model based on software maintainability. In: 28th IEEE International Conference on Software Maintenance, ICSM, pp. 316–325 (2012)
2. Basili, V.R., Caldiera, G., Rombach, D.H.: The Goal Question Metric Approach. John Wiley & Sons (1994)
3. Capiluppi, A., González-Barahona, J.M., Herraiz, I., Robles, G.: Adapting the 'staged model for software evolution' to free/libre/open source software. In: Ninth International Workshop on Principles of Software Evolution, pp. 79–82 (2007)
4. Capiluppi, A., Lago, P., Morisio, M.: Characteristics of open source projects. In: European Conference on Software Maintenance and Reengineering (2003)
5. Capiluppi, A., Stol, K., Boldyreff, C.: Software reuse in open source: A case study. International Journal on Open Source Software and Processes 3(3) (2011)
6. Capiluppi, A., Stol, K., Boldyreff, C.: Exploring the role of commercial stakeholders in open source software evolution. In: Hammouda, I., Lundell, B., Mikkonen, T., Scacchi, W. (eds.) OSS 2012. IFIP AICT, vol. 378, pp. 178–200. Springer, Heidelberg (2012)
7. English, R., Schweik, C.M.: Identifying success and tragedy of floss commons: A preliminary classification of sourceforge.net projects. In: Proceedings of the 29th International Conference on Software Engineering Workshops, ICSEW 2007 (2007)
8. Fioravanti, F., Nesi, P.: Estimation and prediction metrics for adaptive maintenance effort of object-oriented systems. IEEE Transactions on Software Engineering 27(12), 1062–1084 (2001)
9. Gao, Y., Van Antwerp, M., Christley, S., Madey, G.: A research collaboratory for the open source software research. In: First International Workshop on Emerging Trends in FLOSS Research and Development, FLOSS 2007 (2007)
10. Halstead, M.H.: Elements of Software Science. Operating and programming systems series. Elsevier Science Inc., New York (1977)
11. Heitlager, I., Kuipers, T., Visser, J.: A practical model for measuring maintainability. In: Proceedings of the 6th International Conference on Quality of Information and Communications Technology, QUATIC 2007, pp. 30–39 (2007)
12. Howison, J., Crowston, K.: The Perils and Pitfalls of Mining Sourceforge. In: Proc. International Workshop on Mining Software Repositories, MSR (2004)
13. McCabe, T.J.: A complexity measure. IEEE Transactions on Software Engineering 2(4), 308–320 (1976)
14. Oman, P., Hagemeister, J.: Construction and testing of polynomials predicting software maintainability. The Journal of Systems and Software 24(3), 251–266 (1994)
15. Raymond, E.S.: The Cathedral and the Bazaar, revised edition. O'Reilly & Associates, Inc., Sebastopol (2001)
16. Samoladas, I., Stamelos, I., Angelis, L., Oikonomou, A.: Open source software development should strive for even greater code maintainability. Commun. ACM 47(10), 83–87 (2004)
17. Schach, S., Jin, B., Wright, D., Heller, G., Offutt, A.: Maintainability of the Linux Kernel. IEE Proceedings – Software Engineering 149(1) (2002)
18. Schweik, C.M., English, R.: Internet Success: A Study of Open Source Software Commons. MIT Press, Cambridge (2012)
19. Schweik, C.M., English, R., Paienjton, Q., Haire, S.: Success and abandonment in open source commons: Selected findings from an empirical study of sourceforge.net projects. In: 2nd workshop on Building Sustainable Open Source Communities, OSCOMM 2010, pp. 91–101 (2010)

20. Stol, K., Ali Babar, M.: A comparison framework for open source software evaluation methods. In: Ågerfalk, P., Boldyreff, C., González-Barahona, J.M., Madey, G.R., Noll, J. (eds.) OSS 2010. IFIP AICT, vol. 319, pp. 389–394. Springer, Heidelberg (2010)
21. Wiggins, A., Crowston, K.: Reclassifying success and tragedy in FLOSS projects. In: Ågerfalk, P., Boldyreff, C., González-Barahona, J.M., Madey, G.R., Noll, J. (eds.) OSS 2010. IFIP AICT, vol. 319, pp. 294–307. Springer, Heidelberg (2010)
22. Yu, L., Schach, S., Chen, K.: Measuring the maintainability of open-source software. In: International Symposium on Empirical Software Engineering, ISESE (2005)
23. Zhou, Y., Xu, B.: Predicting the maintainability of open source software using design metrics. Wuhan University Journal of Natural Sciences 13, 14–20 (2008)

Community Dynamics in Open Source Software Projects: Aging and Social Reshaping

Anna Hannemann and Ralf Klamma

Advanced Community Information Systems
RWTH Aachen University
Ahornstrasse 55, 52056 Aachen, Germany
{hannemann,klamma}@dbis.rwth-aachen.de

Abstract. An undeniable factor for an open source software (OSS) project success is a vital community built around it. An OSS community not only needs to be established, but also to be persisted. This is not guaranteed considering the voluntary nature of participation in OSS. The dynamic analysis of the OSS community evolution can be used to extract indicators to rate the current stability of a community and to predict its future development. Despite the great amount of studies on mining project communication and development repositories, the evolution of OSS communities is rarely addressed. This paper presents an approach to analyze the OSS community history. We combine adapted demography measures to study community aging and social analysis to investigate the dynamics of community structures. The approach is applied to the communication and development history of three bioinformatics OSS communities over eleven years. First, in all three projects a survival rate pattern is identified. This finding allows us to define the minimal number of newcomers required for the further positive community growth. Second, dynamic social analysis shows that the node betweenness in combination with the network diameter can be used as an indicator for significant changes in the community core and the quality of community recovery after these modifications.

1 Introduction

There are about $300,000$ OSS projects registered in `sourceforge.net`, but only few of them succeed [6]. Most of the Open Source Software (OSS) projects are started by a very small group of people bound by a goal they want to approach with the project. Later on, successfully developing projects gain a community of peripheral developers, bug fixers, bug reporters and peripheral users. This project community needs to achieve a critical mass of people for the project breakthrough. The meaning of OSS community is multifold, e.g. community members bring new ideas to the project, present a kind of social reward for the developers effort and increase the "market shares" of the project by spreading the word [9], [13], [17]. Considering the voluntary nature of OSS development,

E. Petrinja et al. (Eds.): OSS 2013, IFIP AICT 404, pp. 80–96, 2013.

the sustainability of an OSS project depends on the sustainability of its community. The analysis of the OSS community evolution can be used to extract indicators to rate the current stability of community and predict its possible future development.

The study of the OSS movement in general and OSS development principles in particular have evolved to a separate research field of community-intensive socio-technical projects [12]. Plenty of those studies address the evolution of OSS systems [2]. However, the dynamic analysis of the OSS communities - a social component of OSS projects - is seldom. The existing research papers on OSS community dynamics either present a set of static measurements for a certain cut off of a project history [14], [5] or are restricted to the developer sub-communities only [10], [1]. In this paper, we combine the demographic analysis of an OSS project community as an aging population and dynamic analysis of an OSS as a social structure. We apply our approach on the whole communities of three bioinformatics OSS. The selected projects, BioJava, Biopython and Bioperl, are very similar in their goals, scientific communities and infrastructures (all three supported by "The Open Bioinformatics Foundation"). Thus, we hope to overcome the bias of results in case of too different communities in terms of policies, culture, lifetime, domain, organization of the OSS projects.

The rest of the paper is organized as follows. Section 2 presents an overview of the existing OSS community studies: statistical studies of community dynamics are described in Section 2.1 followed by an overview of OSS social evolution studies in Section 2.2. In Section 3 we present our approach to analyze OSS community evolution and the data used for validation. The results are described in Section 4. Section 5 discusses the results and concludes the paper. An outlook is given in Section 6.

2   Related Work

A large number of studies was executed upon publicly available communicational and development repositories of OSS projects during the last decade [12]. Many of those studies address the evolution of OSS system. In the systematic literature review Breivold et al. [2] identify four main research topics on OSS system evolution: software trends and patterns, evolution process support, evolvability characteristics addressed in OSS evolution, examining OSS at software architecture level. The researchers provide an overview of metrics that are used to analyze OSS evolution over time: Software growth metrics, system growth metrics, etc. address only the technical aspects of OSS projects. However, the success of an OSS project depends not only on technical quality of the developing system, but also on the social state of its community [17]. The attention of researchers is also attracted to the analysis of the OSS communities: motivation for voluntarism, participation and interaction patterns, social structure, etc. However, the dynamic analysis of the OSS communities is seldom. No metrics for measuring social quality of an OSS project are developed so far. In Section 2.1

we give an overview of the studies, which address evolution of the community composition. While in Section 2.2 the existing investigations of the community restructuring in social terms are presented.

2.1 Population Evolution

In [17] Ye et al. present a conceptional framework of the OSS evolution. An OSS community is defined as an example of a community of practice (CoP) with the legitimated peripheral participation (LPP) [15]. According to the LPP concept, through continuous learning the newcomers become experienced community members, thus, they move from the periphery to the community center. Ye et al. call this process "role-transformation" and, thereby, extend the static onion-model of the OSS communities by time dimension. Role-transformation in open source leads to evolution of community social structure and composition, which in turn results in evolution of developer skills and organizational principles. The authors also define a term "second generation", which is achieved, when an OSS community core is evolved from a single project leader to a group of core members.

Von Krogh et al. in [14] study the early stage of community establishment in the Freenet project (year 2000). The researchers investigate which behavioral patterns (level of activity and specialization) increase the chances to be granted developer privileges (role-transformation). However, this study is restricted to one OSS project in the early stage.

In contrast to [14], in [5] Jensen et al. study the joining behavior across four different OSS projects. The projects are analyzed not at their early stage, but when they were already widely acknowledged and supported by a bigger community. The authors estimate a "survival rate" of newcomer in the mailing lists: 9.4% of those, who entered the project in three month period (643), were still participating in mailing lists after six month period. However, only 9 month of the projects' history are taken into consideration.

Robles et al. in [11] investigated the meaning of evolution within the Debian project. The finding, that if a package leader leaves a project, the package is very likely to be abandoned in the future, shows the importance to understand and even predict the community restructuring.

In [10] Robles et al. use the term "generation" to describe the projects, where the core developers change over time. The results show, that the core remains stable in very seldom cases (3 of 21 projects) and support the expected strong evolution of the leading group and constant need for the emerging gaps to be filled. However, the study is restricted not only to the developers, but even to the core group of them (the most active 20% of committers).

To summarize, the above described studies consider OSS communities as a population: concepts like "generation", "survival rate", "migration" are applied. Demographic methods and models present one possible basis for quantitative analysis of OSS community evolution.

2.2   Social Dynamics

Beside quantitative analysis of an OSS community, its social state can be estimated. Hereby, an OSS community is mapped to a graph. The nodes of the graph represent OSS project members and the edges between the nodes represent interaction between the project members. Plenty of social network analysis measures can be calculated using OSS community graph. Similarly, for each project member his/her social status can be estimated.

In [1] Bird et al. study the chances of migration from non-developers to full developer among others as a function of social status. Analysis of Apache, Postgres and Python communities shows, that the meaning of different aspects vary significantly from project to project. The evolution of newcomers is not considered.

Further, the dynamic of social characteristics is addressed in [4] by Howison et al. Using the data from `sourceforge.net` bug-tracker from 120 different projects, social networks based on direct interaction on submitted bugs are depicted. In order to analyze the evolution of outdegree centralization, the data is sampled in 90-day overlapping windows. Strong variation in community social structure is detected across different projects and within one project over time. The participation behavior proves to be distributed according to power-law: most of the project members join the project for a short period of time. However, the study considers only a relatively short period of project life time.

In [16] Wiggins et al. adapted the analysis methods from [4] and applied to investigate the centralization dynamics of Gaim and Fire. In this study, the significant evolution of communication centralization is showed. For example, a project management activity can reshape the community to a highly centralized network structure.

To summarize, there is a growing interest in OSS community evolution. Monitoring of community social state can be applied in order to detect important internal/external events and thus, to approach sustainability of OSS communities. Both demographic and social network analysis methods and concepts are applied to analyze OSS communities dynamically. However, most of the existing studies are mainly concentrating on the migration from non-developers to the developers. The whole community is rarely addressed. Often only a short cut off of the project history is used for analysis. To our knowledge, the only studies which combine the community statistical and social evolvement are [4] and [16].

3   Methods

In this study we approach an OSS community as an aging population on the one hand and as a social structure on the other hand. We adapt methods of population projection and dynamic social network analysis and apply them to three bioinformatics OSS projects.

3.1 Data

In this study, we use the data from three well-established bioinformatics OSS projects. Bioinformatics is an interdisciplinary research field, where innovative computer science techniques and algorithms are applied to answer emerging research questions of computational biology. There is a branch of commercial bioinformatics applications. However, according to [7] "most of them are not scientific for the level of data analysis required in bioinformatics research. It was partly the frustration with commercial suits that drove the foundation of the Bio* groups." All open source projects used in this study, BioPerl, BioJava, Biopython, belong to the Open Bioinformatics Foundation. The selected projects are very similar in the problems they address, the community they are intended for, policy and organizational issues they experience. The infrastructure used for the project management all cases is composed of a wikipage, mailing lists and a code repository.

The communication data from the project mailing lists and the development history from the project code repositories for the period of eleven years (2000 − 2010) is crawled, filtered from spam and stored in a local database [3]. Multiple aliases of same individuals are semi-automatically detected and consolidated. We detected 5507 distinct users 3259 of them had written more then one posting and had got at least one reply. The mailing list aliases are mapped to the developer aliases. Further insights in the project history, we collected from the project wikipages and project participants via private emails.

3.2 Analysis Procedures

For our study, we monitored the population evolution over time in combination with the changes in social structure of OSS communities. The data was divided in equal one-year-long periods $\{01.01.x - 31.12.x \| \forall x \in (2000, 2010)\}$.

Population Ecology. In order to study the evolution of OSS communities, we defined the population characteristics in the following way:

Year of Birth is a time point t_{0p_i} when a participant p_i entered an OSS project. In the context of this study it is a time point, when a user has written his/her first posting in a project mailing list.

Age Group $(x; x + 1)$ at time t consists of all active project members, who participate in a project at the given time point for at least x and at most $x + 1$ years. In context of this study, a user is defined to be currently active in a project, if he/she has written at least one posting in a mailing list of a project in the current year.

Survival Rate $(x; x + 1) \rightarrow (x + 1; x + 2)$ is a percentage of active users in the last year in the *age group* $(x; x + 1)$, who are still active in the current year.

For example, in 2006 all project participants who posted their first post in the project mailing list not earlier than 01.01.2006 belong to the $(0, 1)$ age group. In turn, those, who have posted their first post before 01.01.2006, but not earlier than 01.01.2005 and at least one post in the current (2006) year form the $(1, 2)$ age group. As the earliest data set we consider originates from 2000 for all three projects BioJava, Biopython and BioPerl, the "oldest" possible project participants in year 2006 present $(4; 5)$ age group. In year 2007 the survival rate $(0, 1) \rightarrow (1, 2)$ presents a percentage of users from $(0, 1)$ age group in 2006, who are still active.

In order to visualize the population age structure, the population pyramids are applied. The population pyramids present an effective graphical way to visualize the population development and to detect some tends and outliers, which can lead to some environmental and historical events. It can be also help to indicate the likelihood of continuation of population under study. The X-axis of a population pyramid represents age or age-groups, while the numbers of people in each age group is plotted along the Y-axis.

Social Network Analysis (SNA) is applied to study the social characteristics of an OSS community modeled as a graph. Individual participants of a community are modeled as nodes of the graph and their relationship (friendship, family relatedness, etc.) is reflected by network ties. The BioJava, Biopython and BioPerl participants are mapped to the nodes V of the project networks. If at least one thread exists, to which both participants v_i and $v_j \in V$ have submitted at least one posting, the link $(v_i; v_j)$ is added to the graph. The edges are binary: either there is a link or not. To analyze the project networks we applied the following SNA measures[1] [8]:

- *Shortest Path* σ_{st} is the minimal length of the path between two nodes s, t

- *Diameter* is the length of the longest shortest path $d = \max_{s,v \in V} \sigma_{st}$

- *Node Betweenness* is the fraction of shortest paths between two nodes s and t that contain node v_i

$$g(v_i) = \frac{\sigma_{st}(v_i)}{\sigma_{st}}$$

- *Largest Connected* identifies the maximal connected components of a graph

- *Density* is the ratio of the number of edges to the number of possible edges

- *Transitivity* (=Clustering Coefficient) measures the probability that the adjacent nodes of a node are connected

---

[1] `http://www.r-project.org/` is used for calculations.

– *Edge Betweenness Clustering* is a method to detect dense interconnected nodes subsets (communities) within social networks with sparse connection to outside of the cluster.

Dynamic network analysis (DNA) extends SNA with the time domain. To analyze the development of social characteristics of the OSS projects over time, we generated the project networks for each year.

4 Results

The following sections present the results of the previously described dynamic analysis procedures applied to three bioinformatics OSS.

4.1 Demographic Forecast

For each project under study, a number of distinct users in each age group $(x; x+1)$ per year was calculated. Starting from the year 2006, we estimated the survival rates for users of each age group. For example, for 2006 the following survival rates were calculated $(0, 1) \rightarrow (1, 2), (1, 2) \rightarrow (2, 3) \dots (3, 4) \rightarrow (4, 5)$. Accordingly, for year 2010 the survival rates of the oldest project members are represented in $(7, 8) \rightarrow (8, 9)$. On average, our investigations showed a pattern of the survival rates for certain age groups in all three bioinformatics OSS (cf. Figure 1). A ratio P_x of the project participants aged x to $x + 1$ at time t being still active in the age group $x + 1$ to $x + 2$ at time $t + 1$ follows certain rules:

– $P_0 = [(0, 1) \rightarrow (1, 2)] \approx 20\%$

– $P_1 = [(1, 2) \rightarrow (2, 3)] \approx 40\%$

– $P_m = [(x, x + 1) \rightarrow (x + 1; x + 2)] \approx 90\%\ , \forall x > 1$

The results showed, that 20% of people, who were newcomers in the year n, remain active in the year $n + 1$. Out of those, who remained with a project already for one year $((1, 2)$ age group) in the year n, there remain only about 40% in the year $n + 1$. Other age groups have a survival rate of about 90%. The population pyramids of BioJava, Biopython, BioPerl in year 2010 in Figure 1 provide a visual representations of the identified pattern. To summarize, the distribution of survival rates in the investigated OSS projects follows the power law. Additionally, a phenomena of *"rebirth"* can be observed in the OSS projects. Some project participants leave the project for several years and after some period of time come back to the community. In the years of their absence, these users do not appear in our measurements. However, when they reactivate their participation, we still consider the date of the first posting as the date of the entrance into the project. These users represent no newcomers anymore, as they already have some experience with the project. Therefore, it can happen, that the age group $(x + 1; x + 2)$ contains more people, than the age group $(x; x+1)$ contained a year before. Thus, especially for older age groups a survival rate higher than 100% is possible.

This finding leads to the conclusion, that if a user was actively participating in a project for more than two years, he/she will probably get "attached" to it on long-term bases. In turn, the percentage of those who survive over two years is very low. Based on the identified pattern, a minimal number of newcomers required to support the same level of participation and, thus, the continuation of project population in the next year can be estimated as follows:

$$|newcomer|_{t+1} >= |(0;1)_t| * 0.2 + |(1;2)_t| * 0.4 + \cdots + |(x; x+1)_t| * 0.9 \quad (1)$$

The history of newcomer numbers can be investigated in order to uncover the events, which influenced the rate of user inflow in a project. In Figure 1 the newbie numbers in all three projects under study are illustrated. The highest inflow of new users in all thee projects can be indicated during $2001 - 2004$. This observation can be linked to the fact, that in those years bioinformatics won a lot of attention due to the announcement of sequencing of the human genome on June 26, 2000[2]. Also the "Bioinformatics Open Source Conference" started in year 2000, attracting the attention of scientists to the open source software for computational biology. We can conclude, that the newcomer rates depend among others on the events within the project domain outside the project community.

Despite the rise of newbie numbers in all three projects during the mentioned time period, the absolute numbers differentiate considerably in BioJava (over 100), Biopython (less than 100) and BioPerl (over 250). In turn, different newbie numbers result in different absolute numbers of users, who get involved in the project on long-term bases, even if the percentage of survival is almost the same (cf. Figure 1). This occurrence can be linked to the different development stages of three projects at the mentioned time period. While BioJava and Biopython were started at around 1999, the BioPerl has been already developed since 1995. Hence, in early years of 2000, the BioPerl was the most-established project in comparison to the other two and could attract more people, even that the topics addressed by all three are quite similar. Thus, we observe interplay among similar OSS project: "the rich get richer" effect.

4.2 Social Evolution

For every year and for each project we generated a network of the currently active project participants. For every of these networks six SNA measures were calculated: diameter, average path length, maximal betweenness, size of the largest connected component, density, transitivity. Some remarkable outlier values in diameter and maximal betweenness series are identified in Biopython and BioJava projects (cf. Figure 2).

---

[2] http://www.ornl.gov/sci/techresources/Human_Genome/
project/clinton1.shtml

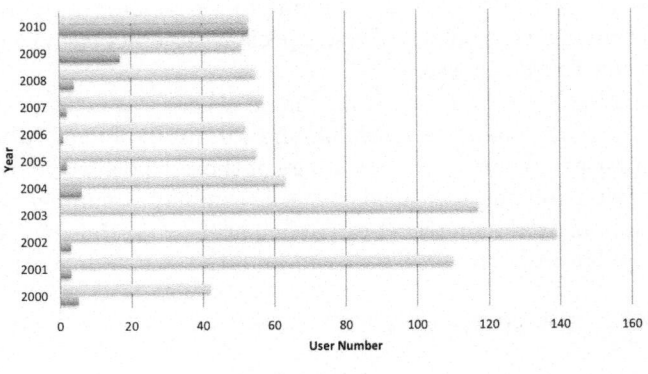

(a) BioJava

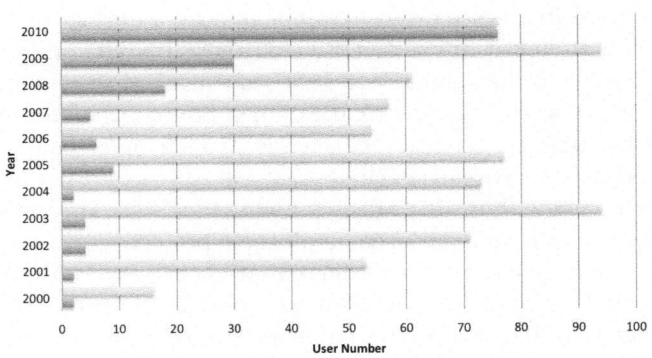

(b) Biopython

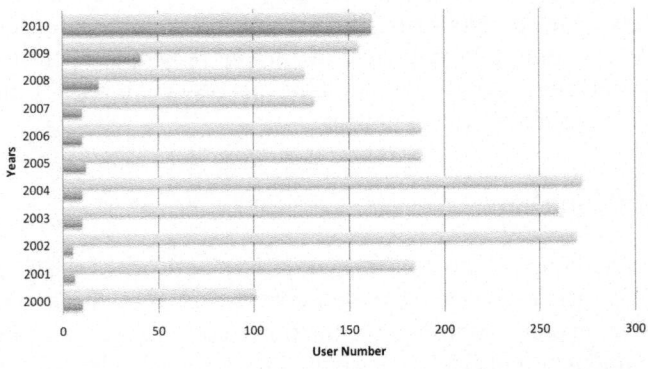

(c) BioPerl

Fig. 1. Newcomers vs. Survived Users

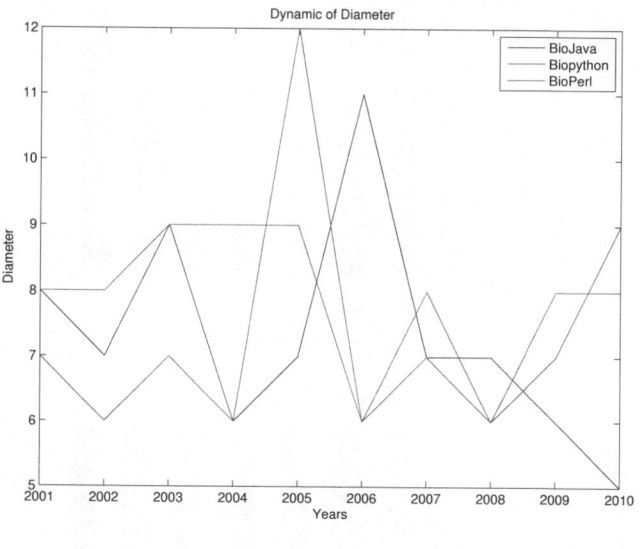

(a) Dynamic of Diameter

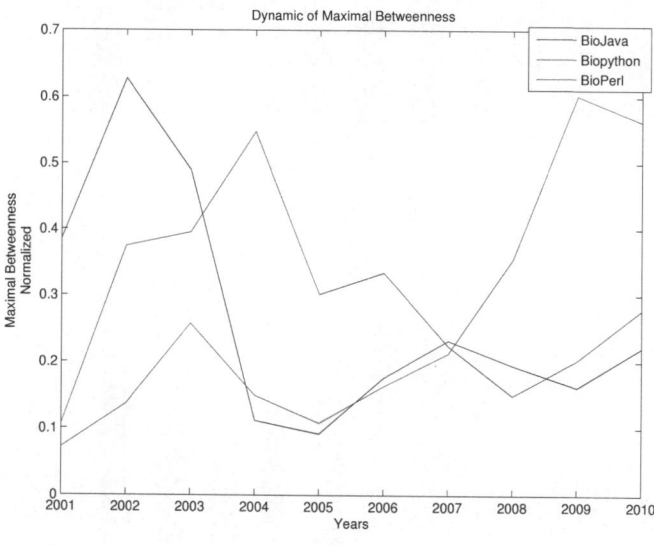

(b) Dynamic of Max Betweenness

Fig. 2. Evolution of Structural Parameters of the Project Social Networks

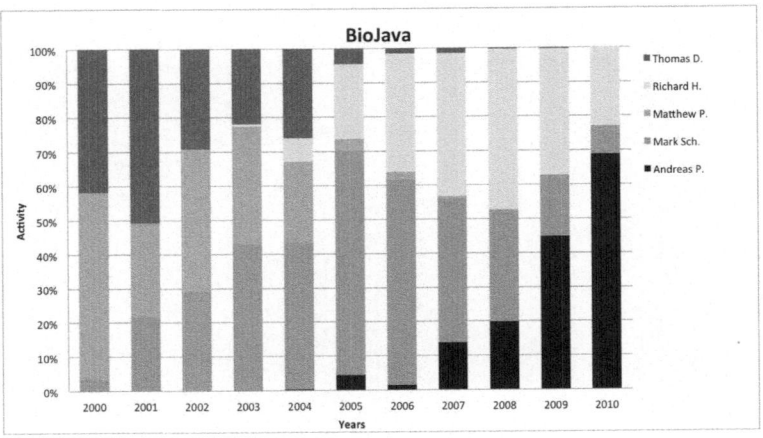

(a) BioJava

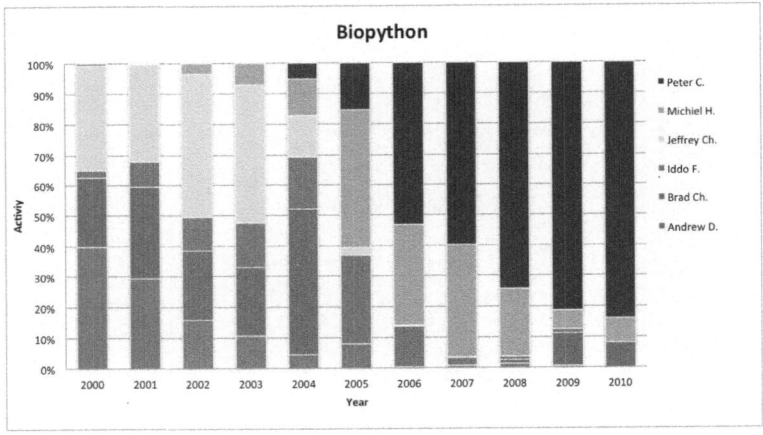

(b) Biopython

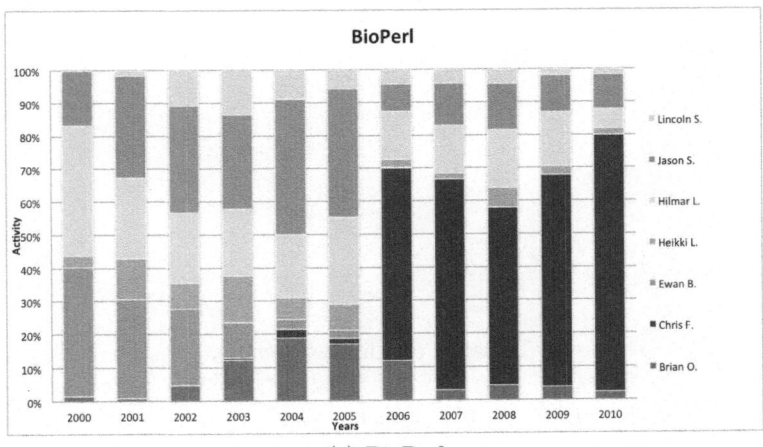

(c) BioPerl

Fig. 3. Participation Activity over Years for Selected OSS Members

In most cases, the diameter value within a network was 6, which is consistent with the well-known small-world phenomena of the social networks [8]. In 2005 in the Biopython network and in 2006 in the BioJava network, the diameter values reached 12 and 11 respectively. In these periods, the networks do not show previous compactness. Noteworthy are the low values of the maximal node betweenness at the same period of time in both projects. Figure 4 shows social networks of the BioJava, Biopython and BioPerl communities in 2006, 2005 and 2004 respectively. The presented networks are clustered using edge betweenness clustering provided by www.yworks.com. The diameter of the node representations reflects its social importance in the network.

Node betweenness is a centrality measure, which determines dominance of a node within a network. Assuming that the information flow takes the shortest path, the node betweenness let us estimate the fraction of information going through a node. However, the information does not always flow along the shortest path and, therefore, the assumption presents only an approximation. Nevertheless, this approximation allows us to estimate quite well the substantial influence of the network nodes. Nodes with high betweenness values often present an interlink between network clusters (community subgroups). Thus, the low value of maximal betweenness can be an indicator for that a central node looses its influences or leave the network. Therefore, we identified the most central and active project members in BioJava, Biopython and BioPerl for each year.

We detected a change of "main actors" within the Biopython community in 2005: Jeffrey C., Andrew D. and Brad C. got "substituted" by Peter C. and Michiel H. However, this takeover was not very smooth. Figure 3(b) presents contribution level of each central member in each year. First after Jeffrey C. and Brad C. had already reduced remarkably their input to the project, Andrew D. and Michiel H. brought the project to its previous progress state. This could be a reason for low maximum betweenness and diameter values. The Biopython network was almost breaking apart, when its core members left the community (cf. Figure 4(a)).

In the BioJava community there were three central members until 2004: Thomas D., Matthew P. and Mark Sh. In 2005, two of them, Thomas D. and Matthew P., left the project (cf. Figure 3(a) and Figure 4(b)). This period is marked by low maximal betweenness and low value of transitivity, but by almost "normal" diameter value of 7. Hence, a community shrunk due to user "retirement", but it remained joined by the third central member Mark Sh. (who remained in the project from the beginning until present). In2006, many new active "actors" entered the BioJava community. Hereby, the community got less centralized, resulting in a higher diameter value. Later (around 2007), Andreas P. and Richard H. gained the central role in the project. The community again presented a hierarchical, very centralized structure with small diameter and high maximum betweenness values.

In BioPerl, in 2003 − 2005, the diameter value raises only up to 9. The maximal betweenness values during the period are very high. This period overlaps with the highest newbies inflow in BioPerl (cf. Figure 1(c)), which resulted in the

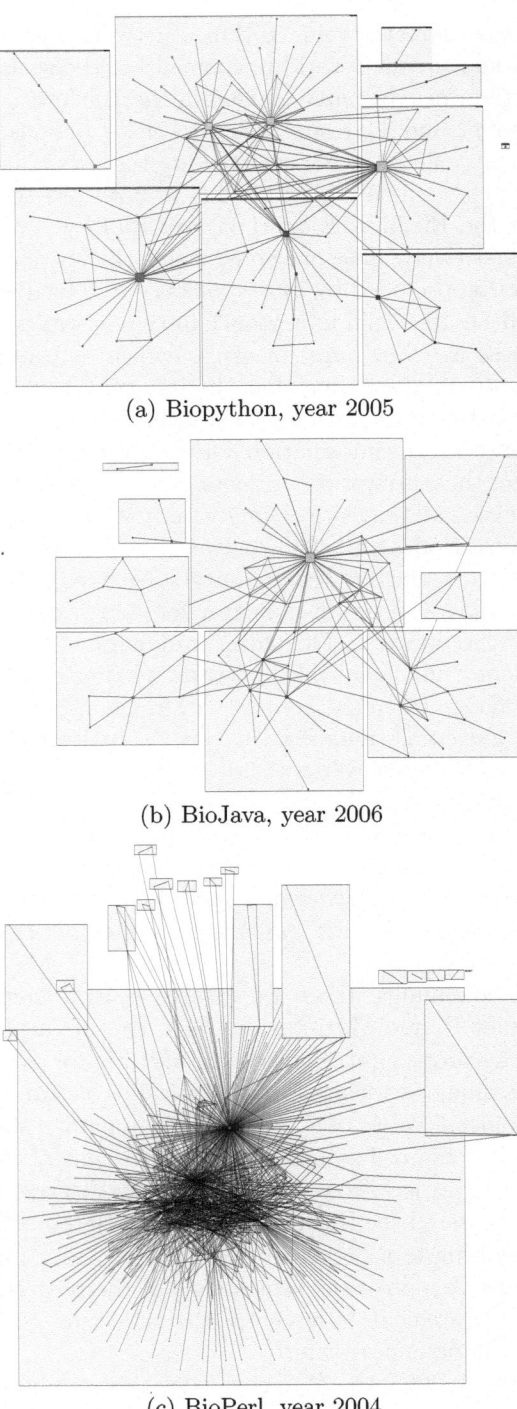

(a) Biopython, year 2005

(b) BioJava, year 2006

(c) BioPerl, year 2004

Fig. 4. Project Social Networks

community expansion (and thus, in higher diameter values). The power within the community stayed in the hands of the same leading people. The community expansion just increased their "power" (resulting in increase of maximum betweenness). There was also a switch in roles among the "main actors" in BioPerl (cf. Figure 3(c)). Until 2006 the maximal node betweenness is gained by Jason S. In 2004, Chris F. enters the BioPerl and achieves the maximal betweenness in the 2006. However, Jason S. continued to contribute to the project actively.

The core of BioPerl is much bigger than in the other two projects. There are on average 24 active distinct developers in BioPerl, while Biopython and BioJava are supported on average by 7 and 11 respectively. A more detailed investigation of the BioPerl community shows, that in contrast to Biopython and BioJava, where only core (very active and socially central actors, experts) and periphery (very passive actors, lurkers) are present, an intermediate layer of "contributors" has been established. Although the project members of this layer put much less effort, than the core, they still provide some active contributions to the project. The edge betweenness clustering of BioPerl network in 2004 detects one very big cluster, which includes almost all project participants (cf. Figure 4(c)). The intermediate layer of active contributors can be a reason for the strong community interconnection and better resistance against "retirement' of core members

4.3   Social Evolution and Demographic Forecast

In Figure 1(b) an increase of the newcomer rate in the year 2009 in Biopython can be observed. At the same time, the rise in commits and releases number per year can be detected starting from 2007 (cf. Figure 5). More detailed investigations show that these changes in release- and effort-culture were introduced by the new leading people in the Biopython community (cf. Figure 3(b)). This organizational and development modifications made the Biopython project more attractive for the newcomers.

5   Discussion and Conclusions

In this paper, we adopted demographic concepts to analyze OSS communities as an aging population and applied several SNA measures to trace social evolution of OSS communities. A survival rate pattern $20 - 40 - 90\%$ was identified within the communities of three bioinformatics projects. Only 20% of the newbies "survive" over their first year in a project, the 40% out of them over the second year followed by about 90% of the previous amount to survive in the next years. This pattern leads to the following conclusions:

– The identified pattern allows to predict the minimal number of newbies required to support the same level of participants in the community.
– There is a very high probability, that a user who remained with an OSS project longer than two years, will remain with the community further.

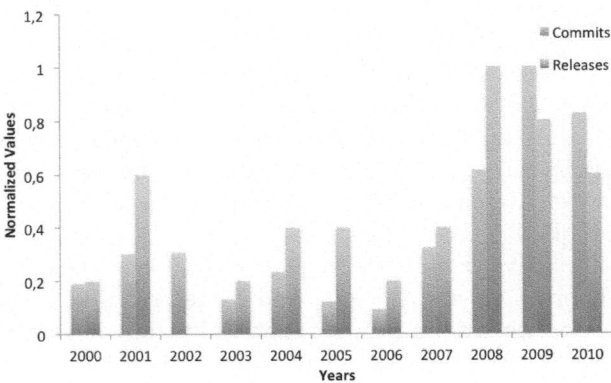

Fig. 5. Biopython: Release and Commit Numbers

- The fraction of the users, who "survives longer" than three years is only about 7, 2%. The very low survival rate is conform to the results presented in [5].
- Within ten years of the project history no maximal possible participation duration was identified, causing the continuous community growth even with slightly decreasing newcomer rates.
- The core group of each OSS project evolves strongly (conform to the results from [10]).
- Retirement of a central community member(s) presents a danger for the project sustainability (conform to the results from [11]).
- There is a phenomena of "rebirth" within an OSS community. Especially those, who get involved deeply in the project for several years and then left it, tend to return to the project later on.
- The number of "oldies" gets continuously bigger. This can lead to seclusion of community against newcomers. The concept of "contribution barrier" from [14] should be extended by social aspects.

The SNA results show, that the combination of increasing diameter and falling maximal betweenness can be used as an indicator for the retirement of the central community member, with a risk of a community to break apart. In the history of all three projects there was a change of the central person within community in about 5 − 6 years. In the BioPerl project the change seems to have no strong effect: the community participants remained strongly interconnected, due to the relatively big and well-developed hierarchical community center. On contrary, the Biopython and BioJava communities show a very loosely structure at the period of the change. BioJava project seems to execute the change more smoothly than Biopython, thanks to the overlap of the central user participation time. Many other active members left the community together with the central actors. The both Biopython and BioJava communities experienced the great restructuring. In Biopython we also observe a complete modification of the development principals. The findings confirm the OSS problem, that the knowledge concentrated in the core of community bringing the danger of its total loss, if the core members leave the project. Especially, considering that the retirement of a central member can induce the further outflow of project members from an OSS project.

Our findings indicate, that a combination of maximal betweenness and diameter values, can be used as metric for measuring social stability of an OSS community. Survival rate and newcomer inflow can be applied in order to detect the important internal/external events.

5.1 Threats to Validity

The presented findings may not be directly transformed to all OSS projects. The bioinformatics OSS projects are mostly driven by bioinformatics scientist, mainly PhD students working on their thesis. Once they finish their PhD, they may loose the interest or/and time for the contributing, which can be one reason for the observed survival pattern. Further, the quality of any dynamic analysis may be influenced by the selected step size. Until now, we performed the population analysis on BioJava communication data cut at the time point of each release. The achieved results are very similar with those presented in this paper. However, there is about one release per year in BioJava. The survival pattern in the projects with another release culture has to be investigated.

6 Future Work

Considering socio-technical nature of OSS projects, social evolution of OSS communities presents a big area for further studies. To validate the results of this study, the proposed measurements should be applied to other OSS projects. Moreover, there is a great deal of possibilities to extend the proposed methods for dynamic analysis of OSS communities by additional parameters. For example, the analysis of participation duration can be combined with the information about participant's activity. For each OSS project member we can define a time series: a sequence of contribution numbers within uniform time intervals (e.g. per month). Using statistical methods like Principle Component Analysis, we can detect different "activity-participation duration" patterns.

References

1. Bird, C., Gourley, A., Devanbu, P., Swaminathan, A., Hsu, G.: Open borders? Immigration in open source projects. In: Proceedings of the Fourth International Workshop on Mining Software Repositories, MSR 2007, pp. 6–13. IEEE Computer Society, Washington, DC (2007)
2. Breivold, H.P., Chauhan, M.A., Ali Babar, M.: A systematic review of studies of open source software evolution. In: Proceedings of the 17th Asia PacificSoftware Engineering Conference, APSEC, pp. 356–365 (November 2010)

3. Hannemann, A., Hackstein, M., Klamma, R., Jarke, M.: Adaptive filter-framework for quality improvement of open source software analysis. In: Software Engineering 2013 (to appear, 2013)
4. Howison, J., Inoue, K., Crowston, K.: Social dynamics of free and open source team communications. In: Damiani, E., Fitzgerald, B., Scacchi, W., Scotto, M., Succi, G. (eds.) Open Source Systems. IFIP, vol. 203, pp. 319–330. Springer, Boston (2006)
5. Jensen, C., King, S., Kuechler, V.: Joining free/open source software communities: An analysis of newbies' first interactions on project mailing lists. In: 2011 44th Hawaii International Conference on System Sciences, HICSS, pp. 1–10 (January 2011)
6. Madey, G., Freeh, V., Tynan, R.: The open source software development phenomenon: An analysis based on social network theory. In: Americas Conference on Information Systems, AMCIS 2002, Dallas, TX, USA, pp. 1806–1813 (2002)
7. Mangalam, H.: The bio* toolkits–a brief overview. Briefings in Bioinformatics 3(3), 296–302 (2002)
8. Newman, M.I.J.: The structure and function of complex networks. SIAM Review 45(2), 167–256 (2003)
9. Raymond, E.S.: The Cathedral and the Bazaar. O'Reilly Media (1999)
10. Robles, G., Gonzalez-Barahona, J.M.: Contributor turnover in libre software projects. In: Damiani, E., Fitzgerald, B., Scacchi, W., Scotto, M., Succi, G. (eds.) Open Source Systems. IFIP, vol. 203, pp. 273–286. Springer, Boston (2006)
11. Robles, G., Gonzalez-Barahona, J.M., Michlmayr, M.: Evolution of volunteer participation in libre software projects: Evidence from debian. In: Scotto, M., Succi, G. (eds.) Open Source Systems, pp. 100–107 (July 2005)
12. Scacchi, W.: The future research in free/open source software development. In: Proceedings of ACM Workshop on the Future of Software Engineering Research, FoSER, Santa Fe, NM, pp. 315–319 (November 2010)
13. von Hippel, E., von Krogh, G.: Open source software and the "private-collective" innovation model: Issues for organization science. Journal on Organization Science 14(2), 208–223 (2003)
14. von Krogh, G., Spaeth, S., Lakhani, K.R.: Community, joining, and specialization in open source software innovation: a case study. Research Policy 32(7), 1217–1241 (2003)
15. Wenger, E.: Community of Practice: Learning, Meaning, and Identity. Cambridge University Press, Cambridge (1998)
16. Wiggins, A., Howison, J., Crowston, K.: Social dynamics of floss team communication across channels. In: Russo, B., Damiani, E., Hissam, S., Lundell, B., Succi, G. (eds.) Open Source Development, Communities and Quality. IFIP, vol. 275, pp. 131–142. Springer, Boston (2008)
17. Ye, Y., Nakakoji, K., Yamamoto, Y., Kishida, K.: The co-evolution of systems and communities in free and open source software development. In: Koch, S. (ed.) Free/Open Source Software Development, pp. 59–82. Idea Group Publishing, Hershey (2004)

Exploring Collaboration Networks
in Open-Source Projects

Andrejs Jermakovics, Alberto Sillitti, and Giancarlo Succi

Free University of Bolzano-Bozen, Piazza Domenicani 3, 39100
Bolzano-Bozen, Italy
{ajermakovics,asillitti,gsucci}@unibz.it
http://www.case.unibz.it/

Abstract. Analysis of developer collaboration networks presents an opportunity for understanding and thus improving the software development process. Discovery of these networks, however, presents a challenge since the collaboration relationships are initially not known. In this work we apply an approach for discovering collaboration networks of open source developers from Version Control Systems (VCS). It computes similarities among developers based on common file changes, constructs the network of collaborating developers and applies filtering techniques to improve the readability of the visualized network. We use the approach in case studies of three different projects from open source (phpMyAdmin, Eclipse Data Tools Platform and Gnu Compiler Collection) to learn their organizational structure and patterns. Our results indicate that with little effort the approach is capable of revealing aspects of these projects that were previously not known or would require a lot of effort to discover manually via other means, such as reading project documentation and forums.

Keywords: Collaboration networks, version control systems, open source.

1   Introduction

Analysis of collaboration networks in a development environment can provide decision support for improving the software development process [24]. It has already been widely used in open source [1] and closed source software for exploring collaboration [32], predicting faults [10, 21, 25], studying code transfer [23] and many other activities [4, 7]. Moreover, since software artifact structure is strongly related to the organization's structure (*Conway's Law*) [5] it becomes important to understand the developer networks involved. The analysis of these networks is often leveraged using visualizations and their appearance plays a significant role in how people interpret the networks [14], [20]. It is, therefore, important that the network visualizations are easy to interpret and represent the actual network as closely as possible.

A common problem is that the actual social networks are not known and need to be discovered. Many existing approaches rely on communication archives to discover the

E. Petrinja et al. (Eds.): OSS 2013, IFIP AICT 404, pp. 97–108, 2013.
© IFIP International Federation for Information Processing 2013

networks [1, 6, 29]; however these are not always available and do not necessarily reflect collaboration on code [22]. Additionally mapping people across multiple communication systems (issue trackers, forums, email) involves considerable manual effort [26]. Another possibility is to use dedicated software for tracking development time and pair programming effort [9] but such studies require prior setup.

Most common source of developer networks is the Version Control Systems (VCS) [13, 19, 31]. The underlying idea is that frequent access and modification on the same code implies communication and sharing. The advantages of using VCS is that they are commonly available for all software development activities, can be mined automatically without human involvement and directly reflect collaboration on code.

Once a developer network is constructed it can be analyzed to improve understanding of the software development process and the organizational structure. The recovered organizational structure then can be used in informing new collaborators or observing the integration of new members. Additional applications include tracking code sharing, finding substitute developers with related code knowledge and assembling communities with prior collaboration experience.

In this work we study the collaboration networks of three open source projects in order to learn their organizational structure and collaboration patterns. To do so we use an approach that mines collaboration networks from version control systems and computes similarities between developers based on commits to common files. Once the similarities are computed the network is visualized using a force-directed graph layout.

2   Approach

Our proposed approach [18] uses VCS to mine commits to source code files that developers make. It then computes similarities between committers and visualizes them in a network using similarities as link strengths. In cases when the network is too dense it offers multiple filtering techniques to reduce the number of links.

A crucial part of the approach is the similarity measure because it is used as the basis for visualization and filtering. For our purposes, we adopted an established similarity measure, which is also used in Collaborative Filtering techniques [28], [30] of Recommender Systems. A number of user similarity measures are derived from the ratings that users assign to items. In our case, we use source files as the items and the number of changes as the rating, which is similar to an approach for recommending software components [20].

Cosine similarity between two developers is obtained by calculating the cosine of the angle between their corresponding vectors d_i and d_j:

$$similarity(d_i, d_j) = \cos(d_i, d_j) = \frac{d_i \cdot d_j}{|d_i||d_j|} = \frac{\sum_k d_{i,k} d_{j,k}}{\sqrt{\sum_k d_{i,k}^2 \sum_k d_{j,k}^2}} \tag{1}$$

The similarity accounts for files that were modified only a few times and also for files that many people modify. Thus it is greater if the two developers modified the same files a large number of times and 0 if they did not share any files.

The approach has been previously validated [18] on two projects where the structure was known and was able to discover actual developer networks. It is implemented in a software visualization tool Lagrein [16, 17] which shows software metrics together with collaboration networks. The tool provides interactive exploration of collaboration networks and user adjustable link filtering. Since networks initially appear very dense due to a large number of links, the tool allows removing low weight links to view the network at different levels of detail.

2.1 Network Visualization

A common choice for social network visualizations [12, 29] is to use multidimensional scaling (MDS) [3, 8] or force-directed algorithms for graph layout [11].

Force-directed algorithms model graph vertices as having physical forces of attraction and repulsion. They iteratively compute vertex positions until the difference between desired and actual distances is minimized. Their advantage is that groups with high connectivity are placed together and similar vertices are placed closer than dissimilar ones.

We apply Fruchterman-Reingold [11] force-directed graph layout to the constructed network by setting the link lengths to developer dissimilarity in order to place similar developers together and dissimilar ones apart. The size of each node in the network is proportional to the number of commits the developer made and no link is created between developers with similarity 0. In cases when the visualization appears complex due to a large number of links, we apply filtering to remove low similarity links.

For visual appeal, links are visualized with transparency (using alpha blending). The transparency of a link is proportional to the similarity – high similarity links are solid while low similarity links are transparent. Thus strong links can be spotted immediately and the viewer can see which edges will disappear first during filtering.

Most developer networks are initially too dense due to large number of links. This makes the networks harder to read and hinders force-directed graph layout. For these reasons we filter out low weight edges using a user specified threshold and re-apply graph layout.

3 Case Study: phpMyAdmin Project

Initially, we repeated an existing study [13] of the phpMyAdmin[1] project to compare the resulting developer networks. The project is a web application for administering MySql relational database management systems and is written in PHP, HTML and JavaScript. It lets database administrators create/manage databases and tables, edit data and execute SQL statements. The tool is widely used by system administrators and after fifteen years is a stable and mature product. It has also received multiple awards and several books have been written about its usage. Details about the project's development are outlined in Table 1.

---

[1] http://www.phpmyadmin.net

Table 1. PhpMyAdmin project details

Property	Value
Repository type	Subversion (SVN)
Analyzed period	2001-2004
Codebase size	100 KLOC
Commits	10K
Languages	PHP, HTML, JavaScript
Committers	16

3.1   Project History

The project was started as a web frontend for MySQL in 1998 by Tobias Ratschiller who was an IT consultant at the time. Due to lack of time he abandoned the project but it already was one of the most popular MySQL administration tools having a large number of people willing to contribute (Table 2) and a large number of patches coming in. At that time in 2001 the project was taken over by Marc Delisle, Olivier Müller and Loïc Chapeaux who registered the project on SourceForge.net[2] project hosting site and the development has continued there ever since.

Table 2. PhpMyAdmin project contributors

Contributor name	Commiter id	Role in the project
Marc Delisle	lem9	Project Manager / Founder
Olivier Müller	swix	Developer / Founder
Loïc Chapeaux	loic1	Developer / Founder
Michal Čihař	nijel	Project Manager
Robin Johnson	robbat2	Developer
Garvin Hicking	garvinhicking	Developer
Alexander M. Turek	rabus	Developer

3.2   Collaboration Network

Similarly to our approach, the developer network was extracted from the version control system, however the links were created when two developers committed to the same directory and all links had the same weight. With a network obtained using such approach the authors notice that it is impossible to determine the importance of each developer and conclude that all developers play the same role. They also mention that the network might be misleading due to link computation at directory level. We confirm this observation and discover a different structure in the project's network using our approach for the same period (until 2004).

First we compute the links the same way – at directory level and without assigning weights to them. The resulting network is similar in layout to the network in the previous study and, indeed, no particular structure is evident (Fig. 1) due to the density of edges.

---

[2] http://sourceforge.net/projects/phpmyadmin/

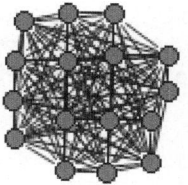

Fig. 1. PhpMyAdmin collaboration network computed at directory level. All contributors appear to have an equal role in the project.

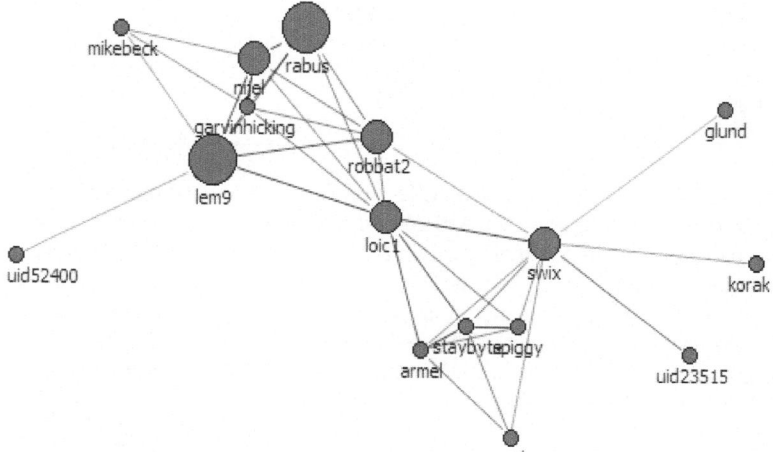

Fig. 2. phpMyAdmin collaboration network computed at file level and filtered links. Some contributors appear having a more central role

Afterwards, we apply the proposed approach and apply link filtering. We can notice that there are two main groups. By looking at the changed files, we noticed that these groups work on different sets of files, however most of these files are located in the root directory of the project. For this reason, link computation at directory level produced dense and compact network and we conclude that the computation is more reliable at file level.

While exploring the modified file list we noticed multiple developers, which are the only committers to some files. They work on their own subset of files and no one else works on these files. They make many commits (large nodes in the graph) and also are well connected to other developers indicating significant collaboration activity. Thus we conclude that all developers do not play the same role and there are some with more central and important roles. We later confirmed this by examining sourceforge.net[3] and project's home page where several such developers (lem9, nijel, swix, loic1) are mentioned as project managers and maintainers.

4   Case Study: Eclipse DTP Project

Having experimentally selected [18] Cosine similarity and filtering as effective methods for discovering team structure we proceeded to apply the technique to the

---

[3] http://sourceforge.net/projects/phpmyadmin/

Eclipse Data Tools Platform (DTP) project[4]. The choice of the project is arbitrary and the goal of the study is to demonstrate the use of the approach in revealing aspects of the organizational structure that are not known beforehand. Details of the project's development are outlined in Table 3.

Table 3. Eclipse DTP project details

Property	Value
Repository type	Concurrent Versions System (CVS)
Analyzed period	2005-2010
Codebase size	1.4 MLOC
Commits	90K
Languages	Java, XML
Committers	25
Subprojects	5

Eclipse Data Tools Platform is a collection of tools and frameworks for database handling and provides an abstract API over database drivers, connections and data so that they can be used in a generic way. It also provides UI inside Eclipse to define database connections and to execute SQL statements. Originally it was started by Sybase in 2005 and later attracted a large community, which is managed by a committee consisting of Sybase, IBM and Actuate. The project is large (1.4 MLOC) and is composed of several subprojects: Connectivity, Enablement, Incubator, Model Base and SQL Development Tools.

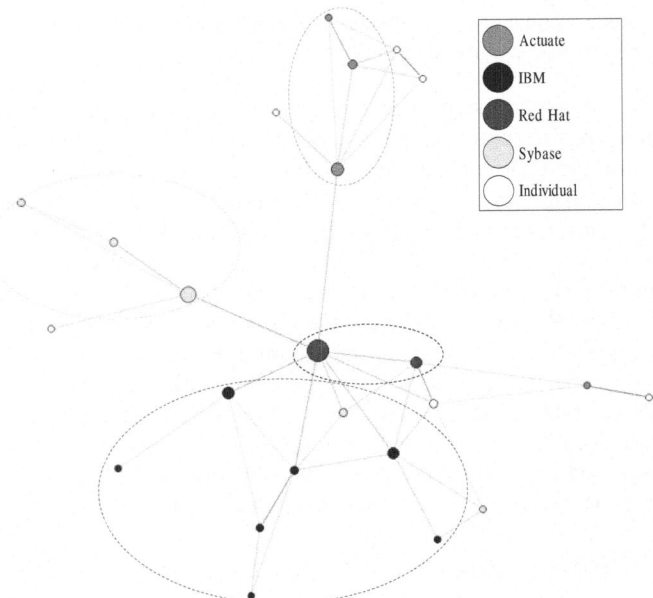

Fig. 3. Eclipse DTP project committer network. There is higher collaboration of contributors within each company.

---

[4] http://www.eclipse.org/datatools/

The Eclipse project provides information on its committers using its Commits Explorer[5]. This application allowed us to learn that contributions to the project have been made by many individual committers and multiple organizations including Actuate, IBM, Red Hat and Sybase. Using its CVS repository we constructed the developer network of 25 people for the period 2005-2010. Fig. 3 shows the resulting network obtained with link filtering and having each company colored in different color.

The visualization of the network allows us to gain quick insight into the organizational structure of the project. We can see a large contribution from IBM in terms of number of people however Red Hat stands in a more central role. An interesting aspect is that contributors do not contribute equally to all parts of the project. They collaborate closely with other contributors from the same company and to a much lesser extent with contributors from other companies.

5   Case Study: Gnu Compiler Collection (GCC) Project

The GNU Compiler Collection (GCC)[6] is a large system of compilers that supports numerous programming languages (C, C++, Java, Objective-C, Fortran, Ada, Go) and compiles to native code of many processor architectures. It is one of the oldest open source projects and has a large number of contributors developing its numerous front-end and back-end projects. It is produced by the GNU Project[7] with Richard Stallman (a.k.a RMS) and now is widely used as the standard compiler on popular Unix-like operating systems, including Linux and BSD.

The organizational process of the project is described as "cathedral" style by Eric S. Raymond [27] due to the fact that the project was under strict control by the Free Software Foundation (FSF). Many developers that were not satisfied with this model started their own forks of projects and formed the EGCS (Experimental GNU Compiler System). EGCS saw more activity than the GCC development and therefore later was made the official version of GCC. As a result the project opened up more and adopted a more "bazaar" style development model to allow more contributions. Studies of the project [33] show that the development process is largely maintenance and less new software creation. The details of the project's development are outlined in Table 4.

Table 4. GCC project details

Property	Value
Repository type	Subversion (SVN)
Analyzed period	1988-2010
Codebase size	8 MLOC
Commits	100 K
Languages	C/C++, Java, Fortran and others
Committers	350

---

[5] http://dash.eclipse.org/
[6] http://gcc.gnu.org/
[7] http://www.gnu.org/

One part of GCC is the GNU Fortran (GFortran) project whose purpose is to develop the Fortran compiler front end and run-time libraries for GCC. GFortran development is part of the GNU Project. Initially in 2000 it was developed by Andrew Vaught as project g95 that was a free Fortran 95 standard compiler using GCC backend. Andrew wrote most of the parser and for a while work on g95 continued to be collaborative until the late 2002 when he decided to be the sole developer of g95. Project GFortran then was forked from the g95 codebase and collaborative development has continued there since together with integration with the GCC codebase. Since the forking both codebases have significantly diverged. Most of the interface with GCC was written by Paul Brook.

Fig. 4. GCC Collaboration network with Fortran community in top-right (red)

We extracted and analyzed their Subversion commit log in the period from 1988-2010 containing commits from 349 committers. From the collaborator network we can immediately see a large and strongly connected core and a lot of scattered contributors in the periphery around the core. We also can see smaller strongly connected groups suggesting that there are sub-communities within the bigger GCC community as observed in other open-source projects [1].

A particularly interesting aspect is that this network also contains a strongly connected group separate from the core (marked red). By looking at the changes of this group, we can see that they are developing the Fortran front-end because most of their commits were to */gcc/fortran* and */gcc/libgfortran* directories. These directories are listed on the project's homepage as the ones where contribution takes place. Thus we can discover that this community is rather closed because it mostly collaborates among its own members and to a much lesser extent with the rest of the GCC contributors.

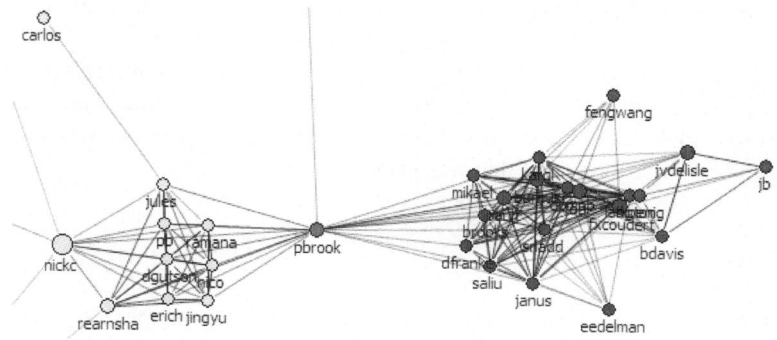

Fig. 5. ARM and Fortran communities in GCC

When we zoom in we can see another closed group to the left of Fortran community. That group (highlighted in yellow) mostly works on the ARM architecture since their commits were in the */gcc/config/arm* subdirectory. One committer (pbrook) stands out in the middle between the ARM and the Fortran communities indicating a lot of involvement in both. We verified this information using the project's contributions page[8], which acknowledges Paul Brook exactly for his work on GNU Fortran and the ARM architecture. He is also listed to have written most of the GFortran code that interfaces with the rest of GCC. Thus by viewing the network we are actually able to identify communities and roles without the need to go through published information or communication archives.

To summarize, by applying the method on open source projects we conclude that it is able to discover various aspects of the projects that were not evident before. We verified them using additional information from the projects however discovering using visualization involves much less effort. These results also added more confidence in the credibility of the approach and we conclude that it can be useful even if the full scope of usefulness is not established.

---

[8] http://gcc.gnu.org/onlinedocs/gcc/Contributors.html

6   Conclusions

In this work we studied collaboration networks of three open-source projects using visualizations. The networks were automatically discovered using an approach that analyses software repositories and finds similarities among developers based on commit counts to common files. Collaborating developers are placed closer together so that clusters and close collaboration becomes noticeable. Initially the networks appear very dense therefore we apply filtering to remove low weight links.

We found in phpMyAdmin project that there are developers with central roles and other contributors with peripheral roles. In Eclipse DTP project we noticed that there are contributions from multiple large companies however more collaboration is happening among developers within each company than between companies. Finally in GCC project we have observed that it consists of multiple sub-communities and that Fortran community is more separated from the other communities.

Overall open source projects vary greatly in their organization and collaboration patterns however these are often not documented. Automatic approaches for discovering collaboration networks can thus shed light on the structure of these projects and reveal information that was previously not known.

References

1. Di Bella, E., Sillitti, A., Succi, G.: A multivariate classification of open source developers. Information Sciences 221(1), 72–83 (2013)
2. Bird, C., Pattison, D., D'Souza, R., Filkov, V., Devanbu, P.: Chapels in the Bazaar? Latent Social Structure in OSS. In: 16th ACM SigSoft International Symposium on the Foundations of Software Engineering, Atlanta, GA (2008)
3. Borg, I., Groenen, P.: Modern Multidimensional Scaling: Theory and Applications. Springer (1997)
4. Coman, I., Sillitti, A.: Automated Identification of Tasks in Development Sessions. In: 16th IEEE International Conference on Program Comprehension, ICPC 2008, Amsterdam, The Netherlands, June 10-13 (2008)
5. Conway, M.E.: How Do Committees invent? Datamation 14(4), 28–31 (1968)
6. Crowston, K., Howison, J.: The Social Structure of Free and Open Source Software. First Monday 10(2) (2005)
7. Di Bella, E., Fronza, I., Phaphoom, N., Sillitti, A., Succi, G., Vlasenko, J.: Pair Programming and Software Defects – a large, industrial case study. IEEE Transaction on Software Engineering, doi: 10.1109/TSE.2012.68
8. Freeman, L.C.: Visualizing Social Networks. Journal of Social Structure (2000)
9. Fronza, I., Sillitti, A., Succi, G.: An interpretation of the results of the analysis of pair programming during novices integration in a team. In: 3rd International Symposium on Empirical Software Engineering and Measurement, ESEM 2009 (2009)
10. Fronza, I., Sillitti, A., Succi, G., Terho, M., Vlasenko, J.: Failure prediction based on log files using Random Indexing and Support Vector Machines. Journal of Systems and Software 86(1), 2–11 (2013)
11. Fruchterman, T.M.G., Reingold, E.: Graph Drawing by Force-Directed Placement. Software-Practice and Experience 21, 1129–1164 (1991)

12. Heer, J., Boyd, D.: Vizster: Visualizing Online Social Networks. In: Proc. of the 2005 IEEE Symposium on Information Visualization, INFOVIS 2005, p. 5. IEEE Computer Society, Washington, DC (2005)
13. Huang, S.-K., Liu, K.-M.: Mining version histories to verify the learning process of legitimate peripheral participants. In: Proceedings 2nd International Workshop on Mining Software Repositories, MSR 2005, pp. 84–88. ACM Press, New York (2005)
14. Huang, W., Hong, S., Eades, P.: How people read sociograms: a questionnaire study. In: Proc. of the 2006 Asia-Pacific Symposium on Information Visualisation, vol. 60, pp. 199–206. Australian Computer Society (2006)
15. Jeh, G., Widom, J.: Simrank: a measure of structural-context similarity. In: KDD 2002: Proceedings of the Eighth ACM SIGKDD International Conference on Knowledge Discovery and Data Mining, pp. 538–543 (2002)
16. Jermakovics, A., Scotto, M., Sillitti, A., Succi, G.: Lagrein: Visualizing User Requirements and Development Effort. In: 15th IEEE International Conference on Program Comprehension, ICPC 2007, Banff, Alberta, Canada, June 26-29 (2007)
17. Jermakovics, A., Moser, R., Sillitti, A., Succi, G.: Visualizing Software Evolution with Lagrein. In: 22nd Object-Oriented Programming, Systems, Languages & Applications, OOPSLA 2008, Nashville, TN, USA, October 19-23 (2008)
18. Jermakovics, A., Sillitti, A., Succi, G.: Mining and visualizing developer networks from version control systems. In: 4th International Workshop on Cooperative and Human Aspects of Software Engineering, CHASE 2011 (2011)
19. Lopez-Fernandez, L., Robles, G., Gonzalez-Barahona, J.M.: Applying social network analysis to the information in CVS repositories. In: Proc. of 1st Intl. Workshop on Mining Software Repositories, MSR 2004, pp. 101–105 (2004)
20. McCarey, F., Cinnéide, M.Ó., Kushmerick, N.: Rascal: A Recommender Agent for Agile Reuse. Artif. Intell. Rev. 24(3-4), 253–276 (2005)
21. Meneely, A., Williams, L., Snipes, W., Osborne, J.: Predicting failures with developer networks and social network analysis. In: SIGSOFT 2008/FSE-16: Proceedings of the 16th ACM SIGSOFT International Symposium on Foundations of Software Engineering, pp. 13–23. ACM, New York (2008)
22. Meneely, A., Williams, L.: Socio-technical developer networks: should we trust our measurements? In: Proceedings of the 33rd International Conference on Software Engineering, ICSE (2011)
23. Mockus, A.: Succession: Measuring transfer of code and developer productivity. In: Proc. of the 2009 IEEE 31st International Conference on Software Engineering, May 16-24, pp. 67–77. IEEE Computer Society, Washington, DC (2009)
24. Petrinja, E., Nambakam, R., Sillitti, A.: Introducing the OpenSource Maturity Model. In: 2nd Emerging Trends in FLOSS Research and Development Workshop at ICSE 2009, Vancouver, BC, Canada (2009)
25. Pinzger, M., Nagappan, N., Murphy, B.: Can developer-module networks predict failures? In: Proceedings of the 16th ACM SIGSOFT International Symposium on Foundations of Software Engineering, SIGSOFT 2008/FSE-16, Atlanta, Georgia, November 09-14, pp. 2–12. ACM, New York (2008)
26. Pinzger, M., Gall, H.C.: Dynamic analysis of communication and collaboration in OSS projects. In: Collaborative Software Engineering, pp. 265–284. Springer (2010)
27. Raymond, E.S.: The Cathedral and the Bazaar. O'Reilly & Associates, Inc., Sebastopol (1999)

28. Resnick, P., Iacovou, N., Suchak, M., Bergstrom, P., Riedl, J.: GroupLens: An Open Architecture for Collaborative Filtering of Netnews. In: Proceedings of CSCW 1994, Chapel Hill, NC (1994)
29. Sarma, A., Maccherone, L., Wagstrom, P., Herbsleb, J.: Tesseract: Interactive visual exploration of socio-technical relationships in software development. In: Proceedings of the 2009 IEEE 31st International Conference on Software Engineering, May 16-24, pp. 23–33. IEEE Computer Society, Washington, DC (2009)
30. Shardanand, U., Maes, P.: Social information filtering: algorithms for automating "word of mouth". In: Proceedings of the SIGCHI Conference on Human Factors in Computing Systems, pp. 210–217. ACM Press/Addison-Wesley Publishing Co., New York (1995)
31. de Souza, C.R., Quirk, S., Trainer, E., Redmiles, D.F.: Supporting collaborative software development through the visualization of socio-technical dependencies. In: Proceedings of the 2007 International ACM Conference on Supporting Group Work, GROUP 2007, pp. 147–156. ACM, New York (2007)
32. Wolf, T., Schröter, A., Damian, D., Panjer, L.D., Nguyen, T.H.: Mining Task-Based Social Networks to Explore Collaboration in Software Teams. IEEE Softw. 26(1), 58–66 (2009)
33. Yamauchi, Y., Yokozawa, M., Shinohara, T., Ishida, T.: Collaboration with Lean Media: how open-source software succeeds. In: Proceedings of the 2000 ACM Conference on Computer Supported Cooperative Work, pp. 329–338. ACM (December 2000)

Socio-technical Congruence in OSS Projects: Exploring Conway's Law in FreeBSD

M.M. Mahbubul Syeed and Imed Hammouda

Tampere University of Technology, Finland
{mm.syeed,imed.hammouda}@tut.fi

Abstract. Software development requires effective communication, coordination and collaboration among developers working on interdependent modules of the same project. The need for coordination is even more evident in open source projects where development is often more dispersed and distributed. In this paper, we study the match between the coordination needs established by the technical domain (i.e. source code) and the actual coordination activities carried out by the development team, such hypothetical match is also known as socio-technical congruence. We carry out our study by empirically examining Conway's law in FreeBSD project. Our study shows that the congruence measure is significantly high in FreeBSD and that the congruence value remains stable as the project matured.

1 Introduction

Investigating socio-technical congruence in software development projects has become an active research area in the last decade [10]. Socio-technical congruence can be defined as the match between the coordination needs established by the technical domain (i.e., the architectural dependency in the software) and the actual coordination activities carried out by project members (i.e., within the members of the development team) [6]. This coordination need can be determined by analyzing the assignments of people to a technical entity such as a source code module, and the technical dependencies among the technical entities [6]. Socio-technical congruence not only has been used as a measure for a number of project properties such as software build success [8] but also as a means for software engineering tasks like architecture recovery [23].

In most of research on socio-technical congruence, Conway's law [4] is often presented as a guide and a basis for the underlying study. Conway's Law in its purest form states that "the organizations that design systems are constrained to produce systems which are copies of the communication structures of these organizations" [1]. In other words, the product architecture often reflects the organizational structure of the development team [1][6]. In [7], Conway's law is considered homomorphic and thus claimed to be true in reverse as well. This means the communication pattern within developer community should reflect the architectural dependency in the software. Thus, the notion of socio-technical congruence is actually a conceptualization of Conway's law.

E. Petrinja et al. (Eds.): OSS 2013, IFIP AICT 404, pp. 109–126, 2013.
© IFIP International Federation for Information Processing 2013

Studying socio-technical congruence in open source software has its own questions and hypotheses, for those products are peer-produced, crowdsourced systems where centralized planning and control of architecture is difficult. Furthermore, the evolution of such systems, and their underlying architecture, is not bound to any pre-defined plans [5]. Surprisingly, this research area has not been given much attention among open source researchers [34].

In this paper, we study Conway's Law and Reverse Conway's Law, as a lens for socio-technical congruence, in the context of open source development projects by proposing a novel evaluation and measurement technique. We further explore the significance of socio-technical congruence as the project matures. To investigate our research problem, we focused on a popular open source project, FreeBSD, which is an advanced operating systems for computing platforms. We carried out our study empirically by analyzing the software repository of the project in a semi-automatic way.

The remaining of the paper is organized as follows. Section 2 introduces a number of key concepts that this study uses. Motivation and related work is presented in Section 3. We then introduce the research questions explored in this paper and our study design in Section 4 and 5 respectively. Results are reported and discussed in Section 6. Possible limitations and threats to validity are highlighted in Section 7. Finally, Section 8 concludes the papers and shed light on future research.

2   Definitions

In this paper we interpreted Conway's law (and reverse Conway's law) as a measure to verify the extent to which the communication pattern of the contributing members is due to the communication needs established by the concrete architecture and vice versa. In examining this the following concepts are defined.

2.1   Developer Contribution

Developer contribution to the software can be defined as the code contribution or any form of commit made to the code base.

2.2   Concrete Architecture

Concrete architecture of a software presents the relationship among components of a software (e.g., modules, files or packages) based on the actual design and implementation. In this work, header file inclusions dependency at code file level were used to derive the concrete architecture. In this architecture two files, and their corresponding packages, were linked if the two files have an inclusion dependency.

2.3   Concrete Coordination Network

Concrete Coordination Network is a social network in which two developers have a relationship if they have communication history as seen by the mailing archives representing the social and technical interactions among the developers.

2.4   Derived Architecture

Derived architecture defines an architecture of the software where any two components (e.g., packages or code files) are related if there are developer(s) who have either (a) contributed to both the components, or (b) have communication at organizational level (e.g., through email). For instance consider that developer D1 has contributed to packages P1 and P2, and developer D2 has contributed to package P3. Also consider that both developers has communication at organizational level as shown in Fig. 1(a). Thus according to the definition, packages P1, P2 and P3 are linked to each others in the Derived Architecture (Fig. 1(b)).

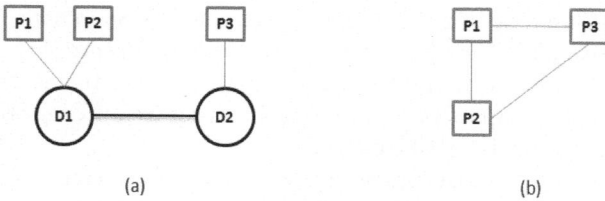

(a)   (b)

Fig. 1. (a) Concrete Coordination Network with contribution to code base (b) Corresponding Derived Architecture

2.5   Derived Coordination Network

Derived Coordination Network is the developer relationship network in which two developers have a relationship if they have contributed either (a) to a common code file or (b) to the code files that have relationships in the concrete architecture. For instance consider that developer D1 and D2 has contributed to package P1 and developer D3 has contributed to package P2. Also consider that P1 and P2 have an inclusion dependency as shown in Fig.2(a). Then, according to the definition developers D1, D2 and D3 will have relationships in Derived Coordination Network as shown in Fig. 2(b).

3   Motivation and Related Work

In this section we discuss the significance of Conway's law and socio-technical congruence in the field of software engineering citing related works from existing literature.

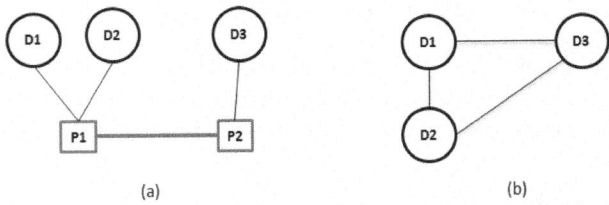

(a)   (b)

Fig. 2. (a) Concrete architecture with contributing developers (b) Corresponding Derived Coordination Network

3.1 Need for Conway's Law and Socio-technical Congruence

Conway's law was stated 30 years ago by Melvin Conway as the means to emphasize the need of coordination in software development [1]. Until then researchers have long argued that the mirroring effect of the software architecture and the communication pattern of the developer community plays a pivotal role in coordinating the development work [9]. A central question arises "Does Conway's law matter in the modern era of software development?". As reported in [10], Conway's law still matters in the domain of software development and the product quality is strongly affected by the organizational structure [11]. Also with the advent of global software engineering where development teams are distributed across the world, the impact of organizational structure on Conways law and its implications on quality is significant [12].

In the domain of software engineering, socio-technical congruence as a conceptualization of Conway's law was first coined in [13]. In this paper, socio-technical congruence was employed as a fine-grained measure of coordination that can be used to diagnose coordination problems in the development team. Also, evidence from studies [13] shows that higher congruence leads to faster completion of modification requests. This concept has been identified as an important element for product design in the field of engineering [14] and management science [15] as well. Researchers also argued that such congruence is a natural consequence and a desired property for collaborative development activities [14], such as software engineering.

3.2 Socio-technical Congruence and OSS Development

In the epoch of OSS projects, there exists a significant number of successful software systems whose volume and complexity are as compound as that of their proprietary counterparts. Such large and successful OSS projects often consist of hundreds and even thousands of developers contributing to the development of the project. Developers working in such projects are not strictly bound to any organizational rules, regulation and structure. Rather they voluntarily join and contribute to the project. OSS developers belong to discrete geographical locations of significant background, timezone, language and cultural distances. Often an OSS project is developed and evolved through the collaboration among the developers using simple communication media like email, wiki, chat [31] as well as revision tracking systems (such as CVS, SVN) to store and access the software code they produce [19].

This unconventional organizational structure and practices of OSS projects combing with the inherent complexity of the software development (as discussed above) brings forth the question, "why such projects succeed and can socio-technical congruence be conceived as an implicit driving force for such success?". Surprisingly, socio-technical congruence as a research area has not been given much attention among open source researchers. In this paper, we infer that socio-technical congruence is an endogenous driver for successful OSS projects, and examines its existence in OSS project though empirical evidences.

4   Research Questions

Our research objective in this paper is to study the applicability of Conway's law as a means of verifying the socio-technical congruence on large, distributed and evolving OSS projects. In great part because of the specific characteristics of the OSS projects and yet having revolutionary success, it is most likely that the OSS development process implicitly encompasses the notion of socio-technical congruence. Thus, we targeted the following research questions.

(a) How does the communication patterns of OSS developer community resemble the architecture of the software?
Conway's law can be interpreted as the first explicit recognition that the communication pattern of the organization has an inevitable impact on the product [20]. Thus there must exist a correspondence between the community structure and the software structure. Our point of interest here is that if such homomorphic force between the software model and its development organization exists in OSS projects, then it could be effectively used to conceptualize the architecture of legacy systems. It can also be used as a metric to assess the quality and maintainability of the system as well.

(b) How does the architecture of the software resemble the collaboration patterns of OSS developer community?
Conway's law pointed out [1] that only the organizational arrangements can be optimized with respect to the system concept. This observation enforces the need for a stable and modular design of the system in order to facilitate effective communication, coordination among the developers. With geographically distributed development setup, as in OSS projects, co-ordination becomes more challenging due to location, time, and cultural differences, and the need for a stable design becomes even more evident [9]. For this kind of organizational setup, a clearly separable and stable architectural design would be the basis for assigning task to the developers [9] and a key to the success of the project. In other words, the collaboration pattern of the developer community should mirror the architecture of the software which should remain stable during the evolution of the project.

(c) Does the socio-technical congruence evolve as the project matures?

Our intension is to examine how the socio-technical congruence evolves as the project matures. We are particularly interested in deriving any visible pattern of such congruence during the evolution. But relating such trends in congruence in OSS projects with its success parameters are out of the scope of this study.

5   Study Design

5.1   Case and Subject Selection

To investigate our research questions, we focused on a popular open source project, FreeBSD, which is an advanced operating system for modern server, desktop, and embedded computer platforms [24]. It is derived from BSD, the version of UNIX developed at the University of California, Berkeley. Selection of this project as a case study was influenced by the facts that FreeBSD's code base has undergone continuous development, improvement, and optimization for thirty years [24]. The project has been developed and maintained by a large team of individuals. Also, FreeBSD has gained considerable attention in earlier research on the evolution of OSS projects [16] [17] [18].

5.2   Data Sources

In literature [10] a great emphasis was given to leveraging software repositories along with the communication data for deriving technical dependencies as well as developers coordination patterns. In OSS projects, repository data is stored and maintained through different data management systems, e.g., source code repository (SVN or CVS), change logs, mailing archive, bug reporting systems, and communication channels. These data sources are highly accepted and utilized medium for empirical studies on OSS projects [25][26][27]. In FreeBSD project, the development and communication history is maintained through SVN repositories and mailing archives. Following is the description of these sources and the data extracted for this study.

1. Source code repository: FreeBSD has two release branches, stable and production releases. In this study, SVN repositories of the stable releases were collected. Fig. 3 provides detail of these stable releases and the data collected from each release.
2. Mailing list archive: In OSS projects, email archives provide a useful trace of the task-oriented communication and co-ordination activities of the developers during the evolution of the project [28]. In the FreeBSD project, email archives are categorized according to their purpose. For instance, there are email for project development (e.g., commits), stable release planning, chat, user emails, bug reports. These archives contain all mailing lists since 1994 and are updated every week [24]. Fig. 4 provides detail on the FreeBSD email archives that were extracted for this study. These email archives contain the

detail of the commit records made for each stable release and are only used by the developer community. These archives thus give more accurate history of contributions than the bug reporting system which is often used by the the passive users for different purposes.

Stable Releases	Release Date	Size (# of code files)	Size (# of packages)	Data Extracted for each code file	Study Purpose
stable-2.0.5	June, 1995	5038	15	1. code or header file name.	1. Identifying developers for
stable-2.1	November, 1995	6831	16	2. File directory path.	each stable release.
stable-2.2	March, 1997	8424	19	3. File package name.	2. Identifying developer
stable-3	October, 1998	6241	14	4. List of included header files.	contribution to each stable
stable-4	March, 2000	15038	19	5. Copyright information	release.
stable-5	January, 2003	17025	19	(name of the copyright holder,	3. Deriving concrete
stable-6	November 2005	18695	19	year, email address).	architecture, and Coordination
stable-7	February 2008	21088	20	6. Number of code files,	Architecture
stable-8	November 2009	22849	20	number of other files, number	
stable-9	January 2012	25583	20	of packages	
Programming language used:	C and C++				
Download source:	http://svn.freebsd.org/base/stable				

Fig. 3. Stable Releases of FreeBSD

Email Collection period:		january, 1994 - january, 2012		
Download Source:		http://docs.freebsd.org/mail/		
Mail type	Year	Mail Archive	Study Purpose	Data Extracted from each email
CVS/SVN commit	1994-1998	cvs-bin, cvs-contrib, cvs-distrib, cvs-doc, cvs-eBones, cvs-etc, cvs-games, cvs-gnu, cvs-include, cvs-kerberosIV, cvs-lib, cvs-libexec, cvs-lkm, cvs-other, cvs-ports, cvs-release, cvs-sbin, cvs-share, cvs-sys, cvs-tools, cvs-user, cvs-	1. Identifying developers for each stable release. 2. Identifying developer contribution to each stable release. 3. Deriving Coordination Network, and Derived Coordination Network.	1. Email subject 2. Sender name 3. Sender email 4. Receiver name, email 5. Date and time Posted (i.e., year, month, day, and gmt)
	1999-2007	cvs-all		
	2008-2012	cvs-all, svn-src-stable-6, svn-src-stable-7, svn-src-stable-8, svn-src-stable-9, svn-src-stable-other		
Discussion	1994-2012	freebsd-chat, freebsd-stable	1. Identifying developers for each stable release. 2. Deriving Coordination Network, Derived Coordination Network.	

Fig. 4. FreeBSD email archives used for this study

5.3   Data Collection Procedure

Data Collection from Source Code Repositories: Each stable release of the FreeBSD project was downloaded from the SVN repository to the local directory. Fig. 3 lists the stable releases and associated detail of each release. To extract data from each of these releases, a parser was written in Java. This parser searched through each directory of a stable release, read through the files in a directory and parsed relevant data. The data that were parsed from each file were listed in Fig. 3. As FreeBSD was written in C and C++, included header files were identified from the #include directive in each code file. The parser excluded all the library header files and kept only the user defined header files. Also the copyright directive in a file contains information of the developer name, email and the copyright year. The parser extracted each of these information from the copyright directive. The developers that were found in this process were considered as the contributors to that file for that stable release.

The parsed data for each stable release was stored in excel files. To read/write excel files Apache POI [29] was used. The number of code files and packages read from each stable release was shown in Fig. 3.

Data Collection from Email Archives: The email archives that concern CVS/SVN commits and general discussions (e.g., on stable releases and the chat entries) were extracted from FreeBSD email archive as shown in Fig. 4. For extracting data from each email entry, a data extraction program was written in Java. This data extractor used the web interface of the email archives (link is provided in Fig. 4). Thus each email was read as an HTML page and the data was extracted using Jsoup html parser [30]. Data that was extracted from each email entry is listed in Fig. 4. This data was then stored in excel files according to the archive name and year. Then the email data was sorted according to each stable release as follows: (a) emails were categorized into a specific release if the release number was mentioned in email subject (e.g., SVN commit emails provide release number in email subject) and (b) other emails (e.g., freeBSD-stable, freeBSD-chat and most of the CVS commit emails) for which the release numbers were not mentioned, the posting dates were checked. In this case, for instance, an email was categorized to stable release 3 if its posting date fall between the release date of stable release 2 and 3. The rationale here is that developers would commit to the code base and discuss on its release strategy before it is officially released.

After categorizing emails to each stable release, the subject of a CVS/SVN commit email was parsed. This subject mentioned the path to the repository to which the commit was made. From this subject, the directory path, package name, and if provided, the name of the modified code file and the stable release number were identified. Sender name for each of these CVS/SVN commit email was considered as a contributor to the code base for that release. Contributors found in this process were combined with the contributors found from the code base to get list of developers who contributed to each stable release. Fig. 5 lists release wise distribution of the number of developers and email entries identified through this process.

Releases	Stable-2.0.5	Stable-2.1	Stable-2.2	Stable-3	Stable-4	Stable-5	Stable-6	Stable-7	Stable-8	Stable-9
# of contributors / release	168	196	325	367	603	693	827	983	1081	1128
# of emails / release	7014	6343	17874	14906	22833	115536	22290	21599	15473	33882

Fig. 5. Number of contributors and emails identified for stable releases

Data preprocessing: Data that was extracted and parsed following the above process contained anomalies data in many cases. For instance, developer names and email addresses might contain punctuation characters like, semi-colons, inverted comas, brackets, unnecessary white space, and hyphens. Furthermore, parsers may parsed data inappropriately in some cases. For example, copyright text "All rights reserved" can be treated as part of developer name while parsing copyright directive from a code file. To clean such anomalies data and punctuation characters, data cleaning programs were written in Java. To ensure the correctness of this process, we performed a manual checking on a randomly selected data to verify their correctness.

5.4   Analysis Procedure

This section discussed the methods used to construct the communication networks, architectures and to measure socio-technical congruence (defined in section 2) utilizing the data collected from the FreeBSD project.

Developer Contribution: Release-wise developer contribution was measured in two ways, (a) from the copyright information provided in each source code file of a release and (b) from the commits made by a developer for a release. Fig. 6(a) shows a sample contribution made by developer *John Birrell* in stable release 3.

Developer	Package	File Dir	File name	Email	Release
John Birrell	3/lib/	3/lib/libc_r/ uthread/	uthread_attr_getstac kaddr.c	jb@cimlogic.com. au	stable-3
John Birrell	3/lib/	3/lib/libc_r/ uthread/	uthread_attr_getstac ksize.c	jb@cimlogic.com. au	stable-3
John Birrell	3/lib/	3/lib/libc_r/ uthread/	uthread_attr_init.c	jb@cimlogic.com. au	stable-3
John Birrell	3/lib/	3/lib/libc_r/ uthread/	uthread_attr_setcrea tesuspend_np.c	jb@cimlogic.com. au	stable-3
John Birrell	3/lib/	3/lib/libc_r/ uthread/	uthread_attr_setdeta chstate.c	jb@cimlogic.com. au	stable-3

(a)

Developer name	Developer name	Relationship weight
J Wunsch	Bruce Evans	15
Peter Dufault	Brian Somers	61
Tom Samplonius	Andreas Klemm	6
Mikael Karpberg	Bill Fenner	3

(b)

Fig. 6. (a) Sample contributions made by developer John Birrell (b) Sample relationships in Concrete Coordination Network

Concrete Architecture: The concrete architecture of a stable release was constructed based on header file inclusion dependency as defined in section 2.2. This inclusion dependency relation was used in earlier works [32] [35] to construct architecture of legacy C/C++ software systems.

Then higher level abstraction of this architecture was built to get the package level concrete architecture. In this architecture, package p1 and p2 had a relationship if file f1 in package p1 had an inclusion dependency with a file f2 in package p2 or vice-versa. Relationship between packages were weighted which was the total number of inclusion relationships that exists between the files in two packages. An example of file level concrete architecture and corresponding package level architecture of stable release 3 is shown in Fig. 7(a) and (b) respectively. Package level concrete architecture was constructed for each stable release.

Source File	Destination File	Source File path	Destination File path
adjkerntz.c	sys/time.h	3/sbin/adjkerntz/adjkerntz.c	3/sys/sys/time.h
adjkerntz.c	sys/param.h	3/sbin/adjkerntz/adjkerntz.c	3/sys/sys/param.h
chkey.c	rpcsvc/ypclnt.h	3/usr.bin/chkey/chkey.c	3/include/rpcsvc/ypclnt.h
ftpd.c	arpa/telnet.h	3/libexec/ftpd/ftpd.c	3/usr.bin/tn3270/distribution/arpa/telnet.h

Source Package	Destination Package	Relationship Weight
3/sbin/	3/sys/	302
3/usr.bin/	3/include/	82
3/libexec/	3/usr.bin/	4

(a)   (b)

Fig. 7. (a) Code file level Concrete Architecture (b) Package level Concrete Architecture

Concrete Coordination Network: Common email conversation in FreeBSD can appear in any of the email archives listed in Fig. 4. This relationship was weighted, meaning that for each new instance of email conversation between the same developers, the relationship weight would be increased by one. For each stable release of FreeBSD, one such Concrete Coordination Network was constructed. Fig. 6(b) shows example relationships in the Concrete Coordination Network of stable release 3. Weight column in this figure shows the number of emails common between the two developers.

Derived Architecture: Derived Architecture was generated based on the definition in Section 2.4. Each package relationship in this architecture was weighted and would increase if either of the two criteria hold for other developers. Both package level and code file leave derived architectures were constructed for each stable release. Fig. 8(a) shows the package level Derived Architecture for stable release 3.

Derived Coordination Network: Derived Coordination Network was generated based on the package level Concrete Architecture and for each stable release following the definition presented in Section 2.5. Each relationship was weighted. Fig. 8(b) shows an example of this network for stable release 3.

Thus this network shows the actual communication need among the developers which is based on the design of the software (i.e., the concrete architecture). This network is essential due to the fact that if two subsystems are to communicate, it is likely to have communication between the developers of the two subsystems [1].

Socio-technical Congruence: To measure socio-technical congruence the following method was applied: common relationships are identified that exists between (a) Concrete Architecture and Derived Architecture, and between (b)

source package	destination package	Relationship weight
3/contrib/	3/etc/	424
3/gnu/	3/release/	251
3/contrib/	3/share/	456

(a)

Developer name	Developer name	Relationship weight
Paul Traina	Michael Smith	21
Sun Microsystems	Philippe Charnier	20
John D. Polstra	Julian R. Elischer	6

(b)

Fig. 8. (a) Derived Architecture (b) Derived Coordination Network

Concrete Coordination Network and Derived Coordination Network. The two sets of relationships identified in this process is termed as congruence.

The former congruence illustrates the match between the architectural dependency and the architecture produced due to the communication structure of the community. And the latter congruence depicts the match between the actual coordination activities in the community and the coordination need established by the architectural dependency of the software. To be precise, these congruences verify Conway's law and the reverse Conway's law, respectively. Both form of congruences were determined for each stable release. A partial snapshot of the congruence between Concrete and Derived Architectures of stable release 3 is shown in Fig. 9.

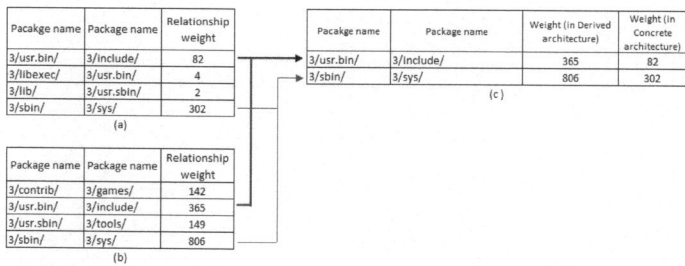

Fig. 9. (a) Concrete Architecture (b) Derived Architecture (c) Congruence

To construct the networks and architectures and to measure socio-technical congruence and Conway's law, Java programs were written.

Result Interpretation: To measure the extent to which Conway's law holds for each stable release of the FreeBSD project, percentile value was calculated for (a) the congruence value and the corresponding Concrete Architecture, and (b) the congruence value and corresponding Coordination Network. These percentile values were plotted in a graph against the stable releases to conceptualize the evolution of the Conway's law and socio-technical congruence in the FreeBSD project.

6 Results

6.1 Resemblance of Communication Pattern to Software Architecture

Our study target in this work was to verify the extent to which the communication patterns of the members of the developer community resembles the actual architectural dependencies. To achieve this, we collected historical data from the FreeBSD project and measured such resemblance for each stable release. The resemblance process consists of determining the concrete architecture and derived architecture for each stable release. Then, the congruence between the two architectures and corresponding percentile measure of Conway's law for each release was measured. The result of this process is reported in Fig. 10. Column 2 and 3 in this figure show the number of relations between packages identified by the respective architectures. The congruence relationships and the percentile value for each release indicate the extent to which the two architectures of the software overlap with each other. Here the percentile value is measured between the congruence and the concrete architecture, because the intension is to measure the extent to which the derived architecture approximates the concrete architecture.

Stable releases	No of Relationships among packages			(%) Conway's law
	Derived Architecture	Concrete Architecture	Congruence	
stable-2.0.5	104	33	22	66,67
stable-2.1	91	38	26	68,43
stable-2.2	211	47	34	72,35
stable-3	153	27	22	81,49
stable-4	153	49	40	81,64
stable-5	136	52	41	78,85
stable-6	136	48	38	79,17
stable-7	190	53	40	75,48
stable-8	193	55	44	80
stable-9	178	56	45	80,36

Fig. 10. Resemblance of communication pattern to software architecture

The percentile values suggest that around 76% to 82% overlap between the two architecutres are found from stable release 3 onward. Whereas for the earlier three releases it is between 66% to 73%. It is worth to mention here that we noted considerable drift in the congruence value for the first three releases of the FreeBSD project. Thus we excluded them from our observation, considering this period as a restructuring and reformation period of FreeBSD after being forked. However, this observation is a positive sign towards the socio-technical congrucence, and can be an implicit charactersitcs of OSS development process. From this result, we can safely say that to a considerable extent the communication of the contributing developers in the community is actually due to the coordination need as identified by the architectural dependency.

Now the question is, does the derived architecture actually resembles the concrete architecture, and can it be used to recover the architecture of the legacy software? By examining Fig. 10 it is evident that the derived architecture is over-estimating the concrete architecture for all the releases. For instance, in stable release 4, the derived architecture identifies 153 relations among the 19 packages, whereas concrete architecture shows only 49. Thus, it is not possible to resemble the concrete architecture from the derived architecture. Yet, the following observation can be offered.

To a great part, the communication pattern of the contributing members within the community is due to the communication needs established by the concrete architecture.

The interdependency among the packages in the concrete architecture influences their contributors to communicate at community level. This supports the existence of Conway's law within the FreeBSD development process. None-the-less, both the architectures overlap considerably. Thus the derived architecture can be used in authenticating the architecture recovered by traditional reverse engineering process.

This over estimation by the derived architecture can be justified in a way that this architecture was derived from the communication record of their contributing developers. And the developers in the community can communicate and collaborate on issues that might be outside of the scope of the actual code implementation and commits. For instance, FreeBSD-chat archive collects only the email threads related to the general discussion. These discussions generate additional relationships among the contributing developers which were not due to only common contribution. In the derived architecture these relationships create additional links between the packages. Yet it can also be possible that some of the links between packages in the derived architecture reflect valid relationships for the release, as the concrete architecture might not identify all the links that actually exists for that release.

6.2   Resemblance of Software Architecture to Communication Pattern

Conventional wisdom supports that the socio-technical congruence measured in reverse (i.e., reverse Conway's law) should hold as well. That is the communication pattern identified by the concrete architecture should simulate the actual communication pattern of the contributing community members. To measure this we constructed the coordination network and the derived coordination network. These networks show the communication among the contributing developers identified by the actual communication through email and by the concrete architecture, respectively. Then the congruence between these two networks and corresponding percentile value was calculated for each stable release. The percentile value indicates the extent to which both networks overlap. Relationships identified by each of these networks are presented in Fig.11.

Stable releases	No of Relationships among contributing developers			
	Derived Coordination Network	Concrete Coordination Network	Congruence	(%) Reverse Conway's law
stable-2.0.5	11017	925	574	62,06
stable-2.1	14884	805	443	55,04
stable-2.2	39059	6614	2165	32,74
stable-3	53152	5635	3980	70,63
stable-4	138228	4195	2983	71,11
stable-5	198602	11590	8253	71,21
stable-6	286244	17113	13634	79,68
stable-7	413188	10828	9453	87,31
stable-8	504458	7167	5768	80,48
stable-9	550427	4073	2857	70,15

Fig. 11. Resemblance of software architecture to communication pattern

It can be noted that the architecture of FreeBSD remains quite stable in terms of number of packages (Fig.3) and their interdependency as identified by the concrete architecture (column 3 of Fig.10). Thus it can be ascertained that

The architectural design of the software remains stable during its evolution.

As can be seen from Fig. 11 the congruence values remain in-between 71% to 88% from stable release 3 to 9 (ignoring the first three releases as discussed in section 6.1). This result is closely tied with the results reported in Fig. 10. This implies that socio-technical congruence in reverse also holds for FreeBSD. And the communication pattern of contributing developer community simulates the underlying architectural dependency of the software to a gereat extent. Yet the derived coordination network is not able to estimate the coordination network, the former network overestimates the later one, similar to the derived architecture. Instead the following observatioin can be offered.

The communication need defined by the architectural design and interdependency among the modules of the software is effectively embedded within the communication pattern of the developer community of the FreeBSD project.

Again the over estimation by the derived coordination network can be vindicated as follows, this network was derived from package level concrete architecture. Thus developers contributing to a package or to the related packages were considered to have communication among them. This lead to a number of relationships among developers in the derived coordination architecture who might not have contributed to the same code files, but to the same packages. Yet these relationships among contributing developers should be taken as a suggestion to improve the coordination further in the community.

6.3   Evolution of Socio-technical Congruence in FreeBSD Project

To conceptualize the evolution of socio-technical congruence in FreeBSD we plotted the congruence values in graph against the stable releases. As shown in

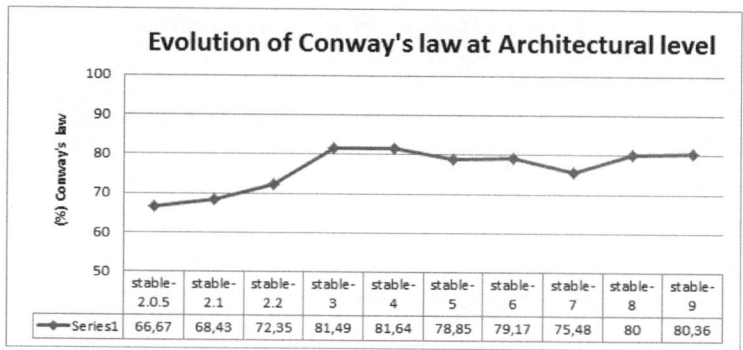

Fig. 12. Evolution of Conway's law at architectural level

Fig. 12 the congruence values remains stable around 76% to 82% starting from stable release 3.

Similar trend can be notified in Fig. 13 where the congruence value remains stable within the range 71% to 88% starting from stable release 3. Based on these observations it can be stated that with the maturation of the project, the communication pattern among developers get more structured following the need of communication based on their tasks. This socio-technical congruence pattern of communication among the community memebrs becomes a traditional practice as the project evolves. Thus it can be affirmed that

The socio-technical congruence in FreeBSD project remains stable during its evolution.

7   Threats to Validity

The following aspects have been identified which could lead to threats to validity of this study.

External validity (how results can be generalized): As case study subject, FreeBSD project was selected, which has been used popularly in the OSS evolution studies. Also, FreeBSD is a large and well established OSS project with over thirty years of evolution history. Yet the findings may not generalize to other OSS projects. This threat can only be countered by doing additional case studies with projects from different domains, which is a part of our future work.

Internal validity (confounding factors can influence the findings): Missing historical data - the study has been able to make use only of available data. It is possible, for instance, that there are commit records and developer chat entries other than that recorded in the emails. Also other email archives may contain

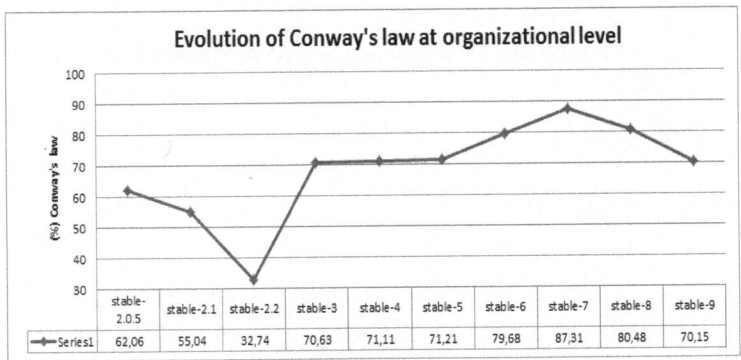

Fig. 13. Evolution of Conway's law at organizational level

relevant data. Thus, we make no claim on the completeness of the email entries with relevance to this study target.

Construct validity (relationship between theory and observation): In this study, part of the email entries were categorized to specific stable release according to their date of post. The reasoning here is that developers commit and discuss on release planning before the product is officially released. Yet, we do not claim the perfection of this approach.

8   Conclusions

In this paper we evaluated the concept of Conway's law as a means of verifying the socio-technical congruence within the context of FreeBSD project. According to our judgment the congruence measure is significantly high in FreeBSD project which has a stable evolution history for the last seven releases of the project. In other words, the communication pattern of the contributing members within FreeBSD community are due to the communication need established by the concrete architecture. Having such high congruence between the code and the community would resolve many contemporary questions that cannot be answered otherwise. For instance, in identifying exact community member(s) to contract for an specific issue [36], it is required to trace which community members collaborates and exchange knowledge based on their task level responsibility.

This congruence is a desired property for collaborative development activities [14] and the reported result conforms the same for collaborative open source community. This result also creates a favorable basis to explore its implications on the OSS projects concerning the quality, success, and sustainability, which were already examined and confirmed in closed source projects.

Also, the results reported in this work hold for a specific OSS project, hence the study suffers from lack of generalizability. Thus a part of our future work is to extend and examine the findings in other OSS project, preferably to the BSD group and operating system domain.

References

1. Conway, M.E.: How Do Committees Invent? Datamation 14(4), 28–31 (1968)
2. Kwan, I., Schröter, A., Damian, D.: Does Socio-Technical Congruence Have an Effect on Software Build Success? A Study of Coordination in a Software Project. TSE 37(3), 307–324 (2011)
3. Ovaska, P., Rossi, M., Marttiin, P.: Architecture as a coordination tool in multi-site software development. Soft. Process: Improvement & Prac., 233–247 (2003)
4. de Souza, C.R.B., Quirk, S., Trainer, E., Redmiles, D.F.: Supporting collaborative software development through the visualization of socio-technical dependencies. In: International ACM Conference on Supporting Group Work, pp. 147–156 (2007)
5. Scacchi, W.: Understanding the requirements for developing open source software systems. IEE Proceedings Software 149(1), 24–39 (2002)
6. Bendifallah, S., Scacchi, W.: Work Structures and Shifts: An Empirical Analysis of Software Specification Teamwork. In: 11th ICSE, pp. 260–270 (1989)
7. Jongdae, H., Chisu, W., Byungjeong, L.: Extracting Development Organization from Open Source Software. In: 16th APSEC, pp. 441–448. IEEE (2009)
8. Raymond, E.S.: The new hacker's dictionary, 3rd edn. MIT Press, Cambridge (1996)
9. Nagappan, N., Murphy, B., Basili, V.R.: Architectures, Coordination, and Distance: Conway's Law and Beyond. Journal IEEE Software 16(5), 63–70 (1999)
10. Kwan, I., Cataldo, M., Damian, D.: Conway's Law Revisited: The Evidence for a Task-Based Perspective. IEEE Software 29(1), 90–93 (2012)
11. Brooks, F.P.: The Mythical Man-Month, Anniversary Edition. Addison-Wesley Publishing Company (1995)
12. Nagappan, N., Murphy, B., Basili, V.R.: The influence of organizational structure on software quality: an empirical case study. In: ICSE 2008, pp. 521–530 (2008)
13. Cataldo, M., Wagstrom, P.A., Herbsleb, J.D., Carley, K.M.: Identification of coordination requirements: Implications for the design of collaboration and awareness tools. In: CSCW, Banff, Canada (2006)
14. Browning, T.: Applying the design structure matrix to system decomposition and integration problems: a review and new directions. IEEE Transactions on Engineering Management 48(3), 292–306 (2001)
15. Sosa, M.E., Eppinger, S.D., Rowles, C.M.: The misalignment of product architecture and organizational structure in complex product development. Management Science 50(12), 1674–1689 (2004)
16. Jingwei, W., Holt, R.C., Hassan, A.E.: Empirical Evidence for SOC Dynamics in Software Evolution. In: ICSM, pp. 244–254 (2007)
17. Herraiz, I.: A statistical examination of the evolution and properties of libre software. In: ICSM, pp. 439–442 (2009)
18. Herraiz, I., Gonzalez-Barahona, J.M., Robles, G., German, D.M.: On the prediction of the evolution of libre software projects. In: ICSM, pp. 405–414 (2007)
19. Fogel, K., Bar, M.: Open Source Development with CVS: Learn How to Work With Open Source Software. The Coriolis Group (1999)
20. Herbsleb, J.D., Grinter, R.E.: Splitting the Organization and Integrating the Code: Conway's Law Revisited. In: ICSE, pp. 85–95. ACM Press, New York (1999)
21. Baldwin, C.Y., Clark, K.B.: Design Rules: The Power of Modularity. MIT (2000)
22. Colfer, L., Baldwin, C.Y.: The Mirroring Hypothesis: Theory, Evidence and Exceptions, Working paper. Harvard Business School (2010)

23. Bowman, I.T., Holt, R.C.: Software Architecture Recovery Using Conway's Law. In: CASCON 1998, pp. 123–133 (1998)
24. FreeBSD (2013), http://www.freebsd.org/
25. Mathieu, G., Mens, T.: A framework for analyzing and visualizing open source software ecosystems. In: IWPSE-EVOL, pp. 42–47 (2010)
26. Daniel, M.G.: Using software trails to reconstruct the evolution of software. Journal of Software Maintenance and Evolution 16(6), 367–384 (2004)
27. Wang, Y., Guo, D., Shi, H.: Measuring the Evolution of Open Source Software Systems with their Communities. ACM SIGSOFT Notes 32(6) (2007)
28. Zhang, W., Yang, Y., Wang, Q.: Network Analysis of OSS Evolution: An Empirical Study on ArgoUML Project. In: IWPSE-EVOL, pp. 71–80 (2011)
29. Apache POI-Java API for Microsoft Documents (2013), http://poi.apache.org/
30. jsoup: Java HTML Parser (2013), http://jsoup.org/
31. Yamauchi, Y., Yokozawa, M., Shinohara, T., Ishida, T.: Collaboration with Lean Media: How Open-source Software Succeeds. In: CSCW, pp. 329–338 (2000)
32. Dayani-Fard, H., Yu, Y., Mylopoulos, J., Andritsos, P.: Improving the build architecture of legacy C/C++ software systems. In: Cerioli, M. (ed.) FASE 2005. LNCS, vol. 3442, pp. 96–110. Springer, Heidelberg (2005)
33. Mahbubul Syeed, M.M.: Binoculars: Comprehending Open Source Projects through graphs. In: Hammouda, I., Lundell, B., Mikkonen, T., Scacchi, W. (eds.) OSS 2012. IFIP AICT, vol. 378, pp. 350–355. Springer, Heidelberg (2012)
34. Bolici, F., Howison, J., Crowston, K.: Coordination without discussion? Sociotechnical congruence and Stigmergy in Free and Open Source Software projects. In: 2nd STC, ICSE (2009)
35. Kazman, R., Carrière, S.J.: Playing Detective: Reconstructing Software Architecture from Available Evidence, Technical Re- p ort CMU/SEI-97-TR-010, Carnegie Mellon University (1997)
36. Syeed, M.M., Altonen, T., Hammouda, I., Systä, T.: Tool Assisted Analysis of Open Source Projects: A Multi-facet Challenge. IJOSSP 3(2) (2011)

Modeling Practices in Open Source Software

Omar Badreddin[1], Timothy C. Lethbridge[1], and Maged Elassar[2]

[1] University of Ottawa
800 King Edward
[2] IBM Ottawa Laboratories
770 Palladium Dr. Ottawa, Ontario, Canada
Ottawa, Ontario, Canada
obadr024@uottawa.ca, tcl@site.uottawa.ca, melaasar@ca.ibm.com

Abstract. It is widely accepted that modeling in software engineering increases productivity and results in better code quality. Yet, modeling adoption remains low. The open source community, in particular, remains almost entirely code centric. In this paper, we explore the reasons behind such limited adoption of modeling practices among open source developers. We highlight characteristics of modeling tools that would encourage their adoption. We propose Umple as a solution where both modeling and coding elements are treated uniformly. In this approach, models can be manipulated textually and code can be edited visually. We also report on the Umple compiler itself as a case study of an open source project where contributors, using the above approach, have and continue to routinely commit code and model over a number of years.

Keywords: Open source, UML, Modeling, Coding, Version Control, Model Merging. Model versioning, Umple, Model Driven Architecture.

1 Introduction

Open-source software (OSS) is witnessing increasing adoption and impact [1]. OSS development communities are collaborative, typically geographically distributed, working together to build software, often over multiple years with hundreds or thousands of contributors. OSS teams share common characteristics. For example, they use open-source version control systems, wikis, issue tracking systems, and automated test suites. Many teams use continuous integration – automated build servers to integrate contributions frequently and generate updated systems within minutes after a new commit.

However, code remains a key development artifact. Documentation and especially models are typically either absent or nearly so. This is despite evidence that model-driven development can increase quality and productivity [2]. In this paper, we propose an approach to help bring modeling to open-source development without disrupting the culture and methods open-source developers have found successful.

The use of modeling (e.g., UML) is considered to be a good practice that is expected to positively affect the quality of software [2]. A recent survey of modeling

E. Petrinja et al. (Eds.): OSS 2013, IFIP AICT 404, pp. 127–139, 2013.
© IFIP International Federation for Information Processing 2013

practices in the industry reveals different levels of modeling adoption [3]. They range from full adoption of model-driven engineering, where engineers rely exclusively on models to generate complete running systems, to using models for documentation only. The survey also reveals that modeling adoption in general remains much lower than what would be desirable.

By only using a set of simple and readily-available tools, OSS communities are able to foster collaboration among a large number of members who often do not know each other. Despite this success, these teams rarely, if ever, use modeling as part of their development activities.

We surveyed the 20 most active open source projects according to Ohloh [4] based on the number of commits. The top of the list is Chromium [5], with about 7 million lines of code, 150,000 commits, and more than 1,300 contributors. Chromium is mostly written in C and C++ (72%). When summing up all hours spent on the development, Chromium consumed 2,000 years of effort. The rest of the list includes projects such as Mozilla Core, WebKit, and GNOME.

The majority of these projects are written in C or C++ (87%). A small percentage of commits (0.3%) were XML based, which could indicate some use of modeling. However, none of these 20 projects listed any modeling notation as a notation where commits were accepted. We can therefore conclude based on this survey that there is no evidence that contributors commit models in any significant numbers. This finding validates our earlier survey results [3] and is in line with other existing observations [6, 7].

Reasons behind this low adoption in the industry in general, and in open source projects in particular, have been investigated in our previous work [3]. In summary, low adoption can be attributed to the following reasons:

- Code generation doesn't work as well as it needs to;
- Modeling tools are too difficult to use;
- A culture of coding prevails and is hard to overcome;
- There is a lack of understanding of modeling notations and technologies;
- The code-centric approach works well enough, such that the return on investment of changing is marginal, yet the risks are high.

The focus of this paper is proposing a new development paradigm that provides tight integration of modeling and coding styles. We demonstrate that this paradigm has the potential of increasing modeling adoption by presenting a model-driven programming environment called Umple, which we developed as an open source project.

2   Proposed Solution

Umple is a fully functional and executable language with a textual syntax that allows uniform code and model development. Umple allows model abstractions from UML to be embedded into code written in Java, PHP and other programming languages. This raises the abstraction level of modern object oriented programming languages to be on par with modeling artifacts. In the remainder of this paper we focus on the Java context.

Umple code can essentially be straight Java code, if desired, but most commonly, it consists of a synergistic mix of Java code, UML associations, and UML state machines all in the same textual format. It is therefore very easy for an open source team to move from Java to Umple. If they do so, their code base tends to shrink considerably as much of their 'boilerplate' Java code can be abstracted out and replaced by more concise modeling constructs.

Umple's compiler and code generator are written in Umple itself. Umple also has a web-based modeling environment that does not require any tool installation.

Umple was developed to help enhance modeling adoption by software engineers in general. It started as a closed source project but was then released as an open source project in 2010. Since then, Umple has had more than 30 contributors who routinely contribute code with modeling elements directly embedded. Umple's integration server runs a suite of more than 2,700 test cases to ensure that the model and code are consistent and produce a working system.

3   Introduction to Umple

A key philosophy behind Umple is that modeling and coding are just different perspectives of the same development practice, with the difference being a question of abstraction. Modeling constructs such as UML associations and state machines are more abstract than traditional code elements like while loops, yet both appear together in Umple code. Complex Umple modeling constructs are typically more readily understood when rendered visually as UML diagrams, while traditional coding constructs are nowadays more commonly best understood when shown as indented text, but it need not be this way only. The Umple environment enables users to model textually and visually (with updates to one view applied instantly to the other view).

Consider the Umple sample code in Listing 1.

```
1    class Person { }
2
3    class Student {
4      isA Person;
5      Integer stNum;
6      status {
7        Applied {
8          quit -> Quit;
9          enroll [!hold] -> Enrolled;
10       }
11       Enrolled {
12        quit -> Quit;
13        graduate-> Graduated;
14       }
15       Graduated {}
16       Quit {}
```

```
17      }
18      * -- 0..1 Supervisor;
19   }
20
21   class Supervisor {
22      isA Person;
23   }
```

Listing 1. Sample Umple code/model [8]

The structure of the code is familiar to a Java programmer. However, many of the lines of this example represent UML elements embedded textually in the code. Line 18 is a UML association, and indicates that class Student can have an optional Supervisor, while a Supervisor can have many Students. Lines 4 and 22 are Umple's way of representing generalization (i.e. designating a superclass). Umple Online [9], the Umple web-based environment, would render the above code as a UML class diagram, as shown in Figure 1.

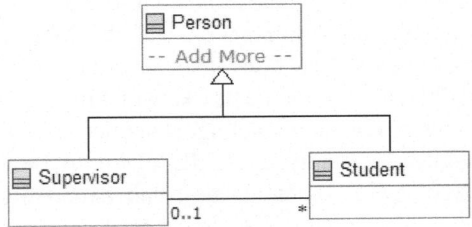

Fig. 1. A Class Diagram in UML

Lines 6 to 17 describe the behavior of the Student class as a state machine, which can be depicted as in Figure 2. When a Student object is created, it goes initially to the Applied state. Depending on the events that occur next, and whether or not the 'hold' boolean variable is true, the Student object moves from one state to another state.

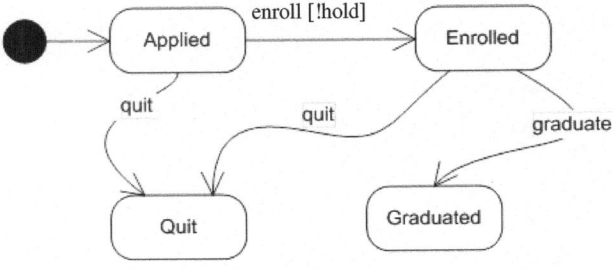

Fig. 2. State Diagram

Umple is not intended to replace the need for visual models. As illustrated in the following sections, the Umple compiler has both a textual and a visual editor. Both views are synchronized automatically, since a change in the model will always have an equivalent change in the textual representation. Of course, not all code changes have an impact on the visual representation, since not all aspects of the code are visualized in every diagram type.

3.1   Code Generation from Umple

The Umple philosophy is to combine code and model into one type of artifact. Hence, Umple does not have the typical process of code generation (model to editable code) nor reverse engineering (edited code to model) found in other modeling tools. An Umple program, consisting of model and code, is compiled into an executable system directly. It is not necessary to reverse engineer Umple code to create a model, since it already is a model.

3.2   Language Independent Modeling

The main strength of UML as a modeling language is being platform and implementation independent. This allows the model in Figure 2, for example, to be used to generate code in Java, C++, or any other programming language. This independence is also maintained in Umple. Users of Umple can chose to write a system in any language of their choice as long as its compiler is available. Umple currently provides full support for Java, PhP and Ruby, with growing support for C++. Umple can also generate XMI and Ecore [10] representations for integration with existing modeling tools.

4   Case Study

In this section, we assess the effectiveness of using model-driven programming languages, such as Umple, to encourage adoption of modeling in open-source projects.

Our case study is on Umple itself as an open source project, hosted in the Google Code repository [11]. The source code of the Umple compiler is written in Umple with Java as the target language and the language of the embedded methods. Contributors need to learn the syntax of Umple before contributing. But since the syntax is very similar to Java and resembles what would appear in a UML diagram, learning Umple does not add significantly to the time needed for contribution.

As with a typical open source project, there is a little up-front effort required to set up the development environment, which includes downloading the code, installing tools such as Eclipse (with the Umple and Jet plugins) and Ant, getting the appropriate project permissions, etc.

Umple was released as open source software in 2010. However, all of the source (model/code) artifacts was stored in a Subversion repository for over 5 years; it is possible therefore to analyse the source changes, including the UML underpinnings of the Umple compiler. Because the model is represented textually in Umple, there is no additional infrastructure investment for model versioning and comparing.

4.1 Objectives and Research Methodology

The objective of this study is to investigate the applicability of model oriented programming in open source projects. This investigation is carried out by analyzing how model orientation was used in developing the Umple platform.

In previous work, we have provided empirical evidence that model oriented code has significant comprehension value over pure Java code [12]. The empirical evidence is a result of a controlled experiment comparing model-oriented code, traditional object-oriented code, and UML models. The experiment included both student and professional participants and proceeded by posing questions on a set of different modeling and coding artifacts. The question and answer sessions were recorded and analyzed to infer comprehensibility of the different code and modeling snippets. The experiment provides evidence that suggests that model oriented code is at least as comprehensible as UML visual models. Therefore, in this paper, we limit our focus to investigation of the applicability of using model orientation in open source environments.

The design of Umple was carried out over more than 5 years. The technology is still under extensive development and iterative improvements. Design of Umple was influenced by the following studies.

- Study of early adopters [13]. This is a study that was conducted during the early design phases where early adopters were interviewed and filled up questionnaire that reflects their attitudes towards model oriented code.
- Experiences of applying Umple in industrial development projects [14]. By using the technology in industrial projects, we were able to refine the design and implementation of the platform. In particular, we improved scalability aspects of the technology.
- User evaluations and experimentation [15]. Such studies provided empirical evidence to support our claims about the comprehension value of model oriented programming technology. These studies have also given us insights on how users actually go about exploring the usage of such technology.

Design is both an art and a science, making it challenging to satisfactorily evaluate design work. Recently, research on design has witnessed a significant uptake in several domains. This increased uptake has encouraged researchers to define a systematic methodology of evaluation design [16]. In summary, this evaluation methodology relies on iterative design evaluation cycles with key stakeholders. This methodology also adopts empirical evaluation of design by measuring to what extent a design satisfies its intended goals.

We adopted the same design evaluation methodology mentioned above in the design of Umple. We implemented a prototype of Umple that embodied many of our design objectives. We used the prototype to iteratively assess to what extent the design met its objectives and we collected feedback and evaluation from users. This case study does not discuss the intermediate designs, but rather focuses on the final design after completing the process of iterative refinement.

4.2   Development Environment

Developers of Umple use a variety of development environments. For simple tasks, the Umple web-based editor [9] can be used to easily write code and visualize the equivalent UML model. Figure 3 is a snapshot of the UmpleOnline system. On the left side there is the code/model textual editor. On the right side, there is the corresponding visualization editor for the model. Edits on either side are automatically reflected on the other side. If a user modifies the default layout of the visual rendering of the model, the new layout information is stored textually. This is to support preserving the layout when a user returns to the same visualization again. This layout information is committed and versioned in the repository.

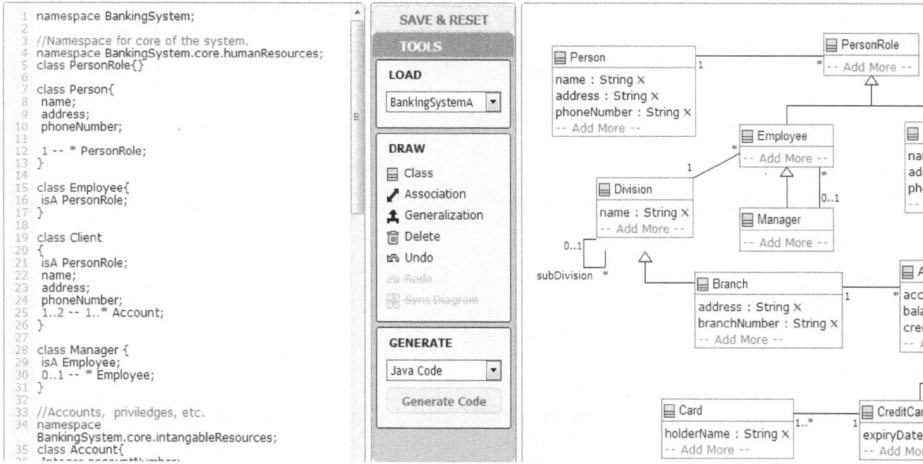

Fig. 3. Umple Online

Umple Online is suitable for a quick demonstration of concepts and for relatively simple development tasks. However, for larger and more elaborate tasks, the Eclipse based plug-in is preferred. The added functionality provided by the plugin includes code highlighting, context assist, outline view, error and problem reporting views, as well as compiling. Finally there is a command line version of the compiler, which is used for automatic building, and is therefore preferred by some developers.

4.3   Developer Contributions

Contributions to Umple are represented in text, as in other open source projects. The key and only difference is that Umple text represents both model and code elements. Once the Umple continuous integration server senses a commit, it automatically triggers a build. The build process first compiles all Umple source files to generate a new executable Umple compiler. Then, the build process runs Umple test cases to verify that the latest commit did not break existing functionality. The new compiler then builds itself, as yet another large test case. If the tests are all successful, the new build is completed and deployed.

4.4   Umple Source Versioning

Umple developers review code and model changes in the same way. Since model and code in Umple are textual; changes can be reviewed using the repository diff functionality (Figure 4).

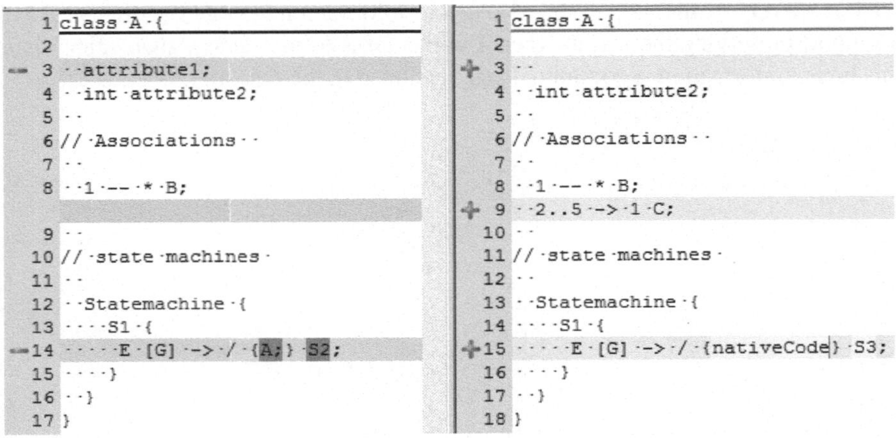

Fig. 4. Code and model revisions

4.5   Quantitative Assessment of Model and Java Code in the Umple Code Base

In this section, we study what portion of our case study Umple code base consists of 'model' code (i.e. Umple's textual rendering of UML), and what portion consists of standard Java code . We also present a brief analysis of how this varies over time.

Our investigation is based on analyzing the revision history of three artifacts (the Umple associations and attributes portion of the metamodel, the state-machine portion of the metamodel, and the parser) as shown in Table 1. The period covered is from October 2008 to February 2012. We chose these artifacts because they are frequently updated, have existed for a long time, belong 'together' in the architecture (the parser populates the Metamodel), and have different distributions of model vs. Java (the metamodel files are mostly model, and the parser is mostly Java). We chose a subset of Umple to simplify the data, and we chose three components to see if the results are consistent between them. This is an exploratory case study only, so we have not attempted to analyse the entire system.

The Umple metamodel is the schema written in Umple of all Umple elements in the system being compiled and is used to define different modeling and code elements within the Umple language. Changes to the metamodel occur when a new Umple language element is defined or when a change is done to an existing element.

The number of lines of code for the associations and attributes portion of the metamodel is 1623, 19% of which are modeling elements and the rest are Java code.

The second artifact is the state machine portion of the metamodel, which is the schema of the state machine related elements. The artifact has 315 lines, 24% of which are model.

The third artifact is the parser, which is a component of the Umple compiler. The parser contains mostly Java code (690 lines), 4% of which is model.

Table 1. Model and code contributions

File	changes	% Model only	% Java only	% Model and Java change	Number of lines (Feb. 2012)		
					Total	Model only (%)	Java only (%)
Attributes and associations metamodel	1414	15%	40%	45%	1623	307 (19%)	1316 (81%)
State machine metamodel	779	18%	25%	57%	315	77 (24%)	238 (76%)
Parser	1242	1%	97%	2%	690	26 (4%)	664 (96%)
Average						**15.6%**	**84.3%**

Comparison of Model vs. Java Code in Terms of the Volume of Their Change Relative to Their Size: The number of changes and the percentages affecting model only, Java only or both are given in the first four columns of Table 1. It would typically be challenging to produce these numbers automatically since Umple treats both model and code uniformly. Hence, in other systems one might have to manually inspect the changed lines or write a special-purpose parser to judge whether they are code or model related. However, we took advantage of the Umple project's coding guidelines, which advise developers to keep modeling elements at the top of the file or in separately-included files whenever possible, to quickly classify the majority of changes. We also used Fisheye [17], a repository visualization tool to help verify our classification estimates. Finally, we verified our numbers by asking three experienced Umple developers to produce them on their own. No significant discrepancies were evident.

Since the Umple metamodel includes a much higher portion of modeling elements than the parser, while the parser includes a much higher portion of Java code than the metamodel, we expected that the changes to those artifacts follow similar proportions (more model changes in the metamodel; more java changes in the parser). Table 1 show that this pattern was indeed observed. In fact, it was valid across different developers. In other words, the change patterns of any particular developer are similar to what is shown in Table 1.

Comparison of Model vs. Java Changes over Time: Umple was initially written purely in Java. Incrementally, more modeling abstractions were added to the language, starting with attributes, then associations, and finally state machines. The more modeling support got added, the more we were able to refactor the code base to take advantage of the modeling abstractions. One would therefore expect to find an upward trend in the percentage of modeling changes and that this trend would persist over time. To our surprise, we noticed a different pattern: modeling changes exhibited a downward trend for most of the time period of our observations (Figure 5). Our explanation is as follows: As the code base was refactored to take advantage of more modeling abstractions, modeling changes were initially extensive as compared to Java changes. But as the refactoring slowed down, more changes occurred to the Java elements to add features, largely algorithms and computations that typically do not involve creating new or changing existing modeling elements.

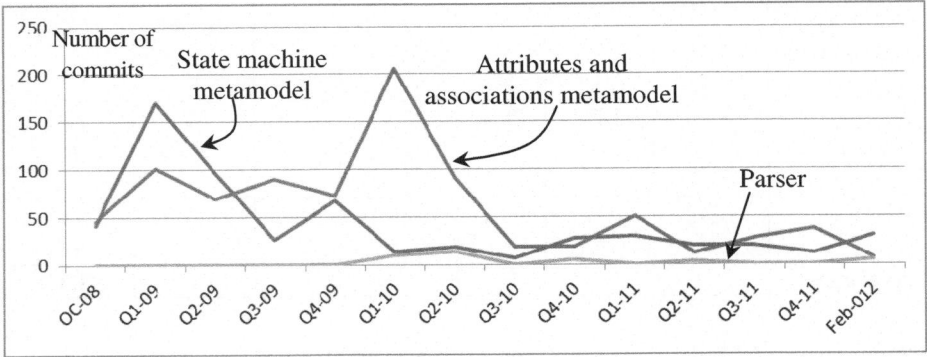

Fig. 5. Model changes trend over time

Figure 5 illustrates the analysis for the same three artifacts; the state machine metamodel, the attributes and association metamodel, and the parser. The figure aggregates model only changes with code and model changes, starting from October 2008 and until February 2012. The data is aggregated quarterly.

The core attributes and association metamodel was developed prior to October 2008. The spike in change activity to Attributes and association metamodel (around Q1 2010) corresponds to refactoring of the metamodel that took place as the responsible researcher was transitioning out. The state machine metamodel was developed during 2009. There was little refactoring performed on this metamodel since it was developed after many modeling abstractions were already supported by Umple. In other words, the state machine metamodel was written in a version of Umple that supported attributes and associations.

The downward trend is more evident in the case of the state machine metamodel than in the attributes and association metamodel. The number of model lines in the parser is minimal; hence, one cannot elicit a trend. With the exception of the refactoring spike in the attributes and association metamodel, the trend would have been also evident in that case too.

Techniques for mining software repositories can recover more trends about the nature and pattern of software development of Umple. The Umple repository and all its versioning history are publicly available for download. This should encourage other independent work to perform such in depth analysis of the repository and report on it.

4.6   Analysis of the Use of Umple to Develop Umple Itself

We now revisit the requirements specified in Section 2, and reflect, in their context, on our experiences developing Umple as an open source project written in Umple itself.

- **Little to no change to existing infrastructure:** At a bare minimum, Umple developers need to simply download a single Jar file (Umple.jar) to use the Umple compiler. This is readily available and works well with other open source infrastructure. Most developers choose to go one step further and work with the Umple Eclipse plugin. However, installing such plugin is a common task to Eclipse-developers.
- **Easy editing paradigm** – textual models: Umple users can use whatever text editor they are familiar with to edit Umple sources. There is no need to use a separate graphical tool to view the Umple-sources in UML notation. Such visualizations can be generated using Umple Online if desired.
- **Versioning, comparing and merging features that operate the same way on model and programming language text:** All Umple sources, whether they include Java or model elements, are represented textually in Umple files and are committed to SVN just like in any other open-source system.
- **Tight integration with code:** In Umple, both model elements and code elements are co-located in the same textual artifact and treated uniformly
- **Semantic completeness:** The Umple compiler completely supports the subset of UML semantics, like multiplicity constraints, bidirectional association referential integrity, and state-machines, expressible in Umple.

5   Related Work

Robbins [6] identifies a set of tools that are absent in an open source community, including requirements and modeling tools. He attributes this absence to a number of reasons, including the fact that open source developers do not have direct paying customers and therefore do not feel the need to follow a rigorous methodology or respect deadlines. He also predicts that many of those missing tools will have a significant positive impact if and when they get adopted by the open source community. This is where the motivation for the research presented in this paper comes from.

Iivari [18] explored why modeling tools are not used in general in software projects. In a study, he reports that 70% of modeling tools are never used after being available for one year, 25% are used by only a single group, and only 5% are widely used. This is despite the fact that the same study reports positive impact of modeling adoption. More than a decade later, modeling tools are still not widely adopted and a significant segment of the software engineering practices are still code centric [3].

6   Conclusion and Future Work

The open source community remains almost entirely code centric. Adoption of modeling practices remains extremely low. Since the open source community is known for its exploration, innovation, and willingness to quickly adopt new technologies, model-oriented programming languages like Umple offer a promising direction. We have presented Umple as a case study of an open source project that has been successfully developed using a model-based programming language (Umple itself). It effectively supports modeling by embedding model elements in code artifacts, and hence in the same repository. Besides using the Umple compiler, which can be invoked from a regular command line shell and from the Eclipse platform, Umple developers only use openly available tools..

The key concept in our approach is the view that model and code can be treated uniformly. While most models are best viewed visually and most code is best viewed textually, the underlying representation of both model and code should be textual, and capable of co-existing in the same textual artifacts. This helps bring modeling to the open source community. To the best of our knowledge, Umple remains the only open source project that is largely model-driven, and where model contributions are performed routinely.

Future work includes more in-depth analysis of the trends of comments of the Umple open source code. Approaches such as mining software repositories can be utilized to uncover trends and patterns.

Future enhancements to Umple include a tool to support incremental reverse engineering from existing systems (umplification) [19]. The key advantage is that systems can be reverse-engineered while being able to instantiate a running system at all stages. Umple is also being extended to include a debugger that can work at the modeling level. This stems from our vision that whatever functionality available to traditional code developers should also be made available when modeling support is added.

References

[1]   Ye, Y., Kishida, K.: Toward an Understanding of the Motivation of Open Source Software Developers. In: Proceedings of the 25th International Conference on Software Engineering, pp. 419–429 (2003)

[2]   Selic, B.: Models, Software Models and UML. UML for Real, 1–16 (2004)

[3]   Forward, A., Badreddin, O., Lethbridge, T.C.: Perceptions of Software Modeling: A Survey of Software Practitioners. In: 5th Workshop from Code Centric to Model Centric: Evaluating the Effectiveness of MDD (C2M:EEMDD) (2010), http://www.esi.es/modelplex/c2m/papers.php

[4]   Ohlo: The Open Source Network, http://www.ohloh.net/ (accessed 2013)

[5]   Google Inc.: Chromium, http://www.chromium.org/Home (accessed 2013)

[6]   Robbins, J.: Adopting Open Source Software Engineering (OSSE) Practices by Adopting OSSE Tools. Perspectives on Free and Open Source Software, pp. 245–264. MIT Press (2005)

[7]   Hertel, G., Niedner, S., Herrmann, S.: Motivation of Software Developers in Open Source Projects: An Internet-Based Survey of Contributors to the Linux Kernel. Research Policy 32, 1159–1177 (2003)

[8]   Badreddin, O., Forward, A., Lethbridge, T.C.: Model Oriented Programming: An Empirical Study of Comprehension. In: Proceedings of the 2012 Conference of the Center for Advanced Studies on Collaborative Research, pp. 73–86 (2012)

[9]   Lethbridge T.C., Forward, A., Badreddin, O.: Umple Language Online, http://try.umple.org (accessed 2012)

[10] The Eclipse Foundation: Package Org.Eclipse.Emf.Ecore, http://download.eclipse.org/modeling/emf/emf/javadoc/2.5.0/org/eclipse/emf/ecore/package-summary.html#details (accessed 2010)

[11] Lethbridge, T.C., Forward, A., Badreddin, O.: Umple Google Code Project (2012) http://code.umple.org

[12] Badreddin, O.: An Empirical Experiment of Comprehension on Textual and Visual Modeling Approaches. University of Ottawa (2012), http://www.site.uottawa.ca/~tcl/gradtheses/obadreldin/

[13] Badreddin, O.: A Manifestation of Model-Code Duality: Facilitating the Representation of State Machines in the Umple Model-Oriented Programming Language (2012)

[14] Badreddin, O., Lethbridge, T.C.: A Study of Applying a Research Prototype Tool in Industrial Practice. In: Proceedings of the Eighteenth ACM SIGSOFT International Symposium on Foundations of Software Engineering, pp. 353–356 (2010)

[15] Badreddin, O., Lethbridge, T.C.: Combining Experiments and Grounded Theory to Evaluate a Research Prototype: Lessons from the Umple Model-Oriented Programming Technology

[16] Verschuren, P., Hartog, R.: Evaluation in Design-Oriented Research. Quality & Quantity 39, 733–762 (2005)

[17] Atlassian: FishEye, http://www.atlassian.com/software/fisheye/overview (accessed 2013)

[18] Iivari, J.: Why are CASE Tools Not used? Communications of the ACM 39, 94–103 (1996)

[19] Lethbridge, T.C., Forward, A., Badreddin, O.: Umplification: Refactoring to Incrementally Add Abstraction to a Program. In: Working Conference on Reverse Engineering, pp. 220–224 (2010)

The Role of Microblogging in OSS Knowledge Management

Jonathan Lewis

Hitotsubashi University, 2-1 Naka, Kunitachi-shi, 186-8601 Tokyo, Japan
jonathan_lewis@mac.com
http://www.lewis.soc.hit-u.ac.jp

Abstract. Given that microblogging has been shown to play a valuable role in knowledge management within companies, it is useful to understand how it is being used in relation to OSS. This project studies tweets related to 12 open source projects and keywords, ranging from web content management systems (CMSes) to general office applications. It found considerable differences in the content and exchange of tweets, especially between specialist products such as CMSes and office suites such as OpenOffice. Tweets concerning the more specialist projects tended to provide information rather than updates on the user's current status. We found a high proportion of event-driven traffic for some CMS projects, and a lower proportion for the office products and groups of projects.

Keywords: microblogging, twitter, knowledge management.

1 Introduction

In any knowledge-intensive project or organization, informal communication is vital to the timely spread of information and ideas. Considerable research has been undertaken on the role of microblogging services such as Twitter in knowledge management within enterprises [1–5]. Many OSS developers and users also use Twitter, but little attention has been paid to the role played by microblogging in exchanging and diffusing knowledge in OSS projects. This study of OSS-related microblogging explores what kind of information is being exchanged on Twitter regarding open source software, and the different ways in which Twitter is being used. In order to answer these questions, a study was made of statuses (Tweets) related to 12 OSS projects, using a taxonomy adapted from previous research on intra-enterprise microblogging. The projects selected had an emphasis on, but were not restricted to, web content management. Table 1 gives an overview of the projects and the numbers of statuses collected, sampled and analyzed.

This paper is organized as follows: Section 2 discusses the selection of projects, presents statistics about the data used, and discusses the challenges in collecting and cleaning Twitter data. Section 3 contains the findings and analysis. Section 4 discusses threats to validity and topics for further research.

E. Petrinja et al. (Eds.): OSS 2013, IFIP AICT 404, pp. 140–152, 2013.

Table 1. Overview of Twitter Statuses Retrieved and Sampled, 7 May-26 Dec 2012

Project/Keyword	Project type (language)	Number of statuses collected	Number tagged English	Number sampled
Joomla	CMS (PHP)	278,821	172,989	1,000
TYPO3	CMS (PHP)	22,800	7,553	1,000
SilverStripe	CMS (PHP)	1,985	1,678	1,000
Drupal	CMS (PHP)	209,901	158,917	1,000
Xoops	CMS (PHP)	1,317	676	676
Plone	CMS (Python)	9,507	6,509	1,000
RoR	Web app framework (Ruby)	24,603	13,781	1,000
PHP	Web scripting language	54,121	32,114	1,000
Apache	Group of software projects	28,3646	165,988	1,000
Mozilla	Group of software projects	30,9958	157,094	1,000
OpenOffice	Office software	35,718	11,185	1,000
libreoffice	Office software	12,905	1,969	1,000
Sum		1,245,282	730,453	11,676

2   Analyzing OSS Microblogging

2.1   Selection of Keywords/Projects

Six web content management systems (CMSes) were selected, five of them written in PHP (Joomla, TYPO3, Silverstripe, Drupal, and Xoops) and one written in Python (Plone).[1] CMSes were selected because they are tightly focused on a particular product used by specialists (mostly website developers and system administrators) but nevertheless have large enough user and developer populations to generate sufficient traffic. Furthermore they can be compared to each other.

The server-side web scripting language PHP and the web application framework Ruby on Rails (RoR) were added in order to compare communications regarding web development using PHP and Ruby.

OpenOffice and libreoffice were included because, compared to the CMSes, they were likely to have more end-users who were not IT professionals. Their inclusion would thus help to highlight the characteristics of microblogging in the more specialist projects.

---

[1] Statuses were also gathered for the keywords 'Geeklog", 'Mambo", 'mojoPortal" and 'WebGUI" in order to analyze the PHP-based content management system of those names, but the keywords were abandoned due to the small proportion of relevant statuses (in the case of Mambo) and the small number of statuses retrieved (in the other cases).

Apache and Mozilla, two umbrella organizations for a number of open source projects, were included because, while being similarly Web-centered to the CMSes, their wider focus promised to show us differences between communication in individual projects and larger open source organizations.

2.2 Selection of Microblogging Service

While Twitter is the most well-known microblogging service, there is an alternative service, identi.ca, which uses open source software and, unlike Twitter, allows users to import and export their data using the FOAF standard. It might be the case that open source users and developers would make greater use of identi.ca for ideological reasons. In order to check whether this is the case, the search APIs of both services were queried for the selected keywords/projects between 15 February and 6 March 2013. The results are shown in Table 2. The results clearly show several orders of magnitude more activity regarding open source keywords on Twitter compared to identi.ca, which justifies the selection of Twitter as the data source for this study.

Table 2. Numbers of Statuses Retrieved from Twitter and identi.ca Search APIs, Feb 15-Mar 6, 2013

Project/keyword	Twitter	identi.ca
Joomla	34,716	10
TYPO3	2,422	0
SilverStripe	457	1
Drupal	24,591	65
Xoops	1,447	0
Plone	1,324	3
RoR	39,916	5
PHP	77,114	875
Apache	43,280	103
Mozilla	41,077	303
OpenOffice	4,160	21
libreoffice	6,567	357
Total	277,071	1,743

2.3 Data Collection

The Twitter Search API was queried approximately every two hours from 7 May to 26 December 2012 for keywords related to the 12 OSS projects. The keywords were not mutually exclusive, so for example a status containing both "PHP" and "Drupal" could be included in both samples.[2] The statuses were saved to a PostGreSQL database. A total of 1,245,282 statuses containing the 12 keywords were collected, as shown in Table 1.

---

[2] In fact, 10 statuses occurred in samples for two keywords/projects.

After collecting the statuses, a random sample of English-language statuses for each keyword was exported from the database for manual coding.[3] A sample size of 1,000 statuses for each project was coded where available, giving a total of 11,676. This compares with the total of 3,152 Twitter posts examined by Ehrlich and Shami, although their sample was not divided into 12 projects.

2.4 Data Cleaning

The sampled data was cleaned by excluding the following kinds of status:

Non-English statuses. The number of non-English statuses in the sample was very low because the sample included only statuses tagged as English language.

Irrelevant statuses. The number of irrelevant statuses was also generally very low, with the exception of Apache, Mozilla and RoR. "Apache" obviously has many other uses, while "RoR" refers not only to Ruby on Rails but also to such things as the Retraining of Racehorses. There were a large number of irrelevant statuses containing the word "Mozilla" because when Firefox users tweeted titles of web pages on any topic the text would include "Mozilla Firefox."

Robot statuses. Many studies of microblogging have focussed on user behavior and accordingly have selected users who were recognizably individual people. Considerable numbers of Tweets, however, are generated automatically. This is also the case where open source software is concerned, and it is a thorny question whether to include them or not. It was decided to exclude these "robot" statuses, above all because they were much more numerous for some keywords/projects than others, making it difficult to compare results. Defining and identifying automatically generated statuses is not easy, but the following categories of statuses were excluded:

1. Machine status Tweets e.g.
   Fedora [f18-arm] :: [97.44%] Completed – [0] Built – [3] Failed :: Task Error [perl-OpenOffice-UNO-0.07-3.fc17]-[1142021]
2. Repository-generated statuses e.g.
   cesag committed revision 1694 to the Xoops France Network SVN repository, changing 1 files: cesag committed revi... http://t.co/nXREVkxj
3. CMS change statuses generated by crawlers detecting changes in web page code e.g.
   http://t.co/YhTLHvCe: Change from NetObjects Fusion to TYPO3 http://t.co/YhTLHvCe #cms
4. Statuses sent automatically when someone posts to a forum e.g.
   XOOPS: Re: Linux Xoops white page issue? [by kidx] http://t.co/MxW4r2Ba
5. Statuses generated by job sites. Based on examination of the samples, these were defined as posts with 'job' or 'elance' (from 'freelance') in the sender's name.

Duplicate statuses. Duplicate statuses, which were defined as those containing identical text (with any urls excluded) and posted by the same user. Statuses containing identical text but sent by different users were labelled as retweets.

Table 3 shows details of data cleaning.

---

[3] 59% of the statuses collected were tagged as being in English.

Table 3. Details of Data Cleaning

Keyword/ Project	Number sampled	Irrelevant	Not English	Robots	Duplicates	Number after cleaning
Joomla	1,000	1	1	323	27	650
TYPO3	1,000	0	3	45	1	951
SilverStripe	1,000	0	3	121	23	854
Drupal	1,000	1	4	147	9	839
Xoops	676	9	39	164	55	417
Plone	1,000	20	7	196	5	772
RoR	1,000	218	7	78	24	673
PHP	1,000	6	8	297	20	674
Apache	1,000	565	5	148	6	277
Mozilla	1,000	236	34	5	0	725
OpenOffice	1,000	0	18	31	49	902
libreoffice	1,000	0	33	266	18	696
Sum	11,676	1,056	162	1,821	237	8,430

2.5   Data Coding

Ehrlich and Shami [6], building on work by Java et al.[7] and by Zhao and Rosson [8], proposed that microblog posts can be sorted into six categories. This study employed Ehrlich and Shami's scheme, which is introduced below along with examples from our data. User names have been changed.

1. Status (giving details of the poster's current activities):

"Doing some module troubleshooting on the @Xoops_forums #XOOPS #imAwesome :P"

2. Provide information (sharing information/URLs, reporting news)

"Get an overview and demonstration of #Acquia Search: http://t.co/ 9I352KgY #Drupal"

3. Directed posts (addressed to one or more other users):

"@userA Ah, well on TYPO3 Sonar you can't - that's decided by the profile. If you want to change it you'd need your own Sonar install imo."

4. Retweets:

"RT @userB: PC World calls out #Plone as one of 10 award-winng apps to try: http://t.co/WOK9mU4Y"

5. Ask question:

"CodeKit users: can I selectively add files from a project? I really don't need it to monitor my entire SilverStripe install, just templates."

6. Directed with question.

> "@userC im just getting into Web Development, but i dont if it would be more begginer firiendly to learn PHP or RoR, help!?"

It was not always easy to decide which category a post should fall into; making a distinction between status and provide information proved particularly difficult, e.g.

> "In thinking caps on Mozilla writeable society session. A few mins, great minds and awesome ideas. See 'em here: http://t.co/dHk1zVSk #pdf12"

In such cases, we put the Tweet into the current status category, which we broadened to include notices and reports of events happening on the day of posting e.g.

> "Great RoR Meetup tonight at @manilla office with @userD and lots of swearing. Good times."

The coding was carried out by the author alone; clearly it would have been better to have three or more coders in order to reduce error and bias. Table 4 shows the numbers of statuses in each category, and Figure 1 displays the same data as proportions.

We also broke down the large "provide information" category into domain-specific subcategories. Table 5 and Figure 2 show the numbers and proportions of subcategories respectively.

3   Results and Analysis

3.1   Status Updates versus Information Provision

Do OSS-related statuses follow general Twitter usage in concentrating on the user's current activities, or do they tend to provide more general information?

Motivation In their study of general Twitter users [9], Naaman et al. used cluster analysis to suggest that 80% of the users sampled were "Meformers", who mostly tweeted about what they were doing, and only 20% were "Informers" forwarding information. In contrast, Ehrlich and Shami [6] found that about 10% of tweets sent by their regular users in IBM were about current status, compared with just under 30% that were providing information. We can therefore hypothesize that, given a more professional context, OSS-related tweets will have a higher proportion of information provision than "Me now" content. However, this is not to deny the potential value of "Me now" posts as a lubricant maintaining easy communication between participants in OSS projects.

Results Percentages of current status updates were between 0.9% and 8.5% (see Table 4 and Figure 1), while those providing information accounted for between 36% and 73% of each sample.

Table 4. Numbers of Statuses in Each Category

Keyword/ project	Ask question	Directed	Directed with question	Provide info	Retweet	Current status	Sum
Joomla	3	28	7	455	146	11	650
TYPO3	57	75	23	321	419	56	951
SilverStripe	9	52	9	381	371	32	854
Drupal	12	71	12	435	272	37	839
Xoops	2	5	2	240	163	5	417
Plone	11	42	8	277	400	34	772
RoR	13	92	13	417	109	29	673
PHP	6	28	3	455	176	6	674
Apache	8	12	4	151	93	9	277
Mozilla	3	30	5	439	224	24	725
OpenOffice	27	132	21	363	285	74	902
libreoffice	34	119	27	259	198	59	696
Sum	185	686	134	4,193	2,856	376	8,430

Table 5. Subcategories of "Provide Information" Statuses

Keyword/ project	Book	Code release	Event	Documentation	General	Jobs	Newsletter	Security	Sum
Joomla	8	42	9	10	208	172	1	5	455
TYPO3	3	40	61	10	182	10	13	2	321
SilverStripe	3	86	39	18	175	18	0	42	381
Drupal	14	34	56	52	160	117	0	2	435
Xoops	1	24	0	101	85	15	4	10	240
Plone	18	37	78	14	106	9	0	15	277
RoR	0	3	9	10	67	328	0	0	417
PHP	11	10	3	21	87	312	0	11	455
Apache	6	22	5	22	72	12	0	12	151
Mozilla	0	28	9	6	384	0	0	12	439
OpenOffice	8	36	4	8	288	4	0	15	363
libreoffice	0	32	5	24	183	2	0	13	259
Sum	72	394	278	296	1,997	999	18	139	4,193

The two office applications both show a higher proportion of current status posts than the other projects. Reading the statuses did indeed suggest a lot of general users posting tweets along the lines of

"man im tryna type this paper but for whatever reason my OpenOffice is gone!"

This supports the hypothesis that statuses written by professionals related to their work tend to be more information providing than "Me now"-ish.

A number of factors help to explain the higher proportions of information providing Tweets in our samples than those found by Ehrlich and Shami. First,

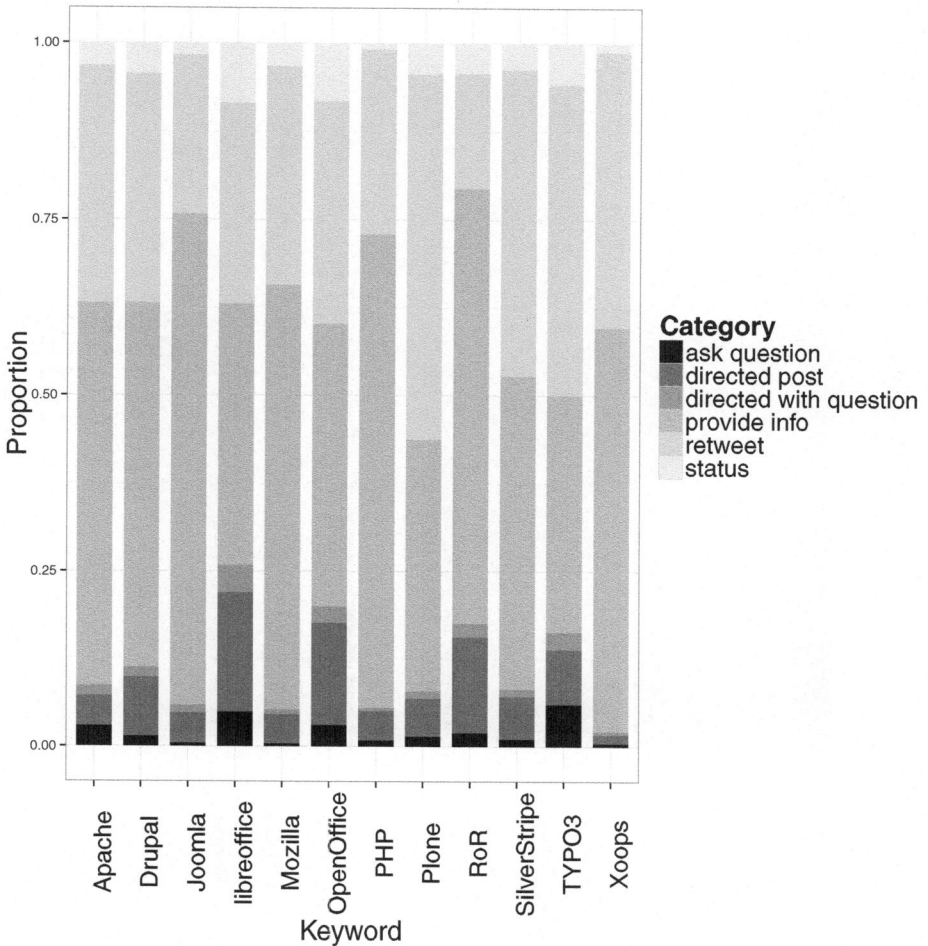

Fig. 1. Categories of Twitter Status

despite excluding many automatically generated job-related posts at the data cleaning stage, 1035 job-related posts remain in the "provide information" category; it is unlikely that Ehrlich and Shami's subjects would be sending many such posts. Second, the "provide information" category includes advertisements for online resources such as articles, books or software, which are also less likely to be sent by Ehrlich and Shami's subjects. Third, Naaman et al. found that tweets sent from mobile terminals are more likely than those sent from computers to be "Me now" rather than "provide information", and we can expect that most of the users and developers of the projects studied will be working on computers. Fourth, Naaman et al. also found that women rather than men are more likely to post "Me now" statuses, and given the high proportion of male participation in most open source software projects this may be having some effect.

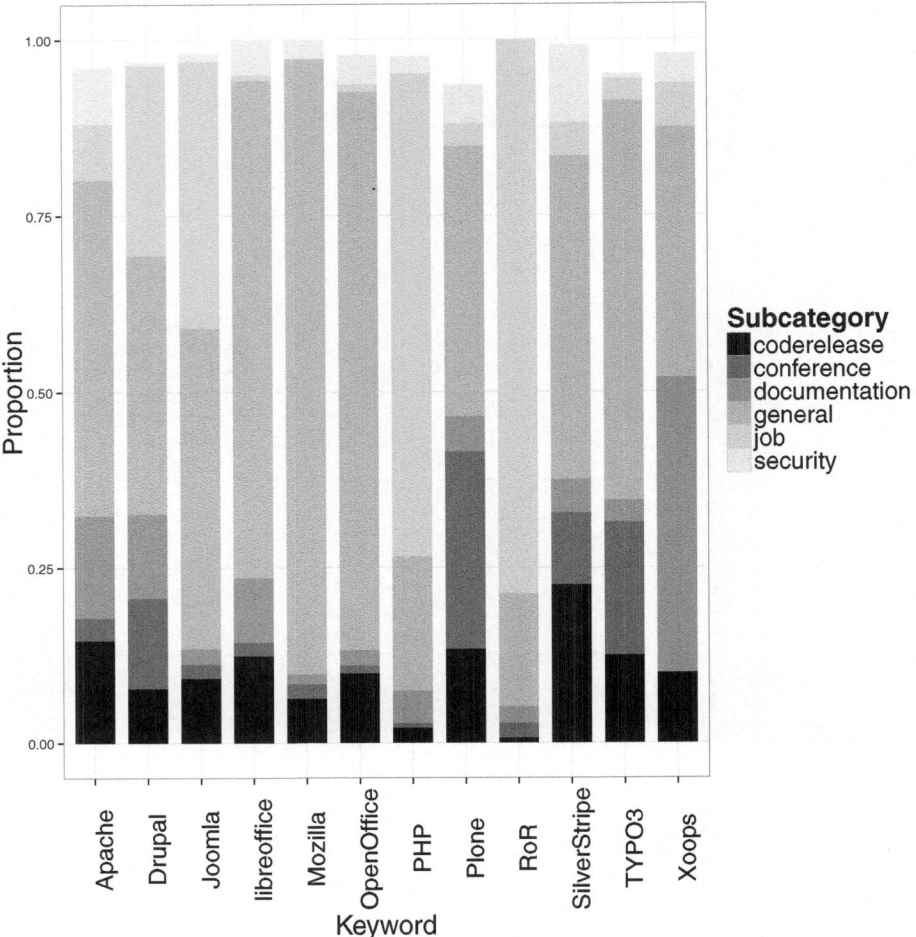

Fig. 2. Main subcategories of "provide information" statuses

3.2   Event-Driven Traffic

How much activity is prompted by events, both off- and online?

Motivation. Research on microblogging has shown that much activity occurs around events, particularly but not confined to offline events such as conferences [10, 11]. Vega et al. [12] found that conference participants tweeted more than usual in the week of the event. Conferences, and smaller events such as sprints and meetups, are the site of intense discussions between participants on all aspects of their project, so we can expect greater Twitter activity to exchange information with other participants and also to communicate what is happening.

Results. Table 5 and Figure 2 show the numbers and proportions of event-related tweets for the 12 project keywords.

Proportions of event-related tweets are low for all keywords except TYPO3 and Plone. In the case of TYPO3, there was something of a spike in activity around the conference held in Stuttgart in early October 2012, while for Plone there was a more pronounced concentration of tweets around the conference held in Arnhem in the same month. While it is not easy to distinguish current status and provide information categories concerning events, for neither project did tweets sharing current status e.g.

> "home and awake after a cool (exhausting) #T3CON12DE - now let's rock #TYPO3, #NEOS and everything like we rocked this conference!"

predominate, suggesting that communication is more focused on providing information about the conference to participants and non-participants e.g.

> "Thanks for attending our talk on #TYPO3 and #TYPO3Neos at #drupalhagen. Our slides are available here https://t.co/j6RJolxx."

It is interesting to note that for both TYPO3 and Plone, when we exclude job-related statuses, we also find that a higher proportion of statuses for these two projects mention "community" than is the case with other projects.[4] Only 4 out of the 35 and 7 out of the 56 statuses for Plone and TYPO3 respectively that mentioned community were event-related, e.g.

> "The #Plone community is just fucking crazy (in a good way). Prost!!!! #beersprint"

Therefore this does not seem to be merely a case of people tweeting about community when surrounded by their fellow developers and users. Further investigation is required to clarify whether this high proportion of event-related statuses and mentions of community is a coincidence, and if not then what is the relationship between the two. While it goes without saying that talking about community does not create one, the spontaneous nature of Twitter makes it a promising medium to explore how open source users and developers think and feel about their projects.

3.3   Rival Products

To what extent do statuses mention non-code related factors such as rival products?

Motivation. In their study of GNOME mailing lists, Shibab et al. [13] found that external factors, and particularly the emergence of rival products, played a significant role in shaping discussions among developers. They used these external developments to explain a decline in the market share of the Evolution

---

[4] We choose to ignore the large number of mentions of "community" for PHP because 24 of the 27 mentions are due to retweeting of a status praising one company's community engagement. The lack of comments on the retweets suggested an advertising campaign.

Table 6. Frequently occuring words in non-job related statuses

Project/ keyword	number of statuses	word	number of occurrences
Joomla	561	wordpress	106
		drupal	31
TYPO3	979	(none)	
Silverstripe	921	wordpress	38
Drupal	765	wordpress	75
		joomla	44
Xoops	525	(none)	
Plone	950	wordpress	36
RoR	368	php	23
PHP	374	apache	110
		mysql	83
		ruby	30
		rails	30
		magento	23
Apache	406	mysql	137
		openoffice	30
Mozilla	729	google	75
		chrome	45
		windows	41
		ipad	32
		microsoft	28
OpenOffice	923	libreoffice	94
		excel	93
		word	68
		microsoft	42
libreoffice	946	openoffice	68
		office	68

mail client as rival products emerged. We can expect that a similar analysis of Twitter activity will show which products are perceived as rivals by those within and without open source projects. These findings, particularly if they could be tracked over years rather than months, would help to explain design decisions and shifts in market share.

Results. We excluded job-related statuses, then counted the occurrences of words in the text of statuses for each keyword/project. Table 6 shows a selection of the technology-related words appearing in the top 50 most commonly used words for each project, along with the number of statuses analyzed. Note that the number of occurrences can be greater than the number of statuses because project names are often used more than once in a single tweet. Some of the words are components or closely related to the projects and some are rival products.

Of the CMSes, statuses regarding all except TYPO3 and Xoops mention rival products, predominantly Wordpress. It would be worthwhile to follow this up with a longitudinal study to establish whether Wordpress is gaining in its position as the chief rival to most open source CMSes. Tweets about the office products, as expected, mention each other and Microsoft Office. It is also interesting to see that statuses on PhP and Ruby on Rails both make significant mention of each other.

4   Threats to Validity and Topics for Further Research

One limitation of this study is that it compares proportions of different kinds of Twitter use across projects/keywords based on samples of similar size, while the absolute numbers of statuses for the different keywords differ greatly. Therefore, while we can conclude that e.g. a higher proportion of Silverstripe-related tweets than Apache-related tweets are concerned with events, that does not mean that Apache users and developers do not make equally active use of Twitter with regard to events, while also using Twitter more actively to e.g. provide links to documentation.

It would be desirable to increase the sample size for each project in order to increase the reliability of the data. It would also be better if the sample came from a full twelve-month period because many projects have large conferences once a year, and the current seven-month period risks excluding some events.

Not all statuses containing those keywords during the period were collected, for two reasons. First, the Twitter Search API does not guarantee to return all statuses for a given period. Second, it was not possible to ensure that the data collection script ran uninterrupted for the entire period. When such interruptions occurred, and the volume of posts was high, due to the limitation placed on the number of results returned from Twitters Search API (1500 in this case), it was not possible to collect all the statuses posted since the previous collection. These gaps might introduce distortions into the findings, for example if they coincide with a major conference or code release related to a particular project, thus missing a spike in microblogging activity. However, the long period of data collection can be expected to reduce the impact and perhaps to even out such distortions. The incompleteness of the data would also be a problem if the study were aiming to do a network analysis of Twitter-based communication in OSS projects, as there would be many missing directed messages and replies. However, as our purpose here is merely to analyze the content of individual statuses, this is not an issue for the current research.[5]

In retrospect, it would have been desirable to include Wordpress, one of the most popular open source CMSes. Unfortunately Twitter's search API does not allow statuses more than a few days old to be collected.[6]

The study could also be improved by obtaining information about numbers of followers and giving greater weight to posts that are more read.

---

[5] In addition, gathering only statuses that contain particular keywords would not capture all the directed Tweets sent between any given set of users.
[6] Some commercial services offer to retrieve historical Tweets.

References

1. Boehringer, M., Richter, A.: Adopting enterprise 2.0: A case study on microblogging. Mensch & Computer 2009: Grenzenlos frei (2009)
2. Reinhardt, W.: Communication is the key-support durable knowledge sharing in software engineering by microblogging. In: Proc. of the SENSE Workshop, Software Engineering within Social Software Environments (2009)
3. Riemer, K., Richter, A., Bohringer, M.: Enterprise microblogging. Business & Information Systems Engineering 2(6), 391–394 (2010)
4. Guenther, O., Krasnova, H., Riehle, D., Schoendienst, V.: Modeling microblogging adoption in the enterprise. In: Americas Conference on Information Systems (AMCIS) 2009 Proceedings, vol. 544 (2009)
5. Riemer, K., Richter, A.: Tweet inside: Microblogging in a corporate context. In: Proceedings of the 23rd Bled eConference, pp. 1–17 (2010)
6. Ehrlich, K., Shami, N.: Microblogging inside and outside the workplace. In: ICWSM 2010 (2010)
7. Java, A., Song, X., Finin, T., Tseng, B.: Why we twitter: understanding microblogging usage and communities. In: Proceedings of the 9th WebKDD and 1st SNA-KDD 2007 Workshop on Web Mining and Social Network Analysis, pp. 56–65 (2007)
8. Zhao, D., Rosson, M.B.: How and why people twitter: the role that micro-blogging plays in informal communication at work. In: Proceedings of the ACM 2009 International Conference on Supporting Group Work, pp. 243–252 (2009)
9. Naaman, M., Boase, J., Lai, C.: Is it really about me?: message content in social awareness streams. In: Proceedings of the 2010 ACM Conference on Computer Supported Cooperative Work, pp. 189–192 (2010)
10. Vega, E.: Communities of Tweeple: How Communities Engage with Microblogging When Co-located. PhD thesis, Virginia Polytechnic Institute and State University (2011)
11. Ebner, M., Mühlburger, H., Schaffert, S., Schiefner, M., Reinhardt, W., Wheeler, S.: Getting granular on twitter: Tweets from a conference and their limited usefulness for non-participants. In: Reynolds, N., Turcsányi-Szabó, M. (eds.) KCKS 2010. IFIP AICT, vol. 324, pp. 102–113. Springer, Heidelberg (2010)
12. Vega, E., Parthasarathy, R., Torres, J.: Where are my tweeps?: Twitter usage at conferences. Paper, Personal Information Management class, Virginia Polytechnic Institute and State University (June 1) (2010),
http://www.socialcouch.com/demos/final_paper_twitter.pdf
13. Shibab, E., Bettenburg, N., Adams, B., Hassan, A.E.: On the central role of mailing lists in open source projects: An exploratory study. In: Proceedings of the 3rd International Workshop on Knowledge Collaboration in Software Development, KCSD, Kyoto, Japan (November 2009)

A Preliminary Analysis of Localization in Free Software: How Translations Are Performed

Laura Arjona Reina[1], Gregorio Robles[2], and Jesús M. González-Barahona[2]

[1] Technical University of Madrid (UPM), Madrid, Spain
laura.arjona@upm.es
[2] GSyC/Libresoft, Universidad Rey Juan Carlos, Madrid, Spain
{grex,jgb}@gsyc.urjc.es

Abstract. Software is more than just source code. There is a myriad of elements that compose a software project, among others documentation, translations, multimedia, artwork, marketing. In this paper, we focus on the translation efforts that free, libre, open source software (FLOSS) projects undergo to provide their software in multiple languages. We have therefore analyzed a large amount of projects for their support and procedures regarding translations, if they exist. Our results show that many, but not all, projects offer some type of support and specify some ways to those wanting to contribute. Usually, projects from a more traditional libre software domain are more prone to ease such tasks. However, there is no general way to contribute, as formats and procedures are often project-specific. We have identified as well a high number of translation-supporting tools, with many projects having their own one. All in all, information about how to contribute is the main factor for having a very internationalized application. Projects accepting and giving credit to contributing translators have high levels of internationalization, even if the process is rudimentary.

Keywords: free software, open source, libre software, translations, internationalization, localization, collaborative development, crowdsourcing, open innovation.

1 Introduction

It is common that free, libre, open source software (FLOSS) projects follow an open development model, accepting contributions from external developers and easing (at least in theory) the entrance of new members. The availability of source code, the use of version control systems, software forges and public mailing lists to manage the project are technical means to put in practice the freedoms that are guaranteed by the license of the software. However, many of these tools, documentation and support are focused on (source code) developers, who have the technical skills to use and understand them. Beyond source code, there is a myriad of elements that compose a software project, such as documentation, translations, multimedia, artwork, marketing, among others.

E. Petrinja et al. (Eds.): OSS 2013, IFIP AICT 404, pp. 153–167, 2013.

. In this paper we put the focus on translations. We analyze how they are managed in a variety of FLOSS projects, if they have a defined process, and the tools and support that are provided. It should be noted that the use of libre software licenses creates a scenario in which any modification to the software is allowed, along with redistribution of those modified versions. This means for example that end-users or any third party may translate the software to their desired language or dialect, without the need of permission. This legal viability is usually viewed as an advantage of libre software versus proprietary alternatives, both by users and by developers. For users, it is a way to guarantee the availability of the software in their language, despite of the interests of the developer group or company. For developers, it is a way to increase the dissemination of the program, attract new users and new contributors to improve the project, specially in the case that the localization processes happens 'inside' the project. In order to ease this, libre software developers have created several means to materialize and take profit of the possibility to internationalize and localize a libre software project, in a similar way to what they do with coding tasks: developing helpful tools, collaborative platforms, giving credit to each contribution and creating a translator community around the project.

The main contributions of this paper are following:

- It provides a complete perspective of translations in FLOSS. To the knowledge of the authors there are few in-depth analyses of the field of translations in libre software.
- It looks if FLOSS projects are open to external contributions in the case of translations, and if they ease this task by providing tools, support and guidance.
- It studies if FLOSS projects have standard procedures and common tools that allow that the knowledge acquired from translating in one project to be re-used in other projects.

The structure of this document is as follows: next, we will introduce some definitions and concepts related to translation tasks. In Section 3 we introduce the research questions that we address in this paper. The next section contains the related research on localization in libre software projects. Then, we describe the sources of information and methodology used to answer the research questions, and show our results in Section 6. Finally, conclusions are drawn and further research possibilities are discussed.

2   Definitions

Software internationalization (often represented by the numeronym i18n) refers to the process to prepare a program to be adapted to different languages, regional or cultural differences without engineering changes [4]. It involves tasks as separating the text strings (those shown to the user in the different interfaces) to be translated, supporting several character sets, using certain libraries to manage dates, currencies or weights.

Software localization (often represented by the numeronym l10n) refers to the process of adapting the software to a particular target market (a *locale*) [4]. It involves tasks as translating the text messages, documentation and published material to the desired language or dialect, adapting graphics, colors and multimedia to the local language or culture if needed, using proper forms for dates, currency and measures and other details.

Crowdsourcing represents the act of a company or institution taking a function once performed by members and outsourcing it to an undefined (and generally large) network of people in the form of an open call [15]. The concept of free software was born to retrieve the spirit of collaboration, so it is very common, specially in the last years, to find libre software projects that build a collaborative web infrastructure to carry out localization tasks (what sometimes is called **crowdtranslation**).

3   Research Questions

In this work, we target following research questions:

3.1   How Do FLOSS Projects Enable Localization?

With this research question we aim to know if FLOSS projects consider localization a separate task of the rest of the source code management. While it is possible to handle localization as any other modification of the source code of a software project, in a well-internationalized software project, the task of translation can be made by conventional users or other people that may not have the programming skills needed for contributing using software development tools.

To answer this question we will look at the websites of several libre software projects and specially at the pages related to how to contribute, and see if there are any special guidelines on how to contribute with translations, comparing the process to follow with the one for contributing with source code. In addition, we will inspect if the objects to be localized are enumerated, and look for the existence of specialized internationalization or localization teams, guidelines and support platforms.

3.2   What Tools and Collaborative Platforms Are Used by FLOSS Projects to Approach l10n Tasks?

The goal of this research question is to gather information about the tools that libre software developers have created to manage the localization process. These tools may be pieces of software such as standalone editors specialized in handling localization files, web platforms, scripts to integrate changes in translations into the source code repository, among others.

To answer this question, in addition to review the related literature, we will investigate libre software catalogs in order to find localization tools and platforms, and will inspect the website of libre software projects to assess if they recommend any particular tool.

3.3   What Are the Results and Consequences of These Approaches to Software Localization?

We plan to count the number of languages to which each software project is translated, and to know if there are significant differences depending of the translation tool or platform used, or other aspects of the localization process. We will review literature in order to find other consequences (economic, social...) of the efforts in localization made by the libre software communities.

4   Related Research

Compared with matters related to source code and even documentation, the number of research articles that address the issue of translations in software is very scarce.

There are some papers that provide some insight on the presence of free software for translations (not necessarily translating libre software) [16]. For instance, Cánovas [1] and Díaz-Fouces [11] show that there are mature, libre software tools aimed for the translation of software. And directories with tools have been published, such as [7,5], including a study of applications for crowdsourcing in translations by the European Commission [3].

From the software engineering perspective, Robles et al. analyzed the KDE desktop environment looking for patterns in different kind of contributions by the type of file (localization files, multimedia, documentation, source code, and others) [21]. From the field of economics, Giuri et al. analyze the division of labor in free software projects and how it affects project survival and performance [14].

In the libre software communities, Gil Forcada, with the feedback from other community members, conducted a GNOME I18N Survey in August 2010, by sending a questionnaire to every GTP (GNOME Translation Project) language coordinator, and collecting answers [10].

Souphavanh and Karoonboonyanan [22] provide a broad perspective on the localization of Free/Open Source Software (FOSS) for the benefit of policy- and decision-makers in developing countries, highlighting the benefits and strategies of FLOSS localization.

5   Methodology

We have gathered the information presented in this work from several publicly available sources: websites of the projects, documentation, mailing lists for translators, and related literature showed in the bibliography.

For each libre software project analyzed, we have written in a research script[1] following aspects: if there is information about how to localize the project, the

---

[1] The research script is publicly available at
http://gsyc.urjc.es/~grex/repro/oss2013-translations
for reproducibility purposes and further research.

recommended tools and website of localization, if internationalization and local-ization teams exist, and other remarkable aspects.

For each libre software tool or web platform analyzed, we have annotated our research script with the following aspects: the type of localization tools (stan-dalone software, plugin, web platform...), the year of first release, the original project for which was developed (if any), the number of projects that use the tool (if it is stated in the main website of the tool), if well-known projects that use the tool, and other remarkable aspects.

6 Results

As a preliminary analysis, we have analyzed 41 libre software projects, from small tools as Mustard -the microblogging client for Android-, to GNU/Linux distri-butions as Debian or Mandriva. We have analyzed groups of "similar" projects as the office suites OpenOffice.org and LibreOffice and the CMS Drupal and Wordpress.

The projects analyzed are listed and grouped as follows[2]:

— Operating Systems (10 projects): Debian, Ubuntu, Fedora, Mandriva, Open-SUSE, Android Open Source, CyanogenMod, Replicant OS, FreeBSD, OpenBSD
— GNU/Linux, cross-platform applications (16 projects): GNOME, KDE, Tux Paint, GNU MediaGoblin, Limesurvey, OpenStack, Wordpress, Drupal, Poo-tle, Scratch, BOINC, LibreOffice, OpenOffice.org, Mozilla apps, Calibre, VLC
— Windows projects (6 projects): Filezilla, Notepad++, 7zip, eMule, Azureus-Vuze, Ares
— Android projects (9 projects): F-Droid, Mustard, K9 Mail, AdAway, Open-StreetMap Android (OSMAnd), Barcode Scanner, aCal, Frozen Bubble, Cool Reader

We have analyzed 22 libre software tools or platforms for supporting the local-ization process. Among them we can find plugins for text editors, standalone programs for localization, and complete online frameworks. They are introduced in the following subsections. We also have compiled a list of 15 more translation tools for further research, which can be found in our research script, along with all the details about the selected projects and localization platforms.

6.1 How Do FLOSS Projects Enable Localization?

Information about How to Contribute Translations
Most of the projects have a dedicated page about how to contribute translations, and many include several objects to localize (in addition to the messages or

---

[2] More details about this sample (selection criteria and other) can be found in our research script.

strings presented to the user, for example the documentation and website). Some projects maintain translations for different releases (the case of Ubuntu) but most of them focus on the development release.

There are some projects with no information about how to contribute, neither code nor translations. This situation is more frequent in the case of libre software created for the Android or Windows platforms than in the case of cross-platform or GNU/Linux tools, we assume that because of *cultural* reasons. In Figure 1 we summarize our findings about this topic.

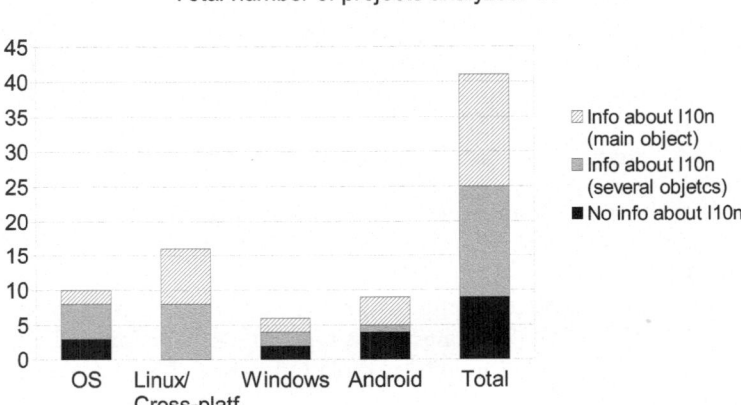

Information on l10n in libre software projects

Total number of projects analyzed: 41

Fig. 1. Information about how to contribute translations

A remarkable exception is the Android Open Source Project, as it does not offer information about the localization of the software. There is a *Localization document*[3] explaining the process that Android developers should follow in order to make their applications localizable; the project has also published the *Hello, L10N* tutorial[4], providing an example of how to build a simple localized application that uses locale-specific resources [20]. However, there is no information about how to contribute translations to Android itself. In some forum threads Jean-Baptiste Queru (Technical Leader of Android OSP at Google) explains that Google translates Android internally, not accepting community contributions[5]. Surprisingly, the libre software forks, CyanogenMod and Replicant OS, do not show either public information about localization. In CyanogenMod the topic has been discussed in several forum threads. However, at this time it still

---

[3] http://developer.android.com/guide/topics/resources/localization.html

[4] http://developer.android.com/resources/tutorials/localization/index.html

[5] See for example: Proposal to add Basque translation to Android Source Code http://tinyurl.com/b2fkpbn; Hungarian localization – questions about legal issues http://tinyurl.com/b9xqrek

does not offer a specific protocol to contribute translations, managing them as any other modification to the source code. It does not have language teams or internationalization delegates either.

Observation #1: Many, but not all, projects offer information and support to contribute translations. Usually those projects from a more traditional libre software domain are more prone to ease such tasks to external contributors.

Existence of Internationalization and Localization Guides and Infrastructure

It is task of the internationalization team to study and decide how the localization of the project is going to be driven, setup the corresponding tools and write the proper documentation for translators and developers.

Most of the projects create language teams and use mailing lists to communicate (the use of the native language in those lists is common), and many software projects define the complete process of localization in a wiki page or website. For example, OpenStack discussed which platform to use: Pootle, Launchpad or Transifex, showing some comparative charts and assessment in their translations wiki page (old version[6]). The current version of the wiki[7] is a comprehensive guide of the localization project, both for translators and for developers. Another example of a complete guide for localization can be found in the Apache OpenOffice.org wiki[8].

Regarding the localization infrastructure, there are different approaches. Some projects use an external, web-based collaborative environment to coordinate the localization teams (for example, OpenStack uses Transifex, and Wordpress uses the official Pootle server). Others deploy an instance of those web-based software in a community server - the Fedora and Mandriva distributions have set up their own Transifex servers, and OpenOffice.org and LibreOffice offer their own, but independent, Pootle servers. Finally, other projects are developing their own localization tools: standalone programs -as Lokalize for the KDE project or the i18nAZ plugin for Azureus/Vuze-, and web based localization platforms, such as Damned Lies[9] -the translation platform developed and used by the GNOME project-, or the Drupal localization website[10] which is used in the Drupal CMS project. The Mozilla project uses (a) Verbatim (their own Pootle server) for the localization of some aspects, (b) an *in-house* developed wiki for the translation of their help documentation, and (c) Narro, an external web-based tool, developed by the Romanian translation coordinator.

There are as well efforts on providing tools for particular tasks of the translation process. One example is the KDE internationalization build system[11] which

---

[6] http://wiki.openstack.org/Translations?action=recall&rev=9
[7] http://wiki.openstack.org/Translations
[8] http://wiki.openoffice.org/wiki/Localization_AOO
[9] http://l10n.gnome.org/
[10] http://localize.drupal.org
[11] http://techbase.kde.org/Development/Tutorials/
Localization/i18n_Build_Systems

basically consists of a script running trough the KDE source code repository server, extracting the localizable strings in the KDE source code and generating the localization templates periodically. This way developers only need to care about writing code with localization in mind, and localizers will always find an updated template with the latest strings to be translated.

For 32 out of 41 projects that have been analyzed, we have obtained the way of submitting translations. Figure 2 shows the results.

How to proceed to contribute translations

Total number of projects analyzed: 32

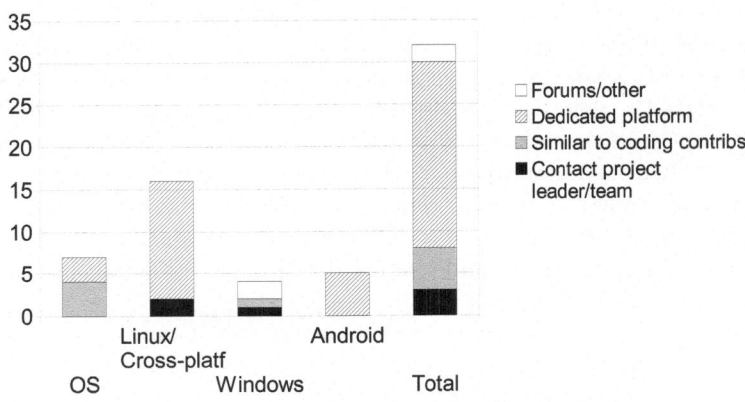

Fig. 2. Means to send translations in libre software projects

Some of the Operating Systems projects use a localization web platform, while others follow a traditional way, similar to code contributions (basically, sending translations via BTS or with mail systems). For GNU/Linux or cross-platform tools we can find that most of them clearly define a platform to manage l10n contributions, but there are some successful projects (in term of number of translations) as Filezilla or Notepad++ that simply explain how to translate the corresponding files and ask to send the contributions to the project leader directly. The Windows specific projects analyzed do not use localization platform for managing translations; however, some of them offer templates in a forum thread and, if required, open another thread for translators to attach their contributions. Finally, for those Android projects that offer information about how to contribute translations, all of them use a dedicated platform, although not the same one (Transifex, Pootle, Weblate or Android-PHP-translator).

Observation #2: There is no standard way to contribute with translations. The tools and procedures, if they exist, are heterogeneous and sometimes even project-specific.

Used and Accepted File Formats for Localization. There are a number of standards to be applied to the task of translation and localization that determine the use of certain file formats to ensure interoperability. Hence, several tools can be used to perform the translation work.

According to the OAXAL framework [9], if we consider the complete process of localization (not only related to software localization), there are certain standard file formats to be used, as `tmx`, `tbx`, and `xliff`. XLIFF (XML Localization Interchange File Format) consists of an XML specification to hold translatable strings along with metadata [8]. This format is frequently used in professional translation, not only in software internationalization. Version 1.2 of XLIFF was approved by OASIS in February 2008.

However, these standards are recent. The libre software community has been concerned with localization from before these efforts, much before the OAXAL framework was designed. Therefore, other kind of file formats became *de facto* standards as the "PO" (Portable Object) file format for software translations.

The GNU Project [12] chose the Gettext [13] tool, implemented originally by Sun[12], to enable the internationalization of GNU software. Gettext explores the source code and extracts all the "printed" strings into a POT file, a template that contains a list of all the translatable strings extracted from the sources.

With time the use of PO files has become a *de facto* standard for libre software internationalization. However we can still find multiple file formats for internationalization of software, documentation and other elements in any libre software development project. For example, the Android Operating System uses "Android Resources" to make the localization of Android applications easy[13].

Observation #3: PO (Portable Object) files are still the *de facto* standard in use in libre software projects, although many projects use their own format. Newer, standardized formats such as XLIFF are seldom used.

6.2   What Tools and Collaborative Platforms Are Used by FLOSS Projects to Approach l10n Tasks?

In general, each language has an independent localization team that agrees on using locale-specific tools, formats, guidelines. Each team is, as well, responsible for the translation, review, and submission.

The tools used by these teams vary from traditional tools such as Poedit and plain text editors (with plugins for handling translation files), to sophisticated web platforms that integrate translation and revision processes, sometimes even automatically committing the changes to the versioning systems.

In our research script we provide a list with all the tools in use, which we have augmented with the most relevant tools referenced in the literature.

---

[12] http://compgroups.net/comp.unix.solaris/History-of-gettext-et-al
[13] http://developer.android.com/guide/topics/resources/localization.html

Text Editor Add-Ons. Emacs[14] and Vim have some tools for working with Gettext:

- **PoMode** for editing .po catalogs, **po-mode+.el** with extra features for PoMode, and
- **MoMode** for viewing .mo compiled catalogs.
- **po.vim** is the Vim plugin for working with PO files (http://www.vim.org/scripts/script.php?script_id=695).

Standalone Tools

- **Poedit**[15] is a cross-platform editor for .po files (gettext catalogs). It allows to configure the tool with the information related to the translator (name and email) and the environment, and every time a file is translated and saved, that information is included in the file.
- **Virtaal**[16] is a more modern translation tool, which allows working with XLIFF files [18].
- **The Translate Toolkit**[17] is a collection of useful programs for localization, and a powerful API for programmers of localization tools. The Toolkit includes programs to help check, validate, merge and extract messages from localizations, as **poconflicts**, **pofilter** or **pogrep**.
- **Pology**[18] is a Python library and a collection of command-line tools for in-depth processing of PO files, including examination and in-place modification of collections of PO files (the **posieve** command), and custom translation validation with user-written rules. The Pology distribution contains internal validation rules for some languages and projects.

Web Platforms for Supporting Translation

In the last years, a number of web based translation platforms have been developed in order to benefit from the advantages of Internet-based collaboration, automate certain tasks and also lower barriers to external contributions. This new method has been called *crowdtranslation* [2].

In many cases, these platforms begin as a web-based infrastructure created for a particular project, and later they are used for other projects too.

- Probably the oldest example of a web based translation platform is **Pootle**[19], which is built on top of the Translate Toolkit. Pootle allows online translation, work assignment, provides statistics and includes some revision checks.

---

[14] http://www.emacswiki.org/emacs/Gettext
[15] http://www.poedit.net/
[16] http://translate.sourceforge.net/wiki/virtaal
[17] translate.sourceforge.net
[18] http://pology.nedohodnik.net/
[19] http://translate.sourceforge.net/wiki/pootle/

- **Launchpad**[20], which is a complete software forge including a powerful web based translation system, was developed by Canonical to handle the Ubuntu development, and initially developed under a proprietary license, but later released under the GNU Affero General Public License, version 3.
- **Transifex**[21] is a newer platform which enhances the translation memory support.
- **Weblate**[22] is a recent tool, developed by Michal Čihař (the phpMyAdmin project leader), which offers a better integration with the git versioning system.

Many different and popular projects decide to host their translations in an external service using one of the above platforms. The already mentioned Damned Lies[23] used in GNOME or the Drupal localization website[24] belong to this group. Wordpress uses the official Pootle translation server[25] (although some languages are handled in GlotPress, an online localization tool developed inside the project), and the FreedomBox Foundation and the Fedora community use Transifex[26] for the localization of their websites.

Observation #4: There is a large amount of translation-supporting tools.

6.3 What are the Results and Consequences of These Approaches to Software Localization?

Results on the Libre Software Projects

In our research script we have annotated the number of languages to which each project is translated. For some cases, the number of languages with more than 50% of the objects translated and the number of languages with more than 90% completion is provided. However, it is difficult to measure the success of the methods and tools used in these terms, since other causes may have to be taken into account.

We have found that the number of language teams or the amount of translations in a libre software projects does not depend on the translation tool(s) used. The most important factor is to have clear specifications on how to contribute with localization tasks. For example, the Notepad++ project recommends to download an XML file, translate it, test it and send it by email to the project leader. With this simple approach, the program has been translated to 66 languages (all the translators are credited in a dedicated page; this may contribute too to attract new translators).

---

[20] http://launchpad.net
[21] http://transifex.com
[22] http://weblate.org
[23] http://l10n.gnome.org/
[24] http://localize.drupal.org
[25] http://pootle.locamotion.org/
[26] http://transifex.net

However, we have identified some projects with users wanting to contribute translations, but without much success. These projects do not offer information on how to translate the software, or if this information is provided it is very sparse. In addition to Android (already mentioned in section 6.1), we have the case of the Ares/Galaxy project: its issue tracking system contains 18 tickets (out of a total of 33) with user-submitted translations to the program; many of them remain unconsidered.

Observation #5: Information about how to translate a libre software is the main factor for having a very internationalized application. Project accepting and giving credit to contributing translators have high levels of internationalization, even if the process is rudimentary.

Other Results or Consequences

Business Opportunities
The experience in the development and participation in localization tasks in libre software projects opens new opportunities for professionals of language management. Marcos Cánovas and Richard Samson have studied the mutual benefits of using libre software in translator training [2], both for trainees and for the libre software community.

Companies specialized in translation and localization of software may cover several cases where the community or company developing a software cannot reach, such as the maintenance of several versions of the localized system, or localization of the software for a specific customer [19].

One example of this is **Acoveo**[27], a company offering a solution for software localization consisting in a Maven and a Jenkins plugin that are offered for free (under the AGPL license) to their customers. The Maven plugin takes care of extracting all the translatable strings of the client's software, and sends the strings to www.translate-software.com, where professional translators will localize them at a certain price per word. The Jenkins plugin allows the customer to control the localization workflow and progress.

Another example is **ICanLocalize**[28] which offers website translations, software localization, Text translations and general translations. They have developed a Drupal module called "translation management"[29], released under the GPL license, and the Wordpress MultiLingual Plugin[30] (which is licensed as GPL and offered at a certain cost, including the fees for the website content translation).

Finally, there is **Transifex**, a libre software project that has become a company offering hosting and support on its platform.

---

[27] http://www.acoveo.com
[28] http://www.icanlocalize.com
[29] http://drupal.org/project/translation_management
[30] http://wpml.org

Localization results as free culture works

In addition to the the localization files of the software, **translation memories** (a database that stores paired segments of source and human translated target segments), **glossaries** (definitions for words and terms found in the program user interface), and **corpora** (large and structured set of texts) may be released as free cultural works too, lowering the barrier for new translations of other projects to the target language. An example of this is the **Atshumato Project**[31]. The general aim of this project is the development of open source machine-aided translation tools and resources for South African languages [6]. Among them, Atshumato releases Translation memories in the Translation Memory eXchange format (TMX) with Creative Commons Attribution Non-Commercial ShareAlike 2.5 license[32] for the following language pairs: ENG-AFR (English to Afrikaans), AFR-ENG (Afrikaans to English), ENG-NSO (English to Sepedi), NSO-ENG (Sepedi to English), ENG-ZUL (English to IsiZulu), ZUL-ENG (IsiZulu to English).

Observation #6: Translation of libre software projects offers new business and cultural opportunities.

---

7   Conclusions and Further Work

In this paper, we have investigated how FLOSS projects manage translations by studying a big number of them for the information and support they provide, and the tools that are being used.

Internationalization and localization in libre software projects are two of their most interesting advantages for dissemination, competition with proprietary alternatives, and penetration in new markets. Therefore, we have seen how most of the libre software projects offering information about how to contribute or join the community, offer information about how to contribute with translations as well. From the projects under study, we have found that the GNU/Linux or cross-platform projects handle translations in a more systematic way (much more standardized than Windows or Android projects), probably due to the tradition of the collaboration spirit of the GNU project and the dissemination of Gettext, and the *cultural* influence of those platforms where contributions have always been welcome.

However, there is big heterogeneity in how projects proceed with translations. Procedures vary from project to project, and no generalized way exists to contribute, as is normally the case for source code. The heterogeneity can

---

[31] http://autshumato.sourceforge.net/, initiated by the South African Department of Arts and Culture and developed by the Centre for Text Technology (CTexT) at the North-West University (Potchefstroom Campus), in collaboration with the University of Pretoria.

[32] The Non-Commercial clause makes them not a completely "free culture work" but allows quite more freedoms to the receiver than traditional copyright application.

be observed as well from the technological point of view. There are many tools that support translations, resulting in a productivity increase for the project, but not allowing translators to reuse their knowledge on other projects. If we compare the tools that exist to contribute source code with the ones that are used for translations, we have not found a concentration of localization tasks in few platforms in the same way as some software forges have concentrated a high number of projects [17]. However, web platforms for translations such as Launchpad (more than 1800 projects) or Transifex (more than 1700 projects) are gaining popularity in recent times and may change this in the near future.

From our analysis of the projects, we have seen that publishing information about how to translate a libre software is the key element to have a project with a large number of translations. This has been found to be true even for smaller projects that use simple ways to accept contributions, even per e-mail or in the e-mail forums. If this practice is augmented with giving credit to the contributing translators, the results have been found to be even better.

Regarding future lines of research, a more comprehensive analysis (involving a higher number of projects) should be performed in order to measure the effect of using different tools and procedures in the localization tasks and management.

We think that due to the availability of the source code of libre software projects, and the fact that many of them use a versioning system that keeps track of the history of changes to all the files, it is possible to inspect the source tree or mine the versioning system logs to get information about the software. This could provide factual details about how localization is driven (for example, looking at changes in the localization files or the information about the translators present in their headers), give hints about vulnerabilities in the process (as, for example, translation files without any change for a long time, which may mean that there are parts of the project that are outdated or not maintained).

Having a distributed team of collaborators, taking benefit of crowdtranslation, increases the number of languages and strings translated but may introduce inconsistencies or quality problems, introducing additional effort for reviewers. It would be interesting to make a comparative analysis on software projects that use the crowdsourcing models with the ones that maintain a stable translation team, in order to see if they evolve similarly o differently in number of languages, size of the translator community, and medium-long term involvement of the contributors).

References

1. Cánovas, M., Samson, R.: Herramientas libres para la traducción en entornos MS Windows. In: Díaz, O., García, M. (eds.) Traducir (con) Software Libre, pp. 33–55. Editorial Comares, Granada (2008)
2. Mugoya, A.: African Apps in a Global Marketplace: ideas, observations, tips and some gripes about the African app industry. Asilia (2011)
3. European Commission. Crowdsourcing translation. Publications Office of the European Union, Luxembourg (2012),
   http://ec.europa.eu/dgs/translation/publications/
   studies/crowdsourcing_translation_en.pdf

4. World Wide Web Consortium. Questions and answers about internationalization (2010), http://www.w3.org/International/questions/qa-i18n.en
5. Cordeiro, G.: Open source software in translator's workbench. Tradumàtica: Tecnologies de la Traducció 0(9) (2011)
6. South Africa; Department of Arts CTexT (Centre for Text Technology, North-West University) and South Africa Culture. Atshumato project (2012), http://autshumato.sourceforge.net/
7. Flórez, S., Alcina, A.: Free translation software catalog. Tradumàtica: Tecnologies de la Traducció 0(9) (2011)
8. Organization for the Advancement of Structured Information Standards (OASIS). Xliff version 1.2. oasis standard (2008), http://docs.oasis-open.org/xliff/xliff-core/xliff-core.html
9. Organization for the Advancement of Structured Information Standards (OASIS). Open architecture for xml authoring and localization reference model (oaxal) tc wiki (2009), https://wiki.oasis-open.org/oaxal/
10. Forcada, G.: Gnome localization update for q1 2012 (2010), https://live.gnome.org/TranslationProject/Survey
11. Díaz Fouces, O.: Ferramentas livres para traduzir com GNU/Linux e Mac OS X. In: Díaz, O., García, M. (eds.) Traducir (con) Software Libre, pp. 57–73. Editorial Comares, Granada (2008)
12. Free Software Foundation. Gnu project, http://www.gnu.org
13. Free Software Foundation. GNU Gettext (1998-2010), http://www.gnu.org/software/gettext/ (updated: June 06, 2010) (accessed January 25, 2012)
14. Giuri, P., Ploner, M., Rullani, F., Torrisi, S.: Skills, division of labor and performance in collective inventions: Evidence from open source software. International Journal of Industrial Organization 28(1), 54–68 (2010)
15. Howe, J.: Crowdsourcing: A definition (2006), http://crowdsourcing.typepad.com/cs/2006/06/crowdsourcing_a.html
16. Mata, M.: Formatos libres en traducción y localización. In: Díaz, O., García, M. (eds.) Traducir (con) Software Libre, pp. 75–122. Editorial Comares, Granada (2008)
17. Mockus, A.: Amassing and indexing a large sample of version control systems: Towards the census of public source code history. In: 6th IEEE International Working Conference on Mining Software Repositories, MSR 2009, pp. 11–20. IEEE (2009)
18. Morado, L., Wolff, F.: Bringing industry standards to open source localisers: a case study of virtaal. Tradumàtica: Tecnologies de la Traducció 0(9) (2011)
19. Parada, C.G.: Free software localization within translation companies. Tradumàtica: Tecnologies de la Traducció 0(9) (2011)
20. Reina, L.A., Robles, G.: Mining for localization in android. In: MSR 2012: Proceedings of the 2012 Workshop on Mining Software Repositories (2012)
21. Robles, G., González-Barahona, J.M., Guervós, J.J.M.: Beyond source code: The importance of other artifacts in software development (a case study). Journal of Systems and Software 79(9), 1233–1248 (2006)
22. Souphavanh, A.: Free/open source software: localization. United Nations Development Programme-Asia Pacific Development Information Programme, New Delhi (2005)

Authoritative Linked Data Descriptions of Debian Source Packages Using ADMS.SW[*]

Olivier Berger[1,2] and Christian Bac[1]

[1] Telecom SudParis, Évry, France
{olivier.berger,christian.bac}@telecom-sudparis.eu
[2] Debian project
obergix@debian.org

Abstract. The Debian Package Tracking System is a Web dashboard for Debian contributors and advanced users. This central tool publishes the status of subsequent releases of source packages in the Debian distribution.

It has been improved to generate RDF meta-data documenting the source packages, their releases and links to other packaging artifacts, using the ADMS.SW 1.0 model. This constitutes an authoritative source of machine-readable Debian "facts" and proposes a reference URI naming scheme for Linked Data resources about Debian packages.

This should enable the interlinking of these Debian package descriptions with other ADMS.SW or DOAP descriptions of FLOSS projects available on the Semantic Web also using Linked Data principles. This will be particularly interesting for traceability with upstream projects whose releases are packaged in Debian, derivative distributions reusing Debian source packages, or with other FLOSS distributions.

Keywords: ADMS.SW, Debian, Linked Data, package, Semantic Web, standard, interoperability, Open Source, Free Software, RDF, DOAP, PTS, FLOSS.

1 Introduction

Asset Description Metadata Schema for Software (ADMS.SW) is a novel ontology developped for describing software packages, releases and projects, which can be applied to describe packages in a Free, Libre and Open Source Software (FLOSS) distribution, using Semantic Web techniques. We consider it is a foundational component that will allow to conduct future Quality Assurance or other large scale FLOSS studies across the Linked Open Data cloud [5].

FLOSS software ecosystems are composed of many different actors collaborating around single programs, from original upstream authors to downstream

---

[*] This is a revised version of a previous paper [2] which was initially accepted at the 8th International Workshop on Semantic Web Enabled Software Engineering (SWESE 2012), but that the authors weren't able to present physically at the workshop.

E. Petrinja et al. (Eds.): OSS 2013, IFIP AICT 404, pp. 168–181, 2013.

packagers in distributions like Debian. Descriptions of FLOSS development artifacts made with standardized and semantic formats like ADMS.SW can help trace some of the process which generally happen in various venues across the ecosystem.

1.1 The Need for Linked Data Descriptions of FLOSS

Constructing models of interactions happening along the FLOSS production lines can be interesting, both for researchers and practitioners. Research in empirical software engineering can for instance involve studies conducted by modeling properties and relations between FLOSS production artifacts and actors.

The Semantic Web techniques bring key benefits in terms of semantic interoperability : using a W3C standard like RDF [16] which is natively extensible helps integrate potentially incoherent data, which fits quite well large scale problems. The size of the communities and diversity of actors and tools present in large FLOSS ecosystems qualify well for such an approach [13].

The Linked Data approach [5], can be very convenient to *interlink* resources representing actors or artifacts belonging to different projects described with RDF. It will allow researchers to integrate in the same "triple store" database, description of FLOSS artifacts or actors with variable structures, still relying on common semantics and a harmonized URI nomenclature that reflects the origin of these resources.

But for FLOSS developers alike, these semantic Web Techniques should offer potential interesting applications, in particular to create new global services that need to interconnect different heterogenous project tools [4]. As an illustration, we can imagine a new "global bug tracking system" that aims at correlating similar bug reports filed in different Linux distributions. It can be helpful to offer better support responses, allowing navigation between reports which may have been related to each-other previously. Such a system will require to interface to lots of different bugtracker APIs. Whereas standards like *Open Services for Lifecycle Collaboration* (OSLC) [3] (which rely on extensible semantic formats based on RDF and REST[1] APIs) can help solve some concrete interoperability issues, they only address parts of the problems (and their deployment is not yet spectacular among FLOSS project). Actually, even once semantically compatible data has been collected, it must be integrated in a coherent data store. And therefore, nomenclature, freshness and accuracy issues still represent interesting challenges. Addressing them is a foundational requirement for large scale applications described above.

1.2 Authoritative Linked Data Descriptors Produced by FLOSS Projects

We postulate that there are higher chances that meta-data is more accurate and up-to-date when it is produced closest to the very heart of the FLOSS projects,

---

[1] REpresentational State Transfer.

than obtained after a series of collection and conversion activities conducted by third parties. Thus, with the Linked Data principles in mind[2], significant artifacts produced by FLOSS projects ought to be complemented with meta-data available at the very same Web domains, as a minimal set of authoritative RDF resources. URIs naming these resources can then be rooted at the project's domain name, and serve to identify its artifacts unambiguously.

As an illustration, Semantic Web resources describing projects from the Apache foundation would be downloaded from RDF documents available on `http://projects.apache.org/` which would identify them for instance with URIs like `<http://PROJNAME.apache.org/>` (or a variant, like `<http://PROJNAME.apache.org/doap#project>`)[3]. Thus, in the description of the Debian packaging the Apache *geronimo* program, we could reference its upstream project (from Debian's point of view) as the RDF resource `<http://geronimo.apache.org/>`.

Our initiative, coupled with other previous and current efforts, will hopefully help achieve a state when almost every FLOSS project are able to publish on their Web sites or development forges, even minimal, but authoritative Linked Data descriptions of the project or its software artifacts, either as *Descriptions Of A Project* (DOAP) [7] or ADMS.SW.

1.3   Goal and Structure of This Paper

This paper will introduce a Linked Data interface based on ADMS.SW, which was deployed on the Debian Package Tracking System (PTS), that produces authoritative meta-data descriptions for the core artifacts produced by the Debian project: *source packages.*

Due to Debian's respected position in the FLOSS ecosystem, such a deployment already covers a great percentage of all FLOSS programs, and can thus be inspirational for many FLOSS projects.

In section 2, we introduce the ADMS.SW specification. Then a brief introduction to the structure of Debian source packages is provided in section 3. Section 4 documents the choices adopted for generating Linked Data representations of Debian source packages and related FLOSS artifacts in the Debian PTS. Section 5 presents a quick review of similar and complementary initiatives, while section 6 illustrates how a trivial project matching can be made with collected Linked Data descriptions.

2   The ADMS.SW Specification

The *Asset Description Metadata Schema for Software* (ADMS.SW) specification[4] is described as : "[...] *a metadata vocabulary to describe software making it possible to more easily explore, find, and link software on the Web."*

---

[2] `http://www.w3.org/DesignIssues/LinkedData.html`

[3] There's actually a DOAP description for Geronimo, linked from `http://projects.apache.org/projects/geronimo.html` — see 5.1

[4] `https://joinup.ec.europa.eu/asset/adms_foss/release/release100`

It is an outcome of the ISA programme (*Interoperability Solutions for European Public Administrations*) of the European Commission, elaborated by a working group of software catalogues and forges experts[5]. Although it is not specifically covering FLOSS software only, ADMS.SW has nevertheless been geared at addressing meta-data of FLOSS projects hosted in public development forges to facilitate their identification and reuse by Public Administrations.

ADMS.SW specifications are published with a complementary OWL ontology, referenced as `http://purl.org/adms/sw/`, to allow the publishing of such meta-data as RDF.

As illustrated in Figure 1, it provides three main entities : *Software Project*, *Software Release*, and *Software Package* to model meta-data about software programs, their versions, and the distribution archives of these.

But it also contains various elements related to *Software Repositories* descriptions in order to facilitate the maintenance of data managed by software catalogues (provenance, timestamping, etc.), based on the RADion common model of ADMS, which describes generic semantic assets.

ADMS.SW 1.0 reuses existing specifications and standards, such as Dublin Core [19], DOAP [7], SPDX™ [9], ISO 19770-2 [8], ADMS [10], and the "Sourceforge Trove software map"[6]. As DOAP is already widely used in practice, ADMS.SW reuses much of its properties. ADMS.SW is also interoperable with the SPDX specification, whose main object, to date, is the description of copyright and license conditions applying to particular software packages or source files.

3   Debian Source Packages

The Debian project[7] creates a Free Software distribution, which contains thousands of FLOSS *binary* packages ready to be installed on various computer architectures. Several versions of the Debian distribution are maintained in parallel, in three main *suites* : 'stable', 'testing' and 'unstable'.

Debian has been studied by many authors, as it represents a good proxy for the entire FLOSS ecosystem, due to the high number of packages it contains, and since its development and Quality Assurance (QA) infrastructure is generally open or easily accessible to researchers in empirical software engineering (see for instance [11] or [6]).

3.1   Structure of Debian Source Packages

Each binary package is actually built from a particular Debian *source* package. Source packages contain "Makefiles" for package generation, `control` files containing different meta-data like versions or package dependency descriptions, and

---

[5] One of the authors was an active member of the working group.
[6] `http://sourceforge.net/apps/trac/sourceforge/wiki/Software Map and Trove`
[7] `http://debian.org/`

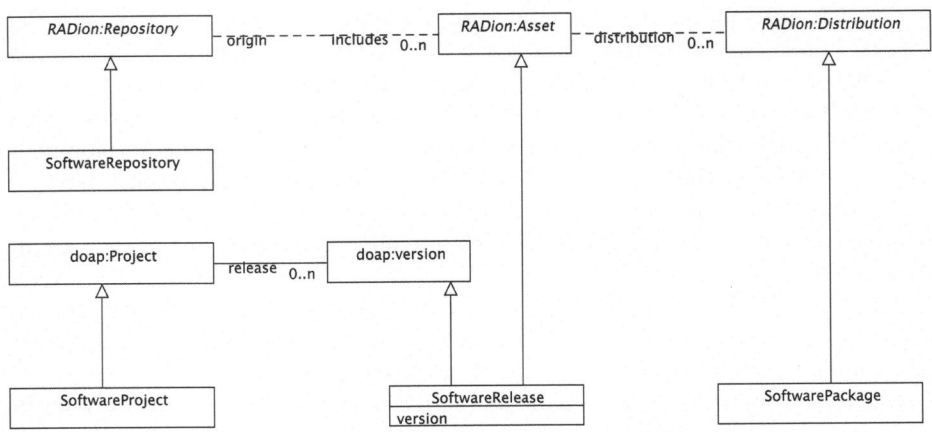

Fig. 1. Simplified UML diagram of the main ADMS.SW entities

other scripts necessary for installation, configuration, upgrade or removal of the binary packages [15]. In addition, it is quite common to include patches applying to the source code of the packaged program, to adjust it to Debian specificities or to include security fixes backported from later upstream releases.

Each revision of a Debian source package is then generally composed of two file archives : one for the source code of the upstream version of the packaged program (ending in `.orig.tar.gz`), complemented by another one for these Debian specific files (ending in `.debian.tar.gz`)[8]. Only the latter Debian specific files archive, and associate meta-data descriptors change between subsequent revisions of Debian source packages of the same version of an upstream program.

3.2   The Debian Package Tracking System

For every Debian source package, the *Debian Package Tracking System* (PTS) provides a Web dashboard (see a screenshot[9] in Figure 2) which displays almost all there is to know about the status of that package [17].

However, its HTML pages are not really exploitable by machines in a direct form, should anyone need to interface the Debian QA system with other services. One such need seems quite obvious for derivative distributions constructed from Debian, like Ubuntu. Therefore, the PTS provides a custom SOAP interface[10], but the lack of standard representation of data retrieved from this API may require another ad-hoc converter to be added to every application wishing to interface with it.

---

[8] As an exception to this general rule, some packages, which are called "native packages", don't have a corresponding upstream project outside Debian and only have Debian specific files.

[9] Taken from `http://packages.qa.debian.org/a/apache2.html`

[10] `http://wiki.debian.org/qa.debian.org/pts/SoapInterface`

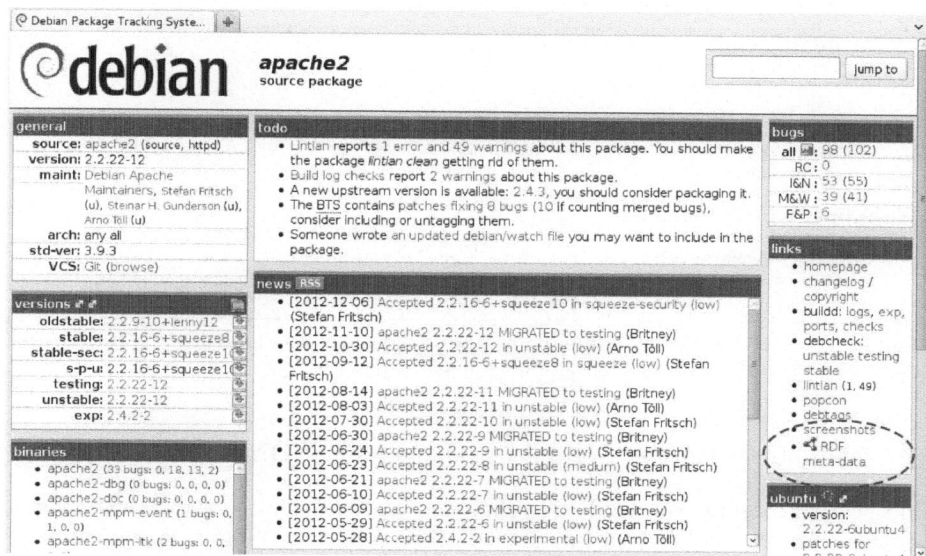

Fig. 2. Apache 2 source package status in the Debian PTS

As an alternative, we have started implementing a Linked Data [5] interface for the Debian PTS, using the ADMS.SW ontology to represent Debian source package facts with the standard, thus interoperable, RDF model.

4   Linked Data Representation of Debian Source Packages

We have improved the Debian PTS to add the generation of RDF descriptions for all Debian source packages.

Every Debian source package, which used to have an HTML page accessible at a URL like `http://packages.qa.debian.org/apache2`, now has a corresponding RDF document available at the same URL, either as Turtle [1] or RDF/XML format. Applying a common Linked Data pattern, HTTP clients will be redirected automatically to the proper HTML or RDF document depending on the *content-type* that is requested by the HTTP client, so that the same URL can be used to represent both the human-readable HTML pages or the machine-processable RDF document.

Thus, each package in Debian can be identified on the Semantic Web with a unique URI like `http://packages.qa.debian.org/SRC-PKG-NAME`, which is dereferenceable as an RDF document.

The example in Listing 1 is an excerpt of such an RDF description, in Turtle, of a particular revision of the Debian source package for `apache2`. Note that URIs based on `http://packages.qa.debian.org/` are converted to `http://p.q.d.o/` for brievity in the rest of this section.

```
<http://p.q.d.o/apache2#apache2_2.2.22-12>
    a admssw:SoftwareRelease ;
    rdfs:label "apache2_2.2.22-12" ;
    dcterms:description "Debian_apache2_source_package_version_
        2.2.22-12" ;
    doap:revision "2.2.22-12" ;
    dcterms:publisher <http://debian.org/> ;
    admssw:status <http://p.q.d.o/#released> ;
    admssw:project <http://p.q.d.o/apache2#project> ;
    admssw:includedAsset <http://p.q.d.o/apache2#upstreamsrc_2.2.22> ;
    admssw:includedAsset <http://p.q.d.o/apache2#debiansrc_2.2.22-12>;
    admssw:package <http://p.q.d.o/apache2#apache2_2.2.22-12.dsc> ;
    dcterms:relation <https://launchpad.net/ubuntu/+source/apache2
        /2.2.22-6ubuntu4> .
```

Listing 1. RDF description available at http://packages.qa.debian.org/a/apache2.ttl of revision 12 of the source package for apache2 version 2.2.22

4.1   Modelling Debian Source Packages with ADMS.SW

This section presents the modelling choices adopted so that every Debian source package can be modeled as interlinked RDF resources. The version numbers reflected in the resource URIs or file names below respect the Debian package versions numbering convention[11].

Figure 3 represents the main resources produced by the PTS for a particular release of the apache2 Debian source package, as found in http://packages.qa.debian.org/a/apache2.ttl (in grey, the "upstream"-related resources).

Every source package has a corresponding *source packaging project* SoftwareProject resource, named <http://p.q.d.o/SRC-PKG-NAME#project>. The different resource URIs which will be expressed below will be fragments to this base URI. *Revisions* of this source package have corresponding SoftwareRelease resources, named as <#SRC-PKG-NAME_DEB-PKG-VERS>. Only one of these (the "latest" one known by the PTS) is fully described as containing (includedAsset) two sub SoftwareReleases :

- one sub SoftwareRelease for the *upstream program's version*, named <#upstreamsrc_UPSTR-VERS>. It comes with additional resources for all *archive files* of the upstream sources as SoftwarePackages (typically named like <#SRC-PKG-NAME_UPSTR-VERS.orig.tar.gz>);
- one for the set of *Debian packaging files*, as <#debiansrc_DEB-PKG-VERS>, with resources for all files comprising the Debian *package source archive* (typically named like <#SRC-PKG-NAME_DEB-PKG-VERS.debian.tar.gz>).
- An additional SoftwarePackage resource is generated for its SRC-PKG-NAME_UPSTR-VERS.dsc file at a URI like <#SRC-PKG-NAME_DEB-PKG-VERS.dsc>.

---

[11] As a short rule, the Debian package revision M of version N of an upstream program P is identified in file names as P_N-M.

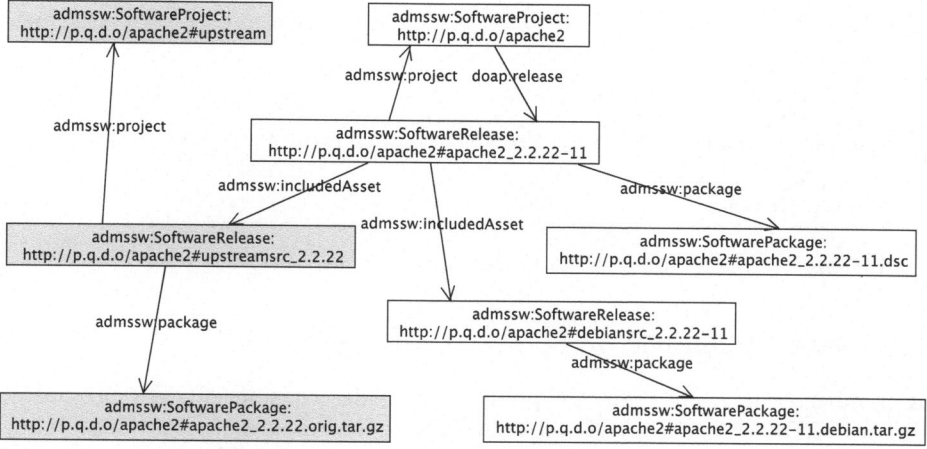

Fig. 3. Relations between resources produced for release 2.2.22-11 of the Debian `apache2` source package

Also produced is one `SoftwareProject` resource for the *upstream project*, named `<#upstream>` whith its `doap:homepage`, if it's known by the PTS (which means it has been documented by the Debian packager appropriately).

Additional complementary resources are produced, and all resources have RDF properties (as mandated in ADMS.SW, mainly reused from DOAP or Dublin Core), all of which it is useless to describe here in detail.

4.2 Deployment on debian.org

The authors have deployed the XSLT stylesheets generating these RDF documents on the PTS service of the Debian project[12]. Alongside the HTML pages of the PTS, the RDF descriptions of Debian source packages are thus refreshed every time new revisions will appear in the Debian archive.

A full RDF dump of all the meta-data is also available to Debian project members[13]. It contains around 2.1 million triples at the time of writing.

5 Complementary Efforts

In this section, we present a few complementary initiatives which describe software packages with RDF vocabularies, using DOAP or ADMS.SW and which could be interesting for interoperability with the Debian PTS.

---

[12] See : `http://packages.qa.debian.org/common/RDF.html`
[13] On `packages.qa.debian.org:/srv/packages.qa.debian.org/`
    `www/web/full-dump.rdf`

```
@prefix doap: <http://usefulinc.com/ns/doap#> .
<http://geronimo.apache.org/>
    a doap:Project .
    doap:name  "Apache Geronimo"@en  ;
    doap:shortdesc  "Java EE Application Server"@en  ;
    doap:description  "Apache Geronimo is an open source server runtime
        [...]."@en  ;
    doap:homepage <http://geronimo.apache.org>  ;
    doap:license <http://usefulinc.com/doap/licenses/asl20>  ;
```

Listing 2. Excerpt from the RDF description of the Apache geronimo project

5.1   DOAP Published by FLOSS Directories

A number of projects maintain public DOAP descriptions of their programs, or other RDF descriptions of meta-data about the releases they produce. They may be interested in complementing descriptions with ADMS.SW, or could offer sources of descriptions that could be interlinked with the ones produced by the Debian PTS.

A quick survey conducted by the authors showed the following sources[14] :

- Gnome project
- Apache project
- PyPI (Python Package Index) directory
- CPAN (Comprehensive Perl Archive Network) directory

Listing 2 shows an excerpt of the DOAP description of the Apache Geronimo project as published by this project[15], and converted to Turtle for readability.

A quick review of samples from these sources showed a lack of consensus on the use of certain meta-data, and that URIs adopted to reference the same projects or programs tend to vary, even for **doap:homepage** URLs (a great portion of these documents are manually crafted, or projects may have various pages that can be considered their *homepage*, in particular when the project is not hosted on its own top level domain).

5.2   Projects Hosted on FusionForge Forges

An ADMS.SW plugin for the FusionForge 5.2 software development forge has also been created by one of the authors[16], in order to allow the description of projects hosted on FusionForge based development forges. It may be

---

[14] These are maintained in `https://github.com/edumbill/doap/wiki/Sites`
[15] Downloaded from
    `http://svn.apache.org/repos/asf/geronimo/site/trunk/doap_Geronimo.rdf`
[16] `http://fusionforge.org/plugins/mediawiki/wiki/`
    `fusionforge/index.php/ADMS.SW_Plugin`

complemented by another FusionForge plugin providing FOAF profiles [12] for project participants, which can enrich the Linked Data representations.

The plugin is still under active development, and targetted at a post 5.2 release of FusionForge, so it will take a certain time until it is deployed on public forges hosting FLOSS projects[17].

5.3   Consuming ADMS.SW in the Joinup Portal

The *Joinup* portal[18] of the ISA programme aims at integrating in a single portal FLOSS descriptions available from different Public Administration forges, by harvesting descriptions of projects directly in their development project spaces, as ADMS.SW descriptions[19].

Whereas the current version of Joinup doesn't rely on Semantic Web techniques for collection of the projects descriptions, it is expected to be improved to evolve towards ADMS.SW consuming in the future. FLOSS Project descriptions would then complement other Semantic Assets (standards, documentation) catalogued and made available on the reference portal at Joinup as semantic assets expressed with the ADMS vocabulary.

5.4   Interlinked Developer Profiles

Project descriptions aren't the only resources that can be interlinked across the FLOSS ecosystem. Iqbal shows in [14] how developer profiles can also be converted to RDF and interlinked to create a more comprehensive view of the developer communities around a project, for instance. This approach usually involves mining repositories or social sites through custom interfaces (via SOAP for instance), and later converting to RDF. But we believe there would be a great benefit in avoiding such potentially error-prone conversions if development platforms would natively produce DOAP/ADMS.SW (or FOAF) descriptions "out of the box", as explained above.

6   Applications

As with every Linked (Open) Data initiatives, the use of standard representations and their availability on the Semantic Web can lead to lots of different uses.

An obvious case of using such ADMS.SW description of Debian source package is the *matching* of Debian packages with other packages/projects described in their respective projects directories, allowing more interlinking of resources.

---

[17] Like Debian's own Alioth forge operated by FusionForge at
     http://alioth.debian.org/
[18] http://joinup.ec.europa.eu/
[19] More details at
     https://joinup.ec.europa.eu/software/federated_forge

```
PREFIX doap: <http://usefulinc.com/ns/doap#>

SELECT * WHERE {
  GRAPH <http://packages.qa.debian.org/> {
    ?dp doap:homepage ?h
  }
  GRAPH <http://projects.apache.org/> {
    ?ap doap:homepage ?h
  }
}
```

Listing 3. SPARQL query matching Apache and Debian projects by common homepages

6.1 Matching Projects / Software across Repositories

The `doap:homepage` of the "upstream" `SoftwareProject` resources generated by the Debian PTS can be an obvious matching key, provided that one has a database of upstream project descriptions (as DOAP[7]).

As an illustration, we demonstrate this by loading DOAP descriptions of projects of the Apache foundation[20], together with a dump of the Debian source package descriptions in a single triple store (virtuoso). The example SPARQL query in Listing 3 shows how to query for such matches between Debian and Apache.

Such a query currently returns 62 matched source packages and Apache upstream projects (see an excerpt in table 1, where URLs have been compacted for brievity).

But the reliability of this matching method isn't very good in practice. There may be many more Apache foundation projects packaged in Debian, but the maintainers may have forgotten to add a homepage link in the package descriptors. Or the URLs mentioned may not be matching, as project homepage naming conventions can vary (and evolve in time).

An alternate matching method could be based on project name litterals, but that isn't always feasable either, due to homonimy for instance. One will refer to [18] for an analysis of this problem.

The *distromatch* project[21], started in 2011, intended to try and help solve these project/packages matching issues, although it is unfortunately not maintained anymore at the time of writing.

In any case, this first quick proof of concept allows us to plan further developments based on such meta-data, which will be tested on real life cases, for instance in constructing RDF harvesters and meta-data aggregators, and eventually merging with initiatives like distromatch.

---

[20] Collected from `projects.apache.org` (see
   `http://projects.apache.org/docs/index.html`)
[21] `http://www.enricozini.org/2011/debian/distromatch/`

Table 1. Matching upstream project homepages with Debian source packages'

dp	h	ap
ivy	ant.a.o/ivy/	ant.a.o/ivy/
apr	apr.a.o/	apr.a.o/
apr-util	apr.a.o/	apr.a.o/
libcommons-cli-java	commons.a.o/cli/	commons.a.o/cli/
libcommons-codec-java	commons.a.o/codec/	commons.a.o/codec/
libcommons-collections3-java	commons.a.o/collections/	commons.a.o/collections/
libcommons-collections-java	commons.a.o/collections/	commons.a.o/collections/
commons-daemon	commons.a.o/daemon/	commons.a.o/daemon/
libcommons-discovery-java	commons.a.o/discovery/	commons.a.o/discovery/
libcommons-el-java	commons.a.o/el/	commons.a.o/el/
libcommons-fileupload-java	commons.a.o/fileupload/	commons.a.o/fileupload/
commons-io	commons.a.o/io/	commons.a.o/io/
commons-jci	commons.a.o/jci/	commons.a.o/jci/
libcommons-launcher-java	commons.a.o/launcher/	commons.a.o/launcher/
. . .	. . .	. . .

6.2   Large Scale Perspective

The RDF-ization of the Debian PTS has just started. Next steps will include modelling of relations between source and binary packages. These will probably require extending ADMS.SW or integrating complementary ontologies.

When deployments of ADMS.SW have been made on software forges (like FusionForge servers), software catalogues (like Joinup) or in other FLOSS distributions, it will become one of the tools allowing automated traceability at large scale of FLOSS releases and associated artefacts, by interlinking their Linked Data resources.

Some interlinking of security advisories, patches, or bug reports (for instance combined with the OSLC-CM standard[22]) should then be easier, and diminish manual intervention needs, for the benefits of all actors along the FLOSS production chains.

6.3   Future Developments

We believe the current early result can be a driving force for more deployments around ADMS.SW as a standardization core. However there seems to be a reluctance in adopting RDF in FLOSS projects, to some extent, maybe linked to an erronous perception that RDF must be expressed as XML (which is certainly not the case, with representations of the RDF model like Turtle [1], which has been adopted as a default for the Debian PTS).

We can foresee that only when novel inter-project "killer" applications making use of such Linked Data will have been developed, will it be possible to convince FLOSS projects that adoption of Linked Data standards descriptions can really be for their own benefit.

It is likely that even when lots of Linked Data descriptions of FLOSS artifacts are made available by major FLOSS projects, achieving effective interoperability

---

[22] http://open-services.net/wiki/change-management/

will require many implementation efforts, far beyond a single actor's reach. More standardisation will be needed, and services will have to be provided to establish trusted reference catalogues of Semantic project descriptors (in the direction set by *Joinup* of the *distromatch* project for instance). Such actors would provide FLOSS "semantic hubs", or project matching "brokers" which could maintain reference interlinking relations for the concurrent Semantic descriptions which were produced in the many venues of the FLOSS ecosystem.

7   Conclusion

We have presented a first significant deployment of an ADMS.SW 1.0 implementation, which illustrates the potential for interlinking large sets of FLOSS project descriptions on the Semantic Web. ADMS.SW allows us to describe relations between projects, programs and their releases so that such entities become part of the Linked Open Data "cloud".

In [4], we envisioned some novel uses of Linked Data representations of FLOSS development artefacts, both for software engineers and researchers observing their efforts. But to achieve the full potential of that approach, the Linked Data representations must be semantically interoperable, authoritative, accurate, and using standard naming schemes for the same resources. We have achieved a first concrete step in this direction, through the current results for the Debian PTS.

The way we did it for the Debian PTS can be inspirational for other FLOSS distributions, either independant, or derived from Debian. By integrating such meta-data generation in the heart of the technical infrastructure of Debian, we hope to establish such an authoritative reference for Debian source packages identification on the Semantic Web.

References

1. Beckett, D., Berners-Lee, T.: Turtle - terse RDF triple language, W3C team submission (2008), http://www.w3.org/TeamSubmission/turtle/
2. Berger, O.: Linked data descriptions of debian source packages using ADMS.SW. In: Kendall, E.F., Pan, J.Z., Stojanovic, L., Zhao, Y. (eds.) SWESE 2012: 8th International Workshop on Semantic Web Enabled Software Engineering, Nara, Japan, pp. 43–55 (2012)
3. Berger, O., Labbene, S., Dhar, M., Bac, C.: Introducing OSLC, an open standard for interoperability of open source development tools. In: ICSSEA, Paris, France (2011) ISSN–0295–6322
4. Berger, O., Vlasceanu, I.V., Bac, C., Dang, Q.V., Lauriere, S.: Weaving a semantic web across OSS repositories: Unleashing a new potential for academia and practice. International Journal of Open Source Software and Processes (IJOSSP) 2(2), 29–40 (2010)
5. Bizer, C., Heath, T., Berners-Lee, T.: Linked Data - The Story So Far. International Journal on Semantic Web and Information Systems (IJSWIS) 5(3), 1–22 (2009)
6. Gabriella Coleman, E.: Coding Freedom: The Ethics and Aesthetics of Hacking. Princeton University Press (2012)

7. Dumbill, E.: Decentralizing software project registries with DOAP. In: Intelligent Search on XML Data - XML (2004)
8. *unspecified authors.* ISO/IEC 19770-2: Software identification tag standard
9. *unspecified authors.* Software Package Data eXchange specification (2011)
10. *unspecified authors.* Asset Description Metadata Schema specification 1.00 (2012)
11. Gonzalez-Barahona, J.M., Robles, G., Michlmayr, M., Amor, J.J., German, D.M.: Macro-level software evolution: a case study of a large software compilation. Empirical Software Engineering 14(3), 262–285 (2009)
12. Graves, M., Constabaris, A., Brickley, D.: FOAF: Connecting People on the Semantic Web. Cataloging & Classification Quarterly 43(3), 191–202 (2007)
13. Howison, J.: Cross-repository data linking with RDF and OWL: Towards common ontologies for representing FLOSS data. In: WoPDaSD (Workshop on Public Data at International Conference on Open Source Software) (2008)
14. Iqbal, A., Hausenblas, M.: Integrating developer-related information across open source repositories. In: 2012 IEEE 13th International Conference on Information Reuse and Integration (IRI), pp. 69–76 (August 2012)
15. Jackson, I., Schwarz, C., et al.: Debian policy manual. version 3.9.4.0 (September 19, 2012), http://www.debian.org/doc/debian-policy/
16. Lassila, O., Swick, R.R., World Wide Web Consortium: Resource description framework (RDF) model and syntax specification. W3C Recommendation (1998)
17. Michlmayr, M.: Managing debian. AUUGN, The Journal of AUUG Inc. 25(3), 9 (2004)
18. Squire, M.: Integrating projects from multiple open source code forges. IJOSSP 1(1), 46–57 (2009)
19. Weibel, S.L., Kunze, J.A., Lagoze, C., Wolf, M.: Dublin core metadata for resource discovery. RFC 2413 (1998)

An Open Source Monitoring Framework
for Enterprise SOA

Nabil El Ioini[1], Alessandro Garibbo[2], Alberto Sillitti[1], and Giancarlo Succi[1]

[1] Free University of Bolzano, Italy
[2] Selex-ES, Italy
{nelioini,asillitti,gsucci}@unibz.it,
alessandro.garibbo@selex-es.com

Abstract. Web services monitoring is currently emerging as an effective way to trace faults in services at runtime. The lack of testing information provided by web services specifications was an indication that other methods need to be used to assess the quality of web services. This is mainly due to the fact that it is difficult to simulate the client infrastructure during testing of web services. Monitoring consists of inspecting services at runtime and taking adequate actions when unacceptable events occur. Monitoring could be performed by different stakeholders and could target different properties of services. Predominantly, monitoring is performed by service providers to manage their internal resources and balance their requests load. In our effort to improve the monitoring infrastructures, we propose a monitoring framework in which all the participants (services providers, services requestors) can contribute to monitoring and at the same time have direct access to the monitoring data. This paper describes a monitoring framework developed as part of NEXOF-RA[1] project. The framework offers a set of capabilities for a collaborative monitoring of web services. The paper presents motivations, system design, implementation and usage of the framework.

1 Introduction

To address the business needs of today's organizations, Web Services (WS) emerge as an enabling technology that allows building flexible systems that integrate multiple pieces of software into one system [12]. Contrary to traditional software development paradigms, where software vendors have to agree on the communication protocols and the interfaces to use, web services improve the collaboration of different software vendors to build the final product by using standardized protocols and interfaces. Nowadays, the effort to push the adoption of web services is twofold. From one side research communities and companies support WS by providing tools that help develop and manipulate web services, and on the other side standardization bodies supply standards to regulate the use of WS [6][7][8][13].

The concept of trust in the domain of services is an important issue, since many services are bound at run time, and the correct behavior of the services is not known a

---

[1] NEXOF-RA project http://www.nexof-ra.eu/

E. Petrinja et al. (Eds.): OSS 2013, IFIP AICT 404, pp. 182–193, 2013.

priori [9]. Being able to give high confidence about the behavior and the quality of a service at run-time can have a great influence on service compositions.

A big challenge with WS is how to trust the claims of services' providers about the quality of their services [14]. In web services, we delegate part of our business logic to an external provider to do it for us. Thus, we have no control of what could happen during the execution of that part of the business logic. One solution to increase customers' trust in the provided services is to provide a monitoring framework where all the stakeholders that take part of a SOA infrastructure are involved in the monitoring process. This way all the stakeholders can collect and use the monitoring data to make decisions about which services to use.

The contribution of this work is twofold. First we are providing a monitoring framework in which the stakeholders have the possibility to specify their monitoring requirements and have access at runtime to the collected data, however, this requires them to adhere to certain practices and collaborate to monitor the used WS. The second contribution is that we are combining the monitoring from the service requestor and service provider point of views. This is done by collecting data from both sides and allow both parties to make use of the data collected by the other party.

The rest of the paper is organized as follows. In section 2 we presented the related work. Section 3 presents an overview of the system architecture. Section 4 discusses the implementation details. Section 5 and 6 show a demonstration scenario and experiments and section 7 concludes and presents future work.

2   Related Work

Existing monitoring techniques differ in many aspects. The main properties that distinguish them from each other are the stakeholders involved, data collection techniques, the degree of invasiveness and the monitoring requirement specification. The spectrum of approaches proposed in the literature spreads along all these dimensions, however, not all the approaches take in consideration all the dimensions.

In the literature many approaches resemble to ours such as SCALEA-G [10], which is a unified monitoring and performance analysis tool for the grid. SCALEA-G uses a different architecture but has similar functionality. IBM Tivoli [11] uses a special integration bus to collect monitoring data so that all the messages passing through the bus are captured. In [4, 5] an approach for monitoring BEPL workflows is presented. A central execution engine intercepts all the passing events and stores them in an event dataset. The probes to be monitored are defined using event calculus.

The main difference between these approaches and ours is that we are providing an approach conformant to a bigger infrastructure, which is the NEXOF-RA. Although the techniques we used might not be new but our goal is to have a framework compatible with the goal of NEXOF-RA, which is establishing strategies and policies to improve delivery of applications and enabling the creation of service based ecosystems where service providers, service requestors and third parties easily collaborate.

3   System Overview

Traditionally system verification and validation (V&V) is a pre-deployment exercise designed to assess the capabilities of systems before putting them into production. In the paradigm of WS and SOA based systems [9], the dynamic nature of these systems requires the extension of the V&V setting to include run-time quality assessment that cannot be applied before deployment.

To ensure the quality of Web Services, we propose a monitoring framework that enables runtime data collection to automatically identify anomalous events defined by any of the stakeholders, aggregates related events and presents data to the interested parties with different levels of granularities.

The framework adopts a proxy-based strategy to collect monitoring data (Figure 1), where each participant in the interaction needs to use a proxy that allows the interception of the messages coming in and out. The framework relies on different receptors implemented inside the proxies to filter out the events of interest and report them to the monitoring server.

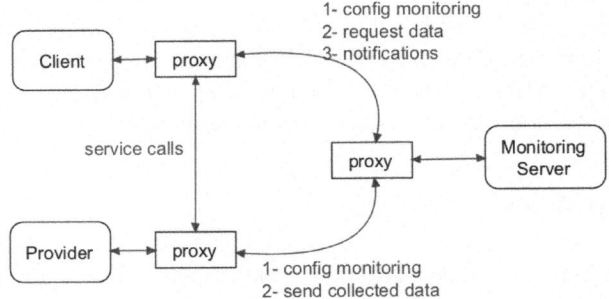

Fig. 1. Proxies for data collection

The framework provides an environment where registered services can be monitored automatically and according to users requirements. The monitoring model is described in the NEXOF-RA Monitoring SOA Enterprise pattern [2]. The main idea of the model is allowing all authorized users to perform two types of monitoring options: push and pull. The push monitoring allows users to register the events of interest to be monitored; if those events occur, all the registered users are notified. The pull monitoring instead, allows authorized users to request log data concerning a specific service.

3.1   Design Choices

The design choices have been shaped to satisfy the requirements defined by the ESOA pattern [2]. Four attributes were given priority.

1. Maintainability: in an infrastructure that meant to be used in a SOA environment, maintainability is an important factor due the size and complexity of the interacting systems. By decomposing the framework into sub-components, maintainability becomes easier [15]. Each of the

sub-components is responsible for a precise set of operations, which are exposed as interfaces to communicate with the rest of the framework. The framework itself looks as a component (a service) from outside, and it communicates with the other components (e.g. proxies collecting data) through a set of pre-defined interfaces (Web Services calls). Therefore, any part of the framework could be updated or modified without affecting the rest of the sub-components.

2. Availability: In a SOA environment, it is critical to understand the availability of the services, mainly because the usual everyday operations may depend on services, which for some reason could be unavailable at some time slots. To this end, the framework needs to be able to monitor all the services that take part of the ESOA environment including the framework itself. As we mentioned before, the framework is built as a set of services, and this allows the framework to monitor its availability.

3. Performance: A drawback of the framework in terms of performance is the overhead generated by the proxies. We have decided to use a proxy-based architecture for collecting data. However, before doing that we have considered other options mainly:

    a.   Monitoring aware middleware [1], relying on a collecting data from interceptors implemented as part of the middleware. This technique has the advantage of being able to monitor detailed information about the services e.g. resources usage, since the interceptors are part of the infrastructure in which services are deployed. However, it imposes a limitation in that it requires all the participants to use the same middleware, in case their existing middleware does not have the monitoring capability, which could have a high cost.

    b.   Central proxy server relying on a central proxy, which can be used by all the participants. This technique represents several challenges. The first one is that it cannot capture precise information about the quality of service. For example, the response time that is captured by the proxy will represent the response time from the proxy to the service and not from the client to the service. The second challenge is that internal quality attributes of the services cannot be captured such as the time needed by the service to process the request internally. For this reason we have decided to choose a proxy-based approach, which does not require the participants to alter their environments as well as it has access to more accurate information, since the proxy is considered to be part of the participants' infrastructures. Of course, there is a cost to pay in terms of the overhead generated by the proxy, however, compared to the advantages we gain, we consider it to be acceptable. Furthermore, the framework offers two strategies for monitoring to deal with how much overhead is generated. The push approach requires much more overhead since each component is required to actively report any event of interest to a specific client. For example, a client requirement might be to be notified if the throughput of the monitored service exceeds 5 ms. In this case the services actively filter out all the incoming requests and in case of an event that exceeds 5 ms, it needs to report it to the monitoring server. The second approach is called the pull approach, and this is a more relaxed approach, in which the service collects the data locally and it is the monitoring server that asks for it when needed.

4. Adaptability: By having a well defined interfaces and separation of concerns, the framework could be adapted and reused in different contexts. Our framework is used to monitor Web Services, however, other types of systems could be used as well. For example, the proxies can be adapted to monitor different types of components instead of Web Services, and communicate the monitored data to the monitoring server.

4   Implementation

The framework architecture features two main components, namely, the monitoring server and the monitoring proxy (Figure 2). The monitoring server provides facilities to store the collected data and serve it to the users when they need it. It also handles notifing the users in case of anomalous events. The current implementation of the monitoring server is done as a web application, and all the interactions with the outside components are done through web services. The monitoring proxy is a Java application that is used by all the participants of the monitored environment. We have extended an existing open source project called membrane router[2] as the monitoring proxy.

4.1   Monitoring Server

It is the central component of the monitoring server. It is implemented as a J2EE application running on top of Apache Tomcat container. The monitoring server offers four operations and requires four operations from the components that need to be monitored.

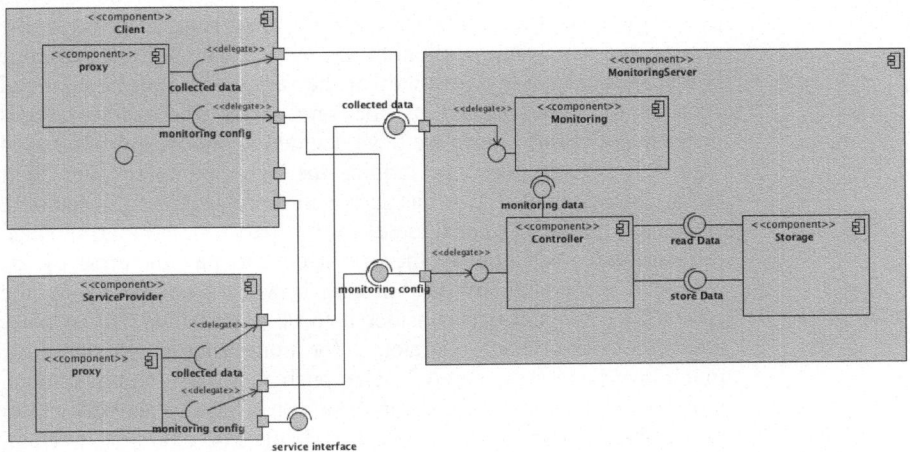

Fig. 2. Architecture overview

---

[2] Membrane Router, http://www.membrane-soa.org/soap-router-doc

- Required operations:
  - ConfigureMonitroingPolicy: sets the monitored component configuration policy such as time slot before sending data to the server;
  - GetLoggedData: pulls all the data from monitored component;
  - IsAuthorized: requests the monitored component if the user who is trying to access monitoring data has authorization to do so;
  - SubscribeEvent: subscribes a new event to be monitored;
  - NotifyEvent: notifies the users who have subscribed to the different events.
- Offered operations:
  - ConfigureMonitringPolicy: enables the users of the monitoring server to set their policy preferences;
  - GetMonitoringData: provides the user with the possibility to pull the monitoring data from the server;
  - SubscribeEvent: allows to specify the events they are interested in;
  - notifyEvent: allows every user (customers and providers) to send a notification to the monitoring server using this interface.

4.2   Monitoring Proxy

The role of the proxy is to collect data from the different participants including service providers, service users and the monitoring server. The data is sent to the monitoring server for storage and analysis. In the current implementation we are using membrane router as the monitoring proxy.

Membrane router is composed of three main parts: 1) the EndpointListener, which waits for the incoming messages 2) the EndpointSender, which sends the messages to their destination and 3) a set of interceptors in between the two end points. The part that we are mostly interested in is the interceptors. In the current implementation we have two interceptors to capture response time and throughput (Figure 3).

The interceptors implement two functionalities:

1. Intercept input messages: this function captures the input messages and adds new headers to them such as the sender id and timestamp
2. Intercept output messages: when a message passes through the router and is processed by the service provider, the provider sends back the response. The response message is captured again and, the headers that have been set in the input message are checked. A practical example that we have used is to calculate the throughput by checking the time elapsed between receiving the input message and receiving the output message.

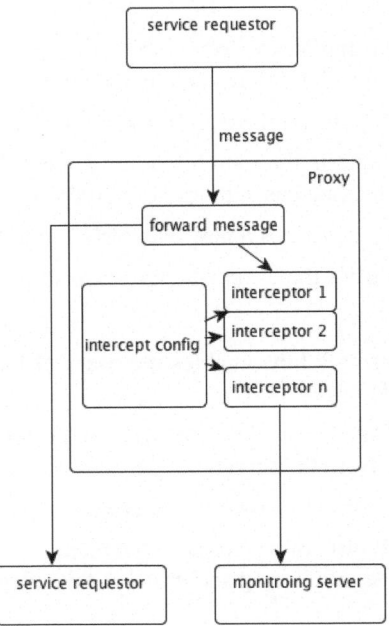

Fig. 3. The proxy architecture

4.3   Data Collection

As we mentioned before the monitoring framework offers two monitoring strategies with a different level of invasiveness and time to react to the events recorded.

The push approach is a timely monitoring strategy, which relies on external data source about the data to collect. The external data source is the set of configurations submitted by the stakeholders interested in monitoring the service. These configurations take the form of a simple triple of the form:

<Property, condition, value>

The property refers to the property to monitor such as response time, throughput, the condition are Boolean expressions (e.g. >, <, =). In the current implementation the Boolean expressions are used to compare the monitored values against. However, to avoid imposing on any specific format for defining the monitoring requirements, it is up to the interceptors' developers to decide how their interceptors receive the monitoring requirements.

The degree of invasiveness has a great impact on the quality of the collected data. The more invasive the technique is, the more data can be collected. Our current implementation is limited in this side, because everything that we collect starts when the service requestor or provider submit the request/response to the proxy. So everything that happens before that such as the internal state of services is not captured. This limitation can be addressed by increasing the level of invasiveness such as the case of [13], but a tradeoff needs to be made between the data collected and the implementation cost.

5   Demonstration Scenario

Several scenarios have been considered and tested. In this demonstration, we focus on the two monitoring strategies, namely, the push and the pull. To use the framework some assumptions are needed. We assume that every participant has built the interfaces required to interact with the monitoring server. We also assume that all the participants have deployed the monitoring proxy in their environments.

In the pull strategy, the process is initiated by a user or a group of users setting their configuration policy for some specific service. Once this is done, the monitored service starts collecting the required events. At any point of time, users who have registered to that specific service can make an implicit call asking the monitoring server to pull the data that has been collected so far. This approach has the advantage of instantly showing how the service is performing. Figure 4 presents a sequence diagram of this approach.

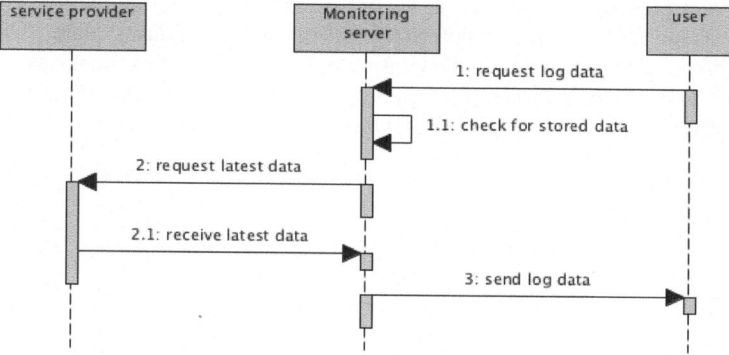

Fig. 4. The pull approach

The push approach on the other hand is initiated by the user registering to a specific event. The monitoring server forwards the registration to the service of interest. The service keeps track of all the users and their events of interest, and once the event occurs, the monitoring server is asked by the service to notify the respective users. The monitoring server is then responsible for notifying the users. The sequence diagram in Figure 5 shows the sequence of activities of the push approach.

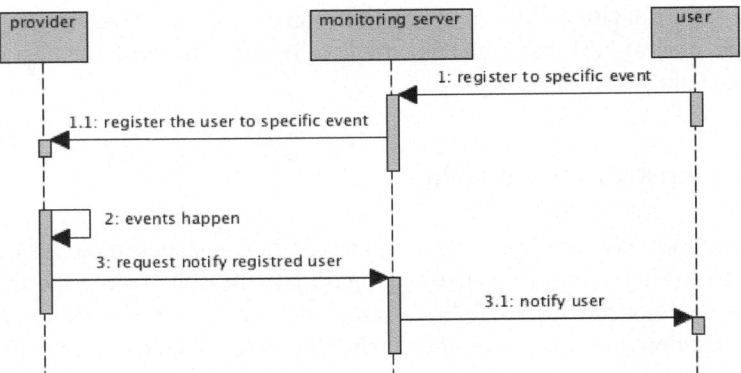

Fig. 5. The push approach

6   Experiments

Starting from the scenarios above we have performed different tests to show how the framework could be used in practice. We have setup a testing environment as shown in Figure 6.

The testing environment is composed of the monitoring server, a service requestor and a service provider. As shown in Figure 6, each one of components has a proxy deployed as part of its infrastructure to collect the monitoring data. The service provider is a web application serving simple web services such as arithmetic operations. The service requestor is a web service-testing tool called SoapUI[3]. SoapUI allows generating SOAP requests to make use of the services exposed by the service

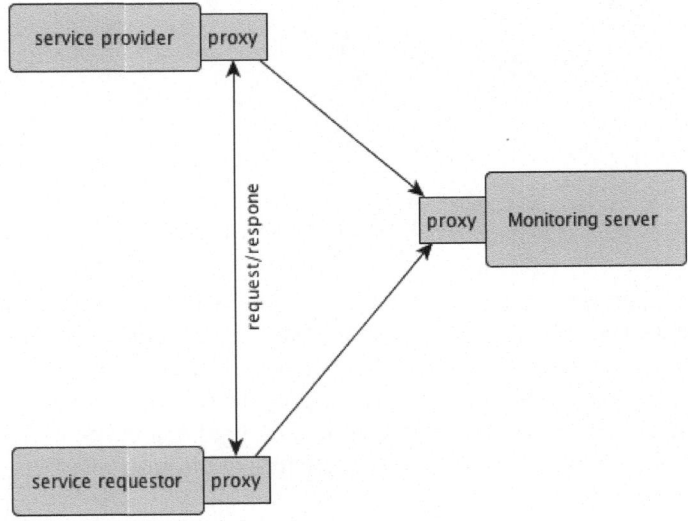

Fig. 6. Testing environment

---

[3] http://www.soapui.org/

provider. The monitoring server uses also a proxy to capture all the requests and responses of the monitoring server. This allows the activities of the server to be monitored also.

In our testing we have primarily focused on the two monitoring strategies, the push and the pull. However, other types of tests were explored. In the following the tests and their results are presented in Table I

Test	Description	Result
Push	The service requestor registers a new event "response time > 5 ms". This means that if the service response time is greater than 5 ms, the service requestor wants to be notified. The monitoring server forwards this information to the service provider proxy to add it to the list of properties to monitor. For testing purposes we have implemented a simple service which takes an integer value as parameter and use it to delay the service response time, for instance if we pass as parameter number 5 the service will have 5 ms as response time. Using SoapUI we have generated 10 SOAP calls with different response times.	The service requestor has been notified every time a request violates the condition specified. The notification was sent by e-mail.
Pull S1	The service requestor can request at anytime the monitoring data collected so far by the proxies. Using SoapUI we generate 10 random requests to the service. On the monitoring server side the database is still empty. The service requestor calls the getMonitoringData service of the monitoring server.	The monitoring server checks its local database, but since no data is available, it requests the data from the proxy. The proxy returns 10 events, which are forwarded to the service requestor and also stored in the database.
Pull S1	We performed the same scenario as S1 but this time we have some existing data in the monitoring server database.	The monitoring server sends back the existing data in the database. Additionally, it sends also the newly collected data by the proxy.
Availability	Once the configuration is set. We shutdown the service provider service.	The provider proxy could not receive any response from the service, so it notifies the monitoring server, which notifies the service requestor.
Overhead	Compare the response time of services with and without proxies. 1000 requests have been sent by the service requestor with and without the proxies	Without the proxies the average response time was 0.12 ms while the ones with the proxies was 0.16 ms.

7   Conclusions

In this paper, we have presented a comprehensive framework for simplifying services monitoring. Our framework adopts the model proposed in the NEXOF-RA Monitoring SOA Enterprise Pattern, which defines the architecture of the monitoring components. The framework has been implemented by integrating different open source components and techniques to increase the level of functionality to the final user. The main advantage of the framework is that it has been implemented as a set of services, which gives it the ability to monitor itself. We have tried to be less invasive as possible to avoid adding extra costs for existing infrastructures. However, this limits the number of events we can monitor. For the future we are working to add more interceptors to the proxies to collect more information. The current implementation is a prototype that we have used to test the different components. The next step we are considering is to perform a larger case study in which real services infrastructures will be used to study the effect of the monitoring on the relations between service requestors and service providers.

References

1. Zheng, Z., Lyu, M.R.: A qos-aware middleware for fault tolerant web services. In: ISSRE, Seattle, USA, pp. 97–106 (2008)
2. Monitoring in Enterprise SOA pattern, http://www.nexof-ra.eu/sites/default/files/Monitoring%20in%20ESOA%20Pattern_v0_7.pdf
3. Baresi, L., Nitto, E.D.: Test and Analysis of Web Services. Springer-Verlag New York, Inc., Secaucus (2007)
4. Mahbub, K., Spanoudakis, G.: A Framework for Requirements Monitoring of Service Based Systems. In: Int. Conf. on Service-Oriented Computing (ICSOC) (2004)
5. Mahbub, K., Spanoudakis, G.: Run-Time Monitoring of Requirements for Systems Composed of Web-Services: Initial Implementation and Evaluation Experience. In: Int. Conf. on Web Services (ICWS) (2005)
6. Web Services Description Language (WSDL 1.1). W3C Note (March 15, 2001), http://www.w3.org/TR/WSDL/
7. Simple Object Access Protocol (SOAP 1.2), W3C Recommendation (April 27, 2008), http://www.w3.org/TR/soap12
8. Di Penta, M., Bastida, L., Sillitti, A., Baresi, L., Maiden, N., Melideo, M., Tilly, M., Spanoudakis, G., Gorroñogoitia Cruz, J., Hutchinson, J., Ripa, G.: SeCSE - Service-centric System Engineering: An Overview. In: Di Nitto, E., Sassen, A.M., Traverso, P., Zwegers, A. (eds.) At Your Service. MIT Press (2009)
9. Damiani, E., El Ioini, N., Sillitti, A., Succi, G.: WS-Certificate. In: IEEE International Workshop on Web Services Security Management (WSSM 2009), Los Angeles, CA, USA (2009)
10. Truong, H.L., Fahringer, T.: SCALEA-G: a Unified Monitoring and Performance Analysis System for the Grid. Scientific Programming 12(4), 225–237 (2004); axGrids 2004 Special Issue
11. IBM Tivoli Composite Application Manager for SOA (2006)

12. Predonzani, P., Sillitti, A.: Components and data-flow applied to the integration of web services. Electronics Society (2001)
13. Petrinja, E., Nambakam, R., Sillitti, A.: Introducing the OpenSource Maturity Model. In: Proceedings of the 2009 ICSE Workshop on Emerging Trends in Free/Libre/Open Source Software Research and Development (FLOSS 2009). IEEE Computer Society, Washington, DC (2009)
14. El Ioini, N., Sillitti, A.: Open Web Services Testing. In: IEEE World Congress on Services (SERVICES), DC, USA (2011)
15. Clark, J., Clarke, C., Panfilis, S.D., Granatella, G., Predonzani, P., Sillitti, A., Succi, G., Vernazza, T.: Selecting components in large COTS repositories. J. Syst. Softw. 73, 323–331 (2004)

Information Security and Open Source Dual Use Security Software: Trust Paradox

Mario Silic and Andrea Back

Institute of Information Management (IWI), University of St. Gallen, Switzerland

Abstract. Nmap, free open source utility for network exploration or security auditing, today counts for thirteen million lines of code representing four thousand years of programming effort[1]. Hackers can use it to conduct illegal activities, and information security professionals can use it to safeguard their network. In this dual-use context, question of trust is raised. Can we trust programmers developing open source dual use security software? Motivated by this research question, we conducted interviews among hackers and information security professionals, and explored ohloh.net database. Our results show that contributors behind open source security software (OSSS) are hackers, OSSS have important dual-use dimension, information security professionals generally trust OSSS, and large organizations will avoid adopting and using OSSS.

Keywords: information security, dual-use technology, open source security software, FLOSS, trust, hacker, Nmap, ohloh.net.

1   Introduction

"Why would thousands of top-notch software developers contribute for free to the creation of a public good?" was a question asked by Lerner and Tirole (2002).

Ten years later, interest for open source software (OSS) development and community collaboration has been taken to another level. Some popular community collaboration web sites, such as SourceForge[2], have over three hundred thousand available projects[3] with over three million developers participating and contributing to this open source community. Moreover, we saw an uptick in the number of companies, creators of some popular closed source software, being involved in OSS. One example is IBM's contribution to Eclipse with over twelve million lines of code[4].

As we saw the phenomenon behind OSS growing, in parallel, the corresponding research was giving more attention to producing important studies. With the rise of the OSS 'movement' (DiBona et al., 1999; Markus et al., 2000; O'Reilly, 2000), different studies saw OSS teams as virtual organizations (Crowston and Scozzi 2002;

---

[1] https://www.ohloh.net/p/nmap
[2] http://sourceforge.net
[3] http://sourceforge.net/about
[4] http://dash.eclipse.org/dash/commits/web-app/
  commit-count-loc.php?sortBy=loc&show=

E. Petrinja et al. (Eds.): OSS 2013, IFIP AICT 404, pp. 194–206, 2013.

Gallivan 2001; Malone and Laubacher 1998; Markus et al. 2000). As such, participants of these organizations are providing their work without financial remuneration or any special interest. Question that many researchers asked is why? Why do developers contribute (Hars and Ou 2002; Lakhani et al. 2003).

Top programmers associated to open source movement are often coming from hacking milieu, and one of the first well-known examples is Linux. Open source software project created by Linus Torvalds, software engineer and hacker, who started the project in 1991 being single contributor. Few years later, Linux project attracted several thousand programmers (Moon and Sproull, 2002) to produce today's one of the most known open source software.

Number of open source projects (e.g. Nmap security scanner) are dealing with information security where their dual use raises trust and security concerns.

On the one side, Black hat hackers can use it to conduct illegal activities against target networks, while on the other side, information security professionals can use it to safeguard their network by discovering security issues and potential threats. In this dual-use context, question of trust is raised. Current research did not explore the link between trust and dual-use context of the OSSS, and we aim to close the existing research gap by exploring the following questions:

Who are the programmers behind open source security software?

Can we trust programmers developing open source dual use security software?

To answer these questions, we will conduct qualitative interviews with fourteen information security professionals who use Nmap OSSS.

We proceed as follows. Firstly, we explore the literature on open source software, dual-use technology and trust theory. Secondly, we present the research methodology outlining data collection and analysis. Thirdly, we discuss the findings of the study. Finally, we conclude by providing some directions for future research, implications for practice, and highlighting limitations of this study.

2   Literature Review

In 1998, Bruce Perens and Eric Raymond, together with other hackers created the "open source" movement (Perens, 1998). The open source movement creations that followed produced a number of open source software with an ever increasing number of contributors. For Linus Torvalds, creator of infamous Linux kernel, the motivation behind it was that it was just "natural within the community" (Torvalds, 1998) or it was "fun to program" (Torvalds and Diamond, 2001). Today's evolution of open source software brought a number of applications in different areas and there is almost no closed software that does not have an equivalent in the open source milieu. One such area relates to information security where different open source security tools appeared. Question of trust is raised as these open source security tools having dual-use behaviour could have potentially undesired consequences on the security of the information system. In the next sections we will discuss open source and information security literature to finish with trust question.

It is also important to define what "hacker" term means. Unfortunately, there is still no consensus among scholars on the final definition as two opposite definitions are today widely used. One definition speaks of an unorthodox, highly talented professional programmer having deep knowledge and understanding of computers. Another definition refers to one who obtains unauthorized, illegal, access to computers. Recently, we saw clearer separation among different hacker subcultures (White hat, Black hat, Grey hat, Blue hat, Neophyte, Script kiddie, Hacktivist, Elite hacker), but in this study, we keep generic "hacker" definition provided above where we see a hacker as a highly talented programmer that can, eventually, conduct some illegal activities.

2.1   Open Source Dual Use and Information Security

Open source software (OSS) phenomena were widely studied in past years. Research mostly focused on incentives and motivations related to career concerns and peer recognition (Lerner et al. 2002, Hann et al. 2004), learning and enjoyment (Lakhani et al., 2002), and private reputations playing a significant role (Lerner and Tirole, 2000). Virtual organizations and teams where members are working in different countries and using collaboration tools to contribute to the open source appeared as an important research area (Hertel, 2002; Hertel et al., 2002).

Intrinsic and extrinsic motivations were studied in a number of empirical studies showing why OSS developers contribute to OSS development (Hars and Ou 2002; Lakhani and Wolf 2005; Roberts et al. 2006; Wu et al. 2007).

From the extrinsic motivation factors, one is related to the "own-use" value, which refers to "internalized extrinsic motives to create OSS for contributors' personal use" (von Krogh et al., 2012). This own-use value is guiding developers to fix bugs and add features they need. This personal use can lead to possible modifications of the source code which could be difficult to identify in millions of lines of code. An open door for possible malicious programming code inside of the OSSS could be opened. Dual-use question and trust in this coding paradigm can be raised.

Dual-use technology (Evans and Hays, 2006) is a term referring to a technology that has two faces: one that can be used for peaceful aims and one that can be used for military aims. One example is Global Positioning System (GPS), originally used for military use, while today it is widely spread in different end user applications in end user aims. According to Eriksson (1999), any action that will try to prohibit the means of information warfare altogether or restricting their availability - are largely impossible due to the ubiquity and dual-use nature of information technology. Reppy (2012) argues that the dual-use nature of cyber technology along with its status as a quasi-public good defines both the source of the benefits of the technology and the limits to government control.

OSSS represents a good example of the dual-use where a number of unanswered and controversial questions arise. Controversies have two sides: on one side, the question can be asked who are the end users of this potentially dangerous security software? Hackers? Information security professionals? On the other side: can you trust these tools if you are using them for peaceful aims?

OSSS can be used by attackers to perform illegal activities by exploiting vulnerabilities identified on the remote systems (Cavusoglu et al. 2007; Cavusoglu et al. 2008) representing the negative side of the use. The positive side would be used to proactively monitor and safeguard network.

This opens a question of trust. Can information security professionals trust software developed mostly by hackers, which at the end are using these same tools to add features they need. This "add features they need" represents an important own-use value factor where past studies showed that developers develop open source software they find useful by adding features they need (Lakhani and von Hippel (2003), Osterloh and Rota (2007), and Raymond (1999)).

2.2   Trust and OSS

McAllister (1995) defines trust as "the extent to which a person is confident in and willing to act on the basis of, the words, actions, and decisions of another". Later, Jarvenpaa generalized this definition to the team level (Jarvenpaa et al. 1998) and this is very valid for OSS teams as what one OSS team member provides as an output from his participation will depend on the efforts and contributions of other team members. Some previous studies showed strong link between trust and project participation decrease (Jarvenpaa and Leidner 1999) followed by important number of changes in project members structure (von Krogh et al. 2003).

For McAllister (1995), affective and cognitive parts of trust are very important. Affective trust is about emotional attachment between two sides: trustor and trust target. Stewart and Gosain (2006) pointed that affective trust can be "relevant to potential developers' psychological and emotional reasons for joining, staying with and contributing to OSS teams". On the other side, cognitive trust specifies rational assessment of the target by the trustor (McAllister, 1995) where utility and reputation motivations appear as key components which lead programmers' project participation.

Gallivan (2001) explored OSS project participants (core developers, peripheral developers and message posters) identifying different types of trust occurring in the relationships between them. Figure 1. shows these three major groups and trust relationships assumed to be reciprocal. Gallivan (2001) also argues that "the OSS movement appears to rely on explicit forms of control to a much greater degree than on trust" which can be explained either by the fact that trust is probably implicit and unacknowledged in the OSS project lifecycle or it can also be that OSS projects avoid to rely on trust as it could make them vulnerable to members' illegal activities.

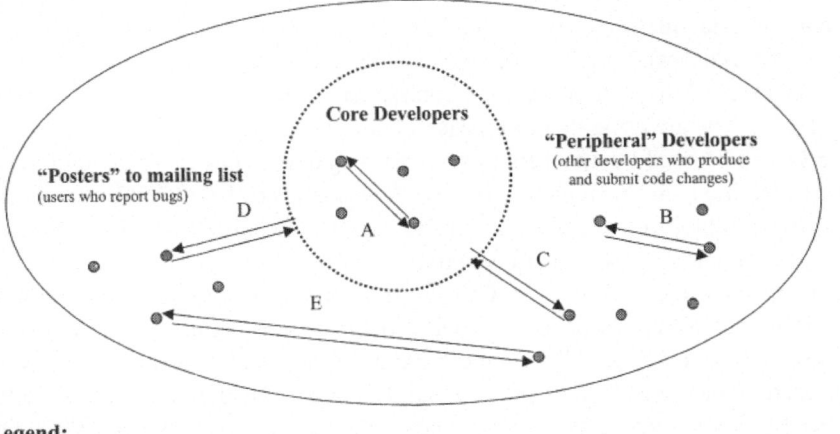

Legend:

A: Trust between Core Developers
B: Trust between Peripheral Developers
C: Trust of Peripheral Developers in Core Developer Group

D: Trust of "Posters" in Core Developer Group
E: Trust between "Posters" and Peripheral Developers

Fig. 1. Structural patterns of trust in open source software projects (Gallivan, 2001)

3   Research Methodology

Our research used ethnographic approach and observations to answer the first research question related to programmers' profiles behind OSSS combined with qualitative interviews and to answer the question related to trust paradox qualitative method was used. In the next sections, we introduce the research setting and explain qualitative and observation approaches used in the paper.

3.1   Research Setting

To investigate our research question we will use open source security tool Nmap, which is a free network security open source scanner. Nmap was created in 1998 by Gordon Lyon who is network security expert, open source programmer, writer, and a hacker. It is used for network scanning and security audits. It is one of the most popular open source security tools. It was also used in popular "The Matrix Reloaded" movie. Reason for Nmap choice is because it is very popular among information security professionals, but it has also wide usage within computer underground community. It also appeared as a good research tool already used in academia (see e.g. Haines et al. 2003). Nmap, being one of the most popular OSSS, is used to set the stage for all interviews and guide all discussions.

To answer the question related to developers behind OSSS, we used observations and qualitative interviews. We analyzed ohloh.net database, large online OSS community with important number of open source projects, of Nmap programmers and randomly identified twenty project contributors. Using internet and Google search tools, we explored profiles of each of the twenty contributors.

3.2   Nmap Security Scanner

Nmap was published in 1997 in famous Phrack (www.phrack.com), an underground magazine with full source code included. Since then, with the help of the computer security community and security enthusiasts, its development continued at an ever increasing pace. Its main purpose is to discover computers and services on the target network. Nmap is an example of the dual-use tool which can be used by hackers in gaining access to unauthorized systems and performing illegal actions. Its typical usage is to discover vulnerabilities on the remote system so they can be exploited by the attacker. On the other side, information security professionals use Nmap to better understand their network, discover potential security issues, and check for eventual vulnerabilities in order to protect their network.

3.3   ohloh.net OSS Community

With its Web 2.0 based application programming interface (API) (Allen et al. 2009) it represents a large OSS community indexing open source software. With over 500,000 OSS, it connects 1.8 million contributors. Ohloh is not a forge (e.g. sourceforge.net). It does not host projects and code, but it connects to project source code repositories and provides analytics insights about project contributors, activity, demographics and code composition.

As explained in the research setting, we use ohloh.net database to identify Nmap contributors in order to explore their profiles and see if programmers belong to hacking milieu.

3.4   Data Collection and Analysis

We gathered data through two different methods. First, we conducted fourteen semi structured interviews between November and December 2012. Second, we used ohloh.net website to complete our first insights on programmers' profiles behind Nmap OSSS. Interviews lasted between 25 to 35 minutes long (on average 28 minutes), totaling 38 pages of transcribed text. Interviewees were chosen from two different categories: information security professional (six interviewees) and programmers (eight interviewees) from different organizations: security companies (36%), large firms (36%), medium size firms (14%), independent experts (14%). Some of the questions we used to conduct interviews were: "In your opinion who are programmers behind open source software?", "How do you see the relationship between trust and open source security tools?", "Did you ever use Nmap to conduct illegal activities?" and "Can programmers inject some malicious code into open source security tools?"

Extracted data from ohloh.net was used to confirm insights from interviews, and after identifying randomly selected twenty contributors from Nmap (https://www.ohloh.net/p/nmap/contributors), we explored their profiles to understand if contributors were hackers. We used observations to identify which contributors described them as being hackers.

We used NVivo software program (version 10) to code the interviews and used exploratory analysis as suggested by Creswell (2002). Data was analyzed and we identified and highlighted different ideas to get some first insights from interviews. Next, we coded different patterns, data, phrases and words and grouped them into defined categories and themes. In this preliminary analysis, two main themes emerged that we further analyzed and discussed in the next sections.

4   Findings

In this section we will explore the findings related to our research questions about programmers' profiles behind OSSS and if we can trust these programmers developing OSSS.

Overall, our findings supported by interviews and data observed from ohloh.net website showed that: 1) Programmers developing open source security tools have important hacking background; 2) Open source security tools have important dual use; 3) Information security professionals generally trust open source security tools and, 4) Large organizations do not trust open source security tools.

To preserve interviewee's anonymity we will proceed as follows: to each interview we will add "INT" with corresponding number between 1 and 14 identifying the interview. For instance, "INT2" will correspond to Interview 2.

4.1   Contributors to Open Source Security Tools Are Hackers

Project members have usually great programming skills and are code addicted. They usually create and code for fun. Interviews and observations of ohloh.net Nmap participants revealed that contributors to open source security tools are hackers. Out of eight programmers we interviewed, seven confirmed that majority of contributors consider themselves as hackers. For one interviewee (INT 3) there is a natural link between being hacker and contributor: "...well, I think you cannot dissociate hacker subculture and the fact you want to create...hacker by its definition is someone who needs to be seen and heard...in that context, we contribute...". For another one (INT2) hackers are at the origin of the OSS movement: "..an example is Linux kernel, it all started as fun and Linux was born...from hacker's coding...this was the origin and now, I see myself as a true hacker, not like some script kiddies...I feel my contribution is visible...". Other interviewees (e.g. INT 4, INT 7, INT 6) also spoke about hacker's heavy involvement in the open source community projects as for them you cannot be programmer without being hacker. When asked about ethical hacking and more precisely if they ever conducted any black hat activities, almost all interviewees confirmed positively highlighting that it is a normal learning process, especially when you are younger and eager to learn faster. One interviewee (INT 4) said "I used to be black hat hacker but its definition is always challenging...I never stolen anything...I did not rob anyone...I wanted to learn and learn faster...today, I see things differently...".

After these first insights from interviewees which clearly pointed to a strong link between contributor and hacker, we analyzed data from ohloh database by exploring randomly selected contributors of Nmap open source security scanner.

By using observations, we explored their profiles and could confirm our initial insights from interviewees, showing that out of 20 contributors representing our sample, 15 declared themselves as hacker.

One example is from Nmap contributor that declared on his website: "I'm a FOSS hacker" or another one stating: "Free Software hacker and Security Enthusiast".

These facts answer our first research question by confirming that programmers behind open source security tools are hackers. However, it is also important to highlight that all interviewees clearly stated that they consider themselves as white hat hackers (hackers that do not conduct illegal activities). This leads to our second research question where knowing that programmers equal hackers we can naturally ask – can we trust them knowing that OSSS have the dual-use side? The answer to this question will be analyzed in the next sections.

4.2   Open Source Security Tools Dual Use

As seen in the previous section, major contributors to OSSS are hackers. Taking into account the fact that dual-use means that hackers can use the tool to conduct illegal activities but also tools can be used for peaceful means by information security professionals, we explored this dual-use paradox by interviewing information security professionals. For one interviewee (INT 9) dual-use can be important threat when using tools like Nmap as you don't have any guarantee behind: *"If I know that my 'enemy' is using the tool to attack my system – the same tool I'm using...there is a problem there..."* Other interviewees (e.g. INT 10 and 12) agreed with this but also added that distinction should be made between very mature projects such as Nmap and some new ones that appeared recently and are still at early development stage: *"...you can't be sure...who knows? Maybe they can modify a piece of code that will impact my network without that I see it immediately...still, I know for mature projects [Nmap] there is very clear code release process...I guess it would be difficult to change something..."* (INT 10).

4.3   Information Security Professionals Generally Trust Open Source Security Tools

Despite dual-use challenge and the fact that open source security tools are developed by hackers, there is a strong direction in trusting open source security tools by information security professionals. Several interviewees highlighted that trust is somehow inevitable and that for well known OSS tools it is part of its fundaments. For one interviewee (INT 14) trust is *"mandatory...without trust any open source project could be challenged"*. For another one (INT 13) *"trust is like a marriage – it is that invisible link you don't check proactively but you also have mechanisms to do it – at the end, we trust but can also check and understand if anything is potentially harming you"*.

When questioned about ways and methods to check eventually the source code of the open source security tool that they are using, most information security professionals agreed that it would be very difficult as *"you need to have the knowledge and also, there are millions of lines of code...it would take you an eternity to check it"*.

Overall, information security professionals generally trust open source security tools but they also recognized that trust cannot be easily checked due to projects' complexity and time constraints.

4.4   Large Organizations Do Not Trust Open Source Security Tools

Our finding from previous section showed that information security professionals generally trust open source security tools despite the facts that there is no easy method to check the trust relationships. However, several information security professionals confirmed that large organizations, per their policy and procedures, do not trust open source security tools and usually outlaw them by forbidding any use of these tools. One interviewee (INT 12) explained that fear is justified as in large organizations it is not easy to control *"if you have 10,000 employees and you allow all of them to use some open source security software, where source code can be literally modified by any of these employees, you can potentially have important security flaw...so what they do – they simply 'outlaw' it by forbidding access to the software"*. Another interviewee (INT 11) challenged this by explaining that a number of governmental organizations implemented open source software and no major issues have been observed: *"take the example of French government where they implemented Linux at large scale and open source kicked out closed source software...there was no big impact on information system security"*. Most of other interviewees had an agreement on the fact that large organizations tend not to trust open source security tools but they also highlighted that more we understand underlying mechanisms behind OSS projects and the way they are controlled, more trust will be there. One interviewee spoke of companies such as RedHat that started as open source companies but are now offering OSS software combined with some trust relationships (INT 9): *"RedHat is the perfect example...today they sell 'trust' combined with free open source system – Linux...large organizations have much higher trust when they know there is a commercial organization that brings trust and guarantee..."*

5   Discussion

In this section we will discuss our findings presented in the previous section. From different interviewees held with information security professionals and hackers, together with data from ohloh database, we found that main contributors to OSSS are hackers. Also, despite dual use side, information security professionals generally have trust in OSSS. However, large organizations avoid OSSS use in their network.

Previous studies that explored questions like 'Who are the developers' provided demographics statistics on programmers of OSS (e.g. Lakhani et al 2002, Hertel et al. 2033) without revealing programmers' profiles such as their hacking background. With our study we provide the answer to this question from a more holistic perspective where we confirm hackers are top contributors to OSSS.

Also, our study confirms previous study (Gallivan, 2001) that speaks of implicit and unacknowledged trust that does not necessarily appear in OSS project descriptions. Harrison and St John (1996) argued that too excessive controls could lead to 'conflict and distrust,' and this is what we saw also in our study, where for contributors, too much of control would be harmful as there seems to be a general agreement on trust level between different process stakeholders. Gallivan (2001) also argued that there is no need for high level trust for collaborative software development and our study further extends this direction by adding relationships between organizational size component and trust. In this relationship, large organizations will refuse OSSS use and adoption unless there is a trusted provider of open source technology (e.g. Redhat) where source code remains free and open but trust component is guaranteed by open source leader.

While some past research on trust confirmed that 'trust building' and 'control mechanisms' are two factors that should ensure confidence in another party's behaviour (Das and Teng, 1998), our research shows that another factor we call 'leader link' should be part of the triangle. This 'leader link' would have compliance and police role by guaranteeing trust to its partners.

6   Conclusion

This study tried to answer two important research questions: who are the programmers behind OSSS; and can we trust programmers developing open source dual use security software? Our study revealed some important findings: contributors behind OSSS are hackers, open source security tools have important dual-use dimension, information security professionals generally trust open source security tools and large organizations will avoid adopting an OSSS.

With the present research we close existing research gap as dual-use technology related to OSSS usage and adoption within organizations, in the context where these same tools developed by hackers did not get significant research focus in literature.

Our findings contain some practical implications for organizations to take into account, especially for large organizations, where we found a need to have 'leader link' involved in 'control' and 'trust' triangle. This leader would bring more trust to open source software and would reduce risk level.

Limitations of this study relate to the fact that we focused only on one (Nmap) OSSS which could have some influence on some insights from interviewees. Moreover, to understand programmers' profiles we relied on what programmers were saying about their background and if they considered themselves as hackers or not. More quantitative approach would be more accurate in this context.

For future research directions, it would be interesting to approach the trust topic more from black hat perspective trying to understand underlying motivations they could have when coding. Also, more in-depth study is welcomed to understand contributors' profiles, their background and trust relationships.

References

1. Allen, J., Collison, S., and Luckey, R.: Ohloh Web Site Api (2009), http://www.ohloh.net
2. Boehm, B.W.: Software Engineering Economics. Prentice Hall (1981)
3. Cavusoglu, H., Cavusoglu, H., Raghunathan, S.: Efficiency of Vulnerability Disclosure Mechanisms to Disseminate Vulnerability Knowledge. IEEE Transactions on Software Engineering 33(3), 171–185 (2007)
4. Cavusoglu, H., Cavusoglu, H., Zhang, J.: Security Patch Management: Share the Burden or Share the Damage? Management Science 54(4), 657–670 (2008)
5. Creswell, J.W.: Educational research: Planning, conducting and evaluating quantitative and qualitative Research. Pearson Education, Inc., Upper Saddle River (2002)
6. Crowston, K., Scozzi, B.: Open Source Software Projects as Virtual Organizations: Competency Rallying for Software Development. IEE Proceedings Software 149(1), 3–17 (2002)
7. Das, T.K., Teng, B.: Between trust and control: developing confidence in partner cooperation in alliances. Academy of Management Review 23, 491–512 (1998)
8. DiBona, C., Ockman, S., Stone, M.: Open Sources. Voices from the Open Source Revolution. O'Reilly & Associates, Sebastapol (1999)
9. Eriksson Anders, E.: Information Warfare: Hype or Reality. The Nonproliferation Review (Spring-Summer 1999)
10. Williams, E.M., Hays Bret, B.: Dual-Use Technology In the Context of the Non-Proliferation Regime, History and Technology (March 2006), doi: 10.1080/07341510500517850
11. Gallivan, M.: Striking a balance between trust and control in a virtual organization: a content analysis of open source software case studies. Inf. Syst. J. 11(4), 277–304 (2001)
12. Gallivan, M.J.: Striking a Balance Between Trust and Control in a Virtual Organization: A Content Analysis of Open Source Software Case Studies. Information Systems Journal 11(4), 277–304 (2001)
13. Haines, J., Ryder, D.K., Tinnel, L., Taylor, S.: Validation of Sensor Alert Correlators. IEEE Security and Privacy 1(1), 46–56 (2003), http://dx.doi.org/10.1109/MSECP.2003.1176995, doi:10.1109/MSECP.2003.1176995
14. Harrison, J.S., St John, C.H.: Managing and partnering with external stakeholders. Academy of Management Executive 10, 46–61 (1996)
15. Hars, A., Ou, S.: Working for Free? Motivations for Participating in Open-Source Projects. International Journal of Electronic Commerce (6), 25–39 (2002)
16. Hars, A., Ou, S.: Working for Free? Motivations for Participating in Open Source Projeets. International Journal of Electronic Commerce 6(3), 25–39 (2002)

17. Hertel, G.: Management virtueller teams auf der basis sozialpsychologischer modelle. In: Witte, E.H. (ed.) Sozialpsychologie Wirtschaflicher Prozesse, pp. 172–202. Pabst Publishers, Lengerich (2002)

18. Hertel, G., Konradt, U., Orlikowski, B.: Managing distance by interdependence: goal setting, task interdependence, and team-based rewards in virtual teams, submitted for publication. Jargon File (2002), The On-Line Hacker Jargon File, Version

19. Hertel, G., Niedner, S., Herrmann, S.: Motivation of software developers in Open Source projects: An internet-based survey of contributors to the Linux kernel. Research Policy 32(7), 1159–1177 (2003)

20. Lakhani, K.R., von Hippel, E.: How Open Source Software Works: 'Free' User-to-User Assistance. Research Policy 32(6), 923–943 (2003)

21. Lakhani, K., Wolf, B., Bates, J., DiBona, C.: Why Hackers Do What They Do: Understanding Motivation and Effort in Free/Open Source Software Projects. The Boston Consulting Group Hacker Survey (2002), http://www.osdn.com/bcg

22. Lakhani, K.R., Wolf, R.G.: Why Hackers Do What They Do: Understanding Motivation and Effort in Free/Open Source Software Projects (September 2003). MIT Sloan Working Paper No. 4425-3. Available at SSRN http://ssrn.com/abstract=443040 or http://dx.doi.org/10.2139/ssrn.443040

23. Lerner, J., Tirole, J.: Some Simple Economics of Open Source. Journal of Industrial Economics 50(2), 197–234 (2002)

24. Lerner, J., Tirole, J.: The Simple Economics of Open Source, NBER Working Paper Series, WP 7600. Harvard University, Cambridge, MA (2000)

25. Malone, T.W., Laubacher, R.J.: The Dawn of the E-Lance Economy. Harvard Business Review 76(5), 144–152 (1998)

26. Markus, M.L., Manville, B., Agres, C.E.: What Makes a Virtual Organization Work? Shan Management Review 42(1), 13–26 (2000)

27. Markus, M.L., Manville, B., Agres, C.E.: What makes a virtual organization work? Sloan Management Review 42, 13–26 (2000)

28. Moon, J.Y., Sproull, L.: Essence of distributed Trust and control in a virtual organization 303 © 2001 Blackwell Science Ltd. Information Systems Journal 11, 277–304 (2000), work: the case of the Linux kernel. First Monday: Peer-Reviewed Journal on the Internet, http://www.firstmonday.org/issues/issue5_11/moon/index.html

29. Moon, J.Y., Sproull, L.: Essence of distributed work: the case of the Linux kernel. In: Hinds, P., Kiesler, S. (eds.) Distributed Work, pp. 381–404. MIT Press, Cambridge (2002), Also available on the World Wide Web: http://www.firstmonday.dk/ issues/issue511/moon/index.html (retrieved October 28, 2002)

30. O'Reilly, T.: Open source: the model for collaboration in the age of the Internet. Computers, Freedom and Privacy (keynote address), Toronto,Canada. O'Reilly Network (2000), http://www.wideopen.com/reprint/740.html

31. Osterloh, M., Rota, S.G.: Open Source Software Development—Just Another Case of Collective Invention? Research Policy 36(2), 157–171 (2007)

32. Perens, B.: The Open Source Definition (1998), http://perens.com/articles/osd.html

33. Raymond, E.S.: The Cathedral & the Bazaar, pp. 19–64. O'Reilly & Associates, Inc., Sebastopol (1999)

34. Reppy, J.: International School on Disarmament and Research on Conflicts, http://www.isodarco.it/courses/andalo12/paper/ISO12_ReppyCyber.pdf

35. Roberts, J.A., Hann, I., Slaughter, S.A.: Understanding the Motivations, Participation, and Performance of Open Source Software Developers: A Longitudinal Study of the Apache Projects. Management Science 52(7), 984–999 (2006)
36. Stewart, K.J., Gosain, S.: The Impact of Ideology on Effectiveness in Open Source Software Development Teams. MIS Quarterly 30(2) (2006)
37. Torvalds, L.: Interview with Linus Torvalds: what motivates free software developers? First Monday 3 (1998), http://www.firstmonday.dk/issues/33/torvalds (retrieved from the World Wide Web, December 14, 2001)
38. Torvalds, L., Diamond, D.: Just for Fun: the Story of an Accidental Revolutionary. Harper Business, New York (2001)
39. von Krogh, G., Haefliger, S., Spaeth, S., Wallin, M.W.: Carrots and Rainbows: Motivation and Social Practice in Open Source Software Development. MIS Quarterly 36(2), 649–676 (2012)
40. Wu, C., Gerlach, J.H., Young, C.E.: An Empirical Analysis of Open Source Software Developers' Motivations and Continuance Intentions. Information & Management 44(3), 253–262 (2007)

Open Standards and Open Source in Swedish Schools: On Promotion of Openness and Transparency

Björn Lundell and Jonas Gamalielsson

University of Skövde, Skövde, Sweden
{bjorn.lundell,jonas.gamalielsson}@his.se

Abstract. We draw from a study aimed to establish the state of practice concerning schools' expectations and provision of IT and software applications in Swedish schools. Analysis focuses on Open Standards and Open Source Software (OSS), and considers educational lock-in. Results consider schools' expectations and provision of software and standards for digital artefacts, and show that schools expect students to use a variety of different software systems including a number of well-known OSS. The study reveals significant misconceptions concerning standards and software applications, characterises problems, and presents some recommendations for action.

1 Introduction

The use of IT and pedagogical software in schools has received significant attention in many countries in a desire to gain positive pedagogical effects and prepare students for society and working life (e.g. Balanskat et al., 2006; IES, 2009; Livingstone, 2012). In acknowledging mixed experiences there is also some research addressing teaching and learning experiences from Open Source Software (OSS) usage at University (e.g. German, 2005; Kilamo, 2010; Lundell et al., 2007) and high school levels (e.g. Lin and Zini, 2008), but there is a lack of research on expectations and provision of open standards and OSS in schools for young students.

As part of a study aimed to establish the state of practice concerning IT usage in Swedish public sector schools with students in ages 7-19, this paper presents novel results from an analysis covering all Swedish schools for young students (ages 7-16). Specifically, results presented concern: provision of OSS applications for use by students; requirements for students related to use of different document formats (standards); requirements for students related to use of software applications for writing essays; and provision of software applications for writing essays. Our analysis provides a state of practice and addresses different implications of educational lock-in and its long-term implications.

A number of factors motivate consideration of Open Standards and OSS in an analysis of IT usage in public sector schools, and there are a number of initiatives and previous research efforts related to the study.

First, skills development in the ICT sector has been identified as important, not only for public sector procurement and standardisation, but also for a range of

E. Petrinja et al. (Eds.): OSS 2013, IFIP AICT 404, pp. 207–221, 2013.

different stakeholder groups. We note that the European Commission reports, in its annual scoreboard, that "sufficient ICT skills" is an area of major concern as half of "European labour force does not have sufficient ICT skills to help them change or find a new job." (EC, 2012)

Second, it is widely acknowledged that there are risks and different types of lock-in effects associated with use of closed file formats (Egyedi, 2007; Ghosh, 2005; Lundell, 2012). One such concern is educational lock-in which may occur in situations when a company sponsors provision of IT and training of teachers (Kirk, 2008), and with such practices there may be significant long-term effects on IT practices.

Third, previous research show that adoption of IT and software systems in the public sector sometimes, perhaps unintentionally, inhibit a fair and competitive market based on important principles of transparency, non-discrimination and equal treatment (e.g. Lundell, 2011). Such practices, with widespread adoption and use of closed standards in the IT area, may significantly reinforce competence development related to certain proprietary technology. Over time, this may contribute to a lack of competence in certain technology areas, with associated risks for lack of skills or an unbalanced pool of skills in the market.

Fourth, despite established principles in European and national law aimed to stimulate a fair and competitive market for public procurement (e.g. Directives 2004/17/EC and 2004/18/EC) it is clear that widespread misconceptions concerning Open Standards and OSS (e.g. FLOSS, 2002) reinforces bad procurement practices in the public sector (e.g. Lundell, 2011).

Fifth, despite a number of national policies and strategies (e.g. UK, 2012; Regeringen, 2009) aimed to achieve a number of desirable effects for the public sector by promotion and use of Open Standards, such as compatibility and interoperability issues (Ghosh, 2005), there are also other potential benefits, such as strengthening democracy, which can be achieved by promotion of Open Standards. For example, it has been claimed that standards "are also strongly relevant to democracy to the extent they affect the conditions under which citizens engage in the democratic process." (DeNardis and Tam, 2007)

The rest of this paper is organised as follows. First, we provide a background on the situation in Sweden (2) followed by our research approach (3). Thereafter we make some observations concerning the responsiveness to the study (4), followed by a presentation of the results (5, 6 and 7) of the study. Finally, we discuss results and present conclusions (8).

2   Background

Openness and transparency have been recurring themes in public speeches from representatives for the Swedish government for a number of years. For example, in its 2004 IT bill (2004/05:175), the Swedish government declared that the use of Open Standards and OSS should be promoted (EU, 2005). More recently, in a public speech during the Swedish EU presidency, the responsible minister presented the Swedish position on the importance of openness in the public sector:

"It is my belief that we need a clear definition of openness in the European Interoperability Framework and that the definition of open standards and open source software as defined by the European Interoperability Framework version one has served us well so far. The use of open standards and open source solutions decreases the public sector's reliance on specific vendors and platforms and it increases European competitiveness as well as the transparency" (Odell, 2009)

From a policy perspective, the concept of Open Standard has been clarified in the Swedish context through inclusion of a clear definition of openness, adopted from the EIF version one (EU, 2004), in the first report from the Swedish e-Governance initiative (SOU, 2009). With the clarification of this fundamental concept, important principles underlying the idea of an Open Standard have been established.

First, use of an Open Standard ensures that data can be interpreted independently of the tools used for its generation, something which is particularly important in an educational context as students cannot be expected to buy (or pay for renting) specific proprietary technology when studying in Swedish public schools. In fact, the The Swedish Schools Inspectorate examines an important principle for education in Sweden, namely that "education shall be free of charge" (Skolinspektionen, 2011), and clarifies that costs for calculators used in public schools and costs related to use and insurances of laptops provided to students for use at school and at home cannot be charged for. However, a minor fee (approx. €10) can be accepted on an occasional basis, such as for costs related to a day with outdoor activities.

Second, when a standard is published, its technical specification contains sufficiently detailed information, and it is provided under royalty free conditions (FRAND, 2012) it can be used as a basis for implementation in software systems under different proprietary licenses and different OSS licenses. Such a standard, which adheres to the definition of an Open Standard (SOU, 2009), fulfils fundamental prerequisites of non-discrimination and equal treatment promoted in national policies and directives for public procurement. With Open Standards as a basis for procurement of IT, software systems, and educational (digital) learning objects (i.e. educational material, documents, and data which are maintained in Open Standards) in an educational context, there will be reduced risks for discrimination against students. Such a policy and practice is well in line with a statement from Kroes, then European Commissioner for Competition Policy, in a public speech: "No citizen or company should be forced or encouraged to use a particular company's technology to access government information." (Kroes, 2008)

In the context of the Digital Agenda for Sweden, the Swedish minister responsible for IT has addressed the topic IT usage in schools and education (Näringsdepartementet, 2011). In a public speech, the same minister commented that many schools provide IT equipment to their students, but also stressed: "I would argue that for schools there is much room for improvement in terms of IT use." (Hatt, 2012a) Further, in another public speech on the topic "Every single child has the right to modern IT in schools", the same minister amplified the importance of openness for promotion of democracy in her conclusion: "With openness and transparency, we can strengthen democracy, promote innovation and new jobs." (Hatt, 2012b) In light of this, we note that current practice is far from this vision as the Swedish National Agency for Education is acting just the opposite of these recommendations and the view of the European Commissioner for Competition Policy when they publish information in closed file formats on their website (Skolverket, 2011), and thereby promote use of proprietary licensed software and closed formats.

Recent statistics reported by the Swedish National Agency for Education show that computers are most commonly used when teaching the subject Swedish (as a native language) with students aged 13 to 15 years old (Skolverket, 2010). For this group of students, results for computer usage when teaching Swedish show that 17% of the students "never" and 32% "rarely" use computers, which imply that almost half (49%) of Swedish students rarely or never use computers. It should be noted that writing essays and reports are rather common activities in primary schools, and in light of these results, statements concerning room for improvements in terms of use of IT by the Swedish IT-minister may, perhaps, not be perceived as surprising. Further, according to the chair for the educational commission at Swedish Association of Local Authorities and Regions, most students learn IT at home with associated risks for a digital divide and that there is an urgent need for an IT-strategy for Swedish schools and IT competence in schools (SKL, 2011).

3   Research Approach

Our goal is to establish the state of practice concerning IT usage in Swedish public sector schools, and to address this a study was designed in order to collect responses from all public sector schools in Sweden through data collection via each municipality.

With a tradition of openness and transparency in its Swedish public sector, there are high expectations and a strict policy on governmental responses to questions and requests for public documents: it is expected that all questions are responded to, and requested public documents must be provided.

The study included 12 questions and 4 requests for public documents. The same questions and requests for public documents are used for all schools, and specifically address a number of aspects concerning students' IT usage.

In this paper, we focus on public sector schools for young students (in ages 7-16) and present our analysis of responses related to the following questions:

- Which OSS and IT equipment (i.e. stationary computers, laptops, tablet computers, etc.) are provided to students in schools in your municipality for use in school work? (*see section 5*)
- Which document formats (and versions of these) are students in schools in your municipality expected to manage in order to be able to read, write and edit documents (as well as to be able to exchange these documents electronically with teachers and other students) to be able to engage in school work? (*see subsection 6.1*)
- Which software (and versions of these) are students in schools in your municipality expected to have access to and regularly use in order to be able to read, write and edit documents (i.e. essays, instructions and other texts that students should prepare and communicate with teachers and other students) to be able to engage in school work? (*see subsection 6.2*)

– Which software (and versions of these) are students in schools in your municipality provided access to on stationary computers and on portable computers (i.e. laptops or tablet computers etc.) for use in order to be able to read, write and edit documents (i.e. essays, instructions and other texts that students should prepare and communicate with teachers and other students) to be able to engage in school work? (*see section 7*)

At time for the design of the study, we had informal dialogues with practitioners in the domain, including potential respondents in the study, in order to scrutinise our design and planned actions for data collection. From this we obtained a number of useful insights about the domain which was accounted for in our detailed planning of the study, and in particular concerning detailed planning of the data collection process. As part of this process initial results have been presented and discussed with practitioners and policy makers in several national and EU contexts (e.g. Lundell, 2012b).

When the data collection was initiated (January 2012), Sweden had 9,5 million citizens (in its 290 municipalities) of which 889000 were students (in ages 7-16) in one of the 4616 public sector schools. For data collection, we sent an email containing the questions and requests for documents in plain text to each municipality (290 in all), with follow-up reminders sent over a twelve month period. The text in the email was supplemented with two attachments (one ODF and one PDF/A-1b file) comprising data collection for the study. The instructions clarify, for reasons of privacy, that respondents can reply via email or by sending a letter containing printed documents.

The study resulted in both quantitative and qualitative data. Quantitative data was analysed to gauge the overall position with respect to informed decision making about students' IT usage in public sector schools. The text of responses, together with that of supplied documents, was analysed qualitatively, to give some insight into the real state of practice.

4   Responsiveness to the Study

The request email was sent to the registered address of each municipality. A municipality is required to respond promptly at least with an acknowledgement (usually an acknowledgement is interpreted to mean within 24 hours). If no response was received within four working weeks, then a reminder was sent. This continued with, for each reminder, increased emphasis. After the fourth reminder the email also included a clear request for an acknowledgement of receipt of the email, and after more than twelve months of elapsed time since the initial request (and in one case after thirteen reminders) all municipalities had acknowledged receipt of the email. We note that the fourth reminder resulted in a significant effect and we received many acknowledgements of receipt of the email during a short time-window (slightly more than 4 months after the initial request).

Figure 1 presents an overview of the data collection process (for the 370 days following the initial request). The dashed line shows accumulated proportion of acknowledged receipt of the email over time and the solid line shows the proportion of respondents that have responded to questions in the data collection over time.

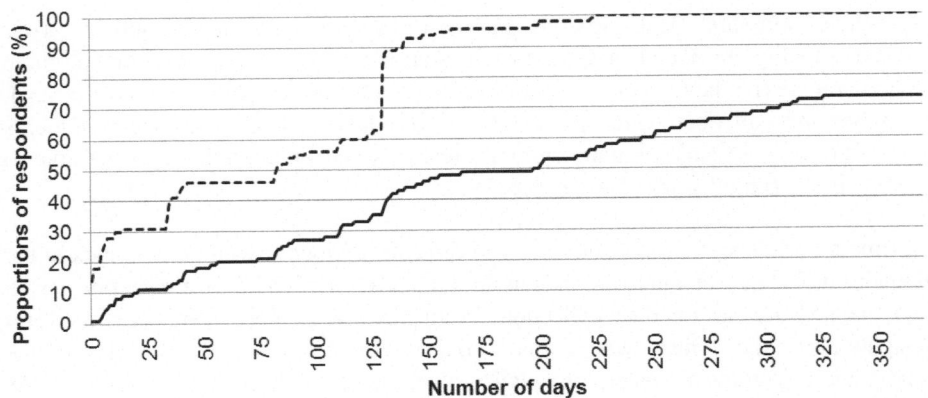

Fig. 1. Overview of the data collection process

Prior to initiating the data collection we anticipated a complex process when collecting data for schools in larger municipalities, but it came as somewhat of a positive surprise to us when we observed that it was not more difficult in comparison to data collection from schools in smaller municipalities.

It should be noted that the email sent for data collection included requests for public documents that they are required by law to respond to (at least with a notification of that requested documents do not exist, or that documents cannot be provided according to a decision in the organisation, e.g. for reasons of national security or privacy).

Initially, some municipalities seem to have ignored the email despite the fact that it contains a request for public documents, whereas yet others explicitly declined to respond. Several provided partial responses, which are probed further. On average, it took 76 days and 2.7 reminders since the initial request before a municipality acknowledged receipt of the email, and even longer before receiving a survey response (at time of writing more than 1800 reminders have been sent concerning the questions in the survey). Many of these reminders contain clarifications and explanations, and a number of telephone conversations have also been used for clarifications.

Some municipalities explicitly declined to respond and others provided partial responses, which were probed further. Some delays were evidently caused by confusion over who should respond, no individual feeling able to respond to all requests. This meant that the email was circulated within and between organisations (as there are also different types of collaborations between schools and municipalities). In many cases this resulted in partial answers being given from different parts of an organisation and from the data collection process it is evident that several individuals were involved. Many respondents expressed reluctance to provide responses and all requested documents, and in some cases even some frustration. In a few cases, respondents (and some non-respondents) even explicitly stated that they have no interest in contributing to the study and no interest to provide requested documents. However, the vast majority of respondents have expressed significant interest in the study and amongst those that have responded several have expressed that they look forward to its results.

Respondents that did not respond to questions and did not provide requested documents gave a number of different explanations, such as one (or several) of the following: lack of time, lack of interest, lack of knowledge, and lack of resources. We also noted that a large proportion of respondents in this group initially reacted positively to the request with statements in the dialogue which indicate that a response is to be expected. However, in many such cases respondents changed their mind and decided not to contribute to the study, and in several cases even made themselves unavailable for further dialogue.

The initial request was responded to by 10% of the respondents. A reminder elicited further responses, resulting in a 19% response rate and after a second reminder, 27% had responded. At time of writing, the response rate for the study is 73%. In addition, some respondents provided requested documents, but did not respond to the questions (6% in total) which implies that we obtained valuable information from 79% of all respondents. On average, it took 138 days and 6.4 reminders since the initial request before receiving these responses.

5   Use of Open Source Software in Schools

Results show that schools typically use several hundreds of software applications and many respondents provided detailed lists of precisely which software they use as requested. However, a number of respondents gave explicit reference to specific software packages (provided by specific suppliers), whereas others explicitly mentioned a handful of software applications with a note that they also use other pedagogical software. From the information provided in detailed lists of software applications used in schools, we find that many schools use a mix of proprietary and OSS licensed software.

From analysis of responses that explicitly mention the OSS used, we find that a number of different OSS applications are provided to students. Table 1 presents an overview of OSS solutions provided by schools which have been mentioned by more than a single respondent. As many respondents did not provide information concerning specific version of the software provided, our overview presents the license used for each software at time of writing.

Amongst other OSS mentioned, responses for use in schools include: CMS and blogging tools (e.g. Wordpress), development environments and platforms (e.g. Eclipse, Netbeans), calculator applications (e.g. KCalc), pedagogical software for astronomy teaching (e.g. KStars), text editors (e.g. NotepadPlusPlus), personal information management tools (e.g. Evolution), text-based web browsers (e.g. Lynx), remote desktop servers (e.g. ThinLinc), libraries and programs for handling multimedia data (e.g. FFmpeg), Linux distributions (e.g. Ubuntu), and e-mail server and web clients (e.g. Zimbra), and administrative software for administration and dialogue between students, their parents and the school (e.g. Unikum).

In acknowledging that not all respondents explicitly mentioned all software they use we note that three OSS projects are the most widely adopted: Audacity, Firefox, and OpenOffice. Further, five additional OSS projects also seem widely used as there are more than a dozen of respondents reporting use of one of these: Amis, Freemind, Gimp, LibreOffice, and VLC.

Table 1. Overview of OSS solutions provided in schools

Software type	Software	License	Link
Sound	Audacity	GPL v2 (or later)	audacity.sourceforge.net/
e-books	Amis	LGPL	www.daisy.org/projects/amis
Graphics	Blender	GPL v2 (or later)	www.blender.org
Text editing	Bluefish	GPL v3	bluefish.openoffice.nl/
Mind mapping	Freemind	GPL v2 (or later)	freemind.sourceforge.net/wiki/index.php/Main_Page
Web browser	Firefox	MPL v2	www.mozilla.org/firefox
Graphics	Gimp	GPL v3	www.gimp.org/
Mathematics	Geogebra	GPL v3	www.geogebra.org/
Graphics	Inkscape	GPL v2 (or later)	www.inkscape.org/
Office suite	LibreOffice	LGPL v3	www.libreoffice.org/
Office suite	OpenOffice	LGPL v3 / Apache license 2.0	openoffice.org/
Desktop publ.	Scribus	GPL v3	scribus.net/
Graphics	TuxPaint	GPL v3	www.tuxpaint.org/
Media player	VLC	GPL v2 (or later) / LGPL v2	www.videolan.org/vlc/
Mind mapping	Xmind	LGPL v2 / EPL v1	www.xmind.net
Archiving	7-zip	LGPL v2 (with unRAR restriction)	www.7-zip.org

From our analysis of responses, we note that several respondents lack (or at least report to us in their response that they lack) documentation of which software they use. From a licensing perspective, such lack of documentation is obviously not an issue, whereas for proprietary licensed software it is important to keep track of precisely which software is being used. For this reason, one may conjecture that the extent to which OSS is used in schools may be (somewhat) underestimated. However, the number of respondents that explicitly commented on their lack of control for which software they use came as something of a surprise to us.

6   Expectations on Use of Document Formats and Software Applications for Writing Essays

As writing essays, reports and other texts is one of the most common activities in primary schools, this section presents results concerning what a school expects from its students concerning use of specific document formats and specific software for writing, editing, and exchanging documents with teachers and other students.

6.1   Expectations on Use of Document Formats for Writing Essays

From analysis of responses related to what schools expect from their students concerning use of specific document formats six broad categories emerged that could be meaningfully interpreted. These six categories represented 93% of all responses concerning what a school expects from its students and below we comment on our analysis of these. For the remaining 7%, it was not possible to give a meaningful interpretation due to lack of information in each response. We make a number of observations from our analysis of responses in the identified six categories.

The first category (39%) includes responses for which it is evident that respondents understand what a document format actually is. For most of the responses in this category commonly used document formats are identified (see Table 2 for an overview of the most common formats). However, there were also some respondents which included file formats primarily aimed at other types of files (in addition to document formats) in their response. File formats primarily aimed at other types of files mentioned in responses include file formats for images (e.g. bmp, jpg, png and gif), video/multimedia (e.g. mpeg4, wmv, avi), and audio (e.g. wav). Several responses include expectations for use of several document formats.

From the second category of responses (29%), it is clear that many of those responding do not understand the concept of document format. Most respondents in this category mention software applications which schools expect students to use for writing documents. Responses include: "MS Office", "Word", "Office", "Open Office", "iWork", "Software which is compatible with MS Office", "Office Pro Plus 2003-2010", "MS Office 2010", "Microsoft Office 2007", "Word 2003", "Office 2003". There are also some responses in this category which included other types of software, file formats (not primarily aimed at editing text), and platforms, such as: "Fronter", "outlook.com", "word and pdf", and "Word for XP". A few responses in this category were more elaborated. For example, one respondent seems to equate "Word" with a document format: "In general it is word and PDF that we expect students to be able to read" and another responded with a policy for its municipality concerning document formats as follows: "The recommended document format in our municipality is Office 2007". As public schools are governed by municipalities, this policy (implicitly) also applies for all schools in this municipality. Others seem to be more aware of their unfamiliarity with the concept of document format. For example, one respondent commented on the lack of understanding and that "most schools use office software. I do not know what the student understands, nor how they have learnt the software. The educators in X-municipality may register for PIM but there is no explicit requirement for the level they are expected to achieve. Today this is up to each headmaster to decide."

The third category (20%) contains responses which refer to specific software with an explicit account for associated format without being specific about which document format they expect students to use (i.e. selection of software implies format). Hence, for these respondents it is clear that consideration of which software the school should expect students to use precedes any decisions on document formats. Several responses in this category were vague and implicitly referred to formats provided by a specific vendor or product. For example, responses in this category include: "Microsoft's", "The formats in Office 2007", "The document formats which are supported by Apple", "The formats supported in Open Office", and "All formats which can be generated by our software".

The fourth category (5%) includes a number of responses which made explicit that the school does not expect students to be able to use specific document formats. Several responses clarified that it does not matter, as illustrated by these responses:

Table 2. Expectations concerning document formats for respondents in the first category

Expected document formats	Percentage of respondents
doc	87
pdf	55
docx	51
odt	29
pages	5
rtf	4

"Nothing is expected", "There are no documented guidelines or requirements", and "We currently do not have any such requirements". Some responses were more elaborated and the responses show some awareness of the challenges associated with different versions of document formats and different versions of software for those formats: "So far it has sometimes been difficult for primary school students and teachers because there are several versions of word processors and suppliers. The primary school currently strives for the iPad and we do not yet know what this will lead to".

Some respondents did not explicitly respond to the specific question concerning document formats, but it was still possible to identify expectations concerning use of document formats. This comprises the fifth category (5%) of responses. From analysis of responses to other questions in the data collection (most notably those related to expectations concerning use of software) we included into this category responses which were explicit about expectations concerning software use. Hence, responses in this category (implicitly) clarified expectations and the responses were similar to those responses that were categorised into the third category (which explicitly expressed expectation regarding document formats). The remaining responses were categorised into the sixth category (2%) and included a few responses in which respondents explicitly express uncertainty.

From these responses, it is apparent that there is confusion concerning what a document format actually is and how choice of such formats may affect users. This includes awareness of the potential impact on students when schools express, explicit or implicit, expectations concerning such formats. In particular, there is considerable confusion amongst respondents concerning the difference between a document format and software systems aimed for reading, writing, and editing of documents.

6.2 Expectations on Use of Software for Writing Essays

Related to the issue of document formats, the study also investigates what a school expects from its students concerning use of specific software applications (and software provided as a cloud service) for writing and managing documents.

From analysis of responses it is clear that a majority of schools expect their students to use (one or several) specific software applications (see Table 3). Some respondents included details concerning which specific version of the software they expect their students to use, whereas others provided no such information.

Table 3. Expectations concerning use of software applications for writing documents

Expected software applications	Percentage of respondents
Microsoft Office	77
OpenOffice	18
LibreOffice	9
iWork	6
Google docs	4
Others (responses include MS Live, Works etc).	2

Table 3 does not distinguish between responses that make a difference between "Microsoft Word" and "Microsoft Office" (with or without specific version number), and all such responses are summarised into one row. Similarly, we do not distinguish between "iWork", "Pages", and "Apple" (these responses are merged into one row, "iWork" in Table 3). Amongst respondents who included expectations concerning specific version, we note that Microsoft 2010, 2007, and 2003 dominate. However, responses that included version also mentioned 97, 2000, and 2002. For "OpenOffice", most respondents did not mention a specific version, but amongst those that did, versions mentioned ranged from "OpenOffice 2.0" to "OpenOffice 3.3". For "LibreOffice", only one response mentioned a specific version (3.4.4).

To gain some additional insights concerning the relationship between expectations for document formats and software we specifically analysed the second category in subsection 6.1 (i.e. the respondents that do not seem to understand the concept of document format) and investigated their expectations for software. From this, we find that 93% of those that do not seem to understand what a document format is expect students to use a proprietary licensed software (e.g. Microsoft Office and iWork), whereas the remaining 7% expect their students to use a software which is licensed under an OSS license (e.g. OpenOffice and LibreOffice) that can be obtained without a license fee.

To further analyse the relationship between expectations for document formats and software we also analysed the first category in subsection 6.1 (i.e. respondents that seem to understand the concept of document format) and investigated their expectation for software. From this, we find that only 3% of respondents expect their students to only use document formats for which there are software applications provided as OSS.

7   Provision of Software Applications for Writing Essays

From our analysis of responses we find that a clear majority of schools provide (one or several) specific proprietary software applications to their students (see Table 4). Some respondents included details concerning which specific version of the software they provide to their students, whereas others provided no such information. Some responses include several software applications (and software provided as a service) that they provide to their students.

Table 4 does not distinguish between responses that make a difference between "Microsoft Word" and "Microsoft Office" (with or without specific version number),

Table 4. Provided software applications for writing essays and other documents

Provided software applications	Percentage of respondents
Microsoft Office	81
OpenOffice	20
LibreOffice	9
iWork	5
Google docs	3
Others (responses include MS Live, Works etc).	2

and all such responses are summarised into one row. Amongst respondents who included expectations concerning specific version, we note that Microsoft 2010, 2007, and 2003 dominate. However, responses that included version also mentioned 97, 2000, and 2002. For "OpenOffice", most respondents did not mention a specific version, but amongst those that did, versions mentioned ranged from "OpenOffice 2.0" to "OpenOffice 3.3". For "LibreOffice", only one response mentioned a specific version (3.4.4).

We analysed the correspondence between responses concerning expectations of file formats and software (as reported in subsections 6.1 and 6.2) with responses concerning the provision (as reported in this section) of software to students for writing and managing documents, and make a number of observations. First, perhaps unsurprisingly, we find that in almost all cases when a school expects its students to use a specific software the school also provides that specific software to its students. However, responses show that some schools expect their students to use specific (proprietary) solutions which the school does not provide to its students. Secondly, there are also schools which expect their students to use specific OSS solutions that they do not provide to their students. It should be noted that in such cases, it is critical that students are allowed and able to adopt and install the specific OSS (that the school expects them to use), either on their own equipment or on stationary computers or laptops provided by the school.

8   Discussion and Conclusions

In a public speech in the Swedish context, the Swedish minister responsible for IT stated (Hatt, 2012a):

"The objective of the Digital Agenda for Sweden is that Sweden will be the best in the world at using digitization opportunities. It is a goal that not only means that we should follow the trend, but we really should be at the forefront of it."

In light of this ambition, it seems clear from the results of the study that current practice is far from this ambition and that Swedish schools face significant challenges concerning IT education and usage.

Concerning use of document formats and software applications, our results show that many schools expect their students to use document formats that are based on a technical specification which "is not complete" and "include references to proprietary technology and brand names of specific products" (EU, 2012). This, in light of presented results, imply that many students are expected to use proprietary software provided from a single vendor. Such expectations from schools are certainly not in line with the regulations from Swedish authorities concerning the requirement that education shall be free of charge for students in Swedish public schools. Further, as such expectations contribute to educational lock-in and clearly are in conflict with national goals concerning use of Open Standards in the Swedish public sector, they also inhibit innovation in society as a whole.

Although our results show that OSS is used to some extent, it is evident that current practice, in the majority of schools, promotes use of software based on proprietary technologies, closed document formats, and a closed mindset for IT usage amongst students. From an educational perspective, a more sustainable strategy would be to utilise solutions based on Open Standards for which there exist OSS implementations. Such a strategy would contribute to transparency and important democratic principles as schools consequently would not (consciously or unconsciously) expect their students to use proprietary software as implied from expectations to use closed file formats. When adopting new forms of open collaboration in educational contexts, involving Open Standards and OSS with its inherent transparency, students' innovative use and exploration of technology may significantly promote learning by active participation.

In the short term, it appears that an effective recommendation for schools based on the results would be to always undertake evaluations of document formats prior to decisions on software applications, and in so doing always consider interoperability and lock-in scenarios.

We acknowledge an inherent uncertainty in our results concerning IT usage in Swedish public sector schools for young students caused by lack of responses from 27% of respondents. Therefore, we undertook a further analysis of different data sources made available by those that did not respond to questions in order to reveal some insights concerning use of specific software in this group. Data sources for this analysis include information provided in response to the initial request for public documents by those that did not respond to questions (in total 6% of all respondents), other information provided via respondents' web sites, and via direct dialogue. This information provided insights into specific instructions for how to use specific software, which software has been adopted and deployed to students, and other statements indicating various decisions concerning use of specific software in the educational environment. From this we conclude that there are strong indications that the proportion of respondents providing proprietary software applications is somewhat underestimated. In addition, we found that this analysis only identified software already explicitly mentioned in responses (and explicitly mentioned in table 4). Further, this analysis also identified an acknowledgement of inherent problems related to use of different file formats, and we also observed explicitly stated expectations concerning use of specific file formats.

To conclude, results from the study suggest that there is significant scope for improvements in the Swedish formal education concerning IT usage. In particular, there are many misconceptions and significant unawareness amongst respondents. Many schools seem unaware of the potential with Open Standards and OSS as enablers for innovative use of IT that does not discriminate any student.

References

Balanskat, A., Blamire, R., Kefala, S.: The ICT Impact Report: A review of studies of ICT impact on schools in Europe, European Schoolnet (December 11, 2006)

DeNardis, L., Tam, E.: Open Documents and Democracy: a Political basis for Open Document Standards, Yale Information Society Project, Yale ISP White Paper (November 1, 2007), Available at SSRN: http://dx.doi.org/10.2139/ssrn.1028073

EC: Digital Agenda: Annual scoreboard confirms need for structural economic reform across Europe and surplus of ICT jobs; big trend towards mobile services and technology, European Commission, IP/12/614, Press Release, Brussels (June 18, 2012)

Egyedi, T.: Standard-compliant, but incompatible?! Computer Standards & Interfaces 29(6), 605–613 (2007)

EU: European Interoperability Framework for pan-European eGovernment Services, European Commission, Version 1.0 (2004), http://ec.europa.eu/idabc/servlets/Doca2cd.pdf?id=19528

EU: From an IT policy for society to a policy for the information society, European Commission (June 30, 2005), http://www.epractice.eu/files/media/media_208.pdf

EU: Guidelines for Public Procurement of ICT Goods and Services: SMART 2011/0044, D2 - Overview of Procurement Practices," Final Report, Europe Economics, London (March 1, 2012), http://cordis.europa.eu/fp7/ict/ssai/docs/study-action23/d2-finalreport-29feb2012.pdf

FLOSS: Use of Open Source Software in Firms and Public Institutions : Evidence from Germany, Sweden and UK , FLOSS Final Report - Part 1, FLOSS – Free/Libre Open Source Software: Survey and Study, Berlin (July 2002)

FRAND: Implementing FRAND standards in Open Source: Business as usual or mission impossible?, EC Workshop, impossible?, Report of FRAND and OS event, Brussels, Belgium (November 22, 2012), http://ec.europa.eu/enterprise/sectors/ict/files/ict-policies/report-from-frand-os-conference-22nov12_en.pdf

Ghosh, R.A.: Open Standards and Interoperability Report: An Economic Basis for Open Standards, FLOSSPOLS, Deliverable D4 (December 12, 2005)

German, D.: Experiences teaching a graduate course in Open Source Software Engineering. In: Scotto, M., Succi, G. (eds.) Proceedings of the First International Conference on Open Source Systems, Genova, Italy, July 11-15, pp. 326–328 (2005)

Hatt, A.-K.: Från Lahore till Ale - It i elevernas tjänst, Public Speech at: 'It i skola och utbildning', Nordiska skolledarkongressen, Gothenburg (March 29, 2012a), http://www.regeringen.se/sb/d/13698/a/189703

Hatt, A.-K.: Vartenda barn har rätt till modern it i skolan, Public Speech at: 'Internetdagarna', Stockholm Water Front Congress Centre (October 23, 2012b), http://www.regeringen.se/sb/d/13698/a/202226

IES: Teachers' Use of Educational technology in U.S. Public Schools: 2009, National Center for Education Statistics, NCES 2010-040, U.S. Department of Education (May 2009)

Kilamo, T.: The Community Game: Learning Open Source Development Through Participatory Exercise. In: Proc. of AMT 2010, Tampere, Finland. ACM Press (October 2010)

Kirk, J.: Microsoft to fund IT training in developing world, IT worldcanada.com, IDG News (January 23, 2008)

Kroes, N.: Being Open About Standards, Brussels, SPEECH/08/317, European Commissioner for Competition Policy (June 10, 2008)

Lin, Y.-W., Zini, E.: Free/libre open source software implementations in schools: Evidence from the field and implications for the future. Computers & Education 50(3), 1092–1102 (2008)

Livingstone, S.: Critical reflections on the benefits of ICT in education. Oxford Review of Education 38(1), 9–24 (2012)

Lundell, B., Persson, A., Lings, B.: Learning Through Practical Involvement in the OSS Ecosystem: Experiences from a Masters Assignment. In: Feller, J., Fitzgerald, B., Scacchi, W., Sillitti, A. (eds.) Open Source Development, Adoption and Innovation. IFIP, vol. 234, pp. 289–294. Springer, Berlin (2007)

Lundell, B.: e-Governance in public sector ICT procurement: what is shaping practice in Sweden? European Journal of ePractice 12(6) (2011), http://www.epractice.eu/en/document/5290101

Lundell, B.: Why do we need Open Standards? In: Orviska, M., Jakobs, K. (eds.) Proceedings 17th EURAS Annual Standardisation Conference 'Standards and Innovation', Aachen. The EURAS Baard Series, pp. 227–240 (2012) ISBN: 978-3-86130-337-4

Lundell, B.: IT Usage in Swedish Primary Schools: Observations on Innovation and Educational Lock-In. In: Coughlan, S. (ed.) The First OpenForum Academy Conference Proceedings, OpenForum Europe, pp. 15–21 (2012b) ISBN: 978-1-300-17718-0

Näringsdepartementet: Rundabordssamtal om it i skola och undervisning, Näringsdepartementet (February 18, 2011), http://www.regeringen.se/sb/d/14390/a/161358

Odell, M.: Innovations for Europe: Increasing Public Value, Public Speech at: 'European Public Sector Award', Maastricht (November 5, 2009), http://www.regeringen.se/sb/d/11678/a/134858

Regeringen: Kommittédirektiv: Delegation för e-förvaltning, Dir. 2009:19 (March 26, 2009), http://www.regeringen.se/content/1/c6/12/40/02/ec50b88b.pdf

SKL: IT en rättighet för elever, Sveriges Kommuner och Landsting, Stockholm (2011), http://www.skl.se/press/debattartiklar/debattartiklar-2011/it-en-rattighet-for-elever

Skolinspektionen: Avgifter i skolan, Informationsblad, Skolinspektionen (December 7, 2011), http://www.skolinspektionen.se/Documents/vagledning/infoblad-avgifter.pdf

Skolverket: Redovisning av uppdrag om uppföljning av IT-användning och IT- kompetens i förskola, skola och vuxenutbildning, Skolverket, Stockholm, Dnr 75-2007:3775 (April 9, 2010)

Skolverket: Hur laddar jag ned dokument från Skolverkets webbplats? , Skolverket (May 19, 2011), http://www.skolverket.se/2.2467/2.2472/2.2475/2.2476/hur-laddar-jag-ned-dokument-fran-skolverkets-webbplats-1.10294

SOU: Strategi för myndigheternas arbete med e-förvaltning, Statens Offentliga Utredningar: SOU 2009:86, e-Delegationen, Finansdepartementet, Regeringskansliet, Stockholm (October 19, 2009), http://www.sweden.gov.se/content/1/c6/13/38/13/1dc00905.pdf

UK: Open Standards Principles: For software interoperability, data and document formats in government IT specifications, Cabinett Office, UK (November 1, 2012), http://www.cabinetoffice.gov.uk/sites/default/files/resources/Open-Standards-Principles-FINAL.pdf

Effect on Business Growth by Utilization and Contribution of Open Source Software in Japanese IT Companies

Tetsuo Noda[1], Terutaka Tansho[1], and Shane Coughlan[2]

[1] Shimane University
nodat@soc.shimane-u.ac.jp, tansho@riko.shimane-u.ac.jp
[2] Founder at Opendawn, Visiting Researcher at Shimane University
and Executive Director / Vice-President Far East at OpenForum Europe
shane@opendawn.com

Abstract. The expanded use of Open Source Software (OSS), and the expansion of the market caused by this adoption has led to a corresponding increase in the number of businesses acting as stakeholders in the field. Some of these are pure users of OSS technology but a great number are developers of such technology, and can be understood to have a substantial investment in this paradigm. It is reasonable to assume that such businesses are rational actors, and that their investment or contribution to the field implies a positive economic benefit either currently obtained or assumed as a return in the future. This paper analyzes how OSS affects Japanese IT companies' business growth both through simple use and by deeper engagement as a stakeholder in OSS community. This is the first time that such a link between the utilization of OSS and economic growth has been explored in the context of Japan, and it can hopefully lay a foundation for further study regarding the real economic value of this approach to software.

1   Introduction

The expanded use of Open Source Software (OSS), and the expansion of the market caused by this adoption has led to a corresponding increase in the number of businesses acting as stakeholders in the field. Some of these are pure users of OSS technology but a great number are developers of such technology, and can be understood to have a substantial investment in this paradigm. The question is why this is so. From the viewpoint of the enterprises (demand side) intending to introduce OSS, the most frequently cited reason for investment is described as cost-reduction. However, the pure cost-reduction on the part of these enterprises (or governmental organizations) may lead to the shrinking of the market of IT companies (supply side). In such an environment it is necessary for supply side IT companies to cultivate new markets to maintain or expand their business. Somewhat ironically, the IT companies are facing the cost pressure from OSS in some cases, and then these companies will need to incorporate outside resources (such as outside OSS developers and their contribution) into their inside product portfolios to maximise their R&D returns.

E. Petrinja et al. (Eds.): OSS 2013, IFIP AICT 404, pp. 222–231, 2013.

In short, supply side companies have to reduce the cost as required by competitive pressure, a pressure partly brought amplified by OSS, and participate in the development processes to ensure their continued competitiveness in the market. This paper analyzes how OSS affects Japanese IT companies' business growth both through simple use and by deeper engagement as a stakeholder in the community.

2   Open Innovation and OSS Business Model

2.1   Open Innovation, and Matter of Free Ride

Chesbrough (2003) describes traditional separate style business strategy as "Closed Innovation", in which enterprises develop ideas, marketing, support, and financing by themselves. And, research and development is almost exclusively performed intra-enterprises. However, the superiority of "Closed Innovation" as an economic model for creativity is being reduced because of the liquidity of labour, improvements in the knowledge power of employees, and the existence of venture capitals to drive new innovation elsewhere. In this context business enterprises have begun to use inflow and outflow of knowledge to fit their purposes, not only accelerate their internal innovation, but encourage the innovation to be used externally. This process is "Open Innovation" which blurs boundaries between business enterprises, and by joining internal resources and external resources together, extra economic values for all parties concerned is generated.

This development style is essentially the same as the longer established OSS development style. OSS is developed by a "Community" of stakeholders, which may be structured as a Bazaar style or a Cathedral style, it tends to be open for all developers, software engineers and business enterprises with an interest in participation, and they can participate or withdraw any stage in the overarching process (though naturally continued participation is incentivised in terms of increase ownership of the technology produced or increased customisation to fit individual use-cases). From the perspective of businesses engaging as stakeholders in this field, they join a community beyond the separated confines of their own organisation in order to absorb the fruit of innovation and developed software from third parties, who participate for similar reasons in turn. It is essentially a situation of enlightened self-interest.

One immediate consideration from this perspective is that the development of OSS technology inherently reduces costs for each stakeholder, with the complete burden of development being shared by all contributors. Conceptualising OSS technologies as platforms on which products or services can be delivered, it is easy to extrapolate that OSS contributions therefore can be directly tied into reductions in the cost of bringing new products and services to market, and therefore provides a market benefit through what can be called a leverage effect.

From a less positive perspective, if we assume rational individuals or business enterprises with to obtain convenience maximization, the obvious next step would be to free ride on OSS development, and seek to obtain the platform benefits without the burden of contribution. However, it is equally true that if every individual (or every business enterprise) behaves rationally, value provided by OSS will immediately drop, and quickly run dry. Ghosh (1998) explains this by introducing a "Cooking-pot Market" model, whereby assumptions of inexhaustible supply via digital copying are off-set by understanding that the cost of development, the human labour involved, is both exhaustible and actually based on technical elites. Therefore, rational business enterprises that want to absorb the outcome of OSS must take part in the OSS development processes and contribute to the future of the platforms.

2.2   Three-step Business Model of OSS

Kunai (2010) categorizes the underlying OSS business model a "Three-step Model" regarding the engagement by business enterprises. As they move up the ladder, though the cost of the development increases, business enterprises can increase the economic effects as shown in Fig. 1.

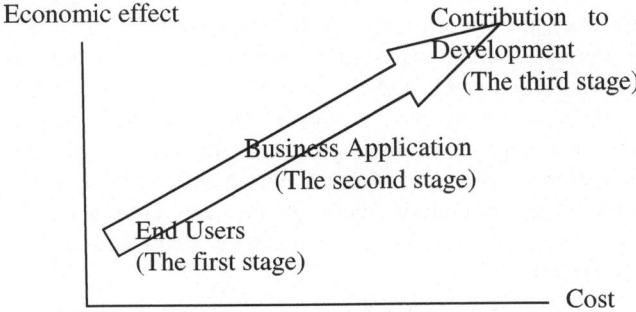

Fig. 1. Three-step Business Model of OSS

In the first stage, business enterprises use OSS as End Users, and they only use OSS in the same was as proprietary software. Their primary purpose is cost reduction, but economic effect is very low. In the second stage they use OSS in a more engaged manner, expanding functional features they need, constructing application software, serving support for their customers, and integrating systems. In this stage, the economic effect is comparatively higher than that of the first stage, though cost rises because of the demand of manpower and equipment to launch and sustain these derivative businesses.

In the third stage they participate in the "mainstream" development process of OSS, and bring forth the highest economic effect. They contribute to the "Community" by providing physical support and financial backing. The development style of this stage is different from to stage two, primarily because they develop software in association with other companies, including their competitors. This is - as referenced before - enlightened self-interest. The "Community" has many resourceful software engineers, who contribute to the development process of OSS by fixing bugs or supplying patches. Those closest to each business sector can address its requirements most effectively, and - on a platform rather than product level - competitors can work together to enable the next generation of their difference products without undertaking 100% of the engineering on their own. In this way business enterprises become to be able to reduce the cost of the demand of manpower and equipment. Moreover, developing with OSS engineers and other companies, they are able to acquire the "Leverage Effect". Thus the underlying hypothesis is that process of "Open Innovation" enables business enterprises to absorb the fruits of the "Community" of OSS. Now, this paper tries to establish this hypothesis by the questionnaire survey of IT companies in Japan.

3   Study Methodology

The methodology we employ in this study is to investigate the effect on the business growth by OSS utilization and contribution in Japanese IT companies (with our primary focus being the supply side of information solutions in business processes).

Box 1: OSS Utilization and Contribution Questionnaire Survey Slips towards Japanese IT Companies

Company profile:
Q1. Home City
Q2. Inauguration of Business
Q3. Main Business Service
Q4. Capital Stock
Q5. Number of Employee
Q6. Number of Developers (programmers, software engineers, etc.)
Q7. Sales Amount
Q8. Growth Rate of Sales (present period)
Q9. Prospect of Sales Growth Rate (subsequent period)
Q10. Growth of Employee Number (present period)
Q11. Prospect of Employee Number's Growth Rate (subsequent period)

Utilization of OSS: (rate of utilization)
Q12. Utilization of Linux
Q13. Utilization of Apache HTTP Server
Q14. Utilization of Database technologies (MySQL, PostgreSQL, etc.)
Q15. Utilization of Programming Language Ruby
Q16. Utilization of Other Programming Languages (Perl, Python, PHP, etc.)
Q17. Utilization of Ruby on Rails

Contribution to OSS Communities: (amount of direct investments
and manpower costs of OSS engineers inside company)
Q18. Contribution to Linux
Q19. Contribution to Apache HTTP Server
Q20. Contribution to Database technologies (MySQL, PostgreSQL, etc.)
Q21. Contribution to Programming Language Ruby
Q22. Contribution to Other Programming Languages (Perl, Python, PHP, etc.)
Q23. Contribution to Ruby on Rails

As is described by Kunai, we assume, "The more IT companies contribute to OSS communities, the more they are able to acquire economic effect".

According to this methodology, we sent out a detailed questionnaire survey to IT companies in Japan, during 2012. The survey slips were sent to 642 companies which accede to Information Industry Association in Japan, and 191 companies gave us replies (collection rate: 29.8%). The survey was conducted in the form of a questionnaire containing the items shown in **box 1**. In the survey we questioned the utilization and contribution of low-level OSS (such as Linux, Database technologies, Programming Languages, etc.). Application-level software (such as ERP, CMS, CRM, etc.) is excluded, because case examples of development of such software are rare in Japanese IT companies. All questions are selected from among alternatives, discrete data.

4   Result and Discussions

4.1   Utilization and Contribution of OSS

In the questionnaire survey, we ask the utilization ratio of OSS - how much percentage of software development is utilized by OSS in total. "100%" in Linux means that the company uses Linux for all the server operating system, and then "50-74%" in Ruby indicates that Ruby is used in the range of 50-74% software development in the company for example. In this company, they probably utilize "other languages" for the rest of 25-50%. The results are shown in Fig.2.

Most Japanese IT companies use OSS in their business field, especially the Linux operating system core components and various Database technologies (MySQL, PostgreSQL, etc.). At the same time, the use rate of Japanese-origin technology like Ruby and its American-based development framework Ruby on Rails are unexpectedly low (Fig. 2). It is because that in the questionnaire survey the poll of IT companies contains wide ranges, including system integrators, software developers, and network service companies. Ruby use is currently limited within the field of web applications development, along with Ruby on Rails.

The survey also revealed that the percentage of companies which contribute to OSS communities is relatively low in Japan (Fig. 3). The terms of currency in the questions were originally in Japanese Yen, however, the temrs are converted into US Dollors (100JPY = 1USD) in order that the readers can capture the volume easily. The result of our study indicates that most of Japanese IT companies use OSS without contributing to OSS development process might show that they are positioned as "free riders" in non-application level. However, the survey also confirmed that, on average, about 20% of IT companies contribute to OSS development process.

The question is therefore what the correlations between the utilization of OSS and the contribution towards OSS are.

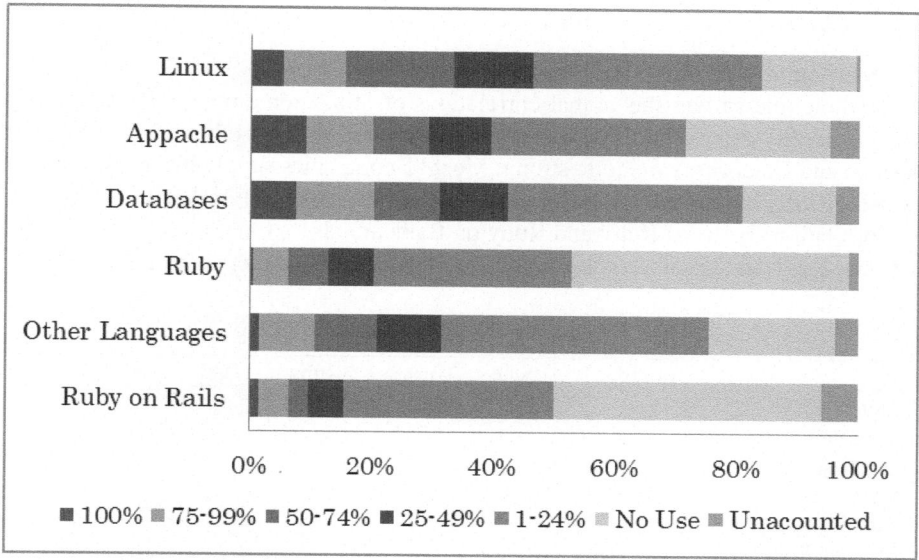

Fig. 2. Utilization of OSS in Japanese IT Companies   n=191

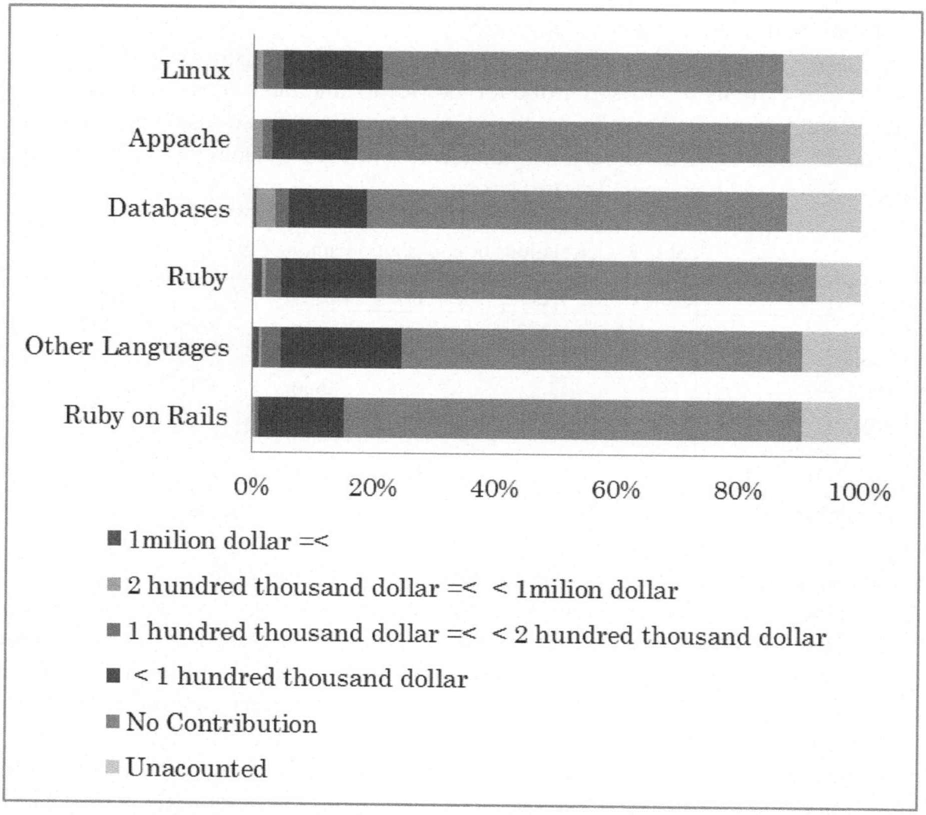

Fig. 3. Contribution to OSS communities in Japanese IT Companies   n=191

4.2   Correlation between Utilization and Contribution of OSS

Correlation of Utilization among OSS

As a whole, the survey shows that correlations of utilization among OSS are strong, and inside this context the, correlation of Linux with regards other OSS (especially Apache and Databases) are quite strong. Most IT companies supply business solutions by using OSS components based on Linux OS and its ecosystem in Japan.

Correlations between Ruby and Ruby on Rails are also strong, though correlations between Ruby and Databases are weak by comparison with other scripting languages.

Table 1. Correlations of utilization among OSS

	Linux	Apache	Databases	Ruby	O.L.	RoR
Linux	-	$.692^{**}$	$.625^{**}$	$.469^{**}$	$.507^{**}$	$.402^{**}$
Apache		-	$.554^{**}$	$.554^{**}$	$.494^{**}$	$.409^{**}$
Databases			-	$.473^{**}$	$.581^{**}$	$.459^{**}$
Ruby				-	$.232^{**}$	$.812^{**}$
Other Languages					-	$.255^{**}$
Ruby on Rails						-

Spearman's rank correlation coefficient ** 1% level of significance

Correlation of Contribution among OSS

Correlations of contribution among stakeholders in OSS are also strong. In the same context, correlations of cross-contribution between Linux and other OSS (especially Apache and various Database technologies) are comparatively strong. It also held true that correlations of Apache between other OSS (various Database technologies and various Scripting Languages) are also strong.

Table 2. Correlations of contribution among OSS

	Linux	Apache	Databases	Ruby	O.L.	RoR
Linux	-	$.836^{**}$	$.773^{**}$	$.616^{**}$	$.696^{**}$	$.447^{**}$
Apache		-	$.765^{**}$	$.580^{**}$	$.702^{**}$	$.430^{**}$
Databases			-	$.550^{**}$	$.802^{**}$	$.526^{**}$
Ruby				-	$.575^{**}$	$.772^{**}$
Other Languages					-	$.622^{**}$
Ruby on Rails						-

Spearman's rank correlation coefficient ** 1% level of significance

Correlation between Utilization and Contribution of Each OSS

As a whole, correlations between utilization and contribution of companies in many OSS technology types are not significant. The exception was that the correlation between Ruby and Ruby on Rails in this context is significant in 1% level. And those of Other Languages between Apache and Databases technologies are rather weak but significant in 5% level.

We are led to the conclusion that in Japan, most of IT companies make use of Linux, Apache, and database technologies. These types of technology as essentially used in the same manner as proprietary software. Of course, these OSS technologies are being developed thorough worldwide communities by the contribution of many engineers and businesses, so many Japanese IT companies gain their value without much pain as "free riders."

In contrast, Ruby has been developed mainly by the Japanese community (approximately half of its developers are Japanese). Justifiably, companies conducting business using Ruby get engaged in the Ruby community around Japan, and by extension they also get engaged in the development process of Ruby on Rails in America. To some extent this is pure self-interest in terms of building the shared platform, and to some extent it shows that Ruby and Ruby on Rails are still very much developing OSS technologies and have not yet gained a stable valuation in business use yet. It is hard to be a free rider at this point in their lifecycle, so adopters are inherently positioning themselves as investors and contributors.

In addition, it is interesting that the correlation between utilization and contribution of other languages (Perl, Python, PHP, etc.) is also shown. Of course, the number of Japanese developers in these languages' communities is small, different from Ruby. This shows that these OSS script languages, including Ruby, have not gained stable valuation in business use yet, either.

Table 3. Correlations between utilization and contribution of OSS

contribution \ utilization	Linux	Apache	Databases	Ruby	O.L.	RoR
Linux	.136	-.002	.004	.128	.083	.110
Apache	.151	.135	.054	.149	.125	.111
Databases	.050	-.016	.052	.132	.098	.105
Ruby	.031	-.013	.007	.324**	.114	.351**
Other Languages	.144	.161*	.189*	.099	.272**	.140
Ruby on Rails	.087	.086	.065	.331**	.159	.420**

Spearman's rank correlation coefficient
** 1% level of significance, * 5% level of significance

4.3   Effect on Business Growth by Utilization and Contribution of OSS

The larger question is how we can survey the effect on business growth by utilization and contribution of OSS, thereby explaining more clearly the actions of the companies in this market as rational actors. We understand that business growth is affected by many factors such as market conditions; however, in order to test our exploratory hypothesis, we investigated the correlations between indicators of business growth and utilization of OSS, and contribution to OSS communities. As a whole the data indicated that a subsequent period prospect of sales growth rate might be impacted by utilization of OSS, and in this context, Ruby favorably compared with other OSS in Japan. At the same time, there is little correlation between indicators of business growth and contribution towards OSS.

The results show that, in Japanese IT companies, the utilization of OSS has an insignificant effect on the present sales growth, but when they use OSS they tend to make allowance for the subsequent sales growth. However, the contribution to OSS communities has an insignificant effect both on the present sales growth and on the subsequent sales growth. As rational economic actors, their investment decisions are impacted by this understanding.

Table 4. Correlations between business growth and utilization of OSS

	Growth Rate of Sales (present period)	Prospect of Sales Growth Rate (subsequent period)	Growth of Employee Number (present period)	Prospect of Employee Number's Growth Rate (subsequent period)
Linux	.191**	.245**	.207**	.133
Apache	.167*	.220**	.079	.066
Databases	.131	.222**	.026	.067
Ruby	.135	.214**	.063	.113
Other Languages	.098	.176*	.052	.092
Ruby on Rails	.055	.178*	.061	.068

Spearman's rank correlation coefficient
** 1% level of significance, * 5% level of significance

Table 5. Correlations between business growth and contribution of OSS

	Growth Rate of Sales (present period)	Prospect of Sales Growth Rate (subsequent period)	Growth of Employee Number (present period)	Prospect of Employee Number's Growth Rate (subsequent period)
Linux	-.091	.007	-.032	-.089
Apache	-.031	.021	-.092	-.127
Databases	-.036	.092	-.083	.020
Ruby	.052	.047	.072	.058
Other Languages	.019	.057	-.029	.002
Ruby on Rails	.034	.075	.018	.049

Spearman's rank correlation coefficient
** 1% level of significance, * 5% level of significance

Conclusion and Challenges for the Future

It has become commonplace for business enterprises to use OSS in their business. The logic we understand as framing this such engagement is that the competitive edge that comes from technical advantages delivered by using OSS, and - using the same logic - it is therefore indispensable for them to contribute or participate in the development process of OSS as Kunai proposes. However, our data shows that major OSS, like Linux, Apache, MySQL, and PostgreSQL, are still utilization objects for Japanese IT companies, or "Frontier" technologies. They have been able to get a competitive edge only by the utilization of OSS, and contribution to OSS projects or communities has not been linked to the business growth for them.

At the same time, exceptionally, Ruby and Ruby on Rails are both utilization and contribution objects for Japanese IT companies. They have to contribute or participate in the development process of both technologies. This appears to be because Ruby and Ruby on Rails are still platforms very much under development and have yet to gain a stable valuation in business use. The contribution to Ruby and Ruby on Rails is not linked to the business growth as other OSS, or motivated by the same adoption criteria.

And, we excluded the survey of application-level software (such as ERP, CMS, CRM, etc.). For the future, case examples of development of such software are expected to increase in Japanese IT companies. Moreover, to survey the effect on business growth we take on growth rate of sales and growth of employee number as indicators of business growth. There are also other indicators to estimate business growth. These are our research challenges for the future.

Our data is not perfect, and the survey included collected data from many types of supply side IT companies is lumping together. The advantage is that this poll of IT companies contains a wide range, and their utilization and contribution of OSS are different from each other but provides a snapshot of the overall market. To analyze the effect on business growth by utilization and contribution of OSS in more detail, and to properly understand the free rider versus investor issue that we have uncovered, will require more assorted statistical analyses. One proposed step for further research is to expand future survey criteria to the demand side of IT businesses, who we might term as consequential OSS users, and who also may contribute to the development process of OSS due to its open nature. Even broader research into non-IT but significant software development areas such as banking or heavy industry could also prove fruitful.

References

[1] Chesbrough, H.: Open Innovation: The New Imperative for Creating and Profiting from Technology. Harvard Business School Press (2003)
[2] Chesbrough, H.: Open Business Models: How To Thriv In The New Innovation Landscape. Harvard Business School Press (2006)
[3] Chesbrough, H., Wim, V., West, J.: Open Innovation: Researching a New Paradigm. Oxford University Press (2008)
[4] Ghosh, R.: Cooking-pot Markets: an economic model for the trade in free goods and service on the internet. First Monday 3(3) (1998)
[5] Kunai, T.: Three-stage approach of Linux Development. Let's go by Linux, vol. 2 (2010)

Misconceptions and Barriers to Adoption of FOSS in the U.S. Energy Industry

Victor Kuechler[1], Carlos Jensen[1], and Deborah Bryant[2]

[1] School of Electrical Engineering and Computer Science
Oregon State University, Corvallis, OR, USA
kuechlej@onid.orst.edu, cjensen@eecs.oregonstate.edu
[2] The Bryant Group, Portland, OR, USA
deborah@debbryant.com

Abstract. In this exploratory study, we map the use of free and open source software (FOSS) in the United States energy sector, especially as it relates to cyber security. Through two surveys and a set of semi-structured interviews—targeting both developers and policy makers—we identified key stakeholders, organizations, and FOSS projects, be they rooted in industry, academia, or public policy space that influence software and security practices in the energy sector. We explored FOSS tools, common attitudes and concerns, and challenges with regard to FOSS adoption. More than a dozen themes were identified from interviews and surveys. Of these, drivers for adoption and risks associated with FOSS were the most prevalent. More specifically, the misperceptions of FOSS, the new security challenges presented by the smart grid, and the extensive influence of vendors in this space play the largest roles in FOSS adoption in the energy sector.

Keywords: Adoption, barriers, energy sector, case studies.

1   Introduction

The energy industry in the United States is changing in many ways. Its growing and diverse energy needs have created a need to collect new types of data and network systems that have historically been "siloed". This new networked grid uses computer-based remote control and automation to intelligently manage the energy as it moves between energy producers and consumers [22]. The American Reinvestment and Recovery Act of 2009 provided $3.4 billion dollars of grant money in the form of the Smart Grid Investment Grant to support the modernization of the power grid [23]. As of July 2012, 99 projects have been funded, all of which deploy smart grid technology with a chief goal to reduce peak and overall electricity demand and operation costs; improve asset management, outage management, reliability, and system efficiency; and reduce environmental emissions [23]. The drive to establish a "smart grid" has introduced new technology, but also created new security risks and challenges [12].

As the modernization of the North American power grid continues, the security of energy delivery systems, control systems, and information sharing must be a high

E. Petrinja et al. (Eds.): OSS 2013, IFIP AICT 404, pp. 232–244, 2013.
© IFIP International Federation for Information Processing 2013

priority. Software, whether supporting operational systems or security technology, is a key element and must be central to any related security discussion. These complex problems require collaboration between regional energy generators, government agencies, standards bodies, and security professionals. Leveraging a community of like-minded individuals who share similar needs and goals can increase the adaptability and flexibility of cyber security initiatives and software within the energy sector.

The free and open source software (FOSS) movement is one of the only distributed software development models that brings together developers from many different domains of knowledge while supporting a common goal of sharing information, collaborating to improve systems, and leveraging diverse knowledge to create some of the most effective software in cost and implementation.

We conducted an exploratory study, funded by the Energy Sector Security Consortium (EnergySec), to map out the use of FOSS software in the energy sector, especially as it relates to cyber security. The motivation for this study was rooted in the common perception that FOSS is less secure due to availability of its source code. Although this perception has existed since the initiation of FOSS, a 2010 study from Boston College supports this claim, concluding that open source software is at greater risk of exploitation [19]. Despite this perception, many government agencies have adopted FOSS, some of which consider FOSS an equal to proprietary software, including the Department of Defense [30].

Through a survey, we identified seven representative organizations and FOSS projects within the energy sector and identified the tools they use, licenses used, legal concern or solutions, and challenges and hurdles they faced or have overcome in adopting FOSS. We conducted semi-structured interviews with key members of each organization or project with a goal to:

1. Understand the extent in which FOSS participates in energy sector, and vice versa
2. Understand the barriers to the adoption of FOSS and the process of contributing to FOSS
3. Record the best practices derived from current initiatives in FOSS, the energy industry, and government.

2   Background

2.1   Introduction to FOSS

FOSS development is a collaborative process, thus understanding its culture is crucial. The open and altruistic nature of FOSS is appealing to many users and developers. FOSS development is predominantly volunteer-driven, built on a model of computer-mediated, asynchronous communication and collaboration. Many people today characterize FOSS in this way.

It may be surprising to learn that large projects like Linux, Firefox, and Apache are the exception rather than the rule; most FOSS projects are developed by a handful of people. In a 2002 study of the most active mature projects (i.e., projects not ramping-up) on Sourceforge.net, the average project has four developers, and the majority has one [14]. In larger projects, more than half of developers only have regular contact with one to five other project members [10].

Because FOSS projects rely on volunteers, users are viewed as potential contributors. Ye and Kishida and Herraiz et al. studied "role transition" from users (using the software, motivating developers) to bug reporters (reporting and documenting problems, submitting feature requests) to active developers (contributing code) [32], [13]. FOSS communities and projects operate as meritocracy, where a programmer's ability and contributions to a project shape how the community perceives them.

FOSS's inherent volunteer nature highlights its adaptability to meet the needs of specific groups and niche markets. Volunteers work, initiate, or develop projects that either meets personal needs or the purpose and goals of other like-minded individuals [16]. FOSS has continually adapted to meet the needs of almost every domain of the software ecosystem. In 2005, Walli et al. evaluated the use of FOSS in U.S. companies. They found that 87% of the 512 companies they surveyed use FOSS [30]. They also discovered that companies and government institutions use FOSS because it reduces IT costs, delivers systems faster, and makes systems more secure. Large companies with annual revenue over $1 billion saved 3.3 million dollars, medium-sized companies saved an average $1 million, and smaller companies (<50 million) saved $520,000. They also discovered that after years of using FOSS software stacks (Linux, etc.) and web server software, companies were beginning to use other FOSS business software instead of proprietary software [30].

In 2007, David Wheeler also found that FOSS has a significant market share and "is often the most reliable software and I many cases has the best performance" [31]. Similarly, in 2011, Coverity compared open source and proprietary software quality and find "open source quality is on part with proprietary code quality, particularly in cases where codebases are of similar size" [5]. The open source ideal has been a part of government in spirit since the 1960s, but only the real potential of FOSS has only been advocated since the late 90s. Several publications, "A Case for Government Promotion of Open Source Software" by Mitch Stoltz; "Open Source Code and the Security of Federal Systems" by a multiagency working group (National Coordinator for Security, Infrastructure Protection, and Counter-Terrorism); "Opening the Military to Open Source" by Maj. Deiferth, USAF; and "The Simple Economics of Open Source" by the Bureau for Economic Research was published in the late 90s and early 2000s. These publications started some of the first serious discussions of FOSS adoption in government and led to a variety of open source solutions being deployed by the U.S. government in the early 2000s. This included the NSA's release of SELinux—an operating system integrated with a suite of FOSS pen testing and security tools, and DHS's Homeland Open Security Technology (HOST) program in 2004.

In 2008, The Open Source Census reported that European government entities had the highest use of FOSS per computer scanned, with an average of 68 different open source packages installed per computer. The United States averaged 51 open source packages per computer [18].

Between 2009 and 2012, several advocacy groups were established to promote the opportunities of FOSS in U.S. government, including Open Source for America—a coalition of companies, academic institutions, communities, and individuals; and

CivicCommons—a community-driven app store that brings people together to share their solutions, knowledge, and best practices to improve government.

In 2003, the Department of Defense approved the use of open source in their agency [26], and later in 2012, they released a memorandum stating that open source and proprietary software are considered equal [30]. NASA also launched code.nasa.gov— a repository of FOSS projects currently in development at NASA.

So far, the energy sector has not been part of the efforts to adopt FOSS.

2.2   Software Security in the Energy Sector

Security, including cyber security, has long been an important concern for the energy sector, given the electric grids' importance as a key infrastructure. In the past, this was in large parts achieved through the isolation of control systems from more publicly accessible and exposed systems, a practice the industry refers to as "siloing." This practice, in theory, means that for control systems, cyber security largely devolved into a problem of physical security.

This model has proven difficult to implement. The temptation or need to network critical systems, be it for monitoring, maintenance, reporting, or to optimize operations means that in practice these systems have been more exposed than the industry has at time been willing to admit.

Robert J. Turk's "Cyber Incidents Involving Control Systems", published in 2005 for the U.S. Department of Homeland Security" summarizes 120 known cyber security incidents [27]. They found that forty-two percent of incidents derived from mobile malware, twenty-eight percent from hacks, twenty-six percent from misconfiguration, and four percent from penetration tests or audits. Thirty-eight percent of these incidents occurred from within the organization, sixty-one from outside the organization, and one percent were unknown. Thirty-three percent of the perpetrators were insiders (contractors, former employees, and current employees), forty-three percent were malware authors, and four percent were foreign nations, competitors and unknowns [27].

In January 2003, the "Slammer" worm disabled the computerized safety monitoring system at the Davis-Besse nuclear power plant in Ohio. Stuxnet is one of the most well-known cyber threats in history. Its primary goal was to reprogram Siemens industrial control systems, but as of September 29, 2010, Stuxnet had infected about 100,000 computers after it escaped on an employee's laptop from Iran. 60% of infected hosts are in Iran, but it has spread to more than 155 countries [8]. Since Stuxnet, other cyber attacks have occurred around the world with both criminal and commercial intent that conduct both espionage (collecting data) and sabotage (destroying data). This includes the Duqa and the Flame virus, a trojan similar to Stuxnet that scans computer systems for key private information on very specific machines around the world.

Hahn and Govindarasu explain that "The coupling of the power infrastructure with complex computer networks substantially expand[s] current cyber attack surface area [...]" [12]. In 2011, the Energy Sector Control Systems Working Group released the "Roadmap to Achieve Energy Delivery Systems Cyber security." This roadmap addresses the growing vulnerabilities in energy delivery systems, including "control systems, smart grid technologies, and the interface of cyber and physical security—where physical access to system components can impact cyber security" [2].

"This update recognizes that smart technologies (e.g., smart meters, phasor measurement units), new infrastructure components, the increased use of mobile devices, and new applications are changing the way that energy information is communicated and controlled while introducing new vulnerabilities and creating new needs for the protection of consumer and energy market information" [2].

The focus on the smart grid and automated control systems like SCADA has opened up for a variety of new threats, business practices, market trends, regulations, and technologies. Among these are a few important issues [2]:

- "Growing reliance on commercial off-the-shelf technologies"
- "Increasing reliance on external providers for business solutions and services, which introduces additional cyber and physical reliability challenges"
- "Increasing interconnection of business and control system networks"
- "Increasing reliance on the telecommunications industry and the Internet for communications"

Though the energy sector does work with unique systems, and have some unique security concerns and requirements, some of these do overlap with general IT security. It is therefore not surprising to find these groups using FOSS tools such as NMAP, OpenADR, OpenPDC, and Hadoop.

The industry has also developed some unique FOSS solutions. In April 2012, Pacific Northwest National Laboratory announced they would be open sourcing a homegrown, host-based security sensor to encourage community feedback and participation. The cyber tool is called the Hone Project and it "pinpoints which applications or processes infected machines and an external network they are using to communicate" [17].

These efforts notwithstanding, there appears to be a marked dearth in energy sector FOSS projects, including cyber security related projects.

3   Study Methodology

Our goal was to catalogue experiences and attitudes with regard to the adoption and development of FOSS in and for the U.S. energy sector, especially related to cyber security. We used a mixed-method study design, implementing both online surveys—to reach a broad audience, and interviews—to gather rich data.

The first step of our process was identifying key FOSS projects, and organizations that operate within the energy sector. We started from a list of contacts from Energy-Sec. We scoured online sources, industry papers, and research articles for others who might provide insight.

Next we emailed each potential contact, explaining the purpose of the study and provided them with a link to our surveys. Two surveys were used, one for people working the energy sector and another for contributors to FOSS projects used in the energy sector. Subjects who identified with both groups filled out both surveys.

Seven semi-structured interviews were conducted with selected survey respondents. Although a regimented series of questions were developed, the semi-structured approach allowed us to explore issues brought up by subjects, or their thinking.

We used open coding as our method of data analysis. Open coding is a method of grounded theory that provides a way for researchers to procedurally organize and analyze qualitative data [3]. We generated codes from our initial survey responses. These codes were discussed among the researchers and used to define categories of comments and concepts in the data. For example, when one participant commented that "business drivers force the energy industry to network their systems [...]," this was tagged with the code "barrier/risk"). Interview transcripts, notes, and surveys answers were analyzed line-by-line and coded independently by two researchers. These codes were compared and refined. This process was repeated until there was sufficient agreement about the codes and their meaning. After all data elements coded, common themes were identified.

The burden of proof is relatively low in exploratory studies; the goal of this study was not to prove anything statistically, but to identify broad themes and concepts. Thus our sample sizes were small, and we did not bother with statistical analysis.

3.1   Sampling

We divided our subjects into three categories: energy producers and grid operators, the solution providers they rely on (IT contractors, software and hardware companies, etc.), and FOSS projects. All three groups were represented in our surveys, and we wanted to make sure all were represented in our interviews. We therefore chose to interview representatives from Portland General Electric, the Tennessee Valley Authority, Utilisec, Dell SecureWorks, GADS/OS, Green Energy Corp, and the Grid Protection Alliance. Table 1 shows how these organizations were classified in our study.

Table 1. List of organizations

Energy Producers	Solutions Providers	FOSS Projects
Portland General Electric	Utilisec	GADS/OS
Tennessee Valley Authority	Dell SecureWorks	Green Energy Corp
		Grid Protections Alliance

Portland General Electric (PGE). PGE serves over 800,000 customers over 52 cities in Oregon and has deployed 825,000 smart meters [24]. PGE can offer insight into their day-to-day operations in both IT and operations from the perspective of a midsize energy provider.

Tennessee Valley Authority (TVA). TVA is owned by the U.S. Government and provides electricity to 9 million people throughout the southeast United States, being the 5th largest provider in terms of revenue [1]. TVA represents a larger energy provider with more diversified resources and needs.

Utilisec. UtiliSec offers cyber security services specifically tailored for electric utilities, with expertise in smart grid security, low-level analysis, and penetration testing. They offer training as well as guidance on real-world systems and security architecture review, penetration testing, and policy composition [28].

Dell SecureWorks®. Secureworks is a provider of information-security-as-a-service, processing more than 13 billion security events and 30,000 malware specimens each day[6]. Dell SecureWorks have extensive experience partnering with utility providers, helping them solve security challenges with industrial control systems and SCADA networks, smart grid technologies, advanced metering infrastructure and other critical IT assets. Currently, they are working on Snort 2.9 (Modbus and DNP3)—a network intrusion detection system for Unix.

GADS Open Source (GADS/OS). GADS/OS is a FOSS project that collects and analyzes performance and event data in a power grid and reports it to NERC. More than 200 companies and 3,800 generating units use GADS/OS in the United States and around the world [9].

Green Energy Corp. Green Energy Corp provides software solutions and software engineering services to communications, utilities, and energy companies. Green Energy Corp developed a FOSS platform called Greenbus, which enables utilities to integrate legacy technologies into their smart grid [25].

Grid Protection Alliance. The Grid Protection Alliance (GPA) is a non-profit aimed at supporting the development of security-related IT solutions for the energy sector [11]. GPA's projects include the PMU Connection Tester, openPDC, openPG, and SIEGate.

4   Findings

FOSS is used more extensively in the energy sector than we initially thought, though most organizations are consumers rather than producers, and most use is behind the scenes. All participants noted, in some fashion, that FOSS was not seen as unreliable or undesirable, though several commented that the FOSS support model could cause problems.

Contributing to FOSS is much more rare than adoption, primarily due to real or perceived intellectual property and liability concerns, uncertainty about how to build community, lack of best practices, and other internal roadblocks. Some concerns were raised about the need to maintain good relations with solution providers and not wanting to appear in direct competition for fear of liability or regulatory oversight. These are common concerns of many industries where there is a lack of strong leadership and examples of FOSS adoption.

FOSS is currently used mostly for ad hoc security solutions. By this we mean that system administrators use one-off FOSS tools to complete small tasks, while proprietary enterprise software is used for critical system management and controls (e.g., SCADA). One participant claimed that "almost every tool used by testers is open source; Backtrack (Linux distribution) is a good example."

On the IT side, use of FOSS seems common, and decisions to adopt FOSS seem to be made based on an assessment of need and availability, as well as vendor support. On the operations side of these organizations, we found that security needs or concerns are downplayed and sometimes ignored due to the supposed separation between IT and production systems. This separation is not always real, and there have been many instances where control systems have been linked to IT systems, either intentionally or accidentally, and security has been breached. As the industry moves to implement a smart grid, the need to network the two sides, as well as consumers and producers, will further weaken the security through isolation model.

4.1   Themes

Eleven codes were generated from the interviews and surveys: *perceptions, future needs or trends, drivers, barriers, risks, potential opportunities, use cases, best practices, ad hoc solutions and policy, reasons for using open source, and business models.* These codes were paired down into two categories: *drivers for adoption* and *risks and barriers.* Table 2 and 3 list each theme that was shared between interviewees or unique to an organization or FOSS project.

Table 2. Drivers for adoption

EP: Energy Producer; **SP:** Solutions Provider; **FP:** FOSS Project; **#:** Number of respondents who agreed			
Theme	**EP**	**SP**	**FP**	**#**
FOSS has greater flexibility and functionality	X	X	X	5
FOSS solutions are already being developed internally	X	X	X	4
Smart grid initiatives require more focus on security	X	X	X	4
Control systems and IT were separate, need to integrate		X	X	4
FOSS decreases license cost	X		X	4
NERC/CIP requires compliance	X	X	X	3
Staff know FOSS tools	X		X	3
FOSS is more secure and reliable	X		X	3
FOSS security tools can be leveraged to face overlapping problems	X	X		3
FOSS decreases vendor lock-in			X	3
Homegrown FOSS solutions are currently being shared	X		X	2
FOSS is currently used ad hoc and in other contexts	X	X		2
FOSS can support niche and legacy systems		X	X	2
Companies will (and can) pay for custom development of FOSS			X	2
FOSS provides a lower support cost	X			1
FOSS provides a lower time to acquisition			X	1

Table 3. Risks and barriers

EP: Energy Producer; **SP:** Solutions Provider; **FP:** FOSS Project; **#:** Number of respondents who agreed				
Theme	**EP**	**SP**	**FP**	**#**
Uncertainty exists about the stability of FOSS for business support	X	X	X	5
Energy sector follows more than it leads, risk averse, regulation driven	X	X	X	5
Distrust between control engineers and other IT professionals	X	X	X	4
Energy producers rely on a small number of vendors. Vendors lack FOSS support	X		X	4
Domain expertise is needed to install/develop core services and standards	X	X	X	4
Lack of solutions (including FOSS) for control systems	X	X	X	4
Reluctance to acknowledge vulnerability of control systems		X	X	4
Energy providers prefer to buy complete solutions	X			1
Jurisdiction (e.g., federal vs. private, regional) issues limit collaboration			X	1

From these codes, we identified themes, significant converging perceptions, drivers, barriers and risks associated with the use and adoption of FOSS in the energy sector. The themes we identified are the following:

4.1.1   FOSS as an "Unknown" or "Hippy Movement"

Many in the energy sector perceive FOSS as a "hippy movement," an ad-hoc effort rather than an effective software model. When FOSS is suggested, most people don't know where the support comes from, which is crucial in energy operations. One FOSS project manager noted that "every client ultimately asks 'how do you stay in business? Will you be there when I need you?'" This same person finds himself doing presentations because people "don't understand open source." One energy producer prefers to pay for something because it guarantees a complete product. This might explain why FOSS is currently used in an ad hoc way with very little, if any, organized discussion of open source adoption aside from small in-house teams or regional collaborators. On the other hand, these perceptions do not apply to more well-known FOSS systems like Linux.

4.1.2   Separation between Controls Engineers and IT

The division of jurisdiction between operations engineers and IT has impeded the broader adoption of FOSS in the energy sector. Systems are being secured by home-grown security teams (often out of the control systems ranks). With the onset of the smart grid, utilities are forced to modernize and network their control systems. Several subjects noted that controls engineers perceive IT engineers as "cowboys". For this reason, many control engineers do not want to let the IT staff "mess around" with security on their systems. In essence, controls engineers try to shut IT folks out of the system. One interviewee noted that there are not enough security professionals in energy sector. Increasing IT numbers could offset these tensions.

4.1.3   Vendor Dependence

It was emphasized that a small number of vendors supply the majority of software solutions to the energy sector. The current mentality is to buy whatever the vendor is supplying rather than advocating for new solutions from these vendors, which means that these vendors decide what software is adopted. Without the support of vendors, FOSS will not be a viable option for security. If a FOSS solution fails, the liability falls on the organization and not the software developers or the vendor. If utilities pool their resources they can get vendors to meet changes and add features they need. As noted by one interviewee, "if you get some of the bigger vendors moving in that direction [of open source] then you will have change."

4.1.4   Legal Concerns

The energy sector is a risk-averse community that follows more than it leads. As one energy producer commented, "the more you use a standard practice, the less questions auditors ask." Regulatory bodies have shaped the adoption and use of software in the energy sector and there are penalties for noncompliance. Common practices, similar tools and methodologies will create simpler audits. This issue presents a variety of legal uncertainty involving the adopting FOSS, which is outside the norm. The energy sector needs one or two strong and influential organizations to prove that FOSS works. Currently, the regional division of the energy sector (e.g., Texas operates independently, the Pacific Northwest collaborates regionally, etc.) does not simplify the task, making it harder to look for role models across regions.

5   Discussion

Our findings show that FOSS is used extensively in the energy sector, though most of it is relatively informal, and few organizations are large-scale users, much less producers of FOSS. As Table 3 demonstrates, interviewees confirmed that FOSS offers significant benefits in cost and flexibility. However, FOSS is still used in most cases as a cursory solution to improve task efficiency or detect network intrusions. FOSS is not used as a primary solution for managing critical systems.

We believe that one of the main reasons for this ad-hoc use of FOSS is a lack of discussion in the energy sector community about the use of FOSS and its potential benefits. Such a FOSS discussion could create a means to petition and influence the market (e.g., vendors, etc.) to deliver more FOSS solutions. The energy community can also leverage best practices, potential opportunities, and the community itself to subdue the risks and barriers that have inhibited FOSS adoption.

One subject noted that there is a lack of documentation that explains how organizations have successfully used FOSS, as well as their reasoning for choosing it. In an effort to broaden their participation in FOSS, the Government of Spain conducted a dossier project in 2010 to catalogue the best practices of FOSS communities and project that are heavily influenced by a public administration [4]. This helped lay the foundations for further adoption. Without sharing case studies, lists of best practices, lessons learned, or advice about legal issues, an organization will find it difficult to justify change. Similarly, the "keeping the lights on" mentality in the energy sector has demonstrated the strong connection between reliability and financial impact. Creating and sharing case studies and best practices will help circulate FOSS's reliability.

FOSS also needs to be recommended by trusted sources. Procuring support of FOSS from larger vendors in the energy sector will drive FOSS acceptance and adoption. Similarly, open sourcing commercial software can open up new revenue streams in consulting and support, which can also improve vendor buy-in.

Opportunities have also surfaced around creating and maturing open standards. Collaboration will help create common practices, tools, and audit procedures that will help shape standards. An example is the Secure Information Exchange Gateway (SIEGate), a FOSS project that provides a secure channel for transporting real-time data between a "utility control center and other control centers, utilities, and regulatory and oversight entities" [21]. This project is a collaborative effort between the Grid Protection Alliance, University of Illinois-Urbana Champaign, Alstom Grid, PJM Interconnection, and the Pacific Northwest National Laboratory. Since the FOSS development model hinges itself on the motto "release early, release often", it is designed to take in changes and deploy them quickly. This creates a responsive environment for implementing policy change and complying with new standards.

Ultimately, one of the most powerful and easiest way to promote the development and adoption of FOSS could be through a top-down initiative and promotion from a regulatory or government agency like the U.S. Department of Energy, much like the U.S. Department of Defense and the U.S. Department of Homeland Security have done for FOSS through the HOST program [14].

6   Limitations

Although we believe the cases examined in this study characterize many of the entities operating in the U.S. energy sector, there are limitations to our work. Firstly, while interviews with individuals within the projects and organizations provided an expansive perspective of FOSS and cyber security, these perspectives are not necessarily representative. Many other organizations operate within the energy sector that did not participate in the study. This includes national labs, electric cooperatives, regulatory bodies and other affiliates. Due to scheduling, policy, or other reasons, representative members of these groups were unable to participate in the study.

That said, and while more study should be undertaken to confirm and expand on their findings, these case studies provide some interesting insight into the barriers and opportunities of FOSS adoption in the U.S. energy sector.

Acknowledgements. We would like to thank EnergySec for funding this project, as well as providing insight into the energy sector. We also appreciate the participation of Portland General Electric, Tennessee Valley Authority, Utilisec, Dell Secureworks®, GADS Open Source, Green Energy Corp, and Grid Protection Alliance.

References

[1] About TVA, http://www.tva.com/abouttva/index.html

[2] Batz, D., Brenton, J., Dunn, D., William, G., Clark, P., Elwart, S., Goff, E., Barrell, B., Hawk, C., Henrie, M., Kenchingon, H., Maughan, D., Kaiser, L., Norton, D.: Roadmap to Achieve Energy Delivery Systems Cyber Security (2011), http://www.cyber.st.dhs.gov/wp-content/uploads/2011/09/Energy_Roadmap.pdf

[3] Berg, B.L.: Qualitative research methods for the social sciences. Allyn and Bacon, Glencoe (1989)

[4] Bryant, D., Ramsamy, P.: Public Administrations Code Release Communities: Dossier ONSFA (2011), http://observatorio.cenatic.es/index.php?option=com_content&view=article&id=728%3Adosiier-nuevo&catid=5%3Aadministraciones-publicas&Itemid=21 (accessed March 23)

[5] Coverity: 2011 Open Source Integrity Report, http://softwareintegrity.coverity.com/coverity-scan-2011-open-source-integrity-report-registration.html

[6] Dell to Acquire Secureworks, http://content.dell.com/us/en/corp/d/secure/2011-01-04-ir-shld-release

[7] Department of Energy Launches Initiative with Industry to Better Pro-tect the Nation's Electric Grid from Cyber Threats, http://energy.gov/articles/department-energy-launches-initiative-industry-better-protect-nation-s-electric-grid-cyber

[8] Falliere, N., Murchu, L.O., Chien, E.: W32. Stuxnet Dossier (2011), http://www.symantec.com/content/en/us/enterprise/media/security_response/whitepapers/w32_stuxnet_dossier.pdf

[9] GADS Open Source, http://gadsopensource.com/

[10] Ghosh, R.A., Glott, R., Krieger, B., Robles, G.: Free/Libre and Open Source Software: Survey and Study, Part 4: Survey of Developers (June 2002), http://www.flossproject.org/report/

[11] Grid Protection Alliance "Grid Protection Alliance" (2012), http://www.gridprotectionalliance.org

[12] Hahn, A., Govindarasu, M.: Cyber Attack Exposure Evaluation Framework for the Smart Grid. IEEE Transactions of Smart Grid 2(4), 835–843 (2011)

[13] Herraiz, I., Robles, G., Amor, J.J., Romera, T., Gonzalez Barahona, J.M.: The Process of Joining in Global Distributed Software Projects. In: Proc. of the Int'l Workshop on Global Software Development for the Practitioner, pp. 27–33 (2006)

[14] Homeland Open Security Technology, http://www.cyber.st.dhs.gov/host/

[15] Krishnamurthy, S.: Cave or Community? An Empirical Examination of 100 Mature Open Source Projects. First Monday 7(6) (2002)

[16] Lakhani, K.R., Wolf, R.G.: The Boston Consulting Group Hacker Survey (2002), http://ftp3.au.freebsd.org/pub/linux.conf.au/2003/papers/Hemos/Hemos.pdf

[17] Messmer, E.: Research lab extends host-based cyber sensor project to open source, http://www.networkworld.com/news/2012/041612-hone-258296.html

[18]   Open Source Census Tracks Enterprise Use of Open Source Globally (2008), http://www.osscensus.org/9.30.08.php

[19]   Ransbotham, S.: An Empirical Analysis of Exploitation Attempts based on Vulnerabilities in Open Source Software. Workshop on the Economics of Information Security (2010), http://weis2010.econinfosec.org/papers/session6/weis2010_ransbotham.pdf

[20]   Robles, G., Scheider, H., Tretkowski, I., Webers, N.: Who Is Doing It? A research on Libre Software developers (2001), http://widi.berlios.de/paper/study.html

[21]   Siegate: Secure Information Exchange Gateway for Electric Grid Operations, http://www.iti.illinois.edu/research/power-grid/siegate-secure-information-exchange-gateway-electric-grid-operations

[22]   Smart Grid, http://energy.gov/oe/technology-development/smart-grid

[23]   Smart Grid Investment Grant Program: Progress Report (2012), http://energy.gov/sites/prod/files/Smart%20Grid%20Investment%20Grant%20Program%20-%20Progress%20Report%20July%202012.pdf

[24]   Smart Grid, Portland General Electric, http://www.portlandgeneral.com/our_company/energy_strategy/smart_grid/default.aspx

[25]   Srivastava, M: Green Energy Corp Introduces Smart Grid Open Source Community, http://smart-grid.tmcnet.com/topics/smart-grid/articles/134784-green-energy-corp-introduces-smart-grid-open-source.html

[26]   Stenbit, J.P.: Open Source Software (OSS) in the Department of Defense (DoD) (2003), http://oss-insti-tute.org/storage/documents/Resources/policy/2003_stenbit_memo.pdf

[27]   Turk, R.J.: Cyber Incidents Involving Control Systems, http://www.inl.gov/technicalpublications/Documents/3480144.pdf

[28]   Utilisec: Electric Utility Cyber Security, http://www.utilisec.com/

[29]   Walli, S., Gynn, D., Rotz, V.: The Growth of Open Source Software in Organization (2005), http://dirkriehle.com/wp-content/uploads/2008/03/wp_optaros_oss_usage_in_organizations.pdf

[30]   Wennergren, D.M.: Clarifying Guidance Regarding Open Source Software (OSS) (2009), http://dodcio.defense.gov/Portals/0/Documents/FOSS/2009OSS.pdf

[31]   Wheeler, D.: Why Open Source Software/Free Software (OSS/FS, FOSS, or FLOSS)? Look at the Numbers! (2007), http://www.dwheeler.com/oss_fs_why.html

[32]   Ye, Y., Kishida, K.: Toward an understanding of the motivation of open source software developers. In: Proc. of the 25th International Conf. on Software Engineering, pp. 419–429 (2003)

A Dual Model of Open Source License Growth

Gottfried Hofmann[1], Dirk Riehle[1], Carsten Kolassa[1], and Wolfgang Mauerer[2]

[1] Friedrich-Alexander-Universität Erlangen-Nürnberg. Computer Science Department,
Martenstrasse 3, 91058 Erlangen, Germany
dirk@riehle.org
http://osr.cs.fau.de/
[2] Siemens AG, Corporate Research and Technologies,
San-Carlos-Str. 7. 91058 Erlangen, Germany
wolfgang.mauerer@siemens.com

Abstract. Every open source project needs to decide on an open source license. This decision is of high economic relevance: Just which license is the best one to help the project grow and attract a community? The most common question is: Should the project choose a restrictive (reciprocal) license or a more permissive one? As an important step towards answering this question, this paper analyses actual license choice and correlated project growth from ten years of open source projects. It provides closed analytical models and finds that around 2001 a reversal in license choice occurred from restrictive towards permissive licenses.

1   Introduction

Research on open source software (OSS) and development processes has gained significant momentum over the last decade. Landmark work was published by Lerner and Tirole in 2003 [1]. A meta-study was conducted by Aksulu and Wade in 2010 [2] to give an overview of the state of the research in the field. Yet many basic questions remain to be answered. One of them is the question of licensing.

When a project has the ability to chose its license freely, license choice is frequently controversial. The same applies to the situation where a project decides to switch from one license to another. Besides philosophical reasons to favor one type of license over another there is the concern whether the chosen license has an impact on the project's success.

Our research question is to understand the relationship between OSS licenses and project growth. In this paper we answer the question of which type of license do people prefer.

Roughly from the early 1960s to the early 1980s sharing of source code for computer programs was commonplace and conducted in an informal manner. This kind of collaboration happened in an academic setting. When commercial companies started to enforce intellectual property rights, the first open source licenses emerged as an effort to retain the collaborative environment by providing a legal framework.

E. Petrinja et al. (Eds.): OSS 2013, IFIP AICT 404, pp. 245–256, 2013.

Among the first of these initiatives was the Free Software Foundation (FSF) [3], which published a first version of the GNU General Public License in 1989 [4]. The GPL includes a clause that forces developers who make changes to the code to release their changes under the same conditions as the GPL. This property of the GPL led to the attribution of the GPL as a 'viral' [5] or 'reciprocal' license. Another term for this kind of licensing is 'copyleft'. For the remainder of this paper, licenses of this kind will be called 'restrictive'.

In 1988, two licenses were first published whose conditions were later coined 'copyfree' or 'permissive', namely the MIT license [6] and the BSD license [7][1]. Both do not require derived work to be licensed under the same terms[2], thus redistributing code for proprietary products is possible.

Later, licenses were created like the GNU Lesser General Public License (LGPL) that are less restrictive than the GPL-like licenses yet still not completely permissive. Projects that use those licenses are not subject of this analysis for the sake of simplicity.

Please note that both license types emerged roughly at the same time, so none of the two types used for the analysis here had a "head-start" over the others, see Fig. 1.

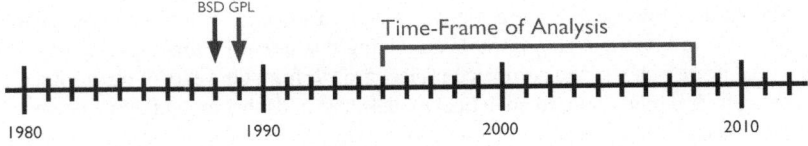

Fig. 1. Time-frame of the analysis

This paper makes the following contributions:

- Two analytically closed models of the total open source growth binned by license-type are proposed.
  - A validation of the models using statistical measures.
  - An estimation of changing-points that separates the growth into two periods.

The rest of the paper is structured as follows. Section 2 reviews related work. Section 3 presents the data source and research method. Section 4 provides the discovered models and statistical validation. We discuss potential limitations in section 5 and present our conclusions in section 6.

2   Related Work

Various studies have been conducted in the past to find out about the rationale behind a license choice. Sen, Subramian and Nelson [8] suggest that "OSS managers who

---

[1] Both licenses are available in multiple versions now, like the 2-clause, 3-clause and 4-clause BSD license or the X11 license.
[2] Yet there are still restrictions like in the 'New BSD License' which does not permit advertising of derived products with the name of the licensor.

want to attract a limited number of highly skilled programmers to their open source project should choose a restrictive OSS license. Similarly, managers of software projects for social programs could attract more developers by choosing a restrictive OSS license". Lerner and Tirole [9] argue that "Projects with unrestricted licenses attract more contributors". In contrast, Colazo and Fang [10] analyzed 44 restrictively- and 18 permissively-licensed projects from the SourceForge database. The restrictively-licensed projects had a significantly higher developer membership and coding activity.

In a series of articles [11] [12] [13], Aslett describes a recent trend in open source licensing that shows that the ratio of permissively- vs. restrictively-licensed projects is slowly shifting in favor of permissive licensing. Source for the data is both the Ohloh.net [14] database and FLOSSmole [15]. The time-frame of that analysis is from 2008 to 2011. We are not verifying these findings as the author looks at trends from 2008 onwards. This paper looks at the developments from 1995 to the middle of 2007 filling the gap left by Aslett.

Deshpande and Riehle [16] use 5122 active and popular open source projects from the Ohloh database as a sample and find that open source in both added SLoC per month and new projects per month shows in total exponential growth.

3   Data Source and Research Method

The sample source of this paper is a snapshot of the Ohloh.net [14] database dated March 2008. The Ohloh database has been collecting data of open source projects since 2005 from publicly visible revision control repositories. Since those repositories provide a history, the available data dates back as early as 1983 [17]. Yet data before 1995 was omitted as it was too sparse to be useful. Data after June 2007 was also omitted as it was not fully collected yet. According to Koch [18], revision control systems (RCS) are a very good source to study open source projects.

Our analysis is data driven: we are discovering existing characteristics in our data rather than starting off with a hypothesis and attempting to invalidate or validate it. We analyze how the total growth of open source projects can be correlated to the chosen type of license and provide closed-form models. We provide details of our final findings and list the models we tried to fit.

3.1   Metrics Employed

To measure growth of the size of projects, we use the metric Source Lines of Code (SLoC) added per month. A SLoC is a line in a commit (code contribution) that is neither empty nor a comment. According Herraiz et. al. [19], SLoC is a good metric to measure project growth. To show this they compared SLoC to various other common metrics of size (number of functions etc.) and complexity (McCabe's cyclomatic complexity, Halstead's length, volume, level etc.) of software projects and found a high correlation between them.

SLoC are calculated using the Unix diff command between two consecutive versions and then removing blanks and comments.

3.2   Growth

To determine the total growth of one license-type, all SLoC of all projects in a license-bin are added up in month-windows after removing the initial month. Removing the initial month is done to reflect the fact that the size at 'birth' of a project is not of interest when measuring growth. Thus the problems of forks and projects that started privately are also addressed[3].

We chose added SLoC per month because it represents all developers as opposed to choosing the number of projects started per month which would only represent those who started a project. Thus our approach is representative of the behavior of the entire developer population.

3.3   Distinction of License-Types

The model for permissive and restrictive licenses in this paper is based on the model proposed by Lerner and Tirole [9]. It was expanded by additional licenses that occur in the data set. All licenses are required to be approved by the OSI. Our sample contains 1861 projects in the category 'permissive' and 3257 projects in the category 'restrictive'. Projects offering both restrictive and permissive licenses are counted in both sets. Projects under 'mildly restrictive' or 'weak copyleft' licenses like the LGPL have been omitted for the sake of simplicity. Table 1 lists the number of occurrences in the sample.

The total number of projects included in the analysis is 5118 which is too large to list the individual projects in here. At its time, it constituted about 30% of all active open source projects.

Table 1. Licenses by Type. Multiple versions of a license are counted as one. For example GPL v1, v2 and v3 are listed as GPL only. Some projects have multiple licenses.

Permissive		Restrictive	
License Name	**Observations**	**License Name**	**Observations**
BSD	730	GPL	3248
MIT	378	CC-BY-SA	24
Apache	479		
zlib/libpng	26		
Public Domain[4]	34		
Artistic License	210		
Python license	17		
Zope	8		
Vovida	1		

---

[3] Note that this does not account for the case when a project becomes open source but the history of the revision control system is preserved or when a fork imports the history, too.

[4] Public Domain is considered a permissive 'license' in this paper.

4   Research Results

Fig. 2 shows the total added SLoC per month for the permissive and restrictive set. For the remainder of this paper, the data for the permissive set in each figure is on the left side and the restrictive set on the right. The blue curve is a smooth nonparametric fit obtained with the Loess method [20]. The curve shape is not influenced by a-priori considerations, it is solely data driven, and can be used as a visual aid in the comparison of descriptive models introduced below. The gray shaded area around the Loess curve represents the 95% confidence interval.

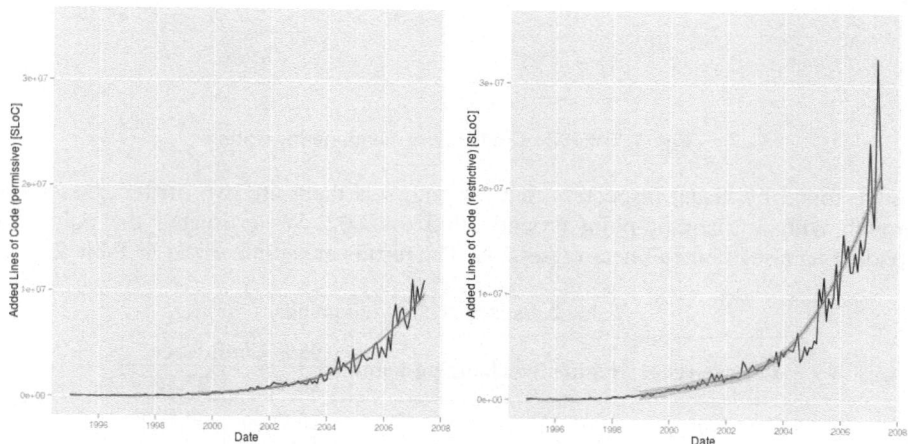

Fig. 2. Total SLoC added per month with blue Loess curve

The form of the monotonically growing Loess curve suggests the following model functions:
*   Logistic (normal and 4-parameter)
*   Gompertz
*   Polynomials: Quadratic, Cubic
*   Exponential

From the functions that returned a fit, we used Pearson's r^2 and visual inspection of the graphs to determine the best fit. For both sets the exponential model returned the highest Pearson's r^2 (0.960 for the permissive and 0.937 for the restrictive set) and best visual compliance. Equation (1) shows the formula for the exponential model.

$$y \sim y0 * \exp(a * x)$$ (1)

As a remedy for the heteroscedasticity that can be seen in Fig. 2 we log- transformed the response. The graphs with Loess curve in blue are shown in Fig. 3.

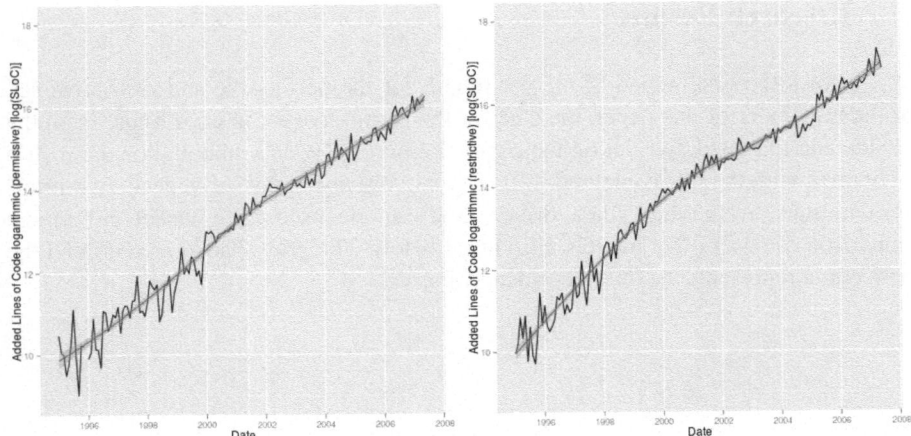

Fig. 3. Total SLoC added per month on log-scale

We found by visual inspection that for both sets there are two distinct periods of growth with a changing-point around 2000 to 2002. We estimated the points by conducting a segmented linear regression. The results are summarized in Table 2.

Table 2. Estimated changing-points

License-type	Estimated changing-point	95% Confidence	
		2.5%	97.5%
Permissive	2001-12	2000-06	2003-05
Restrictive	2000-02	1999-08	2000-08

The ordinary least-squares (OLS) estimator used for the linear regression is sensitive to autocorrelation in the data. We computed the Durbin-Watson-statistic[5] for both segmented linear models which returned significant autocorrelation at lag 1 for the permissive set and marginal autocorrelation at lag 1 for the restrictive set listed in Table 3.

Table 3. Autocorrelation and Durbin-Watson-Statistic for the segmented linear models up to lag 3

License-type	Lag	Autocorrelation	D-W-Statistic	p-value
Permissive	1	0.197	1.560	0.002
	2	-0.086	2.117	0.600
	3	-0.076	2.093	0.590
Restrictive	1	0.137	1.725	0.062
	2	0.038	1.913	0.492
	3	-0.020	1.944	0.670

---

[5] The Durbin-Watson-statistic is approximately 2 for no autocorrelation. Values up to 0 or 4 indicate positive or negative autocorrelation [20].

To take the autocorrelation into account, for both models the two segments were re-fitted using the generalized least-squares (GLS) estimator which works as a maximum-likelihood-estimator even under the presence of correlation. The resulting fits are shown in Fig. 4.

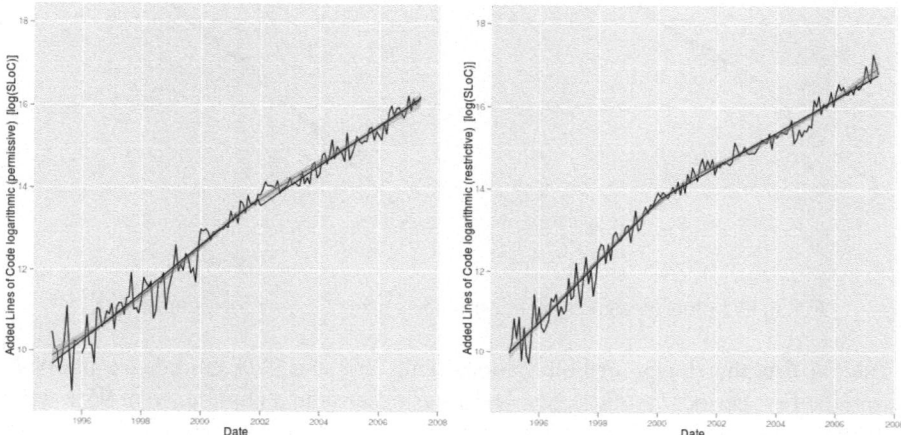

Fig. 4. Segmented linear models on log-scale of total added SLoC using GLS with blue Loess curve

The residuals are shown in Fig. 5 and the quantile-quantile (QQ)-Plots [20] in Fig. 6.

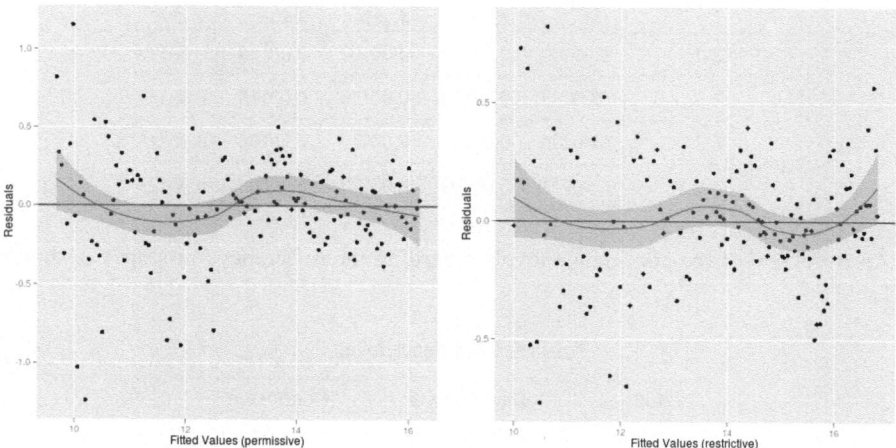

Fig. 5. Fitted values of segmented linear models using GLS on logarithmic data against residuals with Loess-curve in blue

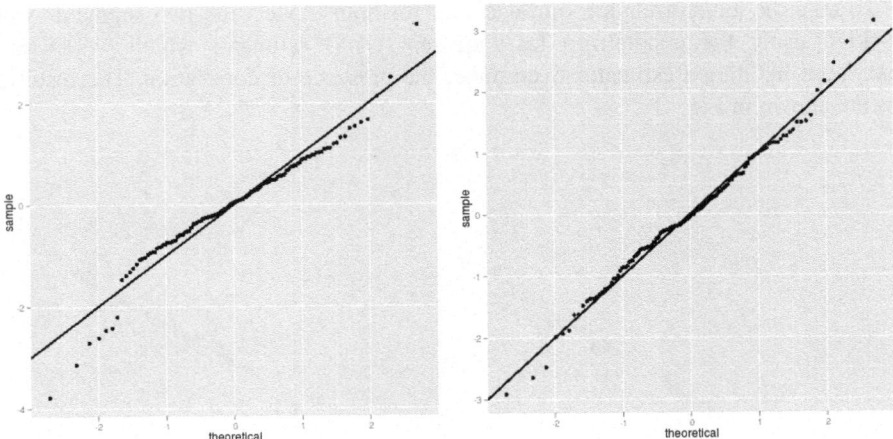

Fig. 6. QQ-plots of segmented linear models using GLS on logarithmic data

Table 4 lists the slopes for both periods with 75% and 95% confidence intervals. During the first period, the restrictive set grows faster with a confidence of 95% while the trend reverses in the second period where the permissive set is growing faster with a confidence of 75%. Note that after the changing-point, both sets grow slower. But the restrictive set shows a stronger slowdown than the permissive one.

Table 4. Comparison of the slope of the segmented linear models using GLS on log-transformed response for the restrictive and permissive set including confidence intervals.

Type	Period	Slope	75%		95%	
			12.5%	*87.5%*	*2.5%*	*97.5%*
Perm.	1	0.00160	0.00153	0.00167	0.00148	0.00172
	2	0.00133	0.00123	0.00143	0.00115	0.00150
Restr.	1	0.00205	0.00198	0.00210	0.00194	0.00215
	2	0.00112	0.00103	0.00122	0.00097	0.00128

An overview of the confidence levels regarding the differences-in-slopes is shown in Table 5:

Table 5. Confidence levels

Period	Total Growth	Confidence
1995-2001	Restrictive > Permissive	> 95%
2001-2007	Restrictive < Permissive	75%

Beyond the changing-point, the different growth speeds can not be distinguished with 95% confidence, yet the results indicate that the initial trend was reversed and the permissive set has been growing faster since then.

Fig. 7 shows the models transformed to the original non-logarithmic scale. The restrictive model visually deviates from the Loess curve towards the end, an effect that is intensified by the high slope in that area. In the future the curves would intersect again.

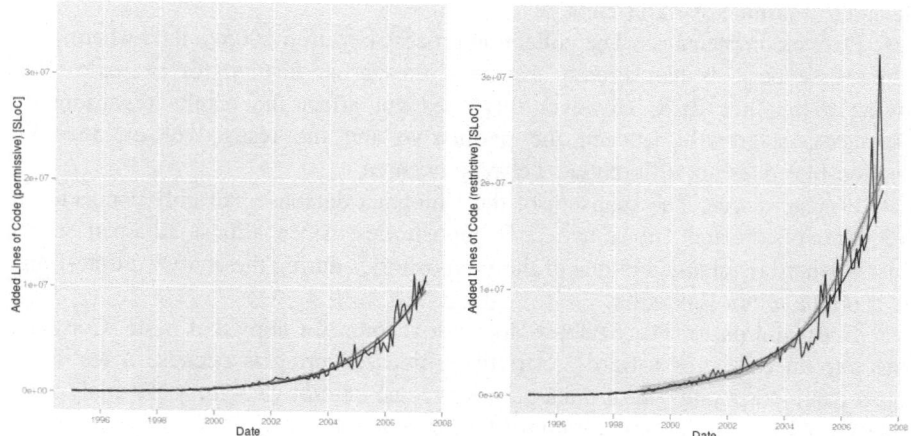

Fig. 7. Segmented linear models on normal scale

Table 6 lists the model fomulas.

Table 6. Models on nomal scale

Type	Model[6]
Perm.	$y = 0.00694 \cdot e^{0.00160 \cdot x} \cdot e^{(-0.000277 \cdot (x - \psi)_t)} \cdot e^{\varepsilon}$
Restr.	$y = 0.00017 \cdot e^{0.00205 \cdot x} \cdot e^{(-0.000922 \cdot (x - \psi)_t)} \cdot e^{\varepsilon}$

The back-transformed models include the error term, because the error roughly has a mean of zero for the linear models on the log-transformed response, which is no longer the case when the models get transformed back to normal scale. An estimate of the bias was conducted using the "smearing estimate of bias" method for residuals that are not normally distributed [21]. The bias needs to be taken into account when the models are used for prediction and is 1.049 (4.9%) for the permissive set and 1.035 (3.5%) for the restrictive one. We emphasize that this correction does, naturally, not eliminate the other complications associated with predictions from non-mechanistic models.

5   Limitations

The quantitative analysis has shortcomings in regard to the database used:

---

[6] $(x - \psi)_t$ defines a function where ψ is the break-point and $(x - \psi)_t$ is 0 for $(x < \psi)$.

- Sample size: The sample constituted of 1861 projects in the category 'permissive' and 3257 projects in the category 'restrictive'. The real number of active projects in both categories was much larger during the analyzed time-frame. Deshpande and Riehle [16] have estimated that the database holds roughly 30% of the active open source projects of the analyzed time-frame, a proportion we consider relevant to examine overall trends.

- Data incompleteness: The collection process began in 2005, a date where some open source projects had already discarded the earlier history, for example when moving to another RCS. However this does not affect the results regarding the differences in growth between the permissive and the restrictive set since the selection-bias does not differentiate between licenses.

- Project source: The snapshot of the Ohloh.net database had only connected to CVS, Subversion and Git source code repositories. Since almost all open source projects where maintained in one of these repositories during the analyzed time-frame this is only a minor limitation.

- Copy and paste: The database does not account for copy and paste. Copy and paste introduces a bias towards restrictively-licensed projects because a restrictive project can incorporate code from a permissive one but not vice-versa. To analyze the influence of this bias is a suggestion for further research.

- Aggregation: Also, we have only been looking at aggregate growth of open source projects, not at the growth of individual projects. We believe this to be justified, given the research question of this work. While some projects are large, the overall project size distribution has a long tail, making it impossible for any single project to have a substantial effect on the overall growth.

- Reproduceability: All data is publicly accessible and can be derived from the projects. The easiest way is to use the original data service, Ohloh.net, which has recently opened API access to its database for the general public.

6   Conclusions

This paper presents an empirical study of open source project growth using a large data set (about 30% of all active open source projects at its time). It repeats the prior finding that open source software code is growing at an exponential rate. It adds to that original finding a higher precision of the closed-form mathematical models of that growth. In addition, the paper looks at a project's open source license choice and provides a growth analysis binned by two dominant license types: permissive and restrictive (reciprocal) licenses. The paper provides analytically closed models for both license types and finds that both models are exponential as well. Surprisingly, both the permissively licensed and the restrictively licensed project data sets are best modeled by two separate exponential models with a changing point at around 2001 for both types of projects. Even more surprising, we find that restrictively licensed projects were growing faster than permissively licensed projects around until that changing point in 2001, and permissively licensed projects have been growing faster since then.

We attribute this finding to the growth of commercially sponsored open source communities, for example, the Linux, Apache, or the Eclipse Foundation [22]. Corbet found that most of the new code written for the Linux Kernel 2.6.20 was paid for by companies [23]. Similarly, in other yet unpublished work we have found an increasing and broad investment of company resources into community-owned open source. Such investments into a common good only make economic sense, if companies can reap benefits through complementary products that build on the common good. A restrictive license would restrict the creation of a competitively differentiated complementary product, so we believe that most companies will prefer a permissive license for the common good. The combined effect of increased commercial investment with the need for competitively differentiated products built on top of that shared investment has lead to an increase of permissively licensed projects and this obviously to such an extent, that number and size of permissively licensed projects have overtaken those of restrictively licensed projects. From this argument, we can only expect this trend to accelerate.

References

1. Lerner, J., Tirole, J.: Some simple economics of open source. The Journal of Industrial Economics L(2) (2002)
2. Aksulu, A., Wade, M.: A comprehensive review and synthesis of open source research 11(11), 576–656 (2010)
3. Free Software Foundation, http://www.fsf.org
4. GNU General Public License v1,
   http://www.gnu.org/licenses/gpl-1.0.html
5. González, A.G.: Viral contracts or unenforceable documents? Contractual validity of copyleft licences. European Intellectual Property Review, 1–20 (2004)
6. MIT License, http://www.opensource.org/licenses/MIT
7. BSD License, http://www.opensource.org/licenses/bsd-license.php
8. Sen, R., Subramaniam, C., Nelson, M.L.: Determinants of the choice of open source software license. Journal of Management Information Systems 25(3), 207–240 (2008)
9. Lerner, J., Tirole, J.: The scope of open source licensing. Source 21(1) (2005)
10. Colazo, J., Fang, Y.: Impact of License Choice on Open Source Software Development Activity. Journal of the American Society for Information Science 60(5), 997–1011 (2009)
11. Aslett, M.: The trend towards permissive licensing (2011),
    http://blogs.the451group.com/opensource/2011/06/06/
    the-trend-towards-permissive-licensing/
12. Aslett, M.: FLOSSmole data confirms declining GPL usage (2011),
    http://blogs.the451group.com/opensource/2011/06/13/
    flossmole-data-confirms-declining-gpl/
13. Aslett, M.: On the continuing decline of the GPL (2011),
    http://blogs.the451group.com/opensource/2011/12/15/
    on-the-continuing-decline-of-the-gpl/
14. Ohloh, the open source network, http://www.ohloh.net/
15. FLOSSmole: Collaborative collection and analysis of free/libre/open source project data,
    http://flossmole.org/

16. Deshpande A., Alto P., Riehle D.: The Total Growth of Open Source. Source (2006), 3 (2008)
17. Luckey, R.: The world's oldest source code repositories (2007), http://meta.ohloh.net/2007/08/worlds_oldest_source _code_repositories/
18. Koch, S.: Evolution of open source software systems – A large-scale investigation. In: International Conference on Open Source Systems (2005)
19. Herraiz, I., Gonzalez-Barahona, J.M., Robles, G., Rey, U., Carlo, J.: Towards a theoretical model for software growth. In: Fourth International Workshop on Mining Software Repositories, MSR 2007 (2007)
20. Fahrmeir, L.: Regression - Modelle, Methoden und Anwendungen. Springer (2009)
21. Newman, M.C.: Regression analysis of log-transformed data: Statistical bias and its correction. Environmental Toxicology and Chemistry 12(6), 1129–1133 (1993)
22. Riehle, D.: The Economic Case for Open Source Foundations. IEEE Computer 43(1), 86–90 (2010)
23. Corbet, J.: Who wrote 2.6.20?, http://lwn.net/Articles/222773/

Towards a Reference Model on How to Utilise Open Standards in Open Source Projects: Experiences Based on Drupal

Jonas Gamalielsson[1], Björn Lundell[1], Alexander Grahn[1], Stefan Andersson[4], Jonas Feist[4], Tomas Gustavsson[3], and Henrik Strindberg[2]

[1] University of Skövde, Skövde, Sweden
{jonas.gamalielsson,bjorn.lundell,alexander.grahn}@his.se
[2] Findwise AB, Göteborg, Sweden
henrik.strindberg@findwise.com
[3] PrimeKey Solutions AB, Solna, Sweden
tomas@primekey.se
[4] RedBridge AB, Kista, Sweden
{stefan.andersson,jfeist}@redbridge.se

Abstract. It is known that standards implemented in Open Source software (OSS) can promote a competitive market, reduce the risk for lock-in and improve interoperability, whilst there is limited knowledge concerning the relationship between standards and their implementations in OSS. In this paper we report from an ongoing case study conducted in the context of the ORIOS (Open Source software Reference Implementations of Open Standards) project in which influences between OSS communities and software standard communities are investigated. The study focuses on the Drupal project and three of its implemented standards (RDFa, CMIS, and OpenID).

1 Introduction

Many organisations are currently restricted in their choice of software because of restrictions imposed by existing systems. There is a lack of interoperability and a risk of different types of lock-in. The use of Open Standards and OSS implementations of standards can reduce the risk of lock-in, improve interoperability and stimulate innovation (Lundell et al., 2012; Friedrich, 2011). Further, it is widely acknowledged that there are challenges in implementing Open Standards (FRAND, 2012) and that standardisation has significant impact in the IT market and is subject to review within the digital agenda in the EU (Europe Economics, 2012). Open Standards, especially when implemented in OSS, have the potential to address challenges such as promoting a healthy and competitive market, reducing the risk for organisations of being technologically locked-in, and creating a basis for interoperability, and offering a basis for long-term access and reuse of digital assets (Lundell et al., 2012). Open standards are especially important for small companies, something which is acknowledged in national IT policies (Gov.uk, 2012).

E. Petrinja et al. (Eds.): OSS 2013, IFIP AICT 404, pp. 257–263, 2013.

In this paper we consider influences between OSS communities and software standard communities. In so doing, we report on an investigation of how communities involved in reporting and handling issues related to the implementation of a standard influence and are influenced by communities involved in the development and maintenance of the standard. We focus on OSS communities for the Drupal implementations of the three software standards RDFa, OpenID and CMIS, and associated software standard communities.

2   Towards a Reference Model for Open Standards and OSS

OSS implementations of software standards have made significant contributions to the establishment of standards (Behlendorf, 2009). Even if a number of standards in the software domain have been adopted and implemented in OSS projects, there is limited knowledge concerning the relationship between standards and their implementations in OSS (FRAND, 2012). Such knowledge is of particular relevance to small companies. For this reason this relationship with associated issues are explored in an ongoing collaborative research project (Lundell et al., 2012). In this research project, we seek to establish a reference model to aid concrete actions for any stakeholder wishing to utilise software standards in an Open Source context. In order to achieve this, we are conducting a number of studies on specific software standards and specific OSS projects.

We draw from an ongoing case study in which we specifically explore the Drupal OSS project and its relationship with three specific standards governed by three different standardisation organisations. By choosing RDFa (a W3C standard), CMIS (an OASIS standard), and OpenID (a foundation governed standard), our study includes investigation of standards provided under different governance models. Further, it was of interest to explore both core and add-on implementations of standards. RDFa and OpenID are both core implementations in Drupal, whereas CMIS is implemented as an add-on. The selected OSS project and the three specific standards represent specific examples of projects which are of interest to the companies involved in the ORIOS (Open Source software Reference Implementations of Open Standards) project. These exemplify core technologies used in the daily business and constitute a relevant set for investigation for all stakeholders involved in the project. Further, the relationship between standards and their implementation is complex (FRAND, 2012), which potentially has significant impact for small companies wishing to use Open Source provided under a copyleft license (Bain, 2012). From this we choose to investigate an OSS project (Drupal) provided under a strong copyleft license.

As part of our approach we first establish a characterisation of the three selected standards and the Drupal project by undertaking an analysis of release history, commits to the source code repository and contributing committers over time. Second, we investigate influences between OSS communities and software standard communities with respect to participation. In so doing, we focus on the three chosen standards using the issue tracking system of Drupal. Third, for RDFa we investigate influences between OSS communities and software standard communities with respect to common issues. The data for the Drupal project was collected from the Drupal website (Drupal.org, 2012), where all issues for Drupal core, RDFa, CMIS and OpenID were used in the analysis. Issue data for all releases of Drupal version 7 was used (including development versions), from the date of the first issue posting until 30 Nov. 2012. The issue data was collected and thereafter parsed and analysed using custom made scripts. More specifically, the timestamp and contributor ID for all issue postings was recorded. In addition, a search for issues in issue tracker, forums and mailing lists was performed by means of manual inspection of content in order to identify issues common to both the Drupal RDFa community and the W3C RDFa community.

3   Results

RDFa is a standard model for interchange of data on the web by embedding of metadata within web documents (W3.org, 2012), and is governed by W3C since 2008. CMIS (Content Management Interoperability Services) is a standard that defines a layer of abstraction for the control of various document management systems and repositories by the use of web based protocols (Oasis-open.org, 2010) and is governed by OASIS since 2010. The OpenID standard for decentralised authentication provides means for proving that an end user is in control of an identifier (Openid.net, 2007) and it is governed by the OpenID Foundation since 2007. All standards investigated in this paper are licensed under royalty-free conditions[1] which allow implementation in GPL licensed OSS projects.

Drupal is a content management platform written mainly in PHP, which is provided under the GPL Open Source license (Drupal.org, 2012). It can be used to create "broschureware" style web sites as well as web sites involving blogs, forums and other forms of collaborative environments. There are more than 600000 users and developers in the Drupal communities. Further, there have been 146 committers who have contributed a total of 88091 commits over 828174 lines of code (Ohloh.net, 2012) to Drupal core. The first commit to Drupal core was contributed in May 2000, and the most recent commit in Dec. 2012. There have been seven first level Drupal releases in the interval Jan. 2001 through Jan. 2011 (v1-3 in 2001, v4 in 2002, v5 in 2007, v6 in 2008, and v7 in 2011). In fact, there have been 113 releases (evenly distributed in time) in total since v1.0 including second and third level releases. The latest release (v7.17) was made available on 7 Nov. 2012.

Figure 1 (top diagram) shows number of issue postings (including issue creation and commenting) for Drupal core. Number of contributors over time for Drupal core

---

[1] RDF: http://www.w3.org/2012/09/rdfa-wg-charter, CMIS: https://www.oasis-open.org/news/pr/oasis-members-approve-content-management-interoperability-services-cmis-standard, OpenID: http://openid.net/intellectual-property/

is shown in the middle diagram in the same figure. An observation is that issues relevant for version 7 of Drupal are raised more than 9 years before the first stable release in Jan. 2011. Further, it is evident that significantly elevated activity precedes the first stable release of Drupal 7, whereafter the activity drops considerably. It can also be noted that there is an increasing trend in terms of number of monthly contributors until the time of the stable release after which the number of contributors stabilizes. Figure 1 (bottom diagram) illustrates number of issue postings over time for the parts of Drupal implementing the RDFa standard (green), the CMIS standard (red) and the OpenID standard (blue). Overall, it can be noted that the issue activity level is more modest for the implementations of the standards when comparing with all parts of the core. We also note that issue postings for OpenID go back to Jul. 2007, whereas issue activity for RDFa and CMIS started considerably later (Oct. 2009 and Mar. 2010, respectively).

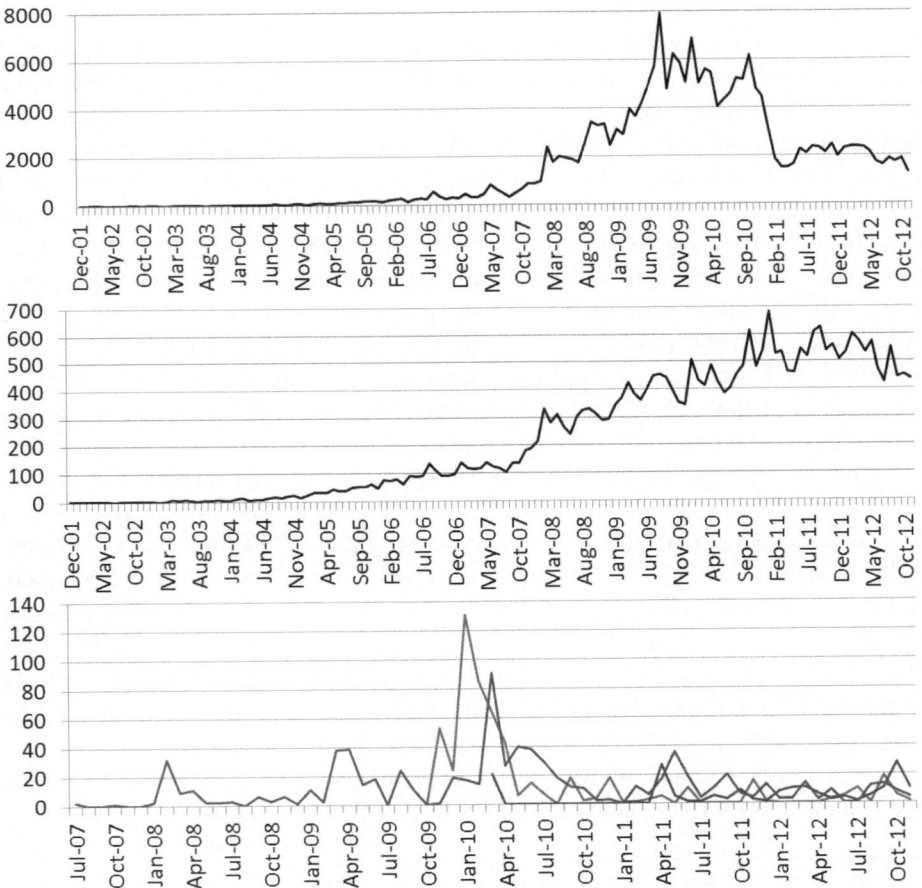

Fig. 1. Number of issue postings (top) and contributors (middle) in Drupal core. Bottom: Number of issue postings for RDFa (green), CMIS (red), and OpenID (blue)

The Venn diagram in Figure 2 provides an overview of the contributions to the Drupal issue tracker. The total number of contributors and postings for RDFa (green circle), CMIS (red circle) and OpenID (blue circle), is shown. Further, the figure illustrates the number of contributors who have contributed to the issue tracker for the seven possible (and mutually exclusive) combinations of the three standard implementations, and also shows (in brackets) the proportion of all postings for the different standards that the contributors in the different project combinations have contributed. Proportions for RDFa, CMIS and OpenID are coloured in green, red, and blue, respectively. It can be observed that the 17 contributors who have been been active in the issue tracker for both RDFa and OpenID have contributed the majority of the postings for RDFa (81,3%) and 30,1% of the postings for OpenID. Hence, there is significant influence between the RDFa and OpenID communities that contribute to the issue tracker. Further, there is very limited influence between CMIS and the other two standards since 98,2% of all CMIS postings are provided by 45 contributors who are only active in CMIS.

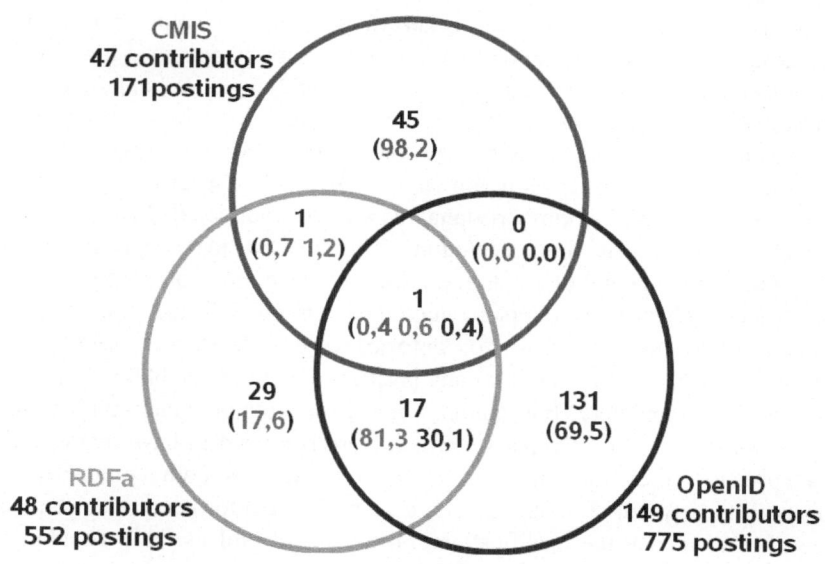

Fig. 2. Contributions to Drupal issue tracker for RDFa (green), CMIS (red) and OpenID (blue)

For the rest of this section we focus on the RDFa standard. When comparing the set of Drupal RDFa issue contributors with the set of participants in the meetings of the RDFa standard working group, there is one individual who is active in both communities. This person has contributed 199 (36%) of all 552 RDFa issue postings and has participated in 33 (31%) of all 104 RDFa working group meetings in the time period Feb. 2010 to Nov. 2012.

Further, RDFa related issues have been identified which appear in both the issue tracker and in the context of the W3C community involved in RDFa standardisation. One example is an issue on how some RDFa content is interpreted in Drupal (and other RDFa parsers) due to the use of XML literals that was raised in Jan. 2010 on the issue tracker. Deep processing of XML literals would be required to solve the problem, something which was currently not supported in the specification of RDFa. The same issue was subsequently acknowledged and discussed at a W3C meeting in Oct. 2010. Another example is an issue from Jan. 2010 concerning the validity of Drupal generated RDFa code, where one RDF validator reports invalid Drupal code for a specific attribute whereas another validator does not (i.e. two different conformance tests produce different results). This issue was afterwards discussed on the public RDFa mailing list at W3C in Apr. 2010. Further, the issue of support for Drupal specific needs and work practices concerning RDFa has been a recurring topic during several W3C meetings.

4   Discussion and Conclusion

Based on our experiences from participation in standardisation processes in different contexts (including OASIS), we acknowledge the inherent complexity of standardisation. It is not uncommon that development of standards is initially driven by needs stemming from specific usage scenarios involving stakeholders in different organisations. Therefore, standards are often subject to subsequent refinement, adaptation, and generalisation to fit new needs and usage scenarios. Our results illustrate this in the identified issue on support for Drupal specific needs and work practices concerning RDFa. Further, standards are often not detailed enough to enable for unambiguous software implementations. This, in turn, may imply that whoever makes the first implementation has precedence in terms of how to interpret a standard, and in particular when such an implementation becomes widely adopted.

Further, our results show that two conformance tests have been used within the Drupal project, which may impact on any business agreement involving Drupal. This imposes further complexity. For example, if a public sector organisation wishes to procure a system based on Drupal for which there is a need to have interoperability with a specific legacy system, it is essential to address both conformance and interoperability between systems. In such a scenario a conformance test used earlier may now be outdated as the specification of the standard evolves. This would increase the complexity even further since requirements on a specific standard are expressed through requirements for interoperability with its legacy system.

In scenarios when there is a lack of interoperability, despite conformance to the standard according to a specific conformance test, there is of course a limit to what a customer can realistically expect from its supplier. Minor issues concerning lack of conformance and interoperability may perhaps be solved in kind through a constructive dialogue between stakeholders involved. However, further development efforts involving additional cost may be necessary in cases when customer expectations significantly exceed what the business agreement advocates.

In addition, for standards which initially address specific usage scenarios, it is often the case that only a subset of the standard is addressed in conformance tests. For some standards, there is also a lack of conformance tests.

In conclusion, our study shows an inherent complexity concerning issues stemming from different stakeholder groups involved in standardisation and software implementation of standards. Further, we observe different kinds of influence both within the Drupal community (between different sub-communities implementing different standards) and between the RDFa community in Drupal and the RDFa standardisation community in W3C. The findings from our analysis of the Drupal project make an important contribution towards a deeper understanding of challenges concerning relationships between OSS software communities and software standard communities.

References

Bain, M.: Scene Setting - Licensing models for standards and for open source. In: EC Workshop: Implementing FRAND Standards in Open Source: Mission Impossible?, Brussels, Belgium, November 22 (2012)

Behlendorf, B.: How Open Source Can Still Save the World. Keynote Presentation. In: 5th IFIP WG 2.13 International Conference on Open Source Systems, OSS 2009, Skövde, Sweden (June 5, 2009)

Drupal.org: Drupal – Open Source CMS (2012), http://drupal.org/ (accessed December 12, 2012)

Europe Economics: Guidelines for Public Procurement of ICT Goods and Services: SMART 2011/0044, D2 - Overview of Procurement Practices, Final Report (2012)

FRAND: EC Workshop: Implementing FRAND standards in Open Source: mission impossible? Brussels, Belgium (November 22, 2012)

Friedrich, J.: Making innovation happen: The role of standards and openness in an innovation-friendly ecosystem. In: Proc. of the 7th International Conference on Standardization and Innovation in Information Technology, SIIT 2011, pp. 1–8 (2011)

Gov.uk: Open Standards Consultation documents (2012), http://www.cabinetoffice.gov.uk/resource-library/open-standards-consultation-documents (accessed December 12 , 2012)

Lundell, B., Abdurahmanovic, A., Andersson, S., Bergström, E., Feist, J., Gamalielsson, J., Gustavsson, T., Kahlbom, R., Papaxanthis, K.: How can Open Standards be effectively implemented in Open Source? Challenges and the ORIOS project. In: Hammouda, I., Lundell, B., Mikkonen, T., Scacchi, W. (eds.) OSS 2012. IFIP AICT, vol. 378, pp. 383–388. Springer, Heidelberg (2012)

Oasis-open.org: The CMIS v1.0 OASIS Standard Specification (2012), http://docs.oasis-open.org/cmis/CMIS/v1.0/os/cmis-spec-v1.0.pdf (accessed December 12, 2012)

Ohloh.net: The Drupal (core) Open Source Project on Ohloh (2012), http://www.ohloh.net/p/drupal (accessed December 12, 2012)

Openid.net: OpenID Authentication 2.0 – Final (2007), http://openid.net/specs/openid-authentication-2_0.html (accessed December 12, 2012)

W3.org: RDFa 1.1 Primer (2012), http://www.w3.org/TR/xhtml-rdfa-primer/ (accessed December 12, 2012)

How to Calculate Software Metrics for Multiple Languages Using Open Source Parsers

Andrea Janes, Danila Piatov, Alberto Sillitti, and Giancarlo Succi

CASE, Free University of Bolzano, Piazza Domenicani 3, Italy
{danila.piatov,ajanes,asillitti,gsucci}@unibz.it

Abstract. Source code metrics help to evaluate the quality of the code, for example, to detect the most complex parts of the program. When writing a system which calculates metrics, especially when it has to support multiple source code languages, the biggest problem which arises is the creation of parsers for each supported language. In this paper we suggest an unusual Open Source solution, that avoids creating such parsers from scratch. We suggest and explain how to use parsers contained in the Eclipse IDE as parsers that support contemporary language features, are actively maintained, can recover from errors, and provide not just the abstract syntax tree, but the whole type information of the source program. The findings described in this paper provide to practitioners a way to use Open Source parsers without the need to deal with parser generators, or to write a parser from scratch.

1 Introduction

Measurement in software production is essential for understanding, controlling, and improving the result of the development process. Since software is highly complex, practitioners need tools to measure and analyze the quality of the source code (see e.g., [1,2,3,4,5]).

To calculate various source code metrics for different programming languages we developed a extensible metrics calculation system based on two component types:

- **parsers**: for every supported language, a parser produces an intermediate representation of the source code, used for further analysis;
- **analyzers**: analyzers take the intermediate representation of the source code and calculate the desired source code metric independently from the originating language.

The main problem we encountered was writing the parsers themselves. This paper describes our findings in the creation of parsers based on Open Source components. Moreover, it gives a brief overview of the architecture the metric calculation system we developed.

Parsing C/C++ is **difficult** [6,7,8] and therefore robust (can recover from errors), fully functional, actively maintained, and Open Source C/C++ parsers

E. Petrinja et al. (Eds.): OSS 2013, IFIP AICT 404, pp. 264–270, 2013.

are hard to find. To cite a Senior Engineer at Amazon.com: "After lots of investigation, I decided that writing a parser/analysis-tool for C++ is sufficiently difficult that it's beyond what I want to do as a hobby." [7].

Due to the inherited syntactic issues from C, for example that "declaration syntax mimics expression syntax [9]" the C++ grammar is context-dependent and ambiguous. This makes the creation of a C++ parser a complex hence difficult task (not to mention the complex template mechanism present in C++). An example for the statement above is that a construct like a*b in C/C++ can either mean a multiplication of a and b or, if a is a type, a declaration of the variable b with type a*, i.e., a pointer to a.

Strictly speaking, a "parser" performs a syntactic analysis of the source code. However, to correctly interpret the parsing results, we needed more than just a syntactic analysis, namely:

1. Particularly for C/C++, preprocessing to expand includes and macros.
2. Semantic analysis, i.e., obtaining type information and bindings is also part of the parsing process. To completely parse C/C++ code, the parser has to resolve the types of all symbols. Resolving bindings means to understand which declaration (e.g., a function, type, namespace) some reference is pointing to.

Moreover, in the particular case which we describe in this article, we had the following additional requirements:

3. The parser has to be able to ignore syntax errors and to continue parsing the remaining source code correctly.
4. C/C++ is continuously developing, and new language features are introduced from time to time, therefore a parser needs to be well-maintained.

Open source compilers like the GNU C compiler (GCC) or LCC are available that fulfill the criteria described above, but—to the best of our knowledge—they do not provide an API to obtain the (intermediate) parsing results. Moreover, LCC supports only C, and not C++.

The availability of a functioning C/C++ parser is important for developers of the Open Source community to evaluate and improve their software [10]. This applies particularly to larger projects which need a quantitative approach to quality. Unfortunately such a parser is so hard to find. To overcome this issue, we evaluated writing a C/C++ parser from scratch (using a parser generator) or to identify or adapt an Open Source alternative. The next section describes how we decided.

2   Related Works

We found the following 7 Open Source parsers for C++: clang [11], cpp-ripper [12], Elsa [13], GCC [14] using the -fdump-translation-unit option, GCC_XML [15], the Eclipse CDT C/C++ parser [16], and Doxyparse used within the Analizo metric system [17], a parser based on Doxygen [18].

The time it takes for existing Open Source communities to develop such parsers as well as comments on various blogs (e.g., [19]) induced us to think that to write a parser from scratch would take us months, if not years:

- it took clang **8 years** from the 1st commit in July 2001 [20] to the release 1.0 in October 2009 [21];
- GCC_XML has a first commit more than **12 years** ago (August 2000) [22] and its authors still do not consider it production-ready, since the current release version 0.9;
- the first release of the Eclipse CDT C/C++ parser was more than **10 years** ago (August 2003 [23]) and it is still constantly updated;
- several projects are **abandoned**, such as cpp-ripper (first and last commit during September 2009 [24]) or Elsa (last release August 2005, after 3 years of development [25]).

Moreover, writing such a parser from scratch, we would need to keep it up-to-date with the new language features introduced for C++, which would require a continuous effort.

Based on such information, we decided not to write the parser from scratch but to select an Open Source C/C++ parser that can be instrumented to correspond to our requirements. Moreover, we added the following requirement for such a parser:

5. To avoid learning new parsing technologies for different languages, we prefer Open Source parser solutions that are able to parse **several** languages, not only C++.

3   Results and Implementation of a Proof of Concept

We evaluated the candidates using the 5 requirements stated above. Three parsers fulfilled the requirements 1–4: clang, the Eclipse CDT parser, and Doxyparse. Because of requirement 4, we excluded parsers that are not maintained anymore:

- GCC_XML does not parse function bodies, a feature we need to calculate software metrics for functions [26].
- GCC, using the option -fdump-translation-unit, is able to "dump a representation of the tree structure for the entire translation unit to a file" [14], but this option is only designed for use in debugging the compiler and is not designed for use by end-users [27].

Doxygen, on which Doxyparse is based, does not parse the source code completely. To calculate metrics, the authors of Doxyparse had to "hack" the code of Doxygen and, for instance, modify the Lex [28] source file for C to support the calculation of McCabe's cyclomatic complexity on the lexical analysis stage. Since the information provided by Doxyparse is not complete, we ruled it out.

Both clang and Eclipse CDT fulfill our requirements 1–4, but only the parsers provided by Eclipse fulfill requirement 5, i.e., it is an environment not only for C/C++, but also for Java, JavaScript, and other languages.

We successfully developed a proof of concept that instruments the Eclipse C/C++ parser. The Eclipse C/C++ parser is installed together with the Eclipse CDT development environment [16]. However, as we found out, it is possible to use it as a Java library, without initializing the whole Eclipse platform. Since **the instrumentation of the Eclipse CDT parser is undocumented**, we briefly describe here how we accomplished this.

To use the parser in our application, we added the CDT core library org.eclipse.cdt.core_*.jar, as well as the other libraries in the CDT installation folder on which the plugin depends, to the classpath of our application.

As shown in listing 1.1, we pass to the parser a list of preprocessor definitions and a list of include search paths (lines 3 and 4). By extending `InternalFileContentProvider` and using this class instead of the empty files provider we are able to instruct the parser to load and parse all included files (line 6).

`InternalFileContentProvider` allows the use of the interface `IIncludeFileResolutionHeuristics`, which can be implemented to heuristically find include files for those cases in which include search paths are misconfigured. To use the C parser instead of C++, the GCCLanguage class should be used instead of the GPPLanguage class (line 10).

```
1    private static IASTTranslationUnit parse(char[] code) throws Exception {
2        FileContent fc = FileContent.create("/Path/ToResolveIncludePaths.cpp", code);
3        Map<String, String> macroDefinitions = new HashMap<String, String>();
4        String[] includeSearchPaths = new String[0];
5        IScannerInfo si = new ScannerInfo(macroDefinitions, includeSearchPaths);
6        IncludeFileContentProvider ifcp = IncludeFileContentProvider.getEmptyFilesProvider();
7        IIndex idx = null;
8        int options = ILanguage.OPTION_IS_SOURCE_UNIT;
9        IParserLogService log = new DefaultLogService();
10       return GPPLanguage.getDefault().getASTTranslationUnit(fc, si, ifcp, idx, options, log);
11   }
```

Listing 1.1. Calling the CDT parser

Listing 1.2 shows a C++ parsing example. It outputs "C C f f ", i.e., each encountered name in the abstract syntax tree of the parsed code.

The parser returns an abstract syntax tree (AST) as the result of parsing the code. The AST is the representation of the structure of the program as a tree of nodes. Each node corresponds to a syntactic construct of the code, e.g. a function definition, an if-statement, or a variable reference. This AST is used to calculate metrics, e.g., one could count all conditional statements to estimate McCabe's cyclomatic complexity.

We briefly evaluated the functioning of the Eclipse C/C++ parser by parsing the Linux kernel version 2.6.27.62. It worked without problems out of the box. The parser counted 19,744 files, 8.4M lines of code, and 2.6M logical lines of code. It took 11 minutes to parse and calculate metrics on 2 CPUs and 3 minutes on 12 CPUs.

```
1   public static void main(String[] args) throws Exception {
2       String code = "class C { private : C f(); }; int f();";
3       IASTTranslationUnit translationUnit = parse(code.toCharArray());
4       ASTVisitor visitor = new ASTVisitor() {
5           @Override public int visit(IASTName name) {
6               System.out.print(name.toString() + " ");
7               return ASTVisitor.PROCESS_CONTINUE;
8           }
9       };
10      visitor.shouldVisitNames = true;
11      translationUnit.accept(visitor);
12  }
```

Listing 1.2. Parsing "class C { private : C f(); }; int f();"

We successfully applied the same method to instrument the parsers for Java and JavaScript that are part of the Eclipse JDT[1] and JSDT[2] projects, but due to space constraints, we can only provide the UML component diagram of our implementation in figure 1. In this implementation, parser wrappers execute the parsers and convert the output to the intermediate representation used in the system. The analyzer then uses this information to calculate the metrics independently from the source language.

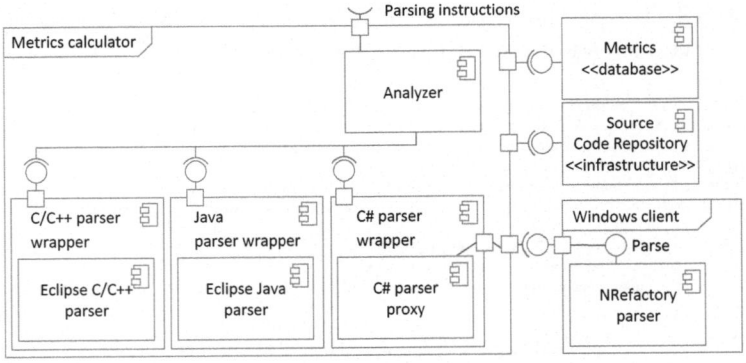

Fig. 1. UML component diagram of the whole metrics calculation architecture

The C# parser (NRefactory [29]) depicted also in figure 1 is written in C# and has to be executed on a Windows machine. This is why we execute it through a proxy on a remote machine.

The component "metrics calculator" wraps all parser wrappers and the analyzer into one component that is able to parse and extract metrics of a variety of languages. It requires the presence of two additional components: a database to store the extracted code structure and metrics, as well as a component to interface the source repository.

---

[1] http://www.eclipse.org/jdt
[2] http://www.eclipse.org/webtools/jsdt

4   Conclusion and Future Works

This article deals with an (apparently) simple problem: to "create or find a working C/C++ parser". We defined four requirements for such a parser which are relevant for us and we think also for the research community: we ask for a parser that supports contemporary language features, is actively maintained, can recover from errors, and provides not just the abstract syntax tree, but the whole type information of the source program.

Due to the complexity of writing a C/C++ parser ourselves, we decided to evaluate existing Open Source parsers adding a fifth requirement: that we look for parser solutions that support multiple languages.

The conclusions of our research are that Eclipse fulfills all five requirements, contains a C/C++ parser, as well as other parsers like Java and JavaScript. Unfortunately there is no official documentation about using the Eclipse parsers as a library outside of Eclipse. In the last section we provide an example of how to achieve this and give a birds-eye view of the architecture of our measurement system that is based on the parsers contained in Eclipse.

In the future we intend to adopt a systematic approach to evaluate the maturity of parsers, e. g., using the Open Maturity Model [30] or automatic measurement techniques [31,32].

References

1. Sillitti, A., Janes, A., Succi, G., Vernazza, T.: Measures for mobile users: an architecture. J. Syst. Archit. 50, 393–405 (2004)
2. Jermakovics, A., Scotto, M., Sillitti, A., Succi, G.: Lagrein: Visualizing user requirements and development effort. In: 15th IEEE International Conference on Program Comprehension, pp. 293–296 (June)
3. Jermakovics, A., Moser, R., Sillitti, A., Succi, G.: Visualizing software evolution with lagrein. In: Companion to the 23rd ACM SIGPLAN Conference on Object-Oriented Programming Systems Languages and Applications, OOPSLA Companion 2008, pp. 749–750. ACM, New York (2008)
4. di Bella, E., Sillitti, A., Succi, G.: A multivariate classification of open source developers. Information Sciences 221, 72–83 (2013)
5. Janes, A., Succi, G.: The dark side of agile software development. In: Proceedings of the ACM International Symposium on New Ideas, New Paradigms, and Reflections on Programming and Software, Onward! 2012, pp. 215–228. ACM, New York (2012)
6. Werther, B., Conway, D.: A modest proposal: C++ resyntaxed. ACM SIGPLAN Notices 31, 74–82 (1996)
7. Birkett, A.: Parsing C++ (2001), http://www.nobugs.org/developer/parsingcpp/index.html (accessed April 14, 2012)
8. Piatov, D., Janes, A., Sillitti, A., Succi, G.: Using the Eclipse C/C++ development tooling as a robust, fully functional, actively maintained, open source C++ parser. In: Hammouda, I., Lundell, B., Mikkonen, T., Scacchi, W. (eds.) OSS 2012. IFIP AICT, vol. 378, pp. 399–399. Springer, Heidelberg (2012)
9. Ritchie, D.M.: The development of the C language, pp. 201–208 (1993)
10. Russo, B., Scotto, M., Sillitti, A., Succi, G.: Agile Technologies in Open Source Development. Information Science Reference - Imprint of: IGI Publishing (2009)

11. clang: a C language family frontend for LLVM, `http://clang.llvm.org` (accessed February 01, 2013)
12. Diggins, C.: cpp-ripper, An open-source C++ parser written in C# (2012), `http://code.google.com/p/cpp-ripper/`
13. McPeak, S.: Elsa: The Elkhound-based C/C++ parser, `http://scottmcpeak.com/elkhound/sources/elsa/` (accessed April 14, 2012)
14. GCC Development Team, GCC, the GNU Compiler Collection, `http://gcc.gnu.org` (accessed April 14, 2012)
15. King, B.: GCC-XML, the XML output extension to GCC, `http://www.gccxml.org` (accessed April 14, 2012)
16. Eclipse CDT (C/C++ Development Tooling) (2012), `http://www.eclipse.org/cdt`
17. Terceiro, A., Costa, J., Miranda, J., Meirelles, P., Rios, L.R., Almeida, L., Chavez, C., Kon, F.: Analizo: an extensible multi-language source code analysis and visualization toolkit. In: Brazilian Conference on Software: Theory and Practice (CBSoft) – Tools, Salvador-Brazil (2010)
18. Doxygen, `http://www.stack.nl/~dimitri/doxygen/` (accessed February 01, 2013)
19. stackoverflow.com, How much time would it take to write a C++ compiler using flex/yacc?, `http://stackoverflow.com/questions/1961604` (accessed February 01, 2013)
20. First revision of clang, `http://llvm.org/viewvc/llvm-project?view=rev&revision=1` (accessed February 01, 2013)
21. Lattner, C.: Llvm 2.6 release! (2009), `http://lists.cs.uiuc.edu/pipermail/llvm-announce/2009-October/000033.html` (accessed February 01, 2013)
22. GCC-XML, the XML output extension to GCC repository, `https://github.com/gccxml/gccxml` (accessed February 01, 2013)
23. Eclipse CDT (C/C++ Development Tooling) repository, `http://git.eclipse.org/c/cdt/org.eclipse.cdt.git/refs/tags`
24. cpp-ripper list of repository changes, `https://code.google.com/p/cpp-ripper/source/list` (accessed February 01, 2013)
25. Elkhound: A glr parser generator and elsa: An elkhound-based c++ parser, `http://scottmcpeak.com/elkhound/` (accessed February 01, 2013)
26. GCC-XML, Frequently Asked Questions, `http://www.gccxml.org/HTML/FAQ.html` (accessed February 01, 2013)
27. Mitchell, M.: GCC Bugzilla – Bug 18279, `http://gcc.gnu.org/bugzilla/show_bug.cgi?id=18279` (accessed February 01, 2013)
28. Lex – A Lexical Analyzer Generator, `http://dinosaur.compilertools.net/lex/` (accessed February 01, 2013)
29. The NRefactory library, `https://github.com/icsharpcode/SharpDevelop/wiki/NRefactory` (accessed February 01, 2013)
30. Petrinja, E., Nambakam, R., Sillitti, A.: Introducing the opensource maturity model. In: Proceedings of the 2009 ICSE Workshop on Emerging Trends in Free/Libre/Open Source Software Research and Development, pp. 37–41. IEEE Computer Society, Washington, DC (2009)
31. Sillitti, A., Janes, A., Succi, G., Vernazza, T.: Monitoring the development process with eclipse. In: Proceedings of the International Conference on Information Technology: Coding and Computing, ITCC 2004, vol. 2, pp. 133–134 (April 2004)
32. Scotto, M., Sillitti, A., Succi, G., Vernazza, T.: A non-invasive approach to product metrics collection. J. Syst. Archit. 52, 668–675 (2006)

The Emergence of Quality Assurance Practices in Free/Libre Open Source Software: A Case Study

Adina Barham

Hitotsubashi University, Graduate School of Social Sciences, 2-1 Naka,
Kunitachi, Tokyo, 186-8601, Japan
adina.barham@yahoo.com

Abstract. As the user base of Free/Libre Open Source Software (FLOSS) diversifies, the need for higher quality is becoming more evident. This implies a more complex development model that includes various steps which were previously associated exclusively with proprietary development such as a formal quality assurance step (QA). However, little research has been done on how implementing formal quality assurance impacts the structure of FLOSS communities. This study aims to start filling this gap by analyzing interactions within such a community. Plone is just one among many FLOSS projects that acknowledged the importance of verification by implementing a quality assurance step.

Keywords: quality assurance, test, social network analysis, information flow.

1   Introduction

A previous preliminary study [1] established that almost one third of the top 50 FLOSS software products ranked by number of downloads on www.ohloh.net had implemented explicit QA procedures. Furthermore, more than a quarter of the top 100 products ranked by number of user have some kind of QA. Verification, and more specifically quality procedures under the FLOSS development model has attracted a lot of interest within the academic community [2-9]. The structure of communities behind FLOSS has also been extensively researched. Studies focus on many community aspects such as structure and dynamics [10], communication patterns between core and periphery [11-12], or migration within the hierarchy of FLOSS projects [13]. However, little research has been done on how implementing formal QA affects the community. This research aims to start filling that gap by improving our understanding of how QA fits into the organizational structure of FLOSS communities.

A single open source project was chosen as a pilot case study in order to develop research questions that can then be applied in a wider comparative study of QA in open source projects. The Python-based content management system Plone was selected because it is a mature project (began in 1999) and because its development process includes a QA step [14]. The QA team has a dedicated webpage where one

E. Petrinja et al. (Eds.): OSS 2013, IFIP AICT 404, pp. 271–276, 2013.
© IFIP International Federation for Information Processing 2013

can find basic information such as activity description, communication channels and team leaders [15]. QA activities include triaging new bugs, validating submitted patches, ensuring that new releases are usable and generally help in the release process.

2   Research Questions

Q1: How is the QA layer included in the Plone community structure? We aim to find out how much contributors work only on QA and how much they work on other aspects of the project. Also, we ask how much peripheral members perform QA tasks. Previous research has approached the latter issue for Firefox and it has been shown that the percentage of periphery contributions is 20-25% [12].

Q2: What are the characteristics of activities performed by members of the Plone QA team? It is logical to draw the conclusion that some members will be more active than others but it would be interesting to investigate if members are equally active on all communication channels or if their tasks are limited to certain areas of the project.

Q3: How does the QA team communicate with other teams? Previous research has shown, that participants who have better access to information are able to contribute more efficiently [16] therefore interrupting the information flow might affect negatively the project's evolution. For this reason it is important to determine if there are any members that control the information flow. Due to the fact that social networks are in a continuous change [17], it might be useful to also establish the stages that the community went through before reaching its current state.

3   Data and Research Method

In order to measure QA activity levels, issue tracker data as well as mailing list data were taken into account. Data was retrieved in December 2012 – January 2013 and stored locally. The issue tracker data contained 13026 bugs with 55883 associated comments, and was downloaded using a web crawler. 29525 e-mails were downloaded from all the Plone mailing list archives that were parsable using MailingListStats [18]. In addition, a list of Plone contributors containing names and nicknames used in code repositories was downloaded from Ohloh.net [19].

Data from the QA mailing list which started in 2011 included 41 members of whom approximately 70% had sent only one e-mail at the time of data collection. Of the remaining 12 members only 1 had sent more than 10 e-mails, 4 were not active on other mailing lists and 7 were not listed as code contributors. The 4 members who were not active on other mailing lists were also not listed as code contributors. However, their activity on the QA mailing list was low: none sent more than 5 e-mails. Therefore QA does not constitute a separate layer in the Plone community.

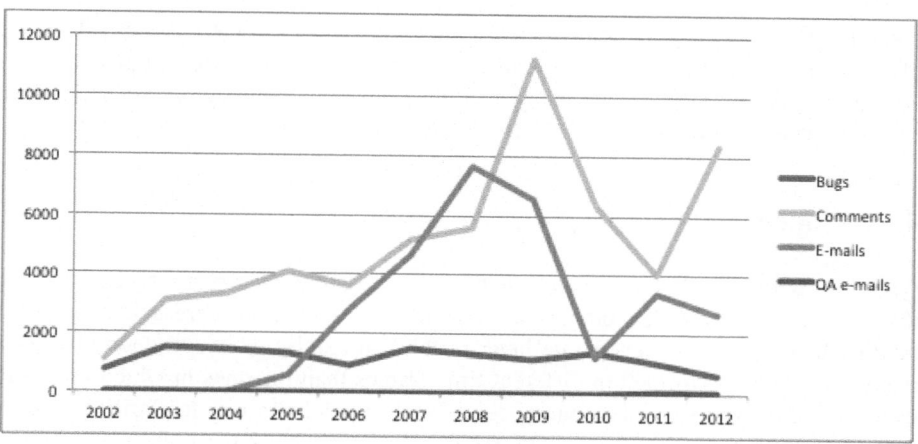

Fig. 1. Clusters within the Plone community

An interesting fact that can be observed from Fig.1 is that there is no correlation between time progression and activity levels. In addition, there seems to be no correlation between the number of bugs posted and the number of associated comments, which leads to the question the reasons behind these spikes in activity levels.

Social network analysis was used to analyse communication patterns within the Plone community. Project participants were represented as nodes (vertices) while interactions were represented as edges (arcs). The weight (value) of the graph's arcs represent the number of interactions between two members.

To create the network graph only authors who had replied to someone were taken into consideration. The next step consisted of eliminating loops or arcs starting and pointing to the same vertex. An additional reduction was performed in order to remove vertices that had no connections with other vertices. The resulted network contains 3414 vertices connected by a total of 16042 arcs of which 5093 have a value greater than 1. This means that 10949 connections (68%) are created by only one interaction. These members are occasional or peripheral contributors. From the remaining arcs 31% have values between 2 and 79 which means that arcs with values between 1 and 79 account for almost 99% of all arcs. The average degree is 9.39, which means that on average, a person interacts with approximately 9 other people. The network was then processed by transforming arcs into edges by summing up their values. Members who interacted with only one other member represented 35% of the whole community. 86% of community members interacted with a lower than average number of members (i.e. < 9).

To assess task distribution among community members the graph was divided into clusters. The cluster that contains QA mailing list members represents 1.06% of the whole community, and contains a sub-cluster of members who do not contribute code accounting for 0.46% of the community.

Social networks are dynamic as they change their structure over time and for this reason it is important to consider time frames [20-21]. Social network analysis methods were applied using 6-month time frames to analyze the states through which the community went after dedicating a communication channel to the QA team. The size of the network varied between 226 and 746 vertices. The variation in size was expected considering the fact that many arcs were created after only one interaction. In addition the highest degree was 7.52 while the lowest was 4.29.

4   Conclusions

Q1: How is the QA layer included in the Plone community structure? Considering that the most active QA members also contributed code and were active on other mailing lists, QA is not a separate layer in the community. However, non-QA tasks might have been performed in different time frames than the ones in which members were part of the QA team; comparing time frames would allow us to clarify this. Furthermore, approximately 70% of QA mailing list members have sent only one 1 e-mail which might suggest that these are periphery members performing QA tasks. Only 30% of QA mailing list participants have not been active on other channels. In addition, members active on the QA mailing list account for only 1% of the whole community.

Q2: What are the characteristics of activities performed by members of the Plone QA team? An interesting phenomenon that occurs within the Plone community is the increase in activity levels that seems not to be linked to time progression. In addition it seems that the number of bugs opened does directly relate to the increase in comment activity levels. This suggests that there are other variables that influence activity levels.

Q3: How does the QA team communicate with other teams? The community seems to form a large component that spans both issue tracker and mailing list with the exception of few small sub-networks. This means that there is a lower risk for some members to control the information flow and to jeopardize the communication flow. However, there is a small group of people that are highly engaged in communicating with other members (86% of community members interacted with less than 9 other members – 9 being the average number of interactions a member has). In line with this conclusion, a large percentage of community members (68%) create links defined by only one interaction. This means that the rest of the community has somewhat stronger connections whereas a small percentage of users (1%) have very strong connections defined by more than 79 interactions. In addition, after analyzing the networks created using time frames, one could reach the conclusion that due to the drastic decrease in community size many participants were occasional contributors or in other words members of the periphery.

5   Limitations and Further Research

A number of limitations should be noted. First, only limited data cleaning was carried out. Second, it is possible that community members have used other communication channels than those listed on the relevant Plone websites. Third, it is possible that some members of the QA team did not actively participate in the mailing list. For these reasons, it would be desirable to conduct follow-up interviews with members of the community. These interviews would also shed light on the reasons for peaks in activity levels.

It could also be useful to re-run the community analysis using smaller time frames as 6 months may be a too big window for a community of this size. In addition, the community evolution could be analyzed using time frames covering the period before the formal adoption of QA in order to track down potential migration from one layer to the other.

A single case study cannot provide a recipe for success that can be applied to all FLOSS projects, but can be used to create hypotheses to be validated in future studies. Based on the findings of this paper the following hypotheses were formulated:

H1: The majority of the QA team members perform non-QA tasks as well.

H2: Approximately 80% of QA tasks are performed by a small percentage of the community.

H3: Increase in activity levels is not linked to time progression.

H4: Members performing QA are not an isolated layer in the community.

References

1. Barham, A.: The emergence of quality assurance in open source software development. In: Proceedings of the OSS 2011 Doctoral Consortium (2011)
2. Halloran, T.J., Scherlis, W.L.: High quality and open source software practices. In: 2nd Workshop on Open Source Software Engineering (2002)
3. Hedberg, H., Iivari, N., Rajanen, M., Harjumaa, L.: Assuring Quality and Usability in Open Source Software Development. In: First International Workshop on Emerging Trends in FLOSS Research and Development, FLOSS 2007, p. 2 (2007)
4. Michlmayr, M., Hunt, F., Probert, D.: Quality practices and problems in free software projects. In: Proceedings of the First International Conference on Open Source Systems, pp. 24–28 (2005)
5. Schmidt, D.C., Porter, A.: Leveraging open-source communities to improve the quality & performance of open-source software. In: Proceedings of the 1st Workshop on Open Source Software Engineering (2001)
6. Chengalur-Smith, I., Sidorova, A., Daniel, S.: Sustainability of Free/Libre Open Source Projects: A Longitudinal Study. JAIS 11 (2001)
7. Spinellis, D., Gousios, G., Karakoidas, V., Louridas, P., Adams, P.J., Samoladas, I., Stamelos, I.: Evaluating the Quality of Open Source Software. In: Proceedings of the International Workshop on Software Quality and Maintainability. Electronic Notes in Theoretical Computer Science, vol. 233 (2009)
8. Aberdour, M.: Achieving Quality in Open Source Software. IEEE Software, 58–64 (2007)
9. Zhao, L., Elbaum, S.: Quality assurance under the open source development model. Journal of Systems and Software - JSS 66(1), 65–75 (2003)
10. Crowston, K., Howison, J.: The social structure of Free and Open Source software. First Monday 10(2) (2004)

11. Oezbek, C., Prechelt, L., Thiel, F.: The Onion has Cancer: Some Social Network Analysis Visualizations of Open Source Project Communication. In: Proceedings of the 3rd International Workshop on Emerging Trends in Free/Libre/Open Source Software Research and Development, FLOSS 2010, pp. 5–10 (2010)
12. Masmoudi, H., den Besten, M., de Loupy, C., Dalle, J.-M.: "Peeling the Onion": The Words and Actions that Distinguish Core from Periphery in Bug Reports and How Core and Periphery Interact Together. In: Boldyreff, C., Crowston, K., Lundell, B., Wasserman, A.I. (eds.) OSS 2009. IFIP AICT, vol. 299, pp. 284–297. Springer, Heidelberg (2009)
13. Jensen, C., Scacchi, W.: Role Migration and Advancement Processes in OSSD Projects: A Comparative Case Study. In: Proceedings of the 29th International Conference on Software Engineering, pp. 364–374 (2007)
14. http://plone.org/
15. http://plone.org/community/teams/qa-team
16. Aral, S., Brynjolfsson, E., Van Alstyne, M.: Productivity Effects of Information Diffusion in E-mail Networks. In: Proceedings of ICIS 2007 (2007)
17. Watts, D.J.: A Twenty-first century science. Nature 445(7127), 489–489 (2007)
18. https://github.com/MetricsGrimoire/MailingListStats
19. https://www.ohloh.net/
20. Howison, J., Wiggins, A., Crowston, K.: Validity Issues in the Use of Social Network Analysis for the Study of Online Communities. Journal of the Association for Information Systems (2012)
21. Christley, S., Madey, G.: Global and Temporal Analysis of Social Positions at Source-Forge.net. In: The Third International Conference on Open Source Systems, IFIP WG 2.13, Limerick, Ireland (2007)

Author Index